What the Hell Is Going On in My Life

Using the "new" astrology to find serious answers

Larry Schwimmer

Other Books by Larry Schwimmer

The Assertive Approach: Do You Lack the Killer Instinct? – S & A Publishing

How To Ask For A Raise Without Getting Fired! And, 24 Other Assertiveness Techniques for the Office – Harper & Row, Publishers

Winning Your Next Promotion in 1 Year (or Less!) – Harper & Row, Publishers

What the Hell Is Going On in My Life?

Using the "new" astrology to find serious answers

by
Larry Schwimmer

Also Available in KINDLE Edition

S & A Publishing, San Francisco, CA

S & A Publishing

> Also Available in KINDLE Edition

What the Hell Is Going On in My Life? – Using the "new" astrology to find serious answers

© 2013 Copyright, Larry Schwimmer

All right reserved. No part of this book may be reproduced or transmitted in any form or by any means, electronic, mechanical, photocopying, recording, or otherwise, without written permission from the publisher or author. A reviewer may quote passages.

Requests for permission to make copies of any part of this book should be submitted to the publisher at Larry@AstroDecision.com.

Cover design by Brad Davis

Editors: Beth Kuper and Leslie Rhea Davis

ISBN: 1481163647
ISBN-13: 978-1481163644

First Printing, May 2013

To the love of my life, Leslie Rhea, let me borrow from the words of W.H. Auden and say to you:

You are my North, my South, my East and West,
My working week and Sunday rest,
My noon, my midnight, my talk, my song;
With you in my life, love is always with me.

Acknowledgements

I would like to express my thanks to all the friends and supporters, who have helped and encouraged me throughout my writing process. First of all, I am deeply indebted to the love of my life, Leslie, who first heard about my idea to write this book as we walked along the beach together. She wisely encouraged me to broaden the scope of this book from using astrology to make decisions – to using astrology to understand your *life*. I am eternally grateful for her excellent counsel. Additionally, in the early stages, as I sought to find the right order for the ideas that I wanted to express, she made some excellent organizational suggestions that helped me write this book in a free-flowing, yet logical fashion.

Most authors are lucky if they can find one great editor. I was blessed to have two. First, I want to give special thanks to my editor, Beth Kuper, a friend for 30 years, who has been my biggest fan, yet never hesitating to disagree if she thought I was wrong, but always giving me insightful editing suggestions. She was of invaluable assistance because of her deep understanding of astrology. Beth is every author's dream because she's been encouraging and tireless in her willingness to help me make this an excellent book.

I want to acknowledge my second editor, Leslie Rhea Davis whose multiple talents include being a fantastic book editor. She made one brilliant suggestion after another, calling me to task whenever my message wasn't clear, making sure my examples were on point, and always reminding me to talk to my reader. Her skillful editing assistance made me write a better book, much like a coach who motivates an athlete to function at his highest performance. Thanks to her, I am very proud of the book, I've written.

Then there are those special friends who were willing to read sample chapters and give me their invaluable feedback, which eventually guided me to the book's final creation today. I want to thank my dear friend June Maguire who made some brilliant editorial suggestions, especially from the perspective of the "non-astrology" reader. Thanks, also to many wonderful friends: Steve Hull, Matt Weatherby, Peter Pope, and Barry Bookman, all who took time out of their lives just to read sample chapters and give me their valuable feedback. Thank you to LeeAnn Lannom, librarian at Vanderbilt University for her skillful research assistance and my special thanks to my brilliant stepson, Brad Davis for his design genius in creating my book cover.

I am eternally grateful for a whole host of astrology teachers who have taught me and shared their brilliance. I want to especially acknowledge Ruby Holladay who has been my fabulous teacher, mentor, and friend for many years always encouraging me and helping me develop my talent as an astrologer. I also want to thank another wonderful astrologer who is no longer here on earth, Hannibal Giudici. He was a gifted astrologer who taught me a great deal as well. Of course, I will never forget my first astrology reading with Christine Rechter, a brilliant astrologer, teacher, and great friend. Wherever you are, thank you!

In addition, there are a whole host of fellow astrologers and colleagues who have taught me, and inspired me over these 35 years, either directly or through their books. I want to thank Robert Hand, James Braha, Frances Sakoian, and Louis Acker. I offer special thanks to the brilliant mundane, financial astrologers, Arch Crawford, Ray Merriman, and Manfred Zimmel. In their niche, they are captains of industry and I tip my hat to them.

My heartfelt thanks to every one of you for helping me create this book.

Table of Contents

Preface xiii

Introduction xix

"What is the *NEW* Astrology?" xxv

Part I   The Secret To Knowing What Is Going On In Your Life 1

Part II Using Astrology As A Decision-Making Tool 7

Part III The Magic of Transits 15

Part IV Free Transit Interpretation 35

Part V   The 5 Planets Affecting Your Life 39

Part VI What The HELL Is Going On In My Life? 45

    1st House: Personality & Appearance 46

    2nd House: Money & Values 95

    3rd House: Communications 132

    4th House: Family & Home 171

    5th House: Love Life & Creativity 200

    6th House: Health & Work 240

7th House:	Relationships, Marriage & Partnerships	271
8th House:	Sex Life, Investments & Transformation	323
9th House:	Travel, Education & Philosophy	358
10th House:	Career & Status	393
11th House:	Friends, Hopes & Dreams	436
12th House:	Psychology & Secrets	468

Part VII Applying the NEW Astrology to Your Life 505

Preface

How I Came To Write This Book

As a reader, I always wondered how authors came to write their books. Let me tell you what inspired me: It was the result of my first experience with astrology, almost 40 years ago, and it changed my life forever!

As a young man of 29, my then girlfriend gave me a birthday gift of a reading with an astrologer in Chicago. As a skeptical person who didn't believe in astrology, my first reaction was: *"Girlfriend, why did you waste your money buying me that birthday gift?"* (Fortunately, I was smart enough to keep that thought to myself.)

With trepidation, I went to my astrology reading, which turned out to be an appointment with destiny. I was working in a senior marketing position with Nabisco at the time, making a good living, hanging out with fun friends, and enjoying the new home I'd purchased on the north side of Chicago, near Wrigley Field. Life was good.

After getting a marketing degree and doing M.B.A. graduate work at Northern Illinois University, my first experience was as an entrepreneur. Now, I was working in the business world as a corporate executive. I was happy with my job, but also wondering what might lay ahead in my future.

I sat down with the astrologer, my arms folded like a true skeptic with body language that said, *"OK, I am not saying a word or giving you any hints about my life. Let's hear what you have to say, Madame astrologer."* She looked at an astrology chart with strange symbols, and replied, "Larry, your life will be radically changing over the next three years. Here is what I see happening for you. . ." Her omniscient forecasts and predictions were bold and left me shaken with disbelief. Here's what she said during our conversation:

What the Hell Is Going On in My Life?

Astrologer: *Based on the planetary cycles in your birth chart, you will be leaving your job within the next 12 months. You'll start a new business and begin a new career that will involve teaching, public speaking and writing books. It will be directed at the masses. You will achieve fame and fortune from your work.*

Larry: *What you are saying makes no sense. The only mass group I've been a part of was at Wrigley Field, watching the Chicago Cubs play baseball. I have no plans to leave my job. I've never ever taught anyone anything in my whole life. And I've never done any public speaking. I've certainly never written a book or even thought of writing one.*

Astrologer: *Well you will. These things will all happen.*

Larry: *But it takes a lot of extra money to start a business, which I don't have right now.*

Astrologer: *That won't be a problem because the money and the opportunity will be provided for you.*

Larry: *But, I still don't understand?*

Astrologer: *You will. . . over time.*

At this point, I'm thinking, "I'm with a nutty." I should just courteously get up and thank her for her time. But I stayed, heard her out, and left her office shocked and bewildered.

A few months after my astrology reading, I started wondering if I was meant to do more with my life than just a 50-60+ hour job at Nabisco. I knew I wanted to do more than the work I was doing. I thought maybe I was meant to help people in some way. I had graduated college with a psychology minor, and I was always interested in people and what made them tick. I realized that I would enjoy learning more about human behavior, which resulted in my enrolling in a night course on *Human Psychology and Behavior* at the University of Illinois, where I learned about the topic of "assertiveness training." It was fascinating to learn a system of communication, which could effectively resolve inter-personal conflicts with others.

This learning experience got me thinking that this information might be extremely helpful to people in the business and professional world. After all, employees everywhere need to learn how to resolve their conflicts at work, whether dealing with a demanding customer, confronting an aggressive co-worker or asking the boss for a raise.

Simple research revealed, that while there were many psychologists speaking about such issues, there was no one with real business experience discussing them. I wondered whether working people would be interested in learning techniques to resolve conflicts from someone with my credentials, as a successful entrepreneur and corporate executive. I started thinking maybe this could be a new business for me to pursue. I had some obstacles to overcome since I did not have enough seed money to risk starting such a business. Furthermore, I didn't have any experience teaching or even talking to people about conflict resolution techniques.

I proceeded to make application to teach my newly developed course titled *"How to Resolve Conflicts at Work."* Eventually, I was approved to teach it through the adult extension programs at the City Colleges of Chicago and at Northwestern University. The class was a big success and the experience did wonders for my confidence. It gave me the opportunity to find out that I was a natural at teaching and I discovered that I really enjoyed public speaking. My students gave me positive feedback that my down-to-earth style of talking to them was appealing and interesting.

I then put on my "entrepreneur's hat" and starting thinking: How can I turn this course curriculum into a business? This led to my contacting several national companies that offered public seminars. I asked them if they might be interested in marketing my unique, "Conflict Resolution" seminar for business and professional people. Their interest encouraged me and I began to see how the astrologer's predictions might all come together.

Working at Nabisco, I was still interested in changing my career, and I discussed my options with my boss. He and I had gotten along well and we had the kind of honest relationship where I could be truthful about my career plans. I was surprised when he informed me that the company was planning some major management re-shuffling. He asked if I would be interested in leaving the company with a very attractive six-month severance package, including full salary and benefits.

I flashed back to my astrology reading six months earlier, and the astrologer's pronouncement: *"Don't worry about money for your new career, because it will be provided for you."* As I recalled that moment, it was an

What the Hell Is Going On in My Life?

amazing epiphany. I accepted my boss's offer and left to start my next business: presenting public seminars.

Shortly thereafter, I signed a contract with a seminar producer and delivered my first public seminar in Chicago for business people on "How to Resolve Conflict at Work." Within one year I was booked on an 18-city seminar tour, speaking before thousands of business people throughout the United States.

I began writing a book, and eventually Harper & Row published it, *How To Ask For a Raise Without Getting Fired (And 24 Other Assertiveness Techniques for the Office)*. I was now an author. Soon after, I wrote my second Harper & Row book, *Winning Your Next Promotion In One Year (Or Less!)*. In fact, I *did* become a nationally recognized career consultant and expert on conflict resolution, appearing on TV shows such as the *Today Show*, and being featured in newspapers and magazines such as *Time* and *U.S. News & World Report*.

I always remembered that astrologer's prediction of how my life would so radically change: *"Larry, you will start a new business and begin a new career that will involve teaching, public speaking, and writing books. It will be directed at the masses. You will achieve fame and fortune from your work."*

The astrology reading I received was profound and made me realize I had the huge potential to do more with my life than I ever imagined. In fact, the reading made me aware of my undeveloped talents before I even knew they existed. The astrologer's message filled me with immense confidence, painting a bright picture of the successful future ahead of me. She was right. How amazing!

Through that fateful experience, where I stepped out of my little conventional box, opening myself to possibilities I had never once considered, I became interested in astrology and its validity. Even more exciting, I realized how it could provide people with valuable assistance in achieving their dreams and goals – just as it had helped me.

During those many years, I began talking courses, learning all about astrology, and how and why it worked. I was amazed to learn about the many historical figures throughout the centuries, who used astrology to understand what was going on in their lives, and for their decision-making, from Aristotle to Galileo to Sir Isaac Newton. I learned that Benjamin Franklin was an astrologer, and regularly wrote about the use of astrology in *Poor Richard's Almanac*. It was well publicized that President Ronald Reagan used a San Francisco astrologer, Joan Quigley, to pick the best days for meetings, treaty signings, and many matters of state. All these brilliant, innovative, and responsible people used astrology to make important decisions. This impressed me. I wondered how many other people would be interested in this knowledge if they only knew about it?

I thoroughly enjoyed reading scores of astrology books, which taught me the details and interpretation of astrology. I read many that helped me understand my personality and how to forecast future events. However, I never found an astrology book that discussed the practical side of how I could use astrology in my everyday life to *explain the changes taking place in my life, AND to give me the perfect times to make successful decisions.* After 35 years as an astrologer, having analyzed more 3,100 astrological charts, these were the practical, yet powerful ways I used astrology to benefit my clients.

I thought, "Wouldn't it be fantastic if *I* could be the astrologer who wrote a book that helped people make sense of the many changes that were going on in their life? Further, wouldn't it be great if I gave them practical advice on how they could use astrology to pick the right person for a love relationship; choose the best day to find a new job; select the correct date to make a profitable financial investment, and so forth?

So, I decided to be that astrologer. **What the Hell Is Going On in My Life? Using the "new" astrology to find serious answers** was written to help you understand the changes, conflicts, problems, and opportunities that you'll experience in each area of your life: your personality, finances, communications, family, romance, relationships, sex, investments, travel, career, friendships, hopes and wishes, and your personal psychology and deepest secrets.

For you to navigate your life, reach your goals, and fulfill your dreams you will need to make decisions. In this book, I will show you how you can use astrology to understand your life, and make successful decisions at the right time just like Ben Franklin, Ronald Reagan, and many others have done in the past. My hope is that you'll use the information in this book to take control over your destiny so that you live your life to its fullest potential.

Please enjoy the journey through each area of this book.

Introduction

As an entrepreneur and *FORTUNE 500* executive, I've successfully used the *NEW* astrology to understand *what the hell was going on in my life,* and to make important decisions, for the past 40 years. I personally know the application of astrology can make you happier and more fulfilled by understanding yourself, your relationships, and the world around you.

I'm not a strange guru who belongs to a magical cult. I won't tell you to light a candle and pray eight times when you have a problem (although, on some days, that may not be a bad idea!). I am a bottom-line businessman who has worked in executive positions for such companies as *Gillette, Nabisco, Smith-Barney/CitiGroup* and *H&R Block.* I combine a Midwestern upbringing and education, with lots of real world experience, and years of practicing my craft as an astrologer.

I've specialized in providing astrological consulting to individuals, small businesses as well as large corporations. As a featured contributor for *The Huffington Post*, I write about how astrological planetary cycles affect people's lives, as well as world, political, economic, and financial events. (Please visit my web site: AstroDecision.com)

How Is This Book Going To Make Your Life Better?

It's my firm belief that what you'll read in upcoming chapters, offers you a new way to understand what is going on in your life, in all areas. The ups and downs of your life will finally make sense. I'll also show you an innovative way to pick the most favorable timing to make successful decisions. I have always said to my clients: "When the conventional advisors can't help you find the answers, come to me and I'll show you how your own personal astrology chart can give you insight and guidance." The valuable information I have given clients for the past 35 years is contained in this book. The 21st century is the perfect time to look to the *NEW* astrology as a compelling resource to use in your life.

Most people don't know that you can use *NEW* astrology to make the most important decisions of your life. However, the biggest surprise is that it can provide you with the *right time* for making a decision so that you will have the successful outcome you desire. And the good news is that the place to find that perfect timing is contained right in your own birth chart.

As mind-boggling as it may sound, your birth chart contains a personal treasure map of your life and the major events that will take place. Of course, it will be up to you whether you follow that map. You are the one in charge and responsible for your own life. However, if there were actually a way to truly understand *what the hell was going on in your life,* during times when you didn't know – would you be interested in talking to someone who had the answers? If there were actually *a way* to truly insure that your decisions were successful, would you be interested in using that information in your life? If so, please read on.

My Promise To You

To understand how the *NEW* astrology can be used to make better sense of your life, and for decision-making, you must have an open mind. Consider that we live in a complex world of problems and challenges, and we have to manage our lives, career, finances, and personal relationships. Finding solutions to the problems that come up in those areas can be overwhelming. Making the correct decisions is crucial.

This is the perfect time to seek information and look for answers – but not in just the usual places. The use of the *NEW* astrology in your life can bring you insights and solutions you'll find nowhere else: not from your accountant, lawyer, doctor, engineer, parents, friends, minister, rabbi, or even your mate. You may be a skeptic or the typical person whose only experience of astrology has been reading about your *sun sign* in the horoscope section of the daily newspaper to see if you were going to meet Prince Charming, win the lottery, or have an argument with your boss that day. If so – then you haven't experienced the in-depth professional astrology, which is the very subject of this book.

If you are already acquainted with astrology because you've read about it, or because you've consulted an astrologer who analyzed your birth chart, I hope you'll find what I've written helpful to understanding how you can use the *NEW* astrology to better understand your life, and for successful decision-making. This knowledge will give you the power to make positive events happen in your life, instead of just hoping and wishing that good things would happen.

No Technical Astrology

#1. This is not a book for learning complicated or technical astrology. The *NEW* astrology is directed at readers who want a simple explanation of how to use astrology in a practical way in their life (not to learn the technical basics of astrology such as symbols, signs, aspects, charts, calculations, or natal interpretation). I will teach you just enough of the *NEW* astrology so you understand what is going on in your life and how it applies to making successful decisions. In the same way that you don't have to know about the technical workings of your computer to send emails, you don't need to know about the technical aspects of astrology.

Believers & Skeptics Welcome!

#2. It doesn't matter whether you wholeheartedly believe in astrology or whether you are skeptical of it. The successful use of astrology does not require anything other than your willingness to (a) keep and open mind, (b) apply it to confirm that it is useful and works. After all, you don't need to believe in electricity to flip a light switch. You just want the practical benefit that comes from turning on the lights. Astrology can deliver the same practical value to you. All that matters is that you are a pragmatic, rational person who is interested in the benefits, which this unique system of knowledge will bring to your life.

The Three Themes of the Book

The *NEW* astrology can give you accurate and valuable information to understand what is going on in your life. On a personal basis, you can use this information to know yourself better, as well as your needs. On a practical basis this knowledge can be used to solve problems in all areas of your life: your home, work, career, investments, love life, family and children.

Best of all, this information can help you create change in your life by making the right decisions and implementing them at the perfect time. Here are some examples: When is the best time to marry, divorce, make an investment, buy a home, sell real estate, start a business, change your career, take a fabulous vacation, or get rid of an addiction? Using astrology in this practical way is what I have written about in this book.

We will be discussing how to use the *NEW* astrology to:

(1) Know yourself better. So often we go through our lives not understanding what is happening to us. We cannot make sense of inexplicable changes in our moods, ideas, philosophy, as well as the events that are taking place — especially ones that seem to be out of our control. The *NEW* astrology can give you special insight and understanding to make sense of what is going on in your life.

(2) Have more harmonious, enjoyable relationships with others. Sometimes it seems mysterious why you get along with some people and not others. You may wonder why you experience tensions, problems, and conflicts? When they occur, you want to know how to resolve these differences. The *NEW* astrology can provide explanations for what you are experiencing, along with many solutions as well.

(3) Provide you the best dates to make your most important life decisions successful. A major factor in making sense of your life and making good decisions is your ability to understand what influences operate in your life, motivating you to make a particular choice. The *NEW* astrology can be like a trusted friend who offers you wise counsel, and valuable insights to help you make the decision that is right for you.

What Areas of Your Life Will This Book Discuss?

Here are the 12 specific areas we will discuss:

1. **Personality & Appearance.** We will begin by discussing your personality and your appearance, because what you don't know about who you are may be hurting your effectiveness in the world. What has caused your personality to change? If you are not happy with it or the way you look, what can you do to make a desired change?

2. **Money & Values.** When it comes to your values, your possessions, and the money that you make, are you happy with what you have? Do you want more? Is there a better time to get more? What are the

decisions you should be making to live according to your values, yet still enjoy prosperity?

3. ***Communications & Intellect.*** Does your communication style help you or hurt you? How does it affect the decisions you need to make at work, home, play, and in your relationships? How does your mind work? What does your intellect say about you? How can you improve it?

4. ***Family & Home.*** What impact has your family had on your life and beliefs? What kind of family do you want? When should you buy a home? Is real estate a fortunate area for you to invest in? What do you need in your life to feel more emotionally secure?

5. ***Romance & Creativity.*** Is romance likely to come into your life? Are you a romantic person? What kind of romantic partner would you find exciting? Are you a creative person? How can you enhance your self-expression? When should you gamble or take risks?

6. ***Health & Work.*** How about your health? Will you be healthy or will you have health issues? What kind of work do you enjoy doing? What type of people would you most enjoy working? When would be the best time to buy a pet?

7. ***Relationships (Marriage & Partnerships).*** What kind of partner are you seeking to marry or be in a committed relationship? When is the best time to find a mate? How should you go about choosing a business partner who will be compatible with you? If you are in a partnership, how can you make it better or change it, if it no longer works? What is the best time to marry; or divorce if your marriage is over?

8. ***Sex, Investments & Transformation.*** What about your sex life? Do you yearn for the deep sexual connection which soul mates share, or do you need the excitement of serial affairs? What are the best investments for you to make? When is the best time for you to invest successfully? How can you avoid losing money by knowing when you are unlucky? Have you thought about your personal transformation and how you can grow and be happier?

9. *Travel, Education & Philosophy.* Do you enjoy foreign travel? Should you go back to school and get an advanced degree? Do you want to publish a book? What is your philosophy? Are you interested in a spiritual journey?

10. *Career & Status.* What kind of career will you have? When is the best time for you to seek a promotion? If you are not happy with your career, when should you make a change? If you don't have a job, when is the best time to find one? When is the best time to start a business? Are status and reputation important to you?

11. *Friendship, Hopes & Dreams.* What kind of friends are you most compatible with? Would you benefit more if you joined organizations? What are your hopes and wishes? Are you interested in doing humanitarian work to make a difference?

12. *Psychology & Secrets.* What is your psychological make-up? What is there about your personality that everyone else knows except you? Are there any psychic wounds or hidden secrets that are in the way of your happiness? If you face depression, how can you successfully combat it? What kind of spiritual life are you creating?

No matter what your expectations are – you're in for a big surprise, because I will take your mind where it has never been! My sincere hope is that you'll find this information intriguing, illuminating, and liberating because it's exciting to learn something useful that can change your life.

Larry Schwimmer

"What is the NEW Astrology?"

OLD Astrology:

- I want to explain what I mean by the "old" versus the "new" astrology. Books on astrology have been written to teach people the *older*, more traditional way of learning about astrology.

- In the *old astrology* the author teaches you about the planetary symbols, signs, houses, and astrological aspects such as conjunctions, sextiles, squares, trines, and oppositions.

- These books have illustrations of natal, progressed, and transit charts, along with technical explanations explaining how to interpret them. Once you learn how to calculate and interpret planetary aspects, you can then analyze your own natal chart and the charts of other people.

- The *old astrology* is excellent for those people who want to learn many of the technical basics about how it works, as well as for those students who are serious about becoming professional astrologers.

NEW Astrology:

- In my book I am introducing a *new* approach to using astrology in a practical way that doesn't require you to learn the technical side of astrology. I call it the *new* astrology.

- The *new astrology* is directed at readers who want astrology interpreted for them so they can *immediately* use it in their lives. They are NOT interested in learning the technical basics of astrology such as symbols, signs, aspects, charts, calculations, or natal interpretation.

- The *new astrology* is directed at readers who exclaim: *"Please do not give me a lot of complicated astrology-speak. Just tell me what it means to my life, in vivid language that is easy to understand."*

- The *new astrology* is a simple explanation of what is going on in your life every year in such areas as your personality, finances, communication, family, romance, health, work, relationships, sex, investments, travel, education, career, friends, and your personal psychology.

- The *new astrology* shows you how to use astrology to make successful decisions in every area of your life.

- You can use the *new astrology* to find out your best dates to:

    o *Meet a New Romantic Partner*
    o *Find a New Job or Change Careers*
    o *Get Married*
    o *Start a Family*
    o *Buy a Home or Real Estate*
    o *Make a Profitable Investment*
    o *Resolve Health Issues*

SUMMARY: Imagine that there is a large fruit tree in front of you. It has ripe, delicious fruit growing from its branches and you have *three* thoughts as you look at that tree: (1) You want to pluck the fruit and take a big bite. (2) You do not want to learn scientific facts about fruit trees or how to grow them yourself. (3) You just want to eat the fruit and feel satisfied.

There is only fruit in this Book. Welcome to the NEW astrology!

Part I   The Secret To Knowing What Is Going On In Your Life

- "Life is great, but when will I finally settle down, marry and have a family?"
- "I'm frustrated because I'm in a dead-end job."
- "I seem to always be having money problems."
- "When will I meet the love of my life?"
- "Will I ever find my purpose – the thing I am meant to do?"

Did you ever wish you had your own personal advisor who knew you extremely well? This person had clear insight into your unique personality and circumstances. The advisor was always able to explain why certain things were happening in your life, when they would get better, and what you could do to improve them. Best of all, if you needed to make an important decision to change your life for the better – your advisor could tell you the *perfect* time to make your decision so it would be a successful one.

Well, I have great news for you: I can be that advisor for you. And that advice is available to you. It is a system of knowledge that combines science, art, and interpretation, to produce usable, valuable information that you can use to manage your life and make successful decisions at the perfect time. It's called astrology.

It has been used over the centuries by kings, Popes such as Leo X and Paul III, and historical figures from Benjamin Franklin to President Reagan, all who have consulted with astrologers. They trusted that the practice of astrology could provide valuable information to help them manage their affairs and make important decisions. Astrological interpretation offered them insightful analysis of the past, guidance to the future, and wise counsel they could depend on as being accurate. In fact, J.P. Morgan once said, *"Millionaires don't use astrologers, but billionaires do!"*

Who Has Used This "Secret?"

Did you know that these brilliant mathematicians, astronomers and scientists were also astrologers: *Aristotle, Hippocrates, Ptolemy, Copernicus, Nostradamus, Galileo, Johannes Kepler,* (considered to be the father of modern astronomy), *Sir Isaac Newton,* and psychologist, *Carl Jung.* Let's take a look a closer look at a few of the more famous people who have used astrology. Then, ask yourself if you think that these were "ignorant" people or just intelligent, practical people, who were a little ahead of their time.

Benjamin Franklin

Benjamin Franklin was one of the most respected and famous people in colonial America. As history notes, Franklin was a publisher, inventor, and statesman. He was a member of the Continental Congress, which declared independence from Great Britain, as well as a member of the committee for the Declaration of Independence; and one of its major drafters. Eventually, he became the country's first Postmaster General. He was also well known for his scientific discoveries such as electricity in the form of lightning, his inventions of bifocal eyeglasses, the lightning rod and the Franklin stove.

Franklin was also Colonial America's *greatest astrologer*. For 25 years he wrote and published *Poor Richard's Almanac*, a popular, yearly book that made him rich and famous throughout the colonies. *Poor Richard's Almanac* contained the calendar, weather, poems, sayings, astronomical, as well as astrological information. Readers were informed of the astrological position of each planet and the planetary alignments for each day of the year. Franklin himself actually calculated these positions, which demonstrated he was an extraordinarily skilled astrologer.

Franklin Used Astrology for the Declaration of Independence

Historical research indicates that both Franklin and Thomas Jefferson, (who was another all-around philosophical, scientific genius, and fellow committee drafter) conspired to have the Declaration of Independence adopted on July 4, 1776, rather than on the July 2nd date urged by their fellow committee member, John Adams. Franklin knew the importance of choosing favorable astrological timing; and July 2, 1776 was bad!

Instead, he picked a fabulous "astrological day" for America's Founding Fathers to sign the *Declaration of Independence*.

J.P. Morgan

J. Pierpont Morgan was a wealthy American financier at the turn of the 20th century who consulted often with a well-known astrologer, Evangeline Adams. She gave him the best timing to make important investments in such companies as *U.S. Steel Corporation* and the *Great Northern & Pacific Railroad*, as well as the Boer War. His use of astrology for business made him a billionaire, back in the early part of that century when a million dollars was a vast fortune. In fact, Morgan listened to Adams when she expressly told him: "Don't get on the Titanic." He followed her advice, cancelled his reservation, and subsequently saw some of his best friends die on that tragic vessel.

President Charles de Gaulle

Susan Bell, a reporter for *The Independent* (London, UK) in her news story, August 4, 2000: *France's Destiny Was Shaped by De Gaulle's Personal astrologer,* writes: "Former President of France, General Charles de Gaulle, the man who guided France into the Modern era often consulted a personal astrologer throughout his political career before making important decisions. But unlike another French president, Francois Mitterrand – who enlisted the services of the professional astrologer Elizabeth Teissier, - General de Gaulle turned to a fellow soldier, Major Maurice Vasset, who broke his silence on the subject yesterday.

They had a professional relationship that lasted 25 years until De Gaulle's resignation in 1969 after the loss of his disastrous referendum on regional government and senate reform – a poll Major Vasset strongly advised against. The major, now 85, revealed that he had regular astrological consultations with the former president, in an interview with the weekly news magazine Le Nouvel Observateur.

Mitterrand and De Gaulle were following an age-old French tradition in looking to the stars for answers to their most pressing problems."

Walt Disney

Walt Disney was the creative genius who created Mickey Mouse, Donald Duck, Disneyland and a vast entertainment empire. It was well known that Walt Disney used astrological timing for business purposes to assure successful openings for his movies and theme parks. In the process he made millions of dollars using this information.

President Ronald Reagan

It was well known and well documented that Ronald Reagan relied heavily on favorable astrological timing in running the affairs of this country as President of the United States. Here are quotes from his daughter, Patty Davis and his former Secretary of the Treasurer and former Chief of Staff, Donald T. Regan.

"My parents have done what the stars suggested – altered schedules, changed travel plans, stayed home, cancelled appearances." – Patti Reagan Davis in her book The Way I See It

"Virtually every major move and decision the Reagans made during my time as White House Chief of Staff was cleared in advance with a woman in San Francisco [astrologer Joan Quigley] who drew up horoscopes to make certain that the planets were in a favorable alignment for the enterprise." – Donald Regan, Reagan's former Chief of Staff, in his book, *For the Record: From Wall Street to Washington*.

This information, that President Reagan and his influential wife sought the advice of an astrologer, wasn't widely circulated until the publication of Donald Regan's book in 1988. *Time* magazine later identified Ron and Nancy's personal chart reader as San Francisco astrologer, Joan Quigley. President Reagan kept his use of an astrologer private for years, until a member of his Cabinet publicly revealed it. If Reagan could use astrology to make important decisions to run the country, you can use it to "run your life."

On Wall Street

"It's common knowledge that a large percentage of Wall Street brokers use astrology." – Donald Regan, formerly Merrill Lynch, Chairman and CEO, Secretary of the Treasury, and Chief of Staff to President Ronald Reagan.

On Wall Street, business astrologers are referred to as business consultants. "Astroeconomics is like technical analysis 30 years ago. People were using it and nobody talked about it." – Henry Weingarten, financial astrologer turned money manager.

"It's a fairly open secret that a certain segment of fund managers, traders and investors use financial astrology, and eventually it will become mainstream." – Reuters

Businesses in Asia and Europe have been utilizing astrology for centuries. Their formidable business competition is a testimony to their understanding of the art and appreciation of the value of astrological timing using planetary cycles.

Jesus & The Three Astrologers (aka "The 3 Wise Men")

Astrology goes way back in history to the birth of Jesus (and even before). The account of this event is found in the New Testament book of Matthew: *"After Jesus' birth, astrologers from the east arrived one day in Jerusalem inquiring, 'Where is the newborn king of the Jews? We observed his star at its rising and have come to pay him homage.'"* (Matthew 2:1, 2, New American Bible). This translation calls the visitors from the east "astrologers."

The scriptures here use the plural form of the Greek word *ma'gos*. Various Bible translations render it as *wise men, astrologers, stargazers*, or they simply translate it as *Magi*. This word refers to those who give advice and make predictions based on the position of the stars and the planets.

Who Uses Astrology?

It is clear: Some of the most powerful and influential figures in history have used astrology, including presidents, CEOs, billionaires, as well as business owners, managers, executives, sales representatives, artists, musicians, writers, financial planners, economists, lawyers, accountants, psychologists, doctors, and those in numerous other professions. The list of organizations using astrology includes publically traded corporations, hedge funds, small businesses, government, non-profit organizations, and sports teams.

Stepping "Out of the Box" of Ignorance

> *"Sorry…but we made a mistake: We thought the world was flat!"*

After all, there was a time in history when almost everyone thought the world was flat and anyone who thought differently was considered a kook! So, don't forget that *what we believe to be true is subject to change*. It's through centuries of learning and discovery that we go from ignorance to enlightenment to a new awareness. Our beliefs about what is true do change. In the same way, more and more people have recognized what they previously believed about astrology was based on ignorance.

Historical figures and leaders have been using astrology for centuries, unconcerned as to whether it was in or out of favor by the masses. Instead, these visionaries viewed it as a practical, valuable tool for understanding the events of their life, as well as making successful decisions about their activities, relationships, and investments. They knew astrology's value centuries ago and they know its value today because they get great benefit from using it.

Most intelligent, rich, famous, and powerful people in our society see no advantage in letting the public know they use astrology or consult with an astrologer. They have no need to open themselves up to the scrutiny, criticism, or ostracism of narrow-minded people. Their approach is to keep a low profile and just reap the benefits of using astrology. The fact is – clients that I consult with demand strict confidentiality. When it comes to using astrology to manage their affairs and make decisions, they would prefer to keep their use private.

People in the many professions who use astrology do so for three reasons:

- It works.
- It's accurate.
- It helps them manage their life more effectively and make their decisions more successful.

You can enjoy its value in your life as well. This book is your opportunity to step out of the box and defy popular convention. You can make practical use of the same information that rich, powerful, and famous people have used for centuries to manage their life and make successful decisions at the correct time.

Next, Part II discusses the ways most people make their decisions. We will discuss the question: Is there a better way to make successful decisions? Then, I'll give you some examples of the different ways you can use astrology to manage your life and make your decisions successful.

Part II   Using Astrology As A Decision-Making Tool

It's important to finally understand, *what the hell is going on in your life?* However, once you know, the question remains: What are you going to do about it? Hopefully, you'll want to change your circumstances and improve your life. But that's often easier said, than done, plus not a simple process. However, *change* usually begins with evaluating your options, deciding if you want to make a change, and understanding what obstacles you'll have to overcome. Then you have to decide if you're ready to take some sort of action, which may result in making a decision. *This* is where you can use astrology as a decision-making tool to help you.

Decision-making is easy for many of us; however, some people have never learned how to make decisions in a calm, thoughtful manner. In fact, the idea of having to make a decision can raise a person's anxiety level to the point where they end up procrastinating until they are forced to make a decision. Others make decisions impulsively, when they're in an emotional state such as fear, anger or insecurity. Then, there are those who make decisions *verrrrrrry* slowly, only after a long period of examination and thoughtful research, where "analysis is paralysis."

Of course, there is a whole other category of people, not even aware of the fact that their circumstances require a decision to be made. We often look at them and think to our self, *"When is John going to realize that he has to face his problem?"* Unfortunately, John may need to first, "buy a ticket on the clue bus," since *awareness* comes before making a necessary decision.

Many of us tend to make our decisions in a vacuum, all by ourselves, often using bad judgment. Have you ever listened to a friend tell you about a difficult decision they just made? You listened patiently, hearing some real flaw in their logic, then you couldn't stop yourself from kindly asking, "Why did you make that decision?" They answer, "Well, it seemed like a good idea at the time." Or, they said, "I really didn't know a good person to talk to about it. So, I just made the decision myself." Clearly, finding the right person to talk to about your decision can be a problem in of itself. After all, you may confer with someone well meaning, but not well qualified or informed to give you the best counsel. Admittedly, some times it's difficult to get good advice when you have to make an important decision. Often, good decision-making requires planning. However, many of us are not conscious of the need to plan for our important decisions. Instead, we let life happen to us, and then we react. We aren't sure where we are going. We become *destiny-reactors,* instead of *destiny-creators.*

Regardless of whether decisions are made impulsively, thoughtfully, or painfully slow, the biggest problem is they are made at the *wrong time.* The result is upset, disappointment, or failure, which could have been prevented by making the decision at a more favorable time. The use of astrology can help you plan your decisions and give you the perfect time to make the right one. If you are already a great decision-maker, then astrology can provide you with excellent information to make even better decisions.

A Genie and a Roadmap

Imagine taking a long trip in your car. You're not totally sure where you're going, but you're thinking you can figure it out once you get on the road. Then, as you drive for a few hours you start wondering, *"Maybe I'm not exactly sure where I'm headed."* Unfortunately, there are no places to stop and ask for help. Eventually you realize that you're lost. Amazingly, at that very moment, a *genie* magically appears in the passenger seat next to you. He tells you to open your glove compartment, where you'll find a road map with specific instructions, including the dates when you will get to each stop on your journey. The map is your assurance that you'll get to your destinations on time.

As an astrologer, just like the genie, I'll show you how to find your road map, plus use it to guide you to where you want to go. However, the way to get to where you want to go in life is by *the decisions you make.* I'll show you how to make your decisions at a time when they will be most successful.

Your road map to making successful decisions is sitting in a file drawer in your home, a safety deposit box, or in the archives of the hospital where you were born. It is called your *birth certificate*, and it has your precise date, place and time of birth. All you have to do is find it; and I'll show you how you can turn your birth information into a map that shows the major events of your life, and the best times to make those events successful. I'll show you how to use astrology for decision-making.

The good news: You do NOT need to have prior knowledge of astrology. This book will explain everything you need to know to understand the changes you're experiencing in your life, the decisions you may be required to make, and how to make them at the perfect time so they will be successful. The use of astrology is to reveal choices to you – not to make your choice for you. In that sense, as my brilliant astrology colleague Ray Merriman says: *"It is a choice-revealer, not a choice-decider."* Your own free will can always be brought to bear on any situation you face in life. You are the master of your own destiny.

A Good Time & A Bad Time To Start A Job!

Suppose, for example, after interviewing for a new job – you receive an offer. Your new employer calls you on the telephone, giving you a choice of two potential starting dates. You can start your new job in July; a time when your astrological chart indicates is a bad one because you'll work hard for little recognition and great frustration; or you can start in August, a positive date when your astrological chart says you will be successful, well received, and have opportunities for advancement. Assuming your new employer gave you these two choices, which date would you choose to start your new job?

Therein lies the practical value of using astrology for *decision-making*. It can give you the perfect time to make your decision a successful one that will benefit you. Of course, the *choice* is always yours. Yet, while *career* decisions are important, you can also use astrology for decision-making in many other areas of your life.

Personal Decisions: "Is there something wrong with me?"

It's easier to make decisions in an objective way about activities and events when there are no emotions involved. However, decisions you make involving your relationships tend to be more personal and subjective. This is especially true if you have a relationship that is stressful or conflict-ridden. If the differences between you and the other person cannot be resolved, you may be faced with the dilemma of having to decide whether or not to continue that relationship. You will face an even bigger challenge if the discord you're experiencing involves your family. The use of astrology can reveal and explain the source of these personal problems and upsets so that you can better decide how to resolve them.

Brigitte grew up with her parents always thinking she was eccentric, unconventional and strange. Despite trying to win their approval, their behavior towards her was hurtful. They constantly made thoughtless and insensitive remarks about her actions, always disapproving of her personal choices, whether it was the clothing she wore or the men she dated. On many occasions she sat down with her parents to discuss the ways their disapproval upset her, however she was always unsuccessful. Eventually, she fell into the trap of thinking "somehow" she was responsible for their disapproval. Maybe there was something wrong with her?

After a comparison of her astrology chart with her parents' charts, the answer was clear – it was no one's fault. The three charts revealed they had totally different views and morals. Even though Bridget's parents loved her, they were pre-disposed to find her behavior, actions and decisions unacceptable to their standards. The reality: they were unlikely to ever approve of her behavior. Once astrology revealed the personality dynamics between Bridget and her parents, she felt immense relief, realizing she was not responsible for their behavior. She wasn't the problem. The poor communication and incompatibilities between them weren't her fault. There was no point in trying to gain their approval or get them to change their behavior toward her. It was simply better for her emotional and mental health to accept the reality they were just different. She realized that she needed to limit her time in their company. *That* was her decision.

In Bridgett's case, the use of astrology was helpful in making some important personal decisions around her basic questions: "Is there something wrong with me? Will my parents ever approve of my choices? Is it likely they will ever change? Under these circumstances, what is the best decision for me to make as far as spending time in their company?"

Relationship Decisions: "Why can't I find the right woman?"

Many single people spend months, years, and even decades trying to find the right person to date, and eventually marry. Some experience the frustration of continually meeting the *wrong* person, feeling disappointed, and being disillusioned. Just when they think they've found the *right* partner, ultimately it's someone who cannot fulfill their needs.

Don's had his birth chart (also called a natal chart) analyzed to understand his personality strengths, weaknesses, and challenges. He wondered if it might provide some clue as to why his experience was to frequently date women, only to be frustrated because they always seemed to fall short of his expectations and requirements. One woman was really pretty, but lacking intellectual depth; another woman was brilliant but "not his body type." Then another woman was very bright, with a chemistry that "really turned him on," but less age appropriate than he liked. When he finally met a woman who seemed to "have it all," in two months' time she went from being his ideal, to being just another disappointing relationship.

Don's astrological analysis revealed that he had a very critical and perfectionistic attitude toward the women he was romantically interested in. To make matters worse, Thomas had a built-in tendency to over-idealize any potential love interest. He was clearly looking for a lofty, romantic connection with a *mythical Goddess* possessing none of the imperfections of a real human. Therefore, when Don finally found a woman whom he was attracted, he would put her on a pedestal. Ultimately, when she showed herself to be a real person, he was disappointed. He had the astrology chart of a classic, *romance-excitement junkie.* His aphrodisiac was getting high on the excitement of new romances. Frequently, he would meet a woman who seemed ideal, yet even when they were on a date, he would glance across the room, imagining someone who might be more exciting. This basic pattern of dating, having unrealistic expectations, being critical, then ending up disappointed, played out for many years of his bachelor life.

Don's immature attitudes were a perfect recipe for never finding anyone good enough to have a real, mature relationship. Many years of serial dating, and unsuccessful relationships were a validation of how he had acted out his challenging astrology, thus sabotaging his chances of finding a mate. However, underneath the surface, Don's natal chart showed him to be a victim of his own self-critical behavior. Because he was critical of himself, it made it easy for him to require others to be perfect. His astrological analysis explained how his behavior interfered with his ability to enjoy a satisfying relationship. He now had to decide if he was going to do some self-improvement work, in order to truly be available for an intimate relationship with a woman.

Astrology can provide you with the opportunity to do some important self-analysis. You'll gain insights to your personality and behavior that you may never have been aware of. So often we behave unconsciously, in ways that may actually sabotage our relationships, and get in the way of achieving our goals. Astrological analysis may provide you with profound insights that can help you resolve psychic wounds that have haunted you all your life.

Practical Decisions: Buying a House, Investing, Marrying

In real estate, you've heard that the secret to buying the best property is "location... location... location." In astrology, the secret to successful decision-making is "timing... timing... timing!" Let me give you some examples of how events turn out when people are unaware of whether they have *good timing* or not?

Bill and Mary have been shopping for a home for the past year and finally found a home within their price range in an acceptable neighborhood. Their bank financing has been pre-approved and their buyer has accepted their offer. The sale is closed. Within four months of moving into their new home they find out that they not only overpaid, but a multitude of defects in the home will require repair much sooner than they expected. Unfortunately, their contract states the seller is not liable for any of these repairs. Once they moved in, they found the neighborhood not as tranquil as they thought; several of the neighbors play loud music and have late night parties. Now Bill and Mary are regretting their decision to buy this house.

Pete has a good friend, Bob, who invests in the stock market regularly and very successfully. He tells Pete that he can get him shares of a new stock IPO (initial public offering) that is sure to go up by 20 percent within a week of the offering. Pete uses his retirement fund to buy this new stock. Instead of going up 20 percent, the stock goes down 20 percent the first week. Six months have gone by and the stock is down another 20 percent.

Judy decided to marry Victor. Their first few months of married life seemed to be going along fine until Victor shocked her, informing her that he had a child out of wedlock with another woman, many years ago. He neglected to mention this during their courtship. She also recognizes that he has an anger problem frequently flying into rages. Victor had never shown this side of himself during the year they dated. Judy is disappointed and disillusioned, to say the least. She plans to see a divorce lawyer to discuss her marriage situation.

You may be thinking: *"Problems and unfortunate events like these happen to people all the time."* Yes, they do. But they occur most often for those people who think: Timing does not matter; one day is as good as the next; or, the best time to do something is whenever they think it's a good time. WRONG!

The conflicts and problems, which occurred in all three of these situations, might have been avoided if each of these people had not made decisions during a time when their personal astrology was so negative. Instead, they could have chosen to make their decision at a time when their personal astrology was very *"lucky,"* assuring them a successful outcome.

To understand how you can use astrology to manage your life more effectively; and to learn the secret of how astrology can show you the *best time* to make successful decisions, read Part III, *The Magic of Transits*.

Part III   The Magic Of Transits

Barbara was shy and lonely. She told me how much she wanted to find a boyfriend who would be her soul mate. I looked at her birth chart and saw a very lucky astrological event occurring for her in July, one which was likely to produce an exciting and lasting romantic relationship. I encouraged Barbara to take advantage of her astrological good fortune by making a plan to be out in the public at parties, clubs and with friends, socializing from July 8 to July 16. The astrological forecast was a "bulls-eye," because she wrote me several months later saying that she met her new boyfriend on July 12.

Barbara was at a club, dancing with a guy she was not interested in, when suddenly her new boyfriend-to-be, asked to cut-in. That was how it started. Their love relationship developed over the next 12 months. They were married in August 2012. (To read her testimonial, please go to my web site: AstroDecision.com)

To the old Italian singer, Dean Martin. . . *"That's amore."* To me. . . that's a favorable astrological event working its magic! Does it work out so perfectly every time? Of course not. But this astro-event was successful because Barbara was out socializing *during the days that her favorable astrological influence was in effect.*

It's now time to discuss how "astrological events" are created, since they explain a great deal about what is going on in your life. These events are called *"transits,"* and they are produced when a moving planet in the sky forms a relationship with a planet in your birth chart. The interaction of those two planets produces an event that causes *something* to happen in your life.

In simple terms, astrological transits affect you. They produce the many changes that occur in each area of your life and can be used *magically* to bring success to your decisions. For this reason, it's important you understand more about transits and how they come into your life, the kind of influences you can expect from them, and how you can use them to make well-timed decisions. These transits are the *catalysts* or *change agents* that affect you, your relationships, your children, your activities, career, health, investments, and every aspect of your life. They occur during every year of your life. Their effects can be positive, beneficial, fortunate, helpful, and easy; or they can be challenging, negative, upsetting, difficult, disappointing, and even depressing. Of course, there are transits whose influences and effects are in between those two extremes. But make no mistake, these *transits* will explain *what the hell is happening in your life* – any time you want to know.

How Transits Work

- The key is to understand that every year the movement of planets in the sky will create relationships (or interactions) with the planets that are in your birth chart.

- These planetary interactions, called transits, produce events in your life.

- Each year there are many transits occurring in your life.

- These transits affect your life in some way, and will help you better understand what is happening in your life.

- Some of these transits will provide the perfect timing for you to make a change in your life; and implement a decision to create the successful outcome you desire.

The length of time a transit exerts its influence to *produce an event* will vary – depending on the particular planet involved. It can be as short as a few days or as long as long as two years. Fortunately, the *date* of a transit's passage into your life can be seen well in advance of its occurrence. This gives you plenty of *advanced* notice to implement your decision at a time when the transit has the greatest potential to produce successful results for you.

What Areas of Your Life Do Transits Affect You?

Transits affect you in all areas of your life. In astrology *an area of life* is referred to as a *House*. Your astrological birth chart looks like a pie, divided into 12 pieces called Houses. Each House represents a unique area of your life, and we'll talk about all 12 House areas in subsequent chapters.

During your life, the five *outer* transiting planets, *Jupiter, Saturn, Uranus, Neptune,* and *Pluto,* will move into (or "transit") most or all of the Houses in your birth chart. Some of these planets will visit a House area of your life many times, others only a few.

When a planet transits one of the Houses in your birth chart, it causes *special events* to occur in your life as a result of its influence. By understanding how each planet influences you, you'll have a better understanding of the changes you'll experience as you live your life. In addition, this understanding will help you make any important decisions you deem necessary.

Do Planets Really Influence You?

Keep in mind that astrology is based on a *system of knowledge* that says that the planets in the solar system have a highly specialized influence on your behavior, your relationships, and the events that happen in your life. No scientist disputes that phases of the Moon exert influences on the tides and the planting of crops. There is plenty of research that has measured and quantified the effects of Moon in this regard. During the full Moon, many hospital medical staff in ER rooms will attest to the abnormal increase in babies being born, patients requiring immediate medical care, whether due to careless accidents, gunshot wounds or illness. Many police departments frequently staff up because of the higher incidents of violent crime and arson during full Moons. (You may have heard the word *lunatic,* which comes from the Latin *luna*, meaning Moon. It refers to someone who's gone mad because of the effects of the Moon.)

It appears that a full Moon seems to raise the level of feelings, emotions and upsets which cause disturbing, even sometimes, violent interactions with people. Therefore, why would it seem so crazy to imagine that the other planets in the solar system also exert a special influence on us? The answer is: It's not crazy, because they do. Each planet exerts its own unique influence on you and within you. A planet's passage through each House of your birth chart will change you and challenge your life in a particular way. Of course, that doesn't mean that astrology is fatalistic. Your own free can always be brought to bear on any situation. In 1632, Sir Francis Bacon said it well, "Wiser astrologers believe that there is no fatal necessity in the stars, but that they rather incline then compel."

For that reason, I am not saying: "A planet makes you do something." After all, you are in charge, responsible for your behavior and actions. However, I *am* saying that a planet does exert an influence and does produce an effect on you. *If you are aware of that influence and the kind of events that may occur "under that influence," it gives you a tremendous opportunity to produce a favorable outcome for your decision, IF YOU TAKE ACTION!*

Let me give you an analogy, which makes this point crystal clear. Imagine sitting down at a poker game at a casino in Las Vegas. Before you place your bet at the poker table, the dealer says: "I am going to deal you five cards. Four of them will be Aces. Then, you can place your bet." You probably would agree that it would be a pretty positive event to be told, *before you place your bet,* you will be dealt a *winning poker hand.* (Most people would agree that in a straight game of 5-card poker, 4 Aces is a winning hand.) Because you have a likely assurance that you will win the hand, you might capitalize on that information by betting even more money.

Now, imagine siting down at the table in the office of your astrologer. You tell him that you'd like to find a job, make a profitable investment in a stock, or meet someone for a love relationship. Just like the dealer at the card table, you're astrologer says: "I can tell you the perfect time to find a great job, make a profitable investment, or meet someone for a love relationship." I think you'd agree, it would be quite fortunate to know that information in advance. The dealer gave you 4 Aces, and then invited you to bet. Your astrologer gives you a positive transit (like the 4 Aces) and then invites you to make your decision (like your bet). Of course, if you don't bet, (take action) you can't win.

KEY POINT: By having advance notice of the transits that will be occurring in your life every year, you have a tremendous opportunity to understand what is going on in your life, take the appropriate steps to make any changes you deem necessary, AND make decisions that will work out in your favor. That is how you can use the *magic of transits* to your advantage.

How Transits Give You Greater Control of Your Life

Feeling out of control of your life can make you feel uncomfortable, insecure and powerless. Therefore, by understanding how your transits are affecting you, you have the advantage of being aware of what is happening in your life at all times. As a result, you feel more in control. Best of all, you can use this knowledge to take charge, and make necessary decisions, instead of letting circumstances make them for you.

While we should each accept individual responsibility for our life and our actions, it's a great burden off our shoulders, even liberating, to acknowledge that there are outer influences affecting us, and ones we can use to our benefit. These *influences* are the transiting planets. If you're open to this revolutionary new way of understanding your life, it will allow you to finally make sense of what *has* happened, what *is* happening, and what *may* happen in your future. This knowledge will make you feel personally powerful.

So...That's What Was Going On!

Have you ever looked for a job and suddenly found a terrific opportunity to work in the ideal environment at a salary way beyond your expectations? Conversely, have you ever found yourself screaming about a problem you were having, only to look up at the sky and stars, and yell: "Why me? Why me? I don't deserve this! What the hell is going on?" Well, I now have an answer for you: there was a transiting planet going through one of your 12 Houses (i.e. areas of your life) and it may have been there bringing you great luck and opportunity; or it may have there wreaking havoc in your life. Rest assured, either way, that transit was there to teach you a valuable lesson. It may have provided you with an experience to help you evolve, grow, let go, or make a change that eventually would be of great benefit to you. The transit acted as a catalyst to promote change in the affairs of that House. This is one of the ways that astrology and planetary transits can help explain the many passages and changes occurring in your life.

The five planets that will be discussed in this book: *Jupiter, Saturn, Uranus, Neptune,* and *Pluto* each exert their own unique influence and cause various events to happen in the particular House they transit.

Depending on the planet, it will spend anywhere from one year to approximately, 21 years in a House area of your life. If you're aware of the way each planet affects you, you'll have an explanation for many of the changes you'll notice going on in your life. It may provide you with the answer as to why certain areas of your life have worked well for so long; or have been difficult for so long. You'll have the explanation for how it's possible that after years of some aspect of your life being *one way*, you suddenly experience a shift where it changes for the better – or worse. You will know why areas of your life may now be happier, more fun, challenged, stressed, problematic, or even radically altered.

Many people are not conscious of the forces that have created change in their life. They just know that *something* has happened or changed. For some, *change* can be blissful, but for others a bit disorienting, even disturbing. After all, what happened to create these changes?

- We were so much in love, and then things changed.

- I was lonely and depressed, now I am so content and happy in my relationship

- After working for others, I realize that I had to have my own business.

- I used to be very sexual – now I don't seem to have much interest.

- My job used to be so satisfying, now it's not.

- All I cared about was money, now it has less meaning and I want something more in my life.

- I use to be so be so poor, now I can't believe how much money I make!

- He used to be so carefree, now he's overly responsible and goal-oriented.

- My child used to be extroverted, but now he's become shy and quiet.

People who have experienced these personal changes and shifts have their own explanations as to what happened; and so would others, such as doctors and psychologists.

Changes such as these can also be explained by understanding the specific astrological transits that have occurred in your life. Dramatic changes are stimulated when one of the five outer planets *transits* a House in your birth chart. A transit may motivate you to take positive action that you haven't taken for years. For example, "I am tired of feeling fat – I've finally decided to lose 20 pounds." "Or, "Since I am shy and timid – I've decided to join a public speaking group to build up my self-confidence." Or, "I realize that this is the person I want to marry." Or, "I've got no future with this company, I am ready to find a new job." These are perfect examples of how a transit might influence your behavior and motivate you to make a decision to change your life. By the way, these are examples of decisions you might consider when you read about the 1st House, which governs your *personality, appearance and how you present yourself to the world*; or 7th House, which rules *your relationships*; or your 10th House, which governs *your career*.

The aim of this book is to teach you just enough astrology so you understand how astrology and transits work together to affect your life and your decisions:

- The *transits* produce events that explain what is happening in your life.

- The *Houses* in your birth chart tell you the major life areas where changes occur and where you may need to make decisions.

- The use of *favorable transits,* produce successful outcomes for your decisions.

Get Me One Of Those "Happy Transits!"

After my explanation of how transits work in your life, you might be thinking, "This explains what's happening in my life. Now I can make a decision to change ANY circumstance I'm not happy with." For example, suppose you're unhappy with your job and ready to tell your boss to "take this job and shove it," or, maybe you're sick of publishers rejecting your book proposal, which you know has the potential to be a best seller; or you're tired of being single and ready to meet your future partner next week. So, you excitedly read through this book, go to one of the 12 House areas that describe your problem, and make a decision to change your failure into a success. Your plan is to pick out one of those *big, juicy, happy-making transits,* and on the day the transit occurs…*voila:* Your decision produces the most amazing success you have ever imagined!

Unfortunately, successful decisions require more effort than that. Please, forgive me if I've made it sound too simple to use astrology to understand what is going on in your life and for decision-making. It's not hard, but you'll have to be committed to making a positive change in any area of your life that requires attention.

In my 35 years of practicing astrology, I have found that most people are reluctant to change. They don't embrace it, even though, intellectually they recognize that it may be necessary. In fact, quite often people fight change, preferring the status quo. They'd rather stay with the "the devil they know, than the devil they don't know." At least their frustration or unhappiness is predictable.

However, if you're *really* ready to make a change and create something different in your life, the process begins with being clear on *what you want to* change. Then, you can ask yourself: "How can I bring about the change I want? What are my options? What actions can I take that would bring me the result I desire? Which decision would help me reach my goal?" The next step will be to turn your decision to create change – into action by picking a transit that will produce the successful outcome you want. Of course, transits cannot be purchased at the grocery store the moment you need one. So, let me explain how transits enter your life.

How Transits Come Into Your Life

As I mentioned before, planets are always moving in the sky. At some point a transiting planet will move into one of the 12 Houses of your birth chart. Or, we could say, *at some point a transiting planet will move into one of the 12 Houses of your life.* Same thing. The planet will stay there for a varying period of time. (Note: the length of time depends on the rate of speed it takes to complete its cycle around the sun.) For example, let's consider the planet Jupiter. It will spend one year transiting a House in your birth chart and will bring specific Jupiter type influences, effects, and activities to that particular area of your life. (Note: Saturn will spend two and a half; Uranus will spend seven years; Neptune will spend 14 years; and Pluto will spend 21 years in a House.)

Here is another way to express what is happening when a transit visits an area of your birth chart: imagine that a transit is a houseguest who has just arrived at your home. Your guest may be staying in your home for a year or more, and during that time, he will bring many experiences into your life. Now, let's assume that the planet Jupiter is transiting the 7th House of your birth chart during that one year. In astrology the 7th House area of your birth chart concerns your partnerships in life, such as a marriage partner or a business partner. While Jupiter is in your 7th

House, it will transit, or form a relationship with, one of the 10 planets in your birth chart (in astrology, the Sun and Moon are also called planets). An astrologer preparing your transit chart performs a mathematical computation that reveals the exact number of transits that occurs during that year of your life.

In summary: The interaction of a transiting planet creates a relationship with a planet in your birth chart, which produces a transit. This, in turn, produces or influences an event to occur. By knowing more about those transits and the events they produce, you can utilize this knowledge to understand what is happening in your life and make successful decisions.

How Transits Manifest in Your Life

In this book, I am only going to focus on the general effects that will go on when the 5 outer planets transit each of the Houses in your birth chart. In the next chapter, Part IV, you can find out which Houses these planets are transiting in your individual chart by using the FREE Transit Calculator.

But many readers will want to know what effects are produced when one of the 5 outer planets makes an "individual" transit to a natal planet in their birth chart.

So, I would like to go through one example showing how a Jupiter transit might affect you. Let's assume that *Jupiter is transiting one of the natal planets in your birth chart.* This illustration will also show you the value of having your astrologer calculate your personal transits.

Keep in mind that your individual transits can manifest in your life in many ways – on a physical, emotional, mental, spiritual, or event level. Transits can also affect you on several levels at the same time.

For example, if you were shopping for a new car you might feel the effect of a transit on an emotional, physical and event level. Let's consider Jupiter's influence on you during the time you are shopping for a car. You might find yourself feeling very enthusiastic and extravagant as you visit different car dealerships. If, for example, you have Jupiter transiting the planet *Jupiter* in your birth chart, you might be motivated to buy a big, expensive car that you might not otherwise have purchased. You would really be happy that you did, too. Let's leave this car example and talk about how you might be affected if Jupiter made an individual transit to some of the other planets in your birth chart.

On an *emotional* level, a Jupiter transit to the natal *Moon* in your birth chart, might cause you to feel unusually warm, generous, and loving towards your family. Because you are in such a happy, generous mood, you might feel like this would be great time to throw a big family reunion. If you did, it would be a very enjoyable and successful party.

On a *mental* level, a Jupiter transit to the planet *Mercury* in your birth chart might help you at work. It could bring you brilliant thoughts and clever ideas to use in a client presentation winning a big contract for the firm. Your success might result in a bonus or promotion.

On a *spiritual* level, if Jupiter transits the planet *Neptune* in your birth chart, you might find that your compassionate and benevolent nature manifests in a strong desire to volunteer, helping people less fortunate than you. You'd feel extremely gratified doing volunteer work.

On an *event* level, a Jupiter transit to the planet *Venus* in your birth chart might bring a joyous love relationship into your life. For that reason (just like in Barbara's story at the beginning of this chapter), this is an excellent time to be out socializing at singles events. You might meet a wonderful person for romance.

Of course, transits to your birth chart can be positive, neutral, challenging or very negative. In this book our focus will be on using positive transits. Please don't be concerned if this discussion seems confusing or more than you want to know. You don't need to learn any of this. However, out of respect to readers who want a full understanding of how astrological transit interpretation works, I wanted to go through this explanation.

What is important to note are – the many practical and beneficial ways you can use astrology for everything from buying a car, to putting on a great family party, to advancing your career, to making your heart feel good through volunteering, or for finding a love relationship.

Transits Teach You Valuable Lessons

When a planet transits a House, it acts as a *catalyst*, raising issues that relate to the affairs of that House. In fact, it can present you with important opportunities for self-examination. For example, the 2nd House of your birth chart concerns your *values;* so when a planet transits there, its influence may cause you to re-examine, *"What are your values?"* The 8th House concerns *investing* your resources. Therefore, a planet transiting there may cause you to consider, *"How will you invest?"* Transiting planets bring you opportunities to learn, grow, evolve, and ultimately make your life better.

Sometimes learning and growing involve pain, too. However, we have choices about how we learn and the amount of pain that will be involved in our learning. For example, when you were a child you could learn that the stove was hot, by touching the stove and getting burnt – as in *"Ouch!"* Or, you could learn by putting your hand near enough to the stove to feel the heat and say to yourself, "I think I might get burned if I touch this stove. Not going to do it." Or, you might have stayed out of harm's way by listening to your mother when she told you not to touch the stove when the gas flame was on. In that case, you might have said, "Thank you Mom for that great advice." The lesson that each transit teaches you can be learned in the same way that you chose to learn that touching a hot stove might lead to burning your hand.

A famous old singer from the '40s, Sophie Tucker, once said: "I've been rich and I've been poor. And, rich is better!" In the same vein, I say to you: You will have positive transits and you will have negatives transits. You will like the positive ones better! The good news it that while you will grow and benefit from both positive and negative transits, my purpose is to teach you how you can use positive transits to make your most important decisions for successful outcomes.

In addition to choosing a favorable astrological transit, there is one very important element necessary to making your decision successful: *You must create an ACTION PLAN to be implemented during the time of the transit's occurrence in your life.* After all, if you want to win the lottery, actions are required. You have to first buy a lottery ticket, win, and then cash it in. If you want to reap the full benefit of a fortunate transit, you have to execute some sort of action. In fact, you need a plan.

The Use of a Transit Requires an Action Plan!

To take full advantage of a favorable transit, you must execute your plan during the time that the transit's influence is in effect. I call this plan an *"ASTRO ACTION PLAN."* Creating and implementing your Astro Action Plan at the time of your transit is just as important as picking the right transit. This is one of the secrets to insure that your decision will be successful. *Always use an Astro Action Plan in conjunction with a positive transit to produce results.*

I've had clients, for example, who assured me that they "really, really want to find a marriage partner." Yet, during a two week period, when they have the most fantastic transit for bringing a love relationship into their life, they will still work the same long hours at the office; or stay at home and order pizza with friends; or read a good book, instead of being out socializing where they could be meeting Prince (or Princess) Charming. In other words, they squandered the positive effects of a favorable transit that was ideal for bringing a love relationship into their life. They were unwilling to put out a sincere effort towards bringing a love relationship into their lives. That's why a genuine commitment to your goal is necessary. Remember: Even the most positive transit will not work its magic without your wholehearted commitment (remember Barbara's success at the beginning of this chapter). So, a plan of action is mandatory to making your decision successful.

At a transit consultation, often a client will make a decision to change an area of their life. When they make such a resolution, I encourage them to create an Astro Action Plan to be used in conjunction with their transit. Let me give you an example: Robin was unhappy with her job. She was tired of the politics at work, never received credit for the many weekend hours she spent on her projects, and was paid too little. Ironically, she was very popular and well respected by her coworkers and boss.

During her astrology consultation there was an excellent transit occurring over a 30-day time period. It was ideal for her purpose of finding a job and making a career move. Therefore, she made her decision to utilize that 30-day time period to find another job that would be right for her. To make her Astro Action Plan successful, Robin agreed that during the time of the transit, she would minimize her long work hours and her normal social activities. She was also committed to being proactive during the time frame of her favorable transit. Here is the Astro Action Plan we created:

Robin's Astro Action Plan from July 28th to August 27th

1. Update my resume.
2. Update Profile and network on *LinkedIn*
3. Attend 2 association conferences and 2 business networking events.
4. Contact all the executive search firms on my list.
5. Attend 3 job fairs.
6. Contact my professional network: old bosses, colleagues from previous jobs, and mentors who are well connected.
7. Use lunches and personal time off for meetings with mentors, business contacts, and interviews.

During those 30 days Robin enjoyed real success. She was told about 12 opportunities; went on four interviews; received two job offers; and accepted a new position. Of course, using a favorable transit and implementing an Astro Action Plan does not guarantee success. However, it does give a high likelihood of getting optimum results. In Robin's case, the job she accepted came with an increase in responsibility, future promotion prospects, additional compensation, and better benefits.

The real purpose of illustrating Robin's Astro Action Plan is to show you how simple it is to make one. Too many people just let life happen to them, being reactive instead of being pro-active. They may lack the ambition, drive, or confidence to make such a plan. Others are just use to flying by the seat of their pants, hoping that things will just work out. My suggestion to them is this: find a friend, a family member or some responsible person who might be interested in helping you create your plan. The key to a successful Astro Action Plan is: (1) making a plan; and (2) implementing it during the time of the transit. It's that simple.

As Robin's Astro Action Plan illustrates, you do not need a Harvard MBA or a Ph.D. in engineering from MIT to create one that is effective. The primary purpose is having a well thought out plan with the action steps you will take and the activities you will pursue, during the time period in which your transit is in effect. These activities allow you to be pro-active and increase the likelihood of a successful outcome for your decision. Don't forget, as my old boss Bernie once said, 90 percent of life is just showing up." In other words, by just making a sincere effort to follow a plan of action, you can produce results during your transit.

Creating an Astro Action Plan

TIP: Your family, friends, and colleagues at work are the perfect resources to use to create ALL of your Astro Action Plans. Here are the steps to take to create an Astro Action Plan; and the questions you should ask them.

- What problem do I have that I want to resolve? (Be clear)
- What is my goal? (Be clear)
- What decision do I want to make? (Be clear)
- Make a list of family, friends, work colleagues or people in your life that you can sit down and discuss your Astro Action Plan.
- Set up a date for your meeting and interview them.
- Bring a pad of paper, a pen, and take notes.

- During your interview, tell them you've made a decision. And you have a goal you want to achieve. Then you'll say, *"I'd like your help. Please give me any suggestions you think would help me achieve my goal."*
- This will give you ideas, support and encouragement.
- Remember: You don't need to get into any discussion about *transits* or *astrology*; or that you've finally figured out, *what the hell is going on in your life.* You just need to ask for their help. Stay on purpose and focus on the interview only.
- Based on your discussion, you may want to do some further research on the Internet or talk to other people who may be of further help.
- Now with your notes and the feedback you've gotten – you're prepared to create your own *Astro Action Plan.*
- Writing down your Astro Action Plan helps bring it into manifestation and keeps you on target.

Using The Total Process: Decision + Transit + Astro Action Plan

When you want to create change in your life, here are the steps to use. They include, making your decision, choosing a transit, and creating an Astro Action Plan.

1. *Survey.* Take an inventory of the areas of your life where you want to understand what is going on, resolve conflicts, improve your life, or make any big decisions.

2. *Realization.* Come to an honest realization about what you want to make happen in your life.

3. *Decision.* Make a conscious decision. For example: "I realize that I've focused too much on my career. Now, I would like to find a marriage partner."

4. *Schedule a Transit Consultation.* Make an appointment with a professional astrologer for a transit consultation (or consult Part IV in this book to learn about your personal transits) to discuss all the individual transits occurring in your life, how they are

affecting you, and the decisions that you would like to make. This will also be an ideal time for you to bring up any issues that may have frustrated your ability to achieve your objectives in the past.

5. *Choose Your Transits.* Discuss which transits and dates would bring the most success to your decision. Use the best one available; or wait for a more positive one to occur; or make whatever decision you think best under the circumstances. At least you'll have the benefit of understanding, which transits are operating in your life at that time.

6. *Prepare Your Astro Action Plan.* Write the dates that the transit will occur in your calendar. Before the transit occurs, prepare a plan of action you will implement during the time of the transit.

7. *Implementation.* Implement your actions during the time period that the transit is occurring in your life.

The 5 Planets Discussed in Each Chapter of This Book

In this book, I will be discussing the transits made to your birth chart by the outer planets: *Jupiter, Saturn, Uranus, Neptune* and *Pluto*, because their effects are pronounced and occur over a long time period, from one to 21 years. These five planets bring major change to your life when they transit a particular House of your chart (i.e. area of your life). *This book will discuss the many experiences you may have during the entire time the planet transits that House.*

However, when a planet transits a House of your birth chart it may also make an *"individual"* transit to a natal planet in your birth chart. For that specific information, you'll need your astrologer to identify those transits. Let me give you an example of the difference between the general transits discussed in this book and the specific ones that your astrologer can provide you.

For example, let's assume you have Jupiter transiting your 7th *House of Marriage and Partnerships*. This book will describe the experiences you may have during the one year that Jupiter transits your 7th House. You will learn that during that year – you may have an opportunity to meet someone for marriage.

However, if you want to find out the "specific" dates *within* that year that you might have the good fortune to meet a marriage partner, you'll need to have your astrologer calculate them for you (as I did for Barbara in the story at the beginning of this chapter).

Meanwhile, there's great value in your knowing where your 5 transits are in your birth chart. You may learn valuable information about great news or an important event that is coming into your life.

Don't Forget: Part IV – Free Transit Interpretation

By now, you maybe curious to know in which areas of your life, the five planets are transiting? So, you'll be happy to know that the next section, Part IV discusses how you can obtain a list of your personal transits for FREE to use in conjunction with this book. Knowing where your transits are today will shed a great deal of light on, what is going on in your life. Also, in the event that you are not able to see an astrologer right away, you can take your list of the five transiting planets, go to the appropriate chapter in the book, and look up the *interpretation* for that transit. This information will give you some valuable insights about what may be going on in your life at this time. However, please keep in mind: these FREE transits are not meant as a substitute for having an astrologer tell you the specific transits you need to know to make a successful decision.

Make Your Decision On A Sunny Day

A transit consultation is like a weather report. It's up to you if you like it or not, and what you're going to do with it. However, the knowledge of that weather report is valuable information to use in making your decision. In fact, let's use the weather to illustrate a simple decision that everyone can relate to: You want to plan a romantic picnic with someone.

Of course, you want to pick the right day to have it. You can't necessarily go on your picnic just any day. After all, if it were raining and thundering, that wouldn't be a good time. Therefore, a sunny day would be an excellent time for your picnic. That is the exact principle of how you can use transits to make sure you pick the perfect day for your picnic. Planetary influences in your birth chart will give you the best days when it will be sunny and the worst days when it will be raining; and maybe even flooding.

Part III   The Magic Of Transits

Your Free Will

At this point, you might want to ask, "Larry, are you saying that I can't make decisions whenever I want?" And, "Are you suggesting that unless I have a *positive transit* to assist me, I shouldn't bother trying to achieve my goals, resolve my problems or face my challenges?"

Answer: "No!"

The reality is that most people DO make their decisions without any consideration to the favorable timing their transits could provide them. So, your *free will* can always be brought to bear. You can continue making decisions as you always have. *However, our goal is to use astrology, and your transits to help you understand what is going on in your life AND to provide you with the most fortuitous time for making a decision that will have the successful outcome you desire.* Therefore, it is to your benefit to use transits as you plan any major events in your future.

The best transit to produce success for an event may not be occurring in your life for a long time. Therefore, it's important to look at the transits that are happening in your life over several years, in order to properly plan for your major life changes and decisions. As an astrologer, I have a wonderful resource to consult that shows me the *position of the planets* in the future over the next 100 years. It is called an *Ephemeris*. So, it's possible for me to see the many positive transits that you can use, well in advance of when you need to make your decision. Therefore, why not plan for your future?

After all, we plan for future vacations. We plan for the day we will go from living in an apartment to the day we will buy a home. Many of us plan our career. When you meet someone you want to marry, you plan your wedding date. Many of us plan for our retirement. So, it makes perfect sense to make a plan that uses your best transits to make decisions to reach your goals, achieve your dreams, and produce the positive results you want to accomplish.

Know Thyself

You may be one of those rare individuals who really knows himself/herself well. In addition, you may have a special gift that permits you to view yourself objectively. If this is the case, your self-knowledge is, no doubt, invaluable to you. However, most people do not know themselves well. They have no objective way of fully understanding who they are, especially the personality traits that prevent them from being happy and attaining their goals. If you'd like to know yourself better, you may find value in having an astrologer do a personality interpretation of your natal chart. You'll learn a great deal about your pre-programmed nature, how you function, what motivates you, the strengths that benefit you, and the weaknesses holding you back. Without this knowledge you may not be aware of self-defeating behavior patterns that can undermine your success.

Let me give you an example how this pre-programming can affect a person's life by describing a client's experience. Jim was a successful professional. He never seemed to be satisfied with any goal he achieved. Soon after his last achievement, he would begin searching for the next thing he could accomplish that he was sure, would be even "more satisfying." When I analyzed his natal chart I saw the source of his dissatisfaction. His birth chart indicated that he was pre-programmed – "hot-wired," never to be satisfied with his successes. This was his basic nature and personality. No matter what he achieved, he felt like there was always something more important he should be doing *than what he had just done*. Jim was unable to live in the moment and to enjoy the journey of getting to his goal. He was always grasping for the "next thing," sure that he was meant for much greater accomplishment. He thought the next goal would be the one that would bring him the satisfaction he was striving for. This basic nature sabotaged his ability to be happy and fulfilled as he lived his life.

When I pointed out this dynamic in his personality, Jim immediately recognized that it was sadly true. He said, "All my life, I've never been satisfied with any goal I achieved. I was sure there was something more important that I should try to accomplish. If only someone had pointed out this part of my nature – when I was in my 20s or 30s, I am sure I could have broken that behavior pattern. I might have enjoyed my life's accomplishments much more." Here's the reason I wanted to illustrate Jim's experience. You have the option to learn more about who you are and what *runs you*. Then, you can decide if you are "hot-wired" the way you want, or if you want to make some changes in the way you operate your life.

Be Open To Change

You can use astrology to create change in your life if you're committed to taking action. Most people want to maintain the status quo. The temptation is to live with the familiar until it is no longer something a person can live with. Usually, pain, discomfort and failure are what motivate most people to make change through action. Be the exception. Don't wait for those extreme conditions to occur in order to decide it's time for you to find solutions and take corrective measures. Instead, choose to embrace the necessary changes that will make your life work better.

Committing to a Life Action Plan

As you read this book, no matter how well you understand what is going on in your life, it will mean nothing if you don't take some beneficial action – *once you know*. Use your personal astrology to understand the best choices for **YOU** to make. Then, use your positive transits to choose the best time to take action to change and improve your life. In the following chapters we will discuss 12 Houses (or areas) of your life. Get ready to truly understand *what the hell is going on in your life!*

Note: Throughout this book the names, characters and scenarios have been changed to protect client confidentiality.

Part IV Free Transit Interpretation

How to Use This Book

"Where are the transiting planets in my birth chart?"

As you read, ***What the Hell Is Going On in My Life?*** – you will learn how the five transiting planets, Jupiter, Saturn, Uranus, Neptune and Pluto affect every area of your life: *personality, body, finances, values, communication, family, home, romance, work, health, relationships, marriage, sex, investments, transformation, travel, education, career, friends, dreams,* and your personal *psychology* and *secrets*.

In order to make this book useful, interesting and fun – I offer you the opportunity to get a *FREE* list of your personal transits. This list will show the areas in your life where planetary transits will cause change and major events to occur.

Then you can read about the specific transits you're experiencing and learn more about how they will affect you. This information will help you make better sense of your life, help you find answers, and aid you in making important decisions. (*Note: If you have no interest in knowing which planets are affecting your life today, then skip this section and please enjoy reading each chapter.*)

Use your transits to learn about these areas of your life and the best dates to:

- *Meet a New Romantic Partner*
- *Find a New Job or Change Careers*
- *Get Married*
- *Start a Family*
- *Buy a Home or Real Estate*
- *Make a Profitable Investment*
- *Resolve Health Issues*

Instructions for a Free List of Your 5 Transiting Planets:

STEP 1 – To get a free list of the 5 Planets transiting in your birth chart, visit my book web site: **WhatTheHellisGoingOninMyLife.com** or professional services web site: **AstroDecision.com**

STEP 2 – Click the FREE TRANSITS Tab to take you to the FREE Transit calculator.

STEP 3 – Enter your birth information. *(Note: You will need to provide your exact time of birth.)* Click – CALCULATE MY TRANSITS. You'll receive a printout of your 5 transiting planets and the House they are in today.

STEP 4 – Use your transit printout to look up your personal transits in the book.

Find Your Transits Today, In the Past and the Future

You can use the FREE Transit Calculator to tell you where your personal transits are today, in the past and in your future. Just type in the *month, day, year* in the Transit date field. Then, click Calculate my Transits. You will receive a list of the 5 Planets and the House (i.e., area of your life) they are in on that date. Then, look up your personal transits in the book to understand, what is going on in your life.

TODAY'S Transits

Examples:

- Let's say your FREE transit printout indicates that *Jupiter* is transiting your 7th *House of Relationship* today. This is often a lucky time for finding a wonderful love relationship. You can go to the 7th House chapter and read the section on *Jupiter Transiting your* 7th *House* and learn more about how you can use this transit to find a romantic partner.

- Or, maybe your free transit indicates that *Jupiter* is transiting your *10th House of Career,* which could mean that this will be a very fortunate time for you to win a promotion at work. You can go to the 10th House chapter and read the section on *Jupiter Transiting your 10th House* and learn more about how you can use this transit to advance your career.

- If *Saturn* is transiting your 8th House (which rules investments and loans), you may have special obstacles in obtaining a mortgage for a home. You can go to the 8th House chapter and read the section on *Saturn Transiting your 8th House* and learn more about the challenges you can expect.

PAST Transits

- As you read this book, you may look back on your life and ask: *"I wonder what was going on in my life when I quit school…married my 'ex'…or left GOOGLE just before they went public?"* You may find your answers by understanding where your transits were in the past.

FUTURE Transits

- You can use this information to *plan* the best time to make favorable changes in any area of your life whether it's picking the best time to get find romance, get married, invest, buy a home, take a trip or plan cosmetic surgery.

These examples illustrate how you can make practical use of this book by knowing where your transits are located.

Part V   The 5 Planets Affecting Your Life

Learn About These 5 Important Planets

JUPITER

A Jupiter transit stays in each House of your life for about one year. Its journey through a House indicates that this is the area of your life where you're trying to learn and grow, and become a more intelligent and successful individual. Jupiter energies will help you develop a broader perspective, and bring maturity and sophistication to your views, attitudes and personal philosophy.

Jupiter's influence will bring you luck and opportunity in the matters of this House. You'll find this to be a pleasant period of time when you feel optimistic and enthused.

Jupiter brings expansion to the affairs of whatever House it's in. Therefore, the area that Jupiter transits tells you where you might take things to excess or become over over-confident. Be careful not to do so.

Think of Jupiter as a friend who teaches you how to improve yourself and also brings you great fortune.

SATURN

A Saturn transit stays in each House of your life for about two and a half years. Its journey through a House indicates that this area of your life is being examined and tested. As a result, you may experience problems or challenges that will force you to make some sort of change. Expect also to feel tension and a sense of responsibility concerning the affairs of this House. This is a serious of time where you're evaluating and considering matters. Saturn's energies represent what you want in life. Its purpose is to help you bring about its manifestation. In that sense, Saturn's effect is to make what you want, "real."

If matters of this House are going well during Saturn's transit here, it's a good sign they're appropriate and should remain in your life. In that case, what you want to happen will manifest if you work hard to bring it about.

However, if the affairs of this House aren't going well, you may find yourself feeling depressed, sad, frustrated, and emotionally upset. This may be a clear sign that you'll have to make a major change. Ask yourself if you're trying to hold onto something that's inappropriate for you? It may even be something you don't really want or need but you may be refusing to let go. If this is the case, you should either make a major readjustment in what you want or give it up. This is the time to make what you want real or cut the "dead wood" out of your life.

Saturn's lessons are hard and if you resist them, they become even harder. But if you learn the lessons and take on greater responsibility, making any necessary adjustments, the rewards that will result later will be with you for life. Saturn rules the bones, and when you know something "in your bones" your determination will help you create a lasting foundation.

Think of Saturn as a teacher guiding you to make a sensible and practical decision that is best for you.

URANUS

A Uranus transit stays in each House of your life for approximately seven years. Its journey through a House indicates that this is the area of your life where you need to embrace newness and change in order to ultimately experience greater freedom.

Uranus' purpose is to challenge the areas of your life that have become rigid. It often does this by bringing events into your life that are surprising, sudden, unexpected, disruptive or upsetting. During a Uranus transit, you'll have experiences that are unusual and out of the order of your everyday life.

When a Uranus transit comes into your life, all that can be said is: Expect the unexpected! Uranus' energies provide you with personal growth and awareness, keeping your life fresh, lively and exciting in the affairs of this House as long as you're willing to be flexible and adaptable.

Think of Uranus as a friend who's there to awaken you in ways you never imagined and give you new freedom from restrictions.

NEPTUNE

A Neptune transit stays in each House of your life for approximately 14 years. Its journey through a House indicates that this is the area of your life where you're likely to be inspired or confused. Neptune's energies give you the ability to be a compassionate person, subordinating your ego desires to the needs of people around you. Neptune's message: "It is no longer just about you – it's about others." Under its influence you can perform great acts of selflessness and sacrifice in service to others. Neptune's energies give you the ability to tap into the mystical, spiritual aspects of life and make a deeper connection to the world you live in.

The House that Neptune transits is where you'll experience faith, creativity and a sense of idealism. It's also the area of your life where you're most likely to deceive yourself or be deceived by others, thus falling prey to mistaken illusions. In matters of this House you maybe unable to see reality, causing you to experience confusion, doubt and fear.

During a Neptune transit, it's not usually a dependable time to make important decisions or permanent commitments concerning the affairs of this House. The problem during this transit is that you're not usually in possession of all relevant facts and pertinent information you may require. Therefore, while you may be right about a belief you have, an action you take, or a decision you make – you won't know for sure until Neptune's transit of this House is finished.

Think of Neptune as a spiritual guide who brings you both dreams and illusions that inspire you but that may or may not be true.

PLUTO

A Pluto transit stays in each House of your life for approximately 21 years. Its journey through a House indicates that this is the area of your life where profound change and transformation must occur. It's also where you want to be in control and where you may get into power struggles with others over matters of this House.

During the many years that Pluto transits each House, you'll experience Pluto's transformational process which will begin with the breakdown or destruction of some aspect of your life that needs to die, followed by a total rebirth that creates something new in its place. Often some significant event or important person comes into your world, bringing a major change that may be beneficial or detrimental, depending on the kind of transformation that's required.

Think of this as a time to build something new! You can no longer fix what has broken down. Just as a demolition crew tears down an old building to construct a new one, Pluto breaks down an old structure in your life, so that a new structure can be built.

The transformational process that Pluto brings is inevitable and cannot be prevented or stopped, because as sure as the night follows the day – it will happen in this area of your life. Take comfort in knowing that this transformational change is vitally important to your evolution as a person.

If you attempt to prevent these changes from happening, you'll only cause the powerful energies of Pluto to build up until they become explosive and produce a disaster in this area of your life. Therefore, you can aid your own transformational process by letting go of the part of your life that must die and embracing the rebuilding process that will be occurring. By the time Pluto's transit through this House is over, the transformation that has occurred will be complete, and of great benefit to you.

Think of Pluto as a powerful friend who tells you that a massive change is required in your life and will be with you throughout the entire process until it's complete.

Part VI   What The Hell Is Going On In My Life?

The 12 Houses of Your Birth Chart

1st House
Personality & Appearance

If you want to make sense of what's going on in your life, the first place to look is your personality. Is it helping or hindering you from getting what you want personally and professionally? Personality comes from the Latin word *persona*, which means, "mask." People are forever wearing masks to fit their mood, attitude and situation. Some individuals have a captivating personality and can take over any room they walk into. Others adapt their personality the way a chameleon changes its colors, if it will get them what they want. Your personality is your calling card in the outer world. It projects the inner parts of your psychological make-up, known as the *self*.

Nothing is quite as unique as a person's personality. Some people are anxious and high-strung while others are relaxed and easy-going. Then there are those who exude confidence, in stark contrast to others who are shy, quiet and somewhat reserved. We are especially aware of people who are aggressive and bullying in their manner. Yet, most of us appreciate people who are friendly, affable and easy to talk to. No two people have the same identical personality.

Most of us are fascinated with the many personalities we encounter in life. How often have you heard someone say, "He has a wonderful personality," "She has no personality," "He has his mother's personality," "She has a boring personality," or "He has such an gregarious personality." Your personality is actually a creation in progress. It undergoes changes as you go through life, especially when a transit affects it. Your personality can either be an asset or a liability. Yet, most people aren't conscious of one of their most prized possessions – their personality. They don't take the time to reflect on how their personality affects their relationships, other people, or life pursuits such as work. In fact, many people get defensive or make excuses when you comment about their personality. Have you ever heard someone say, "Well…that's just the way I am." We are all familiar with the term: personality conflict. How others react to your personality is the first step in discovering which part of it helps you be effective, and which part of it works against your efforts to achieve your goals and make your decisions successful. So, let's discuss more about who you really are.

The 1st House of your birth chart is known as the House of the Self. It describes your outer personality and physical appearance. It represents your identity and the persona that you show the outer world. This includes your attitude, temperament, mannerisms and the overall way that you look at the world. All this adds up to your personality being the very first impression that you give others when they meet you.

This House also represents your sense of self-awareness and how you respond when you're out in public in social situations. Do people experience you as chatty and extroverted or shy and introverted? Are you seen as being intelligent or superficial; intense and deep or easy-going and relaxed? Does the personality that you project to the outer world match or conflict with the real person you are, including you the way you feel inside? You may have heard the expression: "He's being two-faced." Usually that's a pejorative comment that expresses that a person is being hypocritical, saying one thing publicly and yet, privately expressing the opposite view. In contrast, we all know people whom we respect as having integrity because what they say in public matches what they say to us in private. Therefore, it's important for you to understand how others perceive you.

If you're seen as having an *authentic* personality, you're more likely to evoke confidence and receive a positive response from others. The result is your decisions are favored with cooperation and support. By contrast, if your personality is perceived as *inauthentic,* with suspicion and skepticism, your decisions are likely to arouse opposition and not win the support of others. Never forget that for most people: *perception is reality.* Are you being who you really are? This is one of the fundamental questions you must answer if you want to find inner happiness in life and make sense of what's going on in your world.

The 1st House is extremely important because it represents your outer appearance, physical characteristics, (e.g., complexion) physical body, health and the overall way you display yourself to the world. It can indicate whether your energy level is high or low and even predict the likelihood of your being thin or heavy, as you grow older. In this way, this House relates strongly to your health and physical body. Many of the decisions people have to make concern questions about whether they want to change their physical appearance, either through diet, exercise or, through cosmetic surgery.

You Have 3 Faces

Because the 1st House represents your personality (and physical body), it's the most important House in your birth chart. *(Note: The "sign" that rules the first House of your Horoscope, is called the Ascendant or Rising sign.)* As people get to know you they observe that you have three distinct facets to your personality. First, there is your outer facade, which in astrology is known as your *"Ascendant."* It is the persona you show out in public. But it may be different from the basic personality of your *Sun sign*.

Your Sun sign, the second facet of your personality, describes the essence and basic character of your personality. It's also the image that you express to others in the outer world. It is the authentic, essential part of who you really are. The Sun sign indicates where you feel powerful and vital in being who you are. The Sun sign person says, "I may seem indecisive - but when I believe in something I fight for it tooth and nail!"

The third facet of your personality, your *Moon sign,* reflects the personality of your inner emotional state, the way you feel inside. It expresses what makes you feel secure, nurtured and comfortable. It is the inner child within in you. The Moon sign person says, "I may look tough on the outside, but I cry at the movies."

It's especially interesting when you realize that you reveal different sides of your personality (i.e., Ascendant, Sun, and Moon Sign) to various people depending on your relationship with them and vice versa. Let me give you a personal example that illustrates the three different facets of a person's personality.

Years ago a close friend of mine, Kathy, invited me to a cocktail party to meet her friends and business associates. As I socialized at the party, I talked with many people. Often the conversation turned to: "how" we each knew Kathy? In the verbal exchange that followed that question, I would hear different descriptions about Kathy's personality depending on how well the other person knew her. At first the descriptions about her were confusing. Each person seemed to be acquainted with only one facet of her personality. One person, who didn't know her well, said, "Oh, Kathy is really smart, but kind of quiet and detached," (i.e.,

1st House: Personality & Appearance

her Ascendant Sign). Another person who knew her better said, "She is a person of integrity who is passionate when she believes in a cause," (i.e., her Sun Sign). A close girlfriend said, "When Kathy feels comfortable knowing someone she is so warm, caring and nurturing. She'd give you the shirt off her back."(i.e., Moon Sign). Of course, there were people that knew her well and were familiar with the whole range of her personality.

Since many of the people you meet in the outer world won't know you in a deep, personal way, it's important to understand you may be projecting only one facet of yourself. Expressing your total personality can lead to even more satisfying relationships with others.

Your Body in the 1st House

This house rules the head, brain, face, lips and jaw. Since there is nothing more important than your health, pay special attention to these areas of your body whenever a planet transits this House. It may indicate a period of time when you'll experience health benefits, issues or even problems you should be aware of. If you observe anything unusual, you'll have the opportunity to consult with a medical doctor or a health care practitioner.

Your 1st House Decisions

You now understand that 1st House of your birth chart concerns your outer, public personality, and your physical appearance. As you read about the description of this house, it's time to ask yourself a few questions. Do you like your personality? Are you comfortable with the way you project yourself in the outer world? When people meet you – do they like you? Or, do you sense they are uncomfortable in your presence, in some way? Is there anything about the way you project yourself you would like to change? Are you happy with your physical appearance? Are you happy with your hairstyle, your weight and the way you dress? Is it time to join a gym, hire a personal fitness trainer and commit to a regular exercise program? Should you be on a diet or are you perfect just the way you are? What is the biggest change you'd like to make that would improve your personality or physical appearance?

These are all significant questions and your answers may lead you to make important decisions to change your life. Here are a few examples of decisions clients have made based on the activities and issues of the 1st House.

Situation: Bernie has been shy and timid all his life. He has lived with a lack of self-confidence for many years. He's tired of feeling so uncomfortable when he talks to people, so he's decided to confront his problem.

DECISION: *I am going to join a public speaking organization to develop my confidence.*

* * *

Situation: Penelope was never interested in fashion, clothing, make-up or hairstyling. She grew up in a small rural community where physical appearance never mattered. Now that she's started her first job in a big city, she's ready to make a change.

DECISION: *I am ready to hire a consultant to do a total makeover of the way I look and dress.*

* * *

Situation: Ryan is the company "know-it-all." His arrogant attitude turns off co-workers and offends his managers and has resulted in his being passed over for promotional opportunities.

DECISION: *I am ready to see a therapist who can help me change my offensive behavior.*

* * *

Situation: Lana is unhappy working as a hairstylist at a salon that serves older, traditional clientele who have conventional tastes in hairstyles.

DECISION: *I want to find the best time to make a job change so I can work for a modern, contemporary hair salon that caters to young people.*

During the transits of the planets *Jupiter, Saturn, Uranus, Neptune,* and *Pluto,* Bernie, Penelope, Ryan, and Lana will have many opportunities to implement their decisions at a favorable time to produce the outcome they want.

The Transiting Planets Reveal Your Past, Present & Future

Your main focus is using astrology to understand *what the hell is going on in your life.* Once you do – this book will show you the best time to make a decision to change it, should you have a desire to do so. As you read about the five planets transiting the 1st House, notice the way each planet exerts its unique influence and effect, bringing specific opportunities, issues, problems, and events into this area of your life. But if you're curious as to how these planets are personally affecting YOU *today,* in your *past,* or in your *future,* you can find out where each transiting planet is in your birth chart by using the *FREE Transit Calculator* (see Part IV).

> Note: Throughout this book the names, characters and scenarios have been changed to protect client confidentiality.

JUPITER In Your 1st House of Personality & Appearance

A "Lucky" You!

Jupiter's passage through your first House is a time when you're likely to feel optimistic and cheerful. Expect people to shake your hand and say, "He's a really great guy, I enjoyed meeting him," or "She has such a positive personality; it was really great talking with her." The people you meet will bring you good fortune and be of considerable benefit to you. Good luck comes your way, often bringing you material gain as well. People just show up in your life, as if their sole purpose is to help you. For example, this is a period in your life when you may stop off at a coffee shop and bump into a friend you haven't seen in years, who just happens to know of a great job opportunity. Or, as you sit down to enjoy your coffee, you hear two people at the next table discussing a stock tip, which could make you a small fortune.

It's a wonderful time to accomplish your goals by approaching powerful or influential people because they will be of huge assistance to you. They'll see you as being confident with natural leadership ability. You'll be comfortable knocking on the door of the president of your company and saying, "Just thought I'd stop by to bounce an idea off of you and see what you think."

Over the entire year, the people you meet will be, in some way, to your advantage, so it's an opportune year for you to be out in the public meeting people, networking, socializing and making contacts. At work, this is a fortunate time to seek a pay raise or attempt to win a promotion at work. It's the perfect period in your life to take risks because you're likely to succeed. Many opportunities come into your life and you can be confident that you'll be successful in the ones you pursue. You may be honored, receive recognition, or even prestige during this transit.

Now that you know you have this positive power assisting you, ask yourself: How can I use it to achieve my goals?

It Brings Personal Growth

This is the perfect year to engage in personal growth activities that may enhance *you*, so consider this your opportunity to improve your intellect by taking an educational course or some sort of advanced training. It's a period in your life when you should seek a mentor or a life coach and be willing to pay them for their advice because you'll learn a great deal from them. It could also be a fortunate time where you grow psychologically by resolving emotional issues working with a therapist.

Jupiter's beneficence makes this an ideal year to enhance your physical look, whether it's improving yourself through an exercise program to lose weight or by an elective surgery that might benefit your health or enhance your appearance. Jupiter's influence in the 1st House favors all your efforts towards self-improvement.

When Janice discussed her desire for a breast reduction surgery with me, I realized how important the right timing was for her. She explained that for years, whenever she went to the beach, she felt self-conscious in her bathing suit. She wanted to be liked and admired by men, in particular, for her brains and not her chest size. To make matters worse, as she got older, she started having health issues because her back was in constant pain. She had to stop her 5-mile runs and as a result had gained unwanted weight.

During Jupiter's transit to her 1st House she felt a sense of confidence and optimism that the time was right to do corrective surgery. She became very enthusiastic about completing this surgery to improve her appearance and health. At first she was a little uncomfortable because she didn't know a doctor who could perform this procedure. Once she told a few friends about her plans she found one who knew a highly reputable doctor, specializing in this surgery. This is precisely the kind of good luck that occurs with Jupiter's influence. She made an appointment with the doctor, felt great confidence in him and chose him to perform her procedure. Today her life has changed because she's much more confident in the person she now shows the public. She believes that men take her more seriously and she's also back to 5 mile runs and her old weight.

This is an ideal time to engage in any activity that also furthers your personal growth since you're drawn to wisdom and have a thirst for knowledge. In addition, you'll likely win the support of mentors and teachers. So, it's an excellent time to go back to school, take courses or even seminars for higher learning and advanced education.

Jupiter's passage through your 1st House represents the beginning of a cycle of personal growth when you're trying to discover who you are as an individual. You're feeling confident in yourself, the impression you make on others, and eager to have new experiences that will help you grow as a person. For some, this is the time when you're finally ready to let go of immature attitudes that stem from your childhood and early environment, and are no longer appropriate as an adult. What's happening now, on a personal level, is that you're expanding your world-view, and becoming more mature and sophisticated about life in general. This is often a period when a young person, who may have left high school, not knowing what direction to take in life, decides he's now serious about getting a college education or just doing something important with his life. It may be when someone who wasn't sure what career she should pursue is eager to do some thoughtful investigation.

For the duration of this transit you're ready to advance your learning in areas that you've always been interested. If you're so inclined, this is an excellent time for pursuing your interest in philosophy, publishing, law and long-distance travel. Jupiter's influence often brings a greater spiritual or religious appreciation to your life because you're seeking to grow in ways that are beyond the material. These are some of the important areas that favor you during Jupiter's passage through your 1st House.

One caveat: Be careful not to let your self-confidence cause you to be conceited or arrogant where you begin to think that you have all the answers. Also, during this year avoid excessive behaviors, including overeating since Jupiter in the 1st House is often a span of time when you may gain weight.

Jupiter's transit through your 1st House gives you a wonderful opportunity to improve yourself educationally. Hilda came to this country as an immigrant and had to begin work immediately to support her family. She always felt bad about not completing her education by taking English classes to speak the language more properly. During Jupiter's transit of her 1st House she felt great motivation to complete her high school diploma. It was also a fortunate time for her because the company she worked for had a special program, paying her school tuition, and giving her a number of hours off work to allow her to attend her classes.

She enrolled in a GED program to complete her high school degree at night, which included an English language course to perfect her language skills. Within 12 months she had completed her education, received her diploma and elevated her English-speaking and language skills to a much higher level. Hilda felt a great deal of confidence from this achievement and was even more prepared for a promotional opportunity within her company.

It's fair to ask, "Would Hilda have been just as successful if she'd picked another time to pursue her educational goals?" It's hard to know for sure. After all, we know people who attempt to go back to school and for some reason quit because they're distracted from reaching their original goal; or, they begin school and perform poorly and don't earn good grades. Ultimately, they get discouraged and stop their education. That's the danger that comes from picking "any time."

Rather then pick a random time to improve yourself when you may or may not have success, why not choose a positive time when you're much more likely to be successful? That IS the benefit of using your most favorable astrological transits for decision-making. In Hilda's case, she had considered going back to school before. However, at that time, the company didn't have a program to pay for classes and she wasn't permitted to take time off of work. So, for her, the timing didn't feel right. However, those negatives turned to positives when Jupiter transited her 1st House.

I've found that when a transit occurs in someone's life, it brings an influence that's congruent to how that person feel's inside. As an astrologer, I have rarely had the experience of a client feeling miserable during a positive transit or feeling really ecstatic at a time when they were going through a depressing transit. There's a real congruity in how you feel, your motivation level and your desire to achieve a goal. You ambition matches up well with the potential benefit of the transit that's occurring in your life. You'll find that they're in harmony together. For this reason, the decision you make, feels right. Therefore, by taking action at the time of the transit, you tend to experience a successful outcome.

In Hilda's case, typical of Jupiter transiting her 1st House, she was feeling optimistic and confident and had a special thirst for knowledge she hadn't felt in many years. Jupiter transiting her 1st House brought that influence to her life. She also found many individuals in her company supporting her educational goal. Fortunately for her – the company had just started offering a tuition reimbursement program, which is precisely the kind of benefit that falls in the lap of a person when Jupiter passes through their 1st House. So, for Hilda, it felt like the perfect time to act on her desire to complete her education; and, she successfully did.

I've heard successful people say: "The harder I work – the luckier I get!" Well, I say: "The more you use a positive transit in conjunction with your Astro Action Plan – the more your decisions will seem to turn out lucky."

It Brings Self-Confidence & Over-Confidence

When Jupiter transits through the 1st House it gives the person an amazing power of self-confidence, hope and optimism. The results can motivate even a timid, shy person to change who they are. This was the case for Bernie, who grew up shy and lacking confidence. He made sure that his graphics design job allowed him to work alone, away from others, carefully avoiding even small departmental meetings where being among too many people would make him feel anxious.

During his Jupiter transit, he told me that he wanted to confront his worst fear: public speaking. We picked out the perfect transit for him to use to tackle this problem and to optimize his chances of overcoming it. During the transit's influence, he joined a public speaking organization. Admittedly, he was very nervous and uncomfortable at first, but within two months, he was making small speeches before the group. Within four months, he was making graphic design presentations to department heads at work. His public speaking experience taught him that he was no longer the shy little boy who grew up with great feelings of inferiority, instead he was now a very capable and well-respected graphics designer whom people valued. He felt good seeing the respect in the eyes of co-workers during his presentations at work.

People do feel very confident during Jupiter's transit of the 1st House. However, if confidence turns into over-confidence, it can cause a person to behave arrogantly. Worse, if that person already tends to have an egotistical or self-righteous personality, those qualities will be amplified under this transit.

That was the case for Ryan who was known as the company "know-it all." He was bright, intelligent and gifted in many ways but his personality turned people off. They didn't react badly to the content of what he said, instead they reacted negatively to his communication style – the way he said, what he said. The result was co-workers not supporting his project ideas, with discussions frequently turning into fierce arguments. Because he wasn't well liked or given cooperation, Ryan was constantly passed over for promotions. When he saw me for a transit consultation,

1st House: Personality & Appearance

he was frustrated but clueless about how cocky he sounded when he shared his ideas or disagreed with other people's opinions. After looking at Ryan's birth chart, it was clear that he had a quick mind and a great intellect, however, it was equally clear he was a very conceited fellow. Even when he was right, which was often, people would oppose his ideas because his personality was so offensive.

As we discussed his personality problem during his transit consultation, he became a bit defensive. Then, he conceded maybe he did have strong opinions; after all, he knew he was right. As we talked more, I asked him to close his eyes, and to imagine how he might feel, if someone who was *just as sure they were right,* confronted him at work? He smiled and said, *"That would really piss me off!"* He finally understood what I was trying to make him see about his arrogant personality and abrasive communications style; and why others reacted so negatively towards him. Ryan confessed that getting along with others had always been a battle. He realized that it negatively affected his promotional opportunities at work and his personal relationships, which upset him greatly.

Since Jupiter was transiting his 1st House, ready to make a very positive transit in his birth chart – it gave him an ideal opportunity to improve his personality. So, I suggested a human relations course that focused on how to get along with people more harmoniously. Ryan said he'd also found a therapist to discuss the deeper issues of his personality that were behind his aggressive communications style. It turned out that his therapist was a great help, arousing his curiosity and desire to learn more about himself, and why he behaved as he did. This led Ryan to enrolling in a personal growth workshop that he found illuminating, and a special skills course on how to communicate more effectively with people.

Within six months, Ryan's personal therapy gave him more insight into the fact that his arrogance was merely a cover up for his feelings of insecurity and fears of inferiority. His communication class had the effect of making him more aware of the benefits of communicating assertively as opposed to his old arrogant style that sounded like, "I know it all – and you don't."

Did he turn into the most humble man on the planet who people at work loved? No. Ryan's personality issues and his basic personality remained. But he did become more aware; and he did improve. He now does a better job relating to the people he works with. Since his old colleagues know him as the abrasive and arrogant person that he is – he and I started talking about the idea of his seeking a new job, where he could have a fresh start with a new set of co-workers who have no past experience working with him. That's another decision for him to consider.

It Brings Luck & Recognition

When Jupiter transits your first house you feel positive, optimistic and happy. Your popularity may even bring you fame or some type of recognition. Since people genuinely like you, your public persona is well received. I had a client bring her teenage son, Jed, in for an astrology consultation while he was home from his college spring break. He was a likeable, bright, precocious young man. In our consultation, Jed told me that he had been thinking more and more about becoming an editor of a newspaper even though he'd never had any publishing experience. He had worked for his college newspaper but had not pursued his interest any further.

His enthusiasm for publishing made a great deal of sense with Jupiter transiting his 1st House. I explained to him that he had a golden opportunity to learn about publishing by applying for an internship program at a newspaper during his Jupiter transit. I gave him the specific dates to make application. That was all the encouragement he needed. When he returned back to campus he submitted applications for internships at more than 100 newspapers. Sure enough, within 90 days, he was offered a fabulous internship opportunity to work for the editor of a major city newspaper. Jupiter transiting your 1st House is an excellent time to make all sorts of decisions that will produce favorable results.

Considerations, Actions, Decisions During Jupiter in 1st House

1. Improve some part of your personality that will help you be more successful.
2. Improve something about your appearance.
3. Seek a promotion that will allow you to grow as a professional.
4. Go to school or take a class to learn something new.
5. Attend law school or study for some other advanced degree.
6. Enjoy creative writing and consider publishing it.

7. Travel somewhere where you can learn something interesting.
8. Begin a spiritual or religious activity.
9. Begin therapy or some self-discovery process that will help you mature.
10. Engage in some sort of political activity.

SATURN In Your 1st House of Personality & Appearance

Re-Evaluating Your Personality

Saturn in the 1st House begins a two and a half year process of internal growth where you're serious, introspective and ready to look within yourself to discover *who you are*. You may even say, "I don't like who I have become." This is a time when you'll be re-defining and re-structuring your personality, identity, and even your physical appearance so that it reflects who you are.

Because your inner focus is on your personality, character, and the internal makeup of yourself, you'll be acutely aware of your shortcomings, flaws and weaknesses. Make sure not to become critical of yourself or depressed about what you find out because it's all a part of the important process of discovering the real you. What's happening is you're engaged in serious self-evaluation, which makes it the perfect time to rid yourself of any long-held fantasy, illusion or even self-deception you've mistakenly believed to be true for years.

I've had clients who grew up with parents who put them down, telling them they were ugly, fat, stupid or incompetent. Unfortunately, they believed what their parents said about them and grew up with the wrong self-image and even an inferiority complex. Other clients were spoiled and coddled by family who told them they were beautiful, intelligent, gifted and would be hugely successful. Some of these pronouncements were made out of love, wishful thinking, but not necessarily reality. These people need to sort out what is accurate and true. Saturn's influence allows for a process of self-discovery that will ultimately lead to building a new foundation for who you are as a person – a more authentic you.

You'll be letting go of those elements of your personality that no longer fit with the person you've become. In spending many of your past years focusing on school, family, work or other outer activities in the world, you may have lost awareness of who you are and your individual needs. During this transit you'll learn more about your true self and as you engage in personal introspection, you may ask yourself, "What kind of person have I become? What do I want out of life? What have

1st House: Personality & Appearance

I learned from life's experience?" In this process, you may discover you haven't lived according to your own standards; rather, you've lived your life based on your family's values or according to other people's standards. Therefore, use this time to take an objective look and re-evaluate who you *really* are, and makes sure that it honestly reflects you.

Saturn's passage through your 1st House provides you with an opportunity to examine your personality, asking yourself if your self-perception is accurate or inaccurate, and sorting out what's true and what isn't. This is an important time for you to lay a new foundation for who you are, in your own terms, not in someone else's. After all, many people start out their life in a direction that is not of their own choosing, as was the case for Steven.

Steven's family included a long-line of attorneys. Both his father and grandfather practiced law. Now Steven has just graduated law school to become an attorney in his own right. But he is having second thoughts about whether the legal profession is the best career for him and further, he's questioning what he's doing with his life. In fact, he realizes he doesn't want to take the bar exam to complete the process of becoming an attorney. For years his father had encouraged him to get a law degree, so it appeared to be the right career to pursue. However, Saturn going through his 1st House has been a catalyst for him to recognize that being an attorney is not what he wants to do "when he grows up."

Steven now realizes his father cultivated in him many of the personality traits that Steven needed to be a successful lawyer. For years, Steven had been agreeable, fitting into an identity mold he knew would be pleasing to his father and the career that had been planned for him. However, this period of Saturn transiting his 1st House has been a serious time of reflection and self-examination about making his own choices for the first time in his life. When he had a consultation with me, it was clear why he was in such a serious and reflective mood. By discussing his transits, I helped him make sense of his feelings of doubt and regret. He was quick to embrace the idea of sitting down with a career counselor to discuss his real interests and aptitudes. Steven felt this would be a good start toward resolving his internal dilemma, as well as leading him to investigate other career directions he might prefer over practicing law.

Sometimes, during a client consultation, it's apparent that a person is experiencing a major transit, which will motivate them to make a necessary change. The result is that they come to their decision over the period in which the transit exerts its influence, as occurred for Steven. In his case, the transit consultation was a validation of what he was going through. The transit delivered the words to the music of what he was already experiencing and really explained what was going on in his life. (Note: Quite often, as in Steven's case, a person experiences a transit as a process – not an event.)

During the time that Saturn transits your 1st House, you're focused introspectively, investing your energy in your personal growth. For that reason, if you have lots of responsibilities and commitments, it may be hard to concentrate and do your normal routine work in the outer world. You may find that work is actually a distraction from your personal efforts to understand yourself and do important soul-searching. Therefore, the demands of your day-to-day life may create a great deal of inner tension, anxiety, and even pressure within you. Your dilemma is that on one hand, you may have a job to do; yet on the other you feel the need to reflect on the internal changes going on within you. Be aware this is a serious, contemplative time in your life where you're engaged in the process of transforming your personality and finding your life purpose. It's easy to understand why it may be difficult to fully concentrate on work.

If a client is distracted from his job, I encourage him to seek out a therapist so that he will have an outlet for his personal exploration while still being productive at work.

It Brings Restrictions & Limitations

When Saturn transits your 1st House, it's not a beneficial time to start a new job, new business or new venture. It is, however, a valuable period to personally discover your objectives, goals and desires. The purpose of this transit is to take time to re-structure and re-define them, so that you're clear on your life's direction. As your vision for your future becomes clearer, it will take time for your plans to mature, requiring patience and perseverance. The process you're encountering is important because it's likely to lead you to the next major undertaking of your life, maybe even your destiny. It's precisely because you are putting so much of your energy into this self-discovery process that it's a difficult time to achieve your goals in the outer world.

Such a circumstance was well illustrated when I did a transit consultation for Nathan. He was struggling with whether or not it was a good time to open his own restaurant. He enjoyed his past restaurant jobs so much that all he could think about was the day he might have his own operation. He spent many waking hours dreaming about how he might make his desire a reality. Operating a restaurant was a big responsibility and Nathan didn't want start his business and have it fail, so he was contemplating how it all might work: using some of his savings, finding a few investors, searching for a location, and finally opening day. He wanted to know when was the best time to start this venture. After discussing it with him, it was obvious he had many doubts and reservations. For example, Nathan wasn't clear on which recipes to use, his exact menu, or even his ability to manage all elements of the business. He was wondering how he could compensate for areas where he lacked knowledge and experience. Saturn transiting his 1st House was the wrong time for him to start a new business because he would likely encounter many obstacles and serious opposition that would be extremely frustrating, likely leading to failure.

In his case, the value of Saturn's transit through Nathan's 1st House was that it gave him the opportunity to refine his restaurant idea, gain more experience, and put more structure into how he wanted to organize this new venture. In fact, I advised him that waiting 18 more months, when Saturn would no longer be transiting his 1st House, would be a more ideal time to begin his new restaurant.

I also explained that, at that time, when Saturn moved into his 2nd House, he would have to work very hard to achieve success, but if we used a favorable transit, his diligent efforts would be rewarded in the end. He immediately saw the value of using his transits to intelligently plan his future. Meanwhile, Nathan decided to use this time to work at another restaurant where he could learn more of the necessary skills he would need to successfully operate his own restaurant.

Saturn's influence brings restrictions and limitations in your life to test and teach you lessons. What you're likely to learn is that no matter how much energy you expend to accomplish tasks at work or in the outer world – challenges and obstacles stand in your way. You end up receiving very little support from people; and circumstances appear to thwart your efforts to accomplish your goals. This is another reason why this time is not ideal for starting something new. You may notice that this lack of assistance is the exactly opposite of the positive support one receives from Jupiter transiting a person's 1st House. Just by comparing the differing influences of Jupiter versus Saturn one can see clearly why things seem to work better at certain times in your life, yet, not so well at others.

This is a further example of why you must pay attention to timing and be willing to plan — if you want your decisions to work out favorably. A transiting planet in your birth chart will help you decipher how to choose the best times in life to accomplish your goals. A Jupiter transit in your 1st House is normally, a great time to start a new venture. Saturn in the 1st House is not. For that reason, be aware that Saturn's placement here is not a good time to achieve promotions or make significant advancements in your career. In reality, your actions at work often meet with resistance and opposition, to the point where you may begin to have doubts about yourself. It's this constant opposition from the outer world that forces you to reflect on your character and abilities. You may start thinking to yourself, *"Hmm...maybe I don't have all the answers."* Or, *"Perhaps I'm not ready to take on that responsibility."*

The reactions you receive from your day-to-day experiences bring you to the point where you feel a deep need to question and re-examine your ideas and who you are. You might have sobering thoughts such as, *"I can see there might be some problems with this idea."* Or, *"Do I have the right skills to do this?"* While such assessments can be hard on one's ego, the positive benefit is that it helps you further refine your ideas because they are challenged and tested. Best of all, it gives you an opportunity to improve yourself, so that you're up to the challenge. Such was the case for Nathan when he realized he lacked sufficient restaurant experience and needed more.

Alice' story is another example of how important it is to pay attention to your transits in order to be successful and not set yourself up for unnecessary hardship or even failure. Alice was working as an assistant manager for a big retail chain and looking for a promotional opportunity to take over one of their locations as a new general manager. She was well respected and had been assured it was only a matter of time when she would be given an opportunity to run a store outlet. She was excited because she knew several store locations would open up in the coming months, requiring general managers.

Alice came to me to discuss the best time to let her senior management know she wanted to be considered for such a promotion. With Saturn transiting her 1st House for next 12 months, it was not a fortuitous time. In her case, the timing in her chart was bad because it was unlikely that she would receive favorable consideration for a promotional opportunity during this time. Even if she was chosen for a general manager position, her store assignment might provide extremely difficult challenges, perhaps long hours with a limited chance for success and recognition. In essence, she would be setting herself up for difficulties, obstacles and potential failure. Alice would be far more likely to get her promotion and be successful as a general manager if she waited 12 months when Saturn would no longer be transiting her 1st House.

Take Time To Understand Who You Are

Since it is rather difficult to achieve your goals in the outer world at this time, you'll find that your biggest successes may be in working on yourself on a psychological level. Use this time to put forth efforts into better understanding *who you are*. You can gain great insights into yourself by reading self-help books, taking psychology classes, attending personal growth workshops, seeing a therapist, or making an appointment to discuss your personality and transits with an astrologer.

Saturn's presence in your 1st House assists you in developing greater maturity through the self-knowledge you gain at this time in your life. It aids you in determining the parts of your personality that benefit you, should be modified, or "let go," because they are of no benefit to you. Make no mistake: the influence of Saturn requires that you work hard. If you resist confronting unresolved issues within yourself – they will persist. This is a two and a half year period of your life where Saturn's message is: "No pain, no gain!"

Watch Your Health

Also, take extra care of your health during Saturn's transit through your 1st House because it's a period when you're likely to feel tired, lacking energy and vitality. In fact, it's often a time when your body may demand some special attention, especially if you've not been taking care of it with proper exercise and a sensible diet. For this reason, this is an excellent time to correct bad habits, adopt healthier practices, and avoid having too much stress in your life. It's not a good period to over burden yourself with work responsibilities, especially if you have workaholic tendencies. However, one of the unique benefits of Saturn in your 1st House is that it's a time when it is relatively easy to lose weight (i.e., just the opposite of Jupiter in your 1st House).

Great Time To Improve Health & Lose Weight

Marge came to me to discuss her health concerns, which included being a smoker and overweight. She had already tried to quit many times, so she wondered if she had any positive transits that could help her be more successful in quitting smoking and losing weight? The question was timely because Saturn in the 1st House forces you to take responsibility for your health or face the consequences of ignoring it.

I cautioned Marge that if she failed to address her health problems and lifestyle, she would experience many of Saturn's unpleasant tests and lessons. I explained that one of the awesome benefits of Saturn's passage through her 1st House was that it would be a long period of time when she would find it much easier to lose weight. She felt sure that if had the "wind sailing at her back," in other words: some positive support, losing weight wouldn't be so challenging. She was determined that this time she would control her eating habits and weight problems. Saturn transiting her 1st House would give her two and a half years to make her health goals a reality.

Marge joined a gym, hired the services of a personal trainer, who then worked with her on her exercise program and diet. Under her doctor's supervision she was provided nicotine patches, special monitoring, and joined a quit-smoking support group. Marge began losing weight in the first 60 days and quit smoking. Of course, in the final analysis, what's important is her ability to maintain her diet, weight reduction, and stay off cigarettes, over a long period of time. But Marge is off to a good start in making important changes to her health and appearance.

Throughout this book, I will continue to illustrate the opportunistic use of transits to bring success to your decisions. People who use helpful transits to achieve their goals have varying degrees of success ranging from 100 percent success to only moderate success. After all, the planets can't *make you do anything*. In the final analysis *you* must work positively with favorable planetary influences to create the most success. To illustrate the use of transits I have purposely kept the examples, the person's situation, and their decision – simple and clear. After all, please keep in mind, the key point of all the examples in this book: *You'll enhance your ability to create positive change, resolve problems, conflicts, issues, and make successful decisions, if you make use of the favorable transits that are occurring in your life.*

1st House: Personality & Appearance

Are You Having Fun?

Because you're feeling more serious and introspective during Saturn's transit of your 1st House, it's important to bring some balance to your life by including plenty of recreation, fun and entertainment. When you complete the process of Saturn going through your 1st House you'll have made meaningful and lasting changes to your personality, and perhaps, even your physical appearance. You'll feel wiser, more mature, realistic about yourself, and who you are in your own terms. Armed with this new self-awareness, you'll venture out into the world more effectively achieving your goals in a way that is authentically – *you*.

Considerations, Actions, Decisions During Saturn in 1st House

1. Are you being authentically you?
2. Are you depressed or lacking in self-esteem?
3. Would seeking professional help be of value to addressing any of your personality issues?
4. Do you know what you want out of life?
5. Are you in the right career or relationship?
6. Do you have too much responsibility?
7. Do you have the skills and experience to be successful?
8. Do you want to make changes to your health?
9. Do you want to lose weight?

URANUS In Your 1ˢᵗ House of Personality & Appearance

A New, Exciting You

Uranus energies deliver an exciting quality to your life, where you feel like there is only blue sky ahead of you and anything is possible. You'll know when Uranus transits through your 1ˢᵗ House. You're filled with a wellspring of pure energy, ready to break out of any routine you've been in. The influence of Uranus will awaken a deep need within you to be free to express your individuality. Consciously and unconsciously, you'll feel compelled to be true to yourself, living your life according your own desires, interests and preferences. It's like somebody gave you a *"get out of jail free card."* You're feeling like you can do anything you want to do and there's no one to stop you.

Living independently and authentically are of paramount importance to you now. You're in the process of changing your personality by breaking free of any limitations that have been placed on you, which includes escaping from your past as well as the expectations of people in your life, such as loved ones, family, friends, or even co-workers. You may recall having this feeling in your late teens and early 20s when you were chomping at the bit to leave your parent's home and go off on your own.

You're beginning a process where you radically transform the personality (and appearance) you show the outside world, causing people to look at you differently. You might find yourself saying, "Hey check out my new tattoo." Or, "Yeah, that's called a nose ring!" You may act in unexpected ways, even displaying rebellious or radical behavior, which may be disruptive and upsetting for yourself and others. People around you may be disturbed by your behavior because it appears you're just being a "rebel without a cause." But you DO have a cause: freedom. Your feelings of being free, independent and wanting to change things are so strong that you'll even break away from those things which may have been important to you in the past. Be aware that your need to rebel and break free is a sign that change is necessary in your life, whether it's in your relationships, work or, other activities you're engaged in.

1st House: Personality & Appearance

NO Restrictions: My Way Or The Highway

Any relationship, be it a friendship or even marriage that has severely limited or restricted you may break-up or come to an abrupt end during Uranus' transit of the 1st House. This is an outgrowth of your need to fully concentrate on your desire to pursue your life in the direction you want to take it. If you're a young person, this could be the time when you say: "Hey Mom and Dad, I'm moving out of the house. I want to be on my own." It doesn't matter if Mom and Dad don't think you are ready to move out, because you're "moving out!"

People in your life may react to you in a surprised and upset way. Those who are most close to you may feel threatened by your independent and rebellious behavior. However, you won't be dissuaded since this is a time when you'll likely feel confident, trust your own feelings, and certainly not be dominated or intimidated. Instinctually, you realize it's an exciting time for you to pursue your own destiny. You have this feeling that your life has limitless potential. Those relationships that give you the necessary freedom you require maybe changed but will still remain. Alternatively, those relationships that are restrictive will no longer be tolerated. You'll only be satisfied with those relationships that give you the freedom to be yourself.

Annie had been married for 25 years and was always there, taking care of her family's needs. She had worked to support her husband while he went to law school, while raising two children who were now grown. Over the past few years she's felt a deep need to finally be her own person, wanting the freedom to do something different with her life without being responsible or burdened to care for anyone else. During this time, her husband focused on his career paying little attention to her needs, so she's been feeling taken for granted for years.

Annie talked with her husband about her creative desire to paint once again, as she had during her college years. She tried to convey how excited she was about taking advanced painting classes at a nearby fine arts school and developing her talent for painting landscapes with water colors. Annie also explained she was bored with the routine of her life and ready to be free to do what she wanted. At first, her husband pooh-poohed the idea, happy with the status quo, wanting her to continue in her domestic role of taking care of the house and making his meals. When she finally got so angry and upset that she threatened to leave their marriage unless he took her desires seriously, he realized he'd better pay attention. They talked seriously about the ways that she could free herself of domestic responsibilities so she could pursue her classes and interest in painting.

When I looked at her chart, it was easy to see why she was rebelling against her predictable life and boring marriage, so she could be have her freedom. Annie was in the first year of Uranus transiting her 1st House. We discussed her situation and typical of Uranus' *"I've got to do it now,"* influence, Annie was not willing to wait 12 more months for the perfect transit. If you want to conjure up – the restless and eager state of mind you may feel when Uranus is in your 1st House: imagine two vultures sitting on a fence. One bird turns to the other and says: "Patience my ass…I'm gonna kill something!" Uranus brings an impatient energy that compels you to take immediate, often willful action to break free and get what you want.

I explained to her that because of Uranus' influence, her mood and state of mind made perfect sense. However, I urged Annie to take a deep breath, be more patient, and exercise some control over her immediate desire to change her circumstance. She agreed to wait a short amount of time for a more suitable transit to change her life from a domestic wife to professional painter. The influence of Uranus brought Annie a need for liberation from her old life and it motivated her to change it, rebelling against a 25-year marriage that stifled her sense of creativity and individuality. To some family members, it appeared she was acting a little crazy, probably just going through a mid-life crisis. To her, she was gaining her liberation and pursuing an exciting new vocation of expressing herself as a painter.

Uranus' pass through the 1st House is also a time when you give up old habit patterns, personality characteristics and strict routines, in order to create new ways of behaving, which are more liberating. This is an exciting period where you feel alive and invigorated, feeling a sense of emotional detachment from all the old habit patterns you're breaking away from. You find yourself making changes, opening you up to new experiences that are only possible because you've broken away from routine and uninteresting elements of your life. The sense of excitement you feel brings you a new outlook on your life, which makes this an ideal time to explore activities, subjects, opportunities, or people who expose you to new perceptions and ideas that could benefit you in the future. You're drawn to unique ways of improving yourself, as long as they take you away from the usual and the mundane. Because you're excited by anything innovative and ahead of its time, you may be attracted to courses

1st House: Personality & Appearance

and workshops in the personal growth area, or more metaphysical areas such as yoga and even astrology.

In fact, one of Uranus' influences is to bring new, unusual, even exciting people into your life. During its passage through your 1st House, you often find yourself meeting new friends, even young, freedom-loving people, who provide you with stimulation and insight to help you make your discoveries. This is a fabulous time to join organizations and get involved in causes you believe in.

A Time To Be Unconventional & Learn a New Trick

At age 62, Raymond had a pretty conventional life. He enjoyed exercising at the gym regularly, but as he got older, his joints stiffened and he continued to have body aches. His doctor explained that the type of exercise he got at the gym, running on the treadmill, was killing his knees. No matter how much effort he put into watching himself during his workouts, even carefully lifting weights was causing too many aches and pains. One day he was talking to a personal trainer who worked at the gym and Raymond told him about his physical problems and the doctor's recommendation to stop working out at the gym. The trainer said, "My wife is a yoga teacher. That might be a better type of exercise for your body. Why don't you try out her class?" Raymond's first reaction was, "I don't know – that kind of exercise sounds a little strange to me." The trainer took the time to explain more about yoga, its health benefits, especially how it might remedy the physical problems he had. By the time they finished their talk, Raymond promised to try the yoga class the next day.

Raymond's life and his physical body changed after just 30 days of yoga classes and within less than six months his body was limber and loose. He'd lost 10 lbs. and made a whole set of new and caring friends who were totally different than the ones he had all his life. Initially, yoga started out as a substitute form of exercise since his body could no longer tolerate conventional weight lifting and gym workouts. Now it had suddenly turned into a life-style for him.

One of Raymond's new yoga friends made some great suggestions on how to improve his diet and eat more healthfully and another friend introduced him to meditation, which had an amazing calming effect on him. He even met someone that he enjoyed socializing with as a steady companion. Raymond had Uranus going through his 1st House. He told me about his yoga experience, as well as the other fabulous health discoveries, and how they had created an entire change in his life-style. His parting comment to me was, "Who said an old dog can't learn a new trick?" Uranus has paved the way for many a human to learn a new trick.

It Brings Radical & Upsetting Change

Be aware that the period when Uranus' transits through your 1st House can also be disruptive and even upsetting for most people. You may surely cry out: "what the hell is happening in my life," during this time. Uranus' influence takes you out of your comfort zone, which is challenging for many people who want to hang onto the usual and the familiar, instead of allowing change to occur in their life. If you find yourself extremely upset by the feelings you're having and the events that are taking place at this time, ask yourself, what are you afraid of that is preventing you from accepting change or even embracing it? Why do you want to hold onto elements of your life that may actually be restricting you from enjoying new, more invigorating experiences?

If you're like many people, you may have a tendency to want to live with what's familiar, even if it's making you feel upset or restricted. For this reason, the influence of Uranus has a way of bringing disruption into your life in the form of accidents or unexpected events, forcing you to make a change you might not otherwise make. What happens is that your unconscious mind brings forth some problem, crisis, or event that acts as a catalyst for change to occur – since your conscious mind is too afraid to allow the change to occur on its own. Perhaps you're avoiding a necessary change, because making it might feel uncomfortable, too radical or, just too irresponsible. If so – pay attention. Ironically, this is, precisely, the area where Uranus' influence is urging you to create major change in your life.

Hugo had been cheating on his wife, Hannah for several years. When she'd once suspected his infidelity, he denied it. Nevertheless, she warned him that if she found out he was being unfaithful to her, their marriage would be over. That was the one betrayal she could not live with.

For Hugo, he'd resigned himself to the fact that marriage was too restrictive for the freedom he wanted now that he was so wealthy. He had gotten married at a young age and spent his years building his small company into a very large and successful business, so he never had a chance to "play the field" and enjoy being single. Now, was his chance to finally be free. He stayed married because it gave him a sense of security; besides

1st House: Personality & Appearance

divorce would be too costly. As he pulled into his company parking lot, got out of his car, he was unprepared, and in shock when a strange man served him with divorce papers. Hugo had Uranus in his 1st House. His second major surprise occurred when he came home to an empty house, with pictures of his infidelity on the dining room table. His wife left a terse note, advising she had moved out and her attorney would be contacting him on her behalf. Hugo thought he'd been clever but his wife had been even more clever, hiring a detective to follow and take pictures of his peccadilloes. Hugo was going to be a "free man" whether he had planned it that way or not.

Examine your life at this time and ask if there are any aspects of it that are limiting your ability to grow and be more fulfilled? Some people will do this self-assessment during Uranus' passage through their 1st House to consciously decide if any limitations are restricting their freedom to grow and bring new change into their life.

Julie worked her way through high school and college. In the last few years of college, she was sure that she knew what she wanted in life: find an upwardly mobile job, get into a management-training program and climb the ladder of success in some company. However, as she graduated college, Uranus was transiting her first house and her plans radically changed overnight. To the dismay of her parents, Julie used the savings she had accumulated for future living expenses and a car down payment, to finance a year off, traveling through Europe with her boyfriend. There was no talking her out of it. Her parents were convinced that their "level-headed, little Julie" had lost her mind doing something so irresponsible. Ironically, Julie had never felt more excited or alive in her life as she and her boyfriend boarded the plane to their first destination: Paris.

With Uranus transits, expect the unexpected! There's no way to know what kind of unexpected, out-of-the-blue surprising events will happen in your life during Uranus transits. All that can be said is that they're exciting, often disruptive, and usually very liberating.

Considerations, Actions, Decisions During Uranus in 1st House

1. What liberating change do you want to make in your life?
2. What is it that you've never done that you'd like to do?

3. What can you do that would make you feel more free and less restricted?
4. Are their any relationships that are holding you back?
5. Are you doing the work that stimulates you?
6. What would excite you at this time in your life?
7. Would you find it exciting to find a new job or start a new business?
8. Is their any area of your life where you aren't allowing change to occur?
9. Are you upset about anything in your life?

NEPTUNE In Your 1st House of Personality & Appearance

Personality Confusion

During Neptune's passage through your 1st House, you show many facets of your personality to those in the outer world. Parts of your personality are changing, some of them even unintentionally, as you interact with other people. Some of the images you project are the real you and some aren't. You may find your personality having a chameleon-like quality to it during this period of your life. As you read this you may be thinking, "Oh...so that's what's happening in my world because I have been feeling different – even a little strange."

This is an excellent time to get in touch with the real, authentic you and discover who you are in your own terms. This can be challenging because you may find yourself projecting your personality in a way, which is not a true reflection of yourself, in order to be someone you *think* others want you to be. Your personality may be sending out "mixed-signals" to the people you interact with like Benny.

Benny's mother, Amanda, was very distressed as she talked about her teen-aged son. His personality had started changing in ways that she no longer recognized. She said that Benny lacked direction and seemed very confused. One moment he seemed enthusiastic and loving, the next, dejected and a bit depressed. The changes in his personality and behavior were starting to concern her. It all came to a head when she found out that Benny had recently joined a gang at school. When she discussed Benny's gang involvement with the high school principal, she became even more upset as he described the gang, as a group of boys with no serious interests other than getting into mischief.

When I met with Amanda, I discussed Neptune's effect on Benny as it transited his 1st House and how it might manifest in his present behavior. There were several ideas we discussed to help Benny through his time of searching and finding out who he really was? He was obviously, experiencing a great deal of confusion about his own identity. Clearly, Benny needed more outlets in his life to express and learn about himself. Since he couldn't find any for himself, Benny gravitated toward the interest and approval he received from the gang members.

In further conversations with Benny, he shared his hesitations about joining the gang, admitting that at the time, the idea sounded like a good one, but confessed he wasn't totally sure. Yet, he had unintentionally sent the gang members the wrong messages that he was interested. This is just another example of the mixed messages that your personality can exhibit when Neptune transits your 1st House.

In Benny's case, his will was weak and he needed more attention, since his parents both worked and had little time for him. Not being very gregarious, he had few friends – thus he was vulnerable to anyone who showed an interest in him, even an unhealthy group of friends. Benny was clearly confused and needed some guidance to avoid making a bad choice. He was a young kid in the middle of an adolescent identity crisis searching for where to fit in.

By understanding the effects of Neptune going through Benny's 1st House, it helped his parents to be more sensitive to him and make appropriate plans to satisfy his needs. Their first step was to draw his interest away from the attention of the gang by spending more time with him. Secondly, they enrolled him in activities, which allowed him to be creative and stimulate his ability to experience his potential. Their efforts led to Benny joining an active church youth group, and taking special art classes, which played to his interests in drawing and painting. They also arranged to have the school's guidance counselor see Benny each week so he could talk about his perceptions about himself, his family and the activities he was now involved in. Suddenly, Benny had outlets where he could learn more about who he was in a healthy way that furthered his personal growth.

For some people, this is a time when they may feel confused and demoralized to the point where their self-esteem suffers, even feeling depressed. Because of their state of mind, they may be motivated to seek out a person – be it a family member, friend, teacher, or counselor, who can help them work through these feelings. This positive step can aid them in sorting out any confusion in their lives, as long as it doesn't lead to being overly dependent.

The negative influence of Neptune in the 1st House can sometimes result in a weak, dependent person looking for answers from someone, who will ultimately enable their dependency. For example, there are people who are so confused at this time of their life that they look to cults or gurus to give them answers and fix them, which can create a long-term, unhealthy dependency.

Just know that a Neptune transit has a great potential to bring confusion into your life, especially when it goes through the 1st House of your personality. As Neptune affects your identity, it can cause you to feel disoriented, where you become both mentally and emotionally confused about *who you are* (just like Benny). What is happening is that your personality is in a developmental state where you're feeling and thinking differently. You're on the road to finding your true self, but it's a long road, best traveled with self-awareness (that's why I hope this book will help guide you). I tell clients going through this transit, you might feel "spacy" and not very "grounded," as you go through this process of further developing your identify.

Our discussion of Neptune is an excellent example of why it's so valuable to understand more about the influences and effects of a transiting planet as it goes through a major area of your life, such as your personality. I've had many clients who have exhibited strange, even mysterious behavior when Neptune transited their 1st House. If you notice this happening to you it is a wise decision to get some help from family, friends, teachers and even a therapist who you can discuss your feelings and the changes you're experiencing.

It Brings Fantasy & Delusion

Let's continue with Neptune's influence on your personality. Neptune in your 1st House can awaken your idealistic and compassionate nature to the point where you're no longer satisfied with merely focusing on goals of material gain. If you ever felt like you were trying to keep up with "the Jones" in order to afford the latest designer label clothes or the hottest new gadget, this is when you pull the cord on the train and say to the conductor, "Stop the world – I want to get off! There has to be something more important to life than just this." Attempting to be successful in the material world is no longer gratifying enough because your orientation is shifting to developing a new identity that's based on something more satisfying to your psyche.

You're now operating on a higher plane of consciousness. However, your personality, just like a plane, is now flying at an altitude of 30,000 feet in the clouds. So, you're no longer connected to the typical earthly desires you were when you were on the ground. You'll also find yourself becoming more aware of your intuitive abilities. You yearn for greater spiritual development in order to tap into your "higher self, and be more at peace with the world you live in. You're inspired to discover the deeper meaning of life beyond the physical and practical realms. For this reason, you may find yourself feeling disinclined to be very assertive in the outer world, in relationships, work or life in general. People may say of you, "I wonder what's going on with Robert? He used to be a label snob, trying to impress everyone with his Italian designer suits and expensive watches. Now, I see him around town in old jeans, talking about helping others who are less fortunate, and volunteering his time to worthy causes."

You may find that the changes you experience in your personality are confusing to both you and the people you interact with. Thus, you end up inadvertently, deceiving and deluding others; they do the same to you in return. You may have a conversation with a friend, "Good grief, you're spacy." "Really, I was thinking the same thing about you." During Neptune's passage through your 1st House, be aware that your sense of reality is not as accurate or reliable. Instead, you may experience a sense of confusion and loss of objectivity where it becomes more difficult to see external reality as it truly is. Your perception can alternate from seeming very clear to being cloudy, which can result in your making bad choices or even the wrong decisions. It becomes hard to distinguish between what is real and what is only a projection of what you would *like* to be true.

This was the case for Gerald, who was living in an assisted living facility. His wife of 42 years had passed away and he was lonely, trying to adapt to a new life without her. Eventually, he found himself very attracted to one of the very young staff working at the facility. Over the months he fantasized a great deal about her. Soon he was having visions that she might be very romantically interested in him. He was sure that their many exchanges of smiles, and *"hello...how are you?"* and brief conversations were further proof they were falling in love with each other. Eventually, he asked to meet privately with her to declare his love and discuss their future together. She assertively let him know she was very flattered, and explained that it was against the rules for staff to socialize with residents. Gerald was under a very Neptunian delusion but fortunately, a kind, compassionate staff person was there to explain reality and make things clear to him.

1st House: Personality & Appearance

Be Careful Of Investing Under An Illusion Or You May "Lay An Egg"

Have you ever made an investment that worked out so badly that when you recalled it years later – you said, "What was I thinking?" Maybe you should've asked, "Where was Neptune transiting in my birth chart when I made that investment?" Make no mistake, when Neptune is transiting your 1st House, you're likely to see the world through "rose-colored" glasses, leaving you gullible and over-optimistic. You're left wide open to exploitation by people with a self-serving agenda. Therefore, be extremely careful of any unusual ideas or strange schemes others may propose to you during this period of time.

Claire received a call from an investment company promoting a fabulous opportunity to buy a profitable ostrich farm. The salesperson discussed its high returns and the fact that it was an excellent growth business since the demographics showed people were eating more and more healthy meat in their diet. With a high level of enthusiasm for this new opportunity, Claire asked me for my astrological advice on investing in this ostrich farm. Based on her transits and the fact that Neptune was transiting her 1st House, I explained that this was a bad time for her. She wasn't seeing this investment clearly. It might turn out to be a huge disappointment if she invested at this time, plus it was just too risky for someone who wanted to be conservative with her savings. Fortunately, Claire dropped the idea. Six months later she sent me an e-mail telling me that her friend had invested in the same ostrich farm proposition and lost a great deal of money.

Neptune's influence can also cause you to look at life idealistically and often unrealistically. This can lead to making decisions based on what you would *like* to be true, instead of what is *actually* true. Frequently you'll find yourself drawn to activities and projects, because they appeal to you on an idealistic basis, even though they are totally unrealistic. Some people call these projects, chasing windmills. Either way, you're likely to have disappointing results if you pursue them, as I counseled Claire.

Here are a few other schemes that occurred for past clients when Neptune was on the scene. Henry had an opportunity to buy into a windmill farm. Rodney was excited about a chance to invest in an alpaca ranch. Gladys received an offer to invest in a patented process that could turn a special metallic iron ore into gold. Each of these unusual investment opportunities came during the time that Neptune was in their 1st House. Be extra careful about investment opportunities that come your way during this transit. This is not to say that any investment opportunity you hear about during the time Neptune transits your 1st House is a bad investment or a scam. The problem is that you just don't know for sure. The lack of clarity during this period of your life requires you to be extra cautious and diligent, carefully investigating all opportunities before your decision. Ultimately, you may find that something was "hidden" from your view.

It Brings Compassion

In a positive vein, Neptune's influence stimulates your sense of compassion towards others, causing you to experience deep feelings of wanting to help and care for others in their time of need, as was Manny's experience. Newly retired, Manny lived alone and was focused on leading a simple and solitary life. However, when Neptune came into his 1st House he found his sense of compassion and duty so aroused that when he heard his dying uncle Lester had nowhere else to live, he offered to take Lester into his home to care for him. His uncle gladly accepted his invitation. Lester had always been a kind and generous uncle to Manny. And Manny had always loved his uncle for his mentorship during his teen-age and young adult years. Now, at this time in his own life, Manny felt a natural desire to unselfishly care for his elderly uncle.

Manny realized there was more to life than catering to his own needs, however, after a few months, he wished he'd been more realistic about how time-consuming caring for his uncle would be. But once Manny became acclimated to Uncle Lester living with him, he found he had much more to live for than just living for himself.

It Brings Inspiration & Creativity

In addition to increasing your compassion, other very positive features of this transit are that you'll feel inspired, your imagination will be greatly heightened and your perception will be keen. Artistic pursuits such as music, painting, crafts, are all excellent ways to channel the creative influences of Neptune in the 1st House.

Alexia shared with me how much she loved music and playing the piano as a child. She still enjoyed playing the piano in her home, dreaming that one day her newborn son, Timothy, would follow in her footsteps and learn to play as well. Just after he was born, she asked me to analyze his birth chart to determine the ideal time to introduce music into his life. I told her that at the age of 5, when her son had Neptune transiting his 1st House, would be the ideal time for him to be inspired to creatively tap into his musical talent to play piano. She used this fortunate timing to begin his musical lessons and it worked out perfectly. He has now enjoyed taking lessons for the past seven years and is getting ready for a major recital.

It Brings Addiction

Since the 1st House concerns the physical body, when Neptune transits in this area of your birth chart, it's especially important to watch your diet and the type of foods you eat to avoid any toxicity that could lead to health problems. Medicine and drugs can have a powerful effect on your body, so you should be mindful, especially if you have an addictive personality. There can also be a strong desire to escape reality through the unhealthy use of alcohol or other toxic drugs leading to dependency or other harmful effects as Curt experienced.

Curt came to me to discuss his addiction to alcohol, which had always been a problem. His downward spiral continued as he started drinking more during his workday at lunch. Clearly, his dependency had gotten out of hand and he was now experiencing serious troubles because of it. He finally saw reality when his wife said she had enough of his drinking and threatened divorce; and his employer declared his job was at risk if he didn't get some professional help. Curt realized he was trying to escape his depression through drinking.

His addiction was dramatically affecting his life in such negative ways that he realized he could no longer ignore his problem. Neptune transiting his 1st House provided Curt the opportunity to face his addiction and decide whether he wanted to be sober or not. Fortunately, Neptune energies are ideal for healing any illness. He was finally ready to go through a detox treatment at a drug re-hab clinic, sign up for support by joining an Alcoholic Anonymous group, and see a therapist to consciously face the issues that were behind his alcoholism. Curt had deceived himself long enough and now was committed to getting help and treatment before he lost everything.

In summary, there is the possibility that you may face some type of disorientation and personal confusion during this transit. It is a special time where you'll feel inclined to move yourself out of your mundane and ordinary existence. You may also experience a strong spiritual and metaphysical influence that draws your interest to meditation, personal growth workshops or other spiritual pursuits. Your sense of compassion and idealism may also express itself by your desire to volunteer and help others in need.

But be especially sensitive and aware of the fact that during Neptune's transit your personality goes through a period of change where you sort out the parts of your identity that may or may not be truly who you are. Once Neptune leaves this House, you'll have some clarity about *who you really are*.

Considerations, Actions, Decisions During Neptune in 1st House

1. What experiences and activities would help you understand your real personality?
2. What do you feel compassionate or idealistic about?
3. Is there any thing creative or artistic that you want to do?
4. Is there any spiritual or religious activity you want to participate in?
5. Are you inspired to improve your health?
6. Are there any addictions you want to confront?
7. Are you deceiving yourself in any area of your life: family, relationships or work?
8. Carefully evaluate any investments that you are considering.

PLUTO In Your 1st House of Personality & Appearance

Who Will You Transform Into?

When Pluto transits your 1st House you're engaged in the process of re-making and transforming your overall personality and appearance. When you think of what this radical change looks like, imagine Clark Kent changing into *Superman*, David Bannister turning into the *Incredible Hulk*, Eliza Dolittle becoming *My Fair Lady*; or, even the fictional person who meta-morphs into the *Wolfman!*

Even though the changes we're talking about occur over time, they're no less dramatic than those examples. During the years that Pluto transits your 1st House your personality blooms from a seed to a full-blown flower. The process turns a shy person into a self-confident dynamo. It can transform an aggressive bully into an enlightened person who realizes his behavior is destructive to himself and others. It's also possible for someone's personality to turn towards the "dark side" as well. For example, the sweet young teen-ager you went to church with can grow up, becoming a manipulating shrew. The mild-mannered fellow you went to school with can become a con artist. Pluto's energies can be constructive – improving you or destructive, leading you to ruin.

Pluto's effect has a profound impact on you making you aware of the psychological forces that have shaped you into the person you are today. You're able to gain an understanding of the unconscious part of your personality, which in the past may have driven you to act compulsively or behave irrationally in ways you've never fully understood or in ways you knew you shouldn't.

In a positive manner these energies can cause a person to feel a compelling need to always be honest, courageous and loving as their general nature or, to develop into a personally powerful individual who has genuine charisma. However, in a more troublesome way Pluto's effect can also be seen in the person who has a "obsessive-compulsive disorder," (OCD) where anxiety causes uncontrollable, unwanted thoughts along with a need to engage in ritualized behaviors they feel compelled to perform.

An individual living with this personality disorder may know that such behavior is irrational, but even so, they're unable to resist and break free of their habit. Perhaps, you've had the feeling that you were powerless to stop a certain bad behavior, almost as if it were out of your control. An old comedienne, Flip Wilson use to say, "The Devil made me do it!" Pluto's influence will help you understand that *you are doing it*.

In addition to transforming your personality and behavior, Pluto's energies can bring you a rebirth of your vital energy and a rejuvenation of your physical body. Thus, if you've had a horrible accident or injury it can be a time of remarkable healing and recovery where amazing healing and surgery can be done to bring recuperative change to your body. Pluto's energies make it possible for you to drastically alter or re-mold your physical appearance, for example, through significant weight loss or even cosmetic surgery. Miraculous transformation can occur during Pluto's transit through your 1st House.

Overall, it's a time of self-improvement as long as you're open to receiving feedback from others, which is part of making your transformation successful. Some people use Pluto's passage through their 1st House to get feedback from others through personal growth work, whether it's seeing a therapist, reading books or self-discovery workshops. This is your opportunity to purge yourself of old beliefs, attitudes, habit patterns that no longer add value to your personality and character. You can now make deep-rooted psychological changes that have been a part of you, ridding yourself of past behaviors that were unproductive and caused disharmony in your relationships with others. For example, a person may finally realize, "I've always had trouble with authority figures," or "I want to stop being so controlling and manipulative."

A self-examination process is occurring at this time that will allow you to better understand yourself and have more satisfying relationships with others. You may have an epiphany such as, "I never knew how much my behavior was turning people off. Maybe I need some help." If you've been constantly embroiled in power struggles, you now have an opportunity to get to the root of why you've had these interactions with others. You may make an important discovery, "I never realized that my personality was so intimidating to others." Your relationships will become more satisfying and less conflict ridden by having greater awareness and control of the way you express your personality in the outer world.

Because your willpower is strong, you feel more driven to achieve and get your way at this time in your life. You have an intense urge to use your abilities to the fullest in the outer world, operating with high intention to accomplish your goals. This is a time when you're ready to do great things and make your mark in the world. You are intensely ambitious, so this can be an excellent time to enroll in school, begin a new profession, start a business or embark on a transformative activity. You're now ready to exert your will, authority and influence in order to present yourself in a more powerful way.

This is when your life may take a new direction, which may include assuming a position of authority, such as an important leadership position. You have the opportunity to effectively use your talents and gifts to achieve the goals and objectives you seek. Pluto transiting your 1st House is a rare opportunity to bring success to whatever you value in life. At this time you feel a real sense of personal power. Get ready for a fantastic period of your life when you come into your own as Roger did.

You've Got The Power!

When Pluto transited Roger's 1st House he decided he wanted to run for political office. Working hard, develop his speaking, negotiating, diplomacy skills, he was never afraid to "mix it up," and be tough when he needed to. He had worked on several campaigns and was a keen observer of the world of power politics. Roger had made a number of great networking contacts and even lined up potential contributors to his campaign. Members of his party agreed it was time for his star to shine.

Roger's birth chart revealed that he had the good fortune to have Pluto in his 1st House (along with other favorable transits), so it was the perfect time for him to organize and start his political campaign. He worked extremely hard in a very hotly contested campaign, winning the vote and becoming city councilman. Roger's success is a good example of using Pluto's powerful energies to accomplish one's goals.

Whether you exert a positive or negative force in your world depends, to a great extent, on your ability to understand yourself, your motivations and inner drives. The powerful energies of Pluto, which drive your ego, provide you with the opportunity to re-make, re-shape, and transform your personality. If you're open to understanding and improving yourself, you'll emerge a more much effective and personally powerful person than you were before. I have known people who were rather mild mannered, never assuming any leadership responsibility turn into bonified leaders during the transit of Pluto in their 1st House.

It Brings Transformation

Irene was starting her freshman year at a university and wasn't clear on her major or even what career to pursue. As Pluto began its transit to her 1st House, we spoke about how she might experience this transit in her life. For Irene, the Pluto process was a period when she felt an intense curiosity in understanding why people behaved as they did and what made them "tick." This motivated her decision to begin pursuing a bachelor's degree in psychology. She'd had recently attended a personal growth workshop held by a prominent psychotherapist. Her workshop experiences with him were life changing on a deep level and she began reading his books and even corresponding with him. After getting to know her in the workshop, the psychotherapist was very impressed with her contribution.

Irene later wrote him, "You inspired me to want to become a psychotherapist." He wrote back and volunteered to be a mentor and provide her with suggestions and counseling to further her learning and studies. She was excited by both his support, as well as the idea of studying the mysteries of the mind and hidden secrets that are a part of each of our personalities. Irene wanted to pursue this career path because helping people through transformational counseling was the way that she could "make a difference" and contribute to society.

Compel Or Dominate?

Pluto's transit through the 1st House is a crucial time for your growth and development as a person. As you become more self-aware of the strength of your will, your unconscious mind becomes more conscious. This is part of your development toward becoming a more powerful and effective person in life. During this lengthy period of Pluto transiting your 1st House, one of the effects you may notice is your need to control the world around you, whether in your relationships, at home, work or play. This driving need may put a strain on your relationships with others, occasionally causing you to engage in power struggles as well as ego clashes.

Consequently, you may be called to choose between dominating others to your will or using your personal influence to compel them. As you more fully transform your personality, you'll discover you have a greater sense of control, resourcefulness, and influence than you've ever had before. This was the exact situation Jerry found himself in at work.

1st House: Personality & Appearance

Jerry was one of 20 sales people in a highly competitive, commission-driven sales force. When he was selected to be the new sales manager over all his peers, there was a lot of dissension. Some sales people supported his promotion because they liked Jerry; those in fierce competition with him for the sales manager job, did not. Some felt he was talented and deserved the opportunity; others thought he had "played politics" to get it. With Pluto going through Jerry's 1st House it was an excellent time to assume power. But he had to choose whether he would do it by dominating the sales force through intimidation and control – as in, "I'm the boss...and you're not;" or compel them through his personal influence, "I'm the new boss...and I want us to work together to achieve our goals and make our yearly bonus." He wisely chose the latter.

Deep Psychic Wounds

This is a profound period of personal transformation where very personal aspects of yourself, which have been long buried within your psyche, begin to emerge in your life. This may include deep psychic wounds that have been hidden beneath your day-to-day consciousness. If this is the case, this may be when you're forced to confront and eliminate the pain that such a wound has caused. The influence of Pluto is meant to purge problems within you, by bringing them to the "light of the day," in order to confront and resolve them. Fortunately, Pluto's influence will give you the power, will and confidence to face your darkest and deepest wounds and heal them permanently.

This was the case for Kate during Pluto's passage through her 1st House. She started having nightmares and then vivid memories of a childhood incest experience with an uncle who was now dead. She was a 22-year-old woman who had buried her horrible memories as a little girl, deep within her psyche. Her painful recollections started one year ago, after finally finding a wonderful man to share love and an intimate, sexual relationship. Kate believed this was the catalyst for her recent obsession to vividly recall her traumatic childhood experience. Even though she wanted to let "sleeping dogs, lie," she couldn't. It was time talk to someone about her past so that she could purge this memory and heal herself for her own health, as well as her love relationship.

Pluto's influence fills you with an inner power that gives you the courage and strength much like a warrior or gladiator who is ready to go into battle and protect others from harm. One of my client's enlisted in the Marines during Pluto's transit through his first House because his sense of patriotism compelled him to serve in the military and go to some hot spot in the world where he could defend his country from aggressors.

This is a time when you're drawn to understanding the motivation beyond your behavior and actions. For this reason, you may be interested in psychology, spiritual, and metaphysical experiences as well as new ways to regenerate and transform yourself. Since you may be intensely focused on re-shaping and overhauling your personality, there may be periods of time where you withdraw and isolate yourself from others in order to meditate on your life. As you contemplate some very deep and profound issues – you may have friends say, "You seem very intense these days." They are right, because you are.

Take advantage of this opportunity to meditate, participate in a personal growth group or learn about yourself through psychotherapy. After all, this is an intense period of discovery for you. As Pluto passes through your 1st House you'll notice that many facets of your personality, relationships, and even surroundings in the outer world, radically change and even die during this period of your life.

As you experience Pluto going through this House you'll begin a powerful transformation of your personality, that properly channeled, can bring you a new life direction and a greater awareness of *who you really are*.

Considerations, Actions, Decisions During Pluto in 1st House

1. What goal should you pursue to advance your life?
2. Are you interested in a promotion where you can take on more responsibility?
3. Do you want to be more powerful?
4. Do you want to engage in politics?
5. What qualities do you need to purge from your personality?
6. What part of your personality would you like to transform?
7. Do you want to begin therapy or some self-discovery process?
8. Do you want to change your appearance?

Transits to Use for Successful 1st House Decisions

You now understand the areas of life that are featured in your 1st House. We've discussed how each of the five transiting planets exerts its unique influence on the affairs of this House. This will help you better understand the changes you are experiencing, moods you're feeling, and the events taking place. Your awareness of this information may prompt you to:

> 1. *ACCEPT* the way things are and be content with what is going on in your life.
>
> 2. *CONSIDER* that you'd like to make some change, in which case you may evaluate your options and further contemplate your situation.
>
> 3. *DECIDE* that you're ready to make a change, take action, and make a decision pertaining to the affairs of this House.

If you make a decision, you'll want to learn how to pick the best transit to produce a successful outcome for it. Please know that the art of picking and interpreting transits requires very thorough analysis, normally done by a professional astrologer. Therefore, I've kept the discussion of selecting and using transits simple, for illustration purposes.

The key is to remember that each planet has the ability to bring a *different* positive quality of success to your decision. For example, *Jupiter's* effect may provide opportunities to expand and grow; *Saturn's* effect is more practical; *Uranus'* effect is sudden and exciting; *Neptune's* influence may bring you inspiration and idealism; *Pluto* may bring an intense and transformative effect for major change. This knowledge will help you understand how your decisions are affected by these planetary influences.

In the examples below, I chose a planetary transit to produce a favorable result for each individual's particular decision. This will help you see the many possibilities available to create the right outcome and make your 1st House decisions more successful.

Using a positive JUPITER Transit

DECISION: I want to have a breast reduction procedure.

Explanation: Remember Janice who wanted a breast reduction surgery? Since we've already discussed Janice's situation, I've include her Astro Action Plan for your reference.

* * *

Janice's Astro Action Plan

1. Contact my doctor for his suggestions and referral recommendations.

2. Call friends and contacts to get additional doctor referrals and information on the procedure.

3. Interview three doctors who came highly recommended.

4. Give doctors the specific dates for my surgery to be done; and confirm their availability on those dates.

5. Choose the doctor I feel most comfortable with; and schedule my surgery during the time of the transit.

* * *

Using a positive SATURN Transit

DECISION: I want to lose weight and adopt a healthier lifestyle.

1st House: Personality & Appearance

Explanation: We discussed earlier in the Chapter how Marge consulted with me to discuss her health concerns, which included being a smoker and overweight. She had already tried to quit many times and wanted to use a positive transit to finally achieve success in her effort to quit smoking and lose weight.

Let's review why this decision worked out well. First, we took advantage of the fact that Saturn was transiting her 1st House for two and a half years. Secondly, we chose a very favorable transit from Saturn to a planet in her birth chart. The transit we chose, amplified the positive effect of helping her lose weight with the right diet and exercise plan. It brought a real seriousness to her goal providing her with discipline and a sense of commitment to her health-diet program. It was a favorable time to re-shape and re-structure her body and her health.

* * *

Marge's Astro Action Plan

1. Ask all my friends to give me their support and assistance.

2. Join a gym.

3. Spend money, in advance to hire a personal fitness trainer who will work with me at the gym three times a week.

4. Meet with the dietician at the gym to create a diet plan.

5. Meet with the dietician each week to confirm that I'm following the plan.

6. Arrange doctor's supervision and monitoring for nicotine patches and any other care needed.

7. Join a "quit-smoking" support group.

8. Join a "weight-watcher's" support group.

* * *

Using a positive URANUS Transit

DECISION: *I am going to be a painter.*

Explanation: We discussed earlier in the Chapter how Annie, after 20 years of marriage, finally decided to free herself from her unsatisfying domestic responsibilities in order to change her life and become a painter. We chose a Uranus transit that coincided well with a positive change in her domestic responsibilities, thus allowing her the freedom she required. This Uranus transit gave her the courage to confront her husband and assert her need to be free to pursue her passion: painting. A Uranus transit allowed Annie to make a radical change such as this, that she would never had the courage to do otherwise.

* * *

Annie's Astro Action Plan

1. Enroll and meet with my teachers at the art school to select courses.
2. Set up my new routine for domestic responsibilities.
3. Hire a cleaning service to do daily domestic work.
4. Buy art supplies and set up a small studio in my basement.
5. Establish a daily routine to paint.

* * *

Using a positive NEPTUNE Transit

DECISION: *I want my son to have a successful experience learning piano.*

Explanation: We discussed earlier in the Chapter how Alexia wanted her son to have an enjoyable and successful experience taking music lessons and playing the piano at the ideal time. We made sure to start her son's music lessons and piano playing during an excellent Neptune transit, which would allow him to channel his creative and artistic talents. It would provide him immense enjoyment and the potential of falling in love with his musical experience. The influence of this transit would also provide him with the ability to bring discipline and structure to his piano classes. His hard work would likely pay off and encourage his interest further.

* * *

Alexia's Astro Action Plan

1. Research and interview five teachers with special experience teaching very young children.

2. Discuss each teacher's availability to begin teaching during the lengthy period of time that this transit was occurring.

3. Ask each teacher for referrals of parents, I could call to discuss the teacher's success in teaching music.

4. Choose one of the teachers and set up the 1st lesson during the time of the transit.

* * *

Using a positive PLUTO Transit

DECISION: *I want to run for political office.*

Explanation: We discussed earlier in the Chapter how Roger had decided that he wanted to run for political office. When we discussed his planning and the best time, it was important that he had Pluto transiting his 1st House. It was also important that other transits that favored his winning were occurring near the date of the election vote. Since Roger had been seeing me for several years, he had the foresight to plan his election during this time of extremely favorable transits to his 1st House.

The transit we chose had some important influences relevant to politics and influencing the masses. It also gave him great organization ability and the skill to motivate staff. The transit gave him the ability to establish rapport with voters and was also favorable for attracting publicity with the public. Most of all, this transit provided him the power to influence and achieve success through his actions. It was the ideal transit to win an election; and, he did.

* * *

Roger's Astro Action Plan

1. Organize all elements of my campaign: staff, financing, media, public appearances during favorable transits.

2. Make final selection of all staff on my best transit days.

3. Implement campaign efforts, activities during favorable transit dates.

4. Schedule speech and media appearances during the campaign using the best transit dates.

* * *

Don't Forget Your Free Transits...

After reading about the 1st House of your birth chart, you may be curious to know in which Houses, *Jupiter, Saturn, Uranus, Neptune,* and *Pluto* are transiting at this time in your life. If you're interested, you can use the *FREE Transit Calculator* that is discussed in Part IV of this book to get a list of *your* personal transits.

2nd House

Money & Values

The 2nd House of your horoscope raises the question, will you be wealthy or poor – but not just in terms of the money you have. After all, there are poor souls who have plenty of money and there happy ones whose wealth is not in their bank account. For such people, their wealth and riches come from the joy their values bring them. They refuse to become slaves to material goods. You could say their values make them feel rich. Alternatively, there are people who are rich in the talents they have, which bring them great joy and satisfaction.

You'll see that the 2nd House is one of the most important places to look to understand what is going on in your life. No doubt, you'll consult this House often to shed light on personal changes you experience and to make important decisions as they relate to your values, resources, possessions and the money you make. This House raises many questions about your life. Are you the type of person who needs to earn a lot of money and have many possessions to feel secure? Or, are you the type that needs very little in the way of material goods because you're unattached to having possessions? In fact, you may consider them a burden.

In the traditional sense, the 2nd House is known as the House of Values and Resources. It rules such matters as: the money you earn, what you value, whether it's your physical belongings and money, or your personal self-worth, self-esteem and your talents. This House describes your attitude towards money, possessions, and your own sense of security about them. You may have your own unique personal issues concerning money. It's an area of life that evokes strong reactions because matters related to money are of paramount concern for most people. On one hand, having and making money is of practical importance, since most of us have bills to pay and a life to live that requires we have sufficient income. On the other, some people have an excessive need for wealth that drives their life to a point where it's out of balance. The Bible says, "The love of money is the root of all evil," (1 Timothy 6:10). Robert Kiyosaki, author of *Rich Dad, Poor Dad*, says, "The lack of money is the root of all evil." I say, "Greed has killed more men than poison." It's clear that the pursuit of money can be a highly charged issue that affects people's attitudes, relationships and very existence. Clearly, people whose sole focus is the acquisition of wealth have their own set of problems just as poor people who have none.

This House is connected with money is many ways. It gives great insight into how successful you'll be at making money. Will you be someone who makes a lot or someone who struggles, trying to earn enough money to make ends meet? It can tell a great deal about your chances of winning or losing money, if you're a risk-taker, and whether you're likely to have many jobs or career changes. It reveals if you're the type of person who spends your money impulsively the moment you see something you want or someone who is very practical and conservative, buying things only when absolutely necessary or on sale. It confirms if you tend to be selfish with your resources or if you're the generous type who spends money freely, the "big sport," always grabbing for the check when you go out with friends. The 2nd House shows whether you're likely to help others out in difficult times or not.

This House also rules bankers, budgets, monetary gains and losses, and security. Therefore, this House can be involved with the investments that you make; and also reveals much about a person's desire to accumulate personal resources, their aspirations for wealth, material security needs and personal values.

Your Body in the 2nd House

This House rules the face, throat, tongue, nose, ears, lower lip, lower jaw; and base of brain, cerebellum, cervical spine, and neck. Since there is nothing more important than your health, pay special attention to these areas of your body whenever a planet transits this House. It may indicate a period of time when you'll experience health benefits, issues or even problems you should be aware of. If you observe anything unusual, you'll have the opportunity to consult with a medical doctor or a health care practitioner.

2nd House: Money & Values

Your 2nd House Decisions

You now understand that the 2nd House of your birth chart concerns your values, possessions, the money that you earn, the money that you spend, your personal self-worth, self-esteem and your talents.

As you read about this House, think about your own life. Are you satisfied with what you have? Are you happy with your values; and the money that you make? Are you getting enjoyment from the way you spend your money? Are you being paid enough for the work that you do? Are there any talents that you'd like to develop that would enrich you?

These are all significant questions and your answers may lead you to make important decisions to change your life. Here are a few examples of decisions clients have made based on the activities and issues of the 2nd House.

Situation: Timothy works long hours for low pay.

DECISION: *I want to find a new job that pays more money.*

* * *

Situation: Virginia is planning a major expenditure for a new piece of art to complete her home. She tends to buy things impulsively, later feeling "buyer's remorse."

DECISION: *I want to make sure that I'm really happy with my art purchase.*

* * *

Situation: Edward has been working for a financial services firm that, while promising a service for its clients, makes little effort to fulfill their agreements. It has become clear to him that the company's sales and marketing efforts are really geared only toward bringing in profits – not honoring their promises to clients. The company's lack of integrity is in direct conflict to his personal values.

DECISION: *I want to find a more satisfying job with a company that is managed by people of integrity.*

* * *

During the transits of *Jupiter, Saturn, Uranus, Neptune,* and *Pluto* – Timothy, Virginia, and Edward will have many opportunities to implement their decisions at a favorable time to produce the outcome they want.

The Transiting Planets Reveal Your Past, Present & Future

Your main focus is using astrology to understand *what the hell is going on in your life.* Once you do – this book will show you the best time to make a decision to change it, should you have a desire to do so. As you read about the five planets transiting the 2nd House, notice the way each planet exerts its unique influence and effect, bringing specific opportunities, issues, problems, and events into this area of your life. But if you're curious as to how these planets are personally affecting YOU *today,* in your *past,* or in your *future,* you can find out where each transiting planet is in your birth chart by using the *FREE Transit Calculator* (see Part IV).

JUPITER In Your 2nd House of Values & Resources

A Wealthier You

To set the stage for what you can expect when Jupiter transits your 2nd House, just imagine that no matter how much of a struggle it was in the past, all of a sudden, you find yourself lucky in the area of making money. Obstacles you may have encountered in the past fall away. If you're already earning a great deal, Jupiter will expand your earnings even further. When Jupiter transits here, it's an excellent time to add to your material possessions and increase your resources. Because this House concerns your values, it's a very positive time to expand whatever it is you *value*. With this Jupiter transit, you've been given a great opportunity to make advances in this area of your life, so make sure to take advantage of it.

Your possibilities for successfully increasing your wealth may include: asking for a raise you deserve; contacting clients who could buy your product or service; acquiring something of value that will increase its worth over time; or making a beneficial investment of some kind. Jupiter brings you the opportunity to wisely grow your resources.

Of course, if your values are beyond material, for example if they are based on your spirituality, personal convictions, ideas, or some standard of justice, this will be a perfect time in your life to expand this dimension of who you are. If you've had thoughts of growing in these areas, you now have a period in your life when you'll derive great joy from pursuing them wholeheartedly.

Jupiter's placement here gives you the good fortune to increase your financial resources through opportunities that allow you to increase your net worth. Sara, a client of mine was a computer consultant and was having difficulties finding clients and making enough money to support her lifestyle. Fortunately for her, at our annual transit consultation, I saw that Jupiter would be transiting her 2nd House in three months. This meant that she would have an entire year to expand her earnings as a consultant. I advised that her best way to reap the benefits would be to spend the year at professional networking events, attending technical conferences, calling up old clients, asking for referrals from current clients, and being very pro-active in building her client base by making countless sales presentations.

The next 12 months brought her the most lucrative earnings Sara had ever experienced in her entire life. Best of all, she used the benefits of Jupiter in her 2nd House to "stock her pond" with clients, by negotiating long-term contracts where she could be paid consulting fees for years to come.

The only downside is that Jupiter's transit here can cause you to become so over optimistic that you can't see how things could go wrong. So, remember that the opportunity you have to add to your resources carries with it the need to manage them in a prudent way. Often people get greedy under Jupiter's influence. If you feel this happening to you, it's a warning that you may be over-expanding and setting yourself up for a disappointment. After all, if you eat delicious food at a buffet, that's a good thing. If you overeat – a good thing becomes a bad stomach ache. In order to carefully improve and grow your resources, be clear about your goals so that any attempts to expand are thoughtfully considered.

One of the positive and negative facets of Jupiter's influence is that it tends to give a person both confidence and the potential to have grandiose expectations. It's exciting to look forward to something wonderful happening. However, if one imagines a *fantastic* thing will occur, only to have something *nice* occur, it's easy to be disappointed. Jupiter's effect can cause you to set the bar of expectations so high that even a fortunate event becomes disappointing. This was well expressed by a friend's fiancé who said, "Oh what a lovely engagement ring. I see it's 1-carat. To be honest, I was expecting it to be at least 2 carats." Part of Jupiter's lesson is having gratitude for the good fortune you receive and sometimes that includes being humble, satisfied and grateful.

Since the 2nd House also concerns the money that you spend, this maybe a perfect time to make a very expensive purchase, as long as you make sure it's within your means and not just out of some frivolous desire to be self-indulgent. Because you'll likely be feeling optimistic, it's a time to be thoughtful about your motivation for buying anything expensive. Are you buying it because you really want the item? Or, is your motivation to impress others and to increase your social status? This is a great time to be honest with yourself; and then, do what you think best.

During this transit you'll find that material possessions bring you great pleasure and comfort. I had a client who repeatedly expressed his dream of one day, owning a red Corvette. Then, he would quickly comment about how totally extravagant and impractical it would be to buy "that kind of car." He just couldn't allow himself to make the purchase. At his transit consultation, I saw that Jupiter was going through his 2nd House and told him that this would be the perfect year to buy his dream car and receive a great deal of joy from driving it. He quickly agreed and said he was feeling so good about enjoying life that he was ready to buy the red Corvette he always wanted. I believe the positive optimism of Jupiter going through this House allowed him to finally buy that car because he could have easily afforded it many years before. However, Jupiter's influence put him in an economically expansive frame of mind where he could allow himself to spend the money for it.

A Time For Great Opportunity

Jupiter is a planet that provides learning and a philosophical perspective in whatever area of your life it transits. Therefore, during the time that it's in the 2nd House of your birth chart you'll have the opportunity to learn more about how you manage your possessions and make your decisions to spend your money. You'll decide which values and talents you want to cultivate and grow.

A client named, Denise enjoyed her talent for singing at her church every Sunday. However, she longed to take her talent, one of her best resources, and expand its use. She wanted to do more with it than sing with the church choir. Jupiter in her 2nd House was the perfect time to look for opportunities to showcase her vocal talent to others. She found a talent agent to promote her, and quickly thereafter, her agent was successful in getting her bookings to sing at local clubs.

This Jupiter transit teaches you how to wisely manage your material world and resources. You may also learn that instead of earning more money, what you value is more free leisure time, which is what Patrick discovered. He was a successful stockbroker, who finally realized that working 60+ hours a week in a quest to make more and more money was no longer satisfying. So, he advised his manager that despite all his success, he was getting burnt-out working such long hours, and needed to take time out to pursue some other activities, outside of the office. His manager, well aware Patrick was a top producer with workaholic tendencies, was very supportive, giving him his blessings to work less, to pursue other interests. Patrick took advantage of his shorter workweek by regularly playing tennis, taking a Spanish class and bringing more balance to his life. His Jupiter transit taught him to enjoy something else of value besides money.

You can use this lucky Jupiter transit to expand your wealth by investing your money in stocks or real estate or any investment you're interested in. As mentioned, it's an excellent time to buy possessions that you really want such as a client who used this transit to invest in a large stamp collection that he had always wanted. It was the perfect way to invest in something that brought him great pleasure.

Considerations, Actions, Decisions During Jupiter in 2nd House

1. Ask for a raise or some additional benefits.
2. Contact new customers to expand your business opportunities.
3. Find a new job that has a future.
4. Cultivate a talent you have always enjoyed.
5. Buy something you have always wanted that would make you very happy.
6. Start or expand a business.
7. Make an investment in an asset that has growth potential.
8. As you've matured, how have your values changed?

SATURN In Your 2nd House of Values & Resources

The Time to Re-evaluate Your Values and Your Money

When Saturn transits your 2nd House, it's an excellent time to become aware of what you *really* value in your life. How much do you value money and your material possessions? You may come to a realization that your new sports car and your designer clothes are the coolest things in the world and you're happy you can afford them. On the other hand, it may dawn on you that you have way too many clothes in your closets and that big SUV you bought a couple of years ago is more than you want or need. What's going on is that you're examining your values and coming to some conclusions about how you want to live your life.

You may want to examine the importance of your spiritual, religious and moral values, too. This may result in your deciding that attending church service every Sunday is now a priority. Or, that you've been going only to please your parents and it's not something you enjoy doing anymore. You could decide that you won't hang out with certain friends because their ethics don't come up to your standards or to spend more time with others because theirs do.

Society, perhaps even your own family, places a lot of stress on the importance of making money and acquiring material possessions. By taking stock of your personal and spiritual values during this transit, you have an opportunity to better understand what you value – not just what you have been taught to value by others. You're developing greater maturity as you sort out what's important to you.

Be aware that Saturn transiting through your 2nd House can bring you financial restrictions where you find that you have to cut back. It's an ideal time to live on less and you'll realize you really can. In some cases, it's a time, when you may experience financial loss and even hardship. Perhaps, circumstances in your life will require that you live on less or sacrifice more than you are use to. No matter what, it's a period when you must be careful with your finances and conscious of being economical, even if that's not your normal approach to spending money. If you resist being financially prudent, where your sole focus is just on making money, and spending it as usual, you may find that Saturn teaches you a harsher lesson because you may find yourself experiencing serious financial limitations, even losses during the two and a half year duration of this transit. For example, some hardship may come along, perhaps a big expense you never anticipated, during this period of your life. This is the way that Saturn can take you out to the woodshed.

Perhaps, you're already the type of person who doesn't over-value money and material possessions since you realize personal riches come from pursuing other values as well. But even if you are a non-material person you may still feel financially insecure, because the influence of Saturn leaves you "feeling" poorer than you really are. For example, I know someone who has $10,000 in his bank account, but the moment his account goes down to $7,500, he'll tell me he's going to have to *really watch* his spending because he's starting to feel poor. This person acts as if he has no money left and starts feeling financially nervous and uncomfortable. His experience is that he's losing control over his finances, his money and even material possessions. He feels like there is not enough.

This is very symptomatic of Saturn's influence, causing a person to have an irrational fear that he doesn't have enough resources, resulting in his becoming financially insecure. For some people this insecurity seems to take over their life and they become depressed over their financial situation. They need a good dose of perspective, which would help them be more realistic in assessing what they actually have, and considering that it really may be enough. It's a time for such a person to manage his poverty-consciousness by looking in the mirror and saying, "I may feel poor but I'm really not."

I have another friend, who lives with this poverty mentality every day because she has a stressful Saturn aspect in her birth chart. So, whenever she feels an attack of, "Gosh, I'm worried...I feel really poor," she hops in her car and drives over to the poor side of town and observes people who live on far less than she has. By the time she's returned home, she's returned to reality and is grateful for what she has. Saturn has taught her that "poor" is relative, and to be realistic.

The Need to Re-evaluate Life

The purpose of Saturn in your 2nd House is to help you restructure or refine your values on a deeper psychological level, so that you become clear about which ones are important to you. A good story to illustrate this point occurred with my client Ted. He started working at

2nd House: Money & Values

his father's company immediately out of college. Ted wasn't particularly excited about coming into his father's business, but it was a foregone conclusion, since the idea of his taking it over had been discussed for many years. In fact, as he grew up, his father often talked to Ted about running the family business. Ted told me that the "eight scariest words" his father ever said to him, were: *"Son…some day, this will all be yours!"*

When Saturn went through Ted's 2nd House, he became depressed realizing that despite earning an excellent income, working in his father's company wasn't what he wanted to do for his work. It didn't conform to his interests or his values. He was much more excited about a career where he could teach those far less privileged than him. In fact, what he really wanted to do was to be a teacher working with inner city kids. Ted realized that the two and a half year period of Saturn transiting his 2nd House was the perfect time to re-structure his life, what he did for a living, and how he made his money. He wanted to be doing the kind of work that had meaning for him and conformed to the values he thought were important.

Utilize this excellent period in your life to re-organize your resources and make them work for you in a more efficient way. Take Steven, for example. He managed his own real estate property for 15 years, initially buying small homes to re-model and soon graduated to three-flats, then to 12-flats. Eventually, he was so successful that he bought a large 100 unit rental building. However, along the way, he kept his smaller properties, which ended up creating most of the problems and distractions, taking a disproportionate amount of his time. Saturn in the 2nd House was the perfect time to consolidate and sell off those smaller properties that no longer fit his more lucrative business model of operating only larger properties. This restructuring removed a lot of stress from his life and allowed him to use his talents to run the rest of his real estate business more successfully.

The problem for most people who experience Saturn going through their 2nd House is that their insecurities of not having enough or losing their possessions, take over their life. The way to combat these fears and worries is to take any appropriate action necessary to re-structure, re-organize and even eliminate anything that may restrict you or be inconsistent with your values. Remember that one of Saturn's purposes during two and a half year period is for you to seriously observe your whole value system, making sure it serves you. This includes your values toward all your resources: money, possessions, material goods, and your talents.

It Brings a Need to Re-Structure

I recommend to a client that as Saturn approaches their 2nd House to prepare to organize their life, especially their financial resources. Make sure that the financial part of your life will not be a distraction and source of worry or insecurity.

Miriam met with me the year before Saturn was to transit her 2nd House. She always had problems managing her money and over-spending on her credit cards, thus she was perpetually in debt, paying high interest rates on her credit card. Miriam's only asset was a small inheritance, which she never wanted to touch. We discussed that this would be the ideal time to re-organize her credit card debt by taking out a total consolidation loan or using part of her inheritance to pay off all her debt. I explained to Miriam that this Saturn transit was a signal for her to recognize the need to re-structure her finances and perhaps, her values too. Miriam was forever shopping for the latest wardrobe to impress her friends or buying the latest hi-tech toys to compete with the people she worked with. I warned that if she took no action and continued her profligate ways, the influences of Saturn transiting here might create severe problems and limitations for her. Why not use the positive energy of Saturn, which is to re-structure and remove anything that no longer works?

To her credit, she made a decision to use most of her inheritance to pay off all credit card debt. She then decided to enroll in a course that taught her the many benefits of paying cash and avoiding the use of credit cards. Most importantly, the course forced her to look at her upbringing, family conditioning, and belief structures that caused her to overspend. Miriam used this Saturn transit as the time to organize her finances and re-examine her values. She destroyed all her credit cards (except one for emergencies) and took control of her life with that decision.

When my clients experience a Saturn transit going through their 2nd House, I discuss with them the main issues likely to arise around their finances, possessions and values. For most people, the money they have and the money they make, as well as their material possessions, reflects their values on a deep psychological level. Becoming consciously in touch with one's inner values provides a person an opportunity to see if their values and material possessions reflect who they are. What many people discover during this Saturn's transit is that their values, especially toward money and material goods, may not be their own. They may have been passed down from their parents, or from another source from their early youth. Some people were raised or taught to think that the road to inner peace and happiness comes from the acquisition of wealth.

During this transit you may come to the realization that what you have, is all that you want or really need. One of my friends spent years in a job that required a great deal of travel in order to make 30 percent more income. When he reevaluated his personal needs and life style requirements, he decided that he'd be happier if he worked in a non-traveling job, even if it paid him 30 percent less money. Saturn teaches you to take responsibility for your values and be content with what you have.

Considerations, Actions, Decisions During Saturn in 2nd House

1. Reorganize and consolidate your wealth, assets, or property.
2. Carefully analyze any investments you make.
3. Secure your possessions and material goods.
4. Buy warrantees for any expensive equipment you purchase.
5. Reevaluate your talents and consider improving them.
6. Examine your values to make sure they serve you.
7. Pay off debt and loans.
8. Avoid being extravagant.
9. Be economical and make prudent financial decisions.
10. Save for a "rainy" day or something you want to buy in the future.

URANUS In Your 2nd House of Values & Resources

A Time of Radical Change in Your Finances and Values

During the coming years as Uranus transits this House you'll experience radical changes in your values, possessions, financial, and material situation. You're fired! You're hired. You just won the lottery! You found out your old baseball card collection is worth a fortune. When Uranus transited through my 2nd House, I bought a brand new Volvo, and parked it in a lot over night. When I came out the next day it wasn't there. It had been stolen! A week later I was given a promotion and a raise at work.

It's a time when you need to prepare yourself for sudden and even surprising changes in your financial circumstances and resources, which you'll likely encounter over the next seven years. If you're fixed and inflexible in the way you approach your finances and material circumstances, trying to maintain the status quo, you'll be vulnerable to the upsetting effects of Uranus going through your 2nd House. Uranus energies demand that you be adaptable and open to change.

Expect to experience this transit on two levels, internally and externally. The first (internally) is on a deeper, more psychological level, where your values will radically change and be altered. You may come to such realizations as: "All my family cares about is money. I'm tired of the rat race, I don't want to live a material life." Or, "My family was so poor. I am going to make a lot of money and be rich, so that I can have anything I want."

You'll discover new values different from old ones that you may have grown up with. While you can expect to feel this change on an inner level, it will also be reflected on an external level in the new ways you view your possessions and the material world you live in. Your new values may make your current relationship to money, possessions and the material world seem inappropriate to who you are. Imagine waking up from a dream suddenly unconcerned about money, as if it no longer mattered. Perhaps, you'll look at all your adult toys, and wonder, "what was I thinking when I bought all those things?" You may have already discovered that many of your values and attitudes towards material wealth

2nd House: Money & Values

were instilled in you and not your own. If so, you may decide to break free from your attachments and obligations to earning money, acquiring wealth, and material possessions. You might even become, downright, rebellious as you assert your newfound convictions.

During this Uranus transit, I had a client who totally rejected the material values of his rather "blue blood" family, realizing that all the wealth he had grown up with had made him feel empty inside. Instead, he discovered that he enjoyed the life of friends who lived a more Bohemian unconventional lifestyle, with no attachment to money, few permanent ties, wandering, traveling and adventuring, only working when necessary.

You're going through an amazing metamorphosis. Uranus' energies are there to liberate you from old behaviors, in favor of new ones that will bring you greater freedom and independence. If you're open to change, and the new discoveries that are part of Uranus' influence, you'll find excitement from the experiences it will bring to the matters of your 2nd House. However, if you're the type that rigidly holds onto those things that are familiar and comfortable, you'll find the effects of Uranus disruptive and stressful. The choice will be yours.

Either way, Uranus acts as a catalyst for change within us on a conscious as well as an unconscious level. For that reason, if you embrace the change that this transit brings on a conscious level, it will not be quite so disturbing. However, if you're clueless (as in totally unconscious) to the need to change your values, your attitudes towards money, and material possessions, then you may find this transit extremely upsetting to your psyche; and to your material wealth. For example, if material wealth, possessions, and resources have limited your personal growth, Uranus often brings a quick and surprising change, shocking your financial situation. For example, you may find yourself saying, "I can't believe I lost my biggest account! How will I afford keeping up with my lifestyle?" Or, an event can occur in your life, which may actually take away your possessions as one client experienced, "When I came home I discovered my place had been burglarized!" Conversely, if your personal growth requires a certain resource, material goods, or a new resource for you to grow further, Uranus may also bring that to you as well as one client told me, "Larry, I never expected such a big bonus." The influences of Uranus are entirely unpredictable, sudden and quite surprising.

It Brings Surprise

When Uranus transits your 2nd House of values, possessions, finances, material wealth and resources – you may experience a sudden windfall *or* an abrupt loss. For example, you may suddenly make a fortune in a stock investment or lose one.

Martha was an extremely conservative person who always thought the lottery was a waste of money because the odds of winning made it a virtual impossibility. She prided herself on the fact that she would never buy a lottery ticket. One day she walked into a convenience store and as the clerk rang up her purchase, he asked her if she wanted to buy a lottery ticket. He obviously misheard her reply and promptly printed out a ticket, handed it to her and put his hand out for payment. Realizing that the clerk misunderstood her, she surprised herself by saying, "Oh, what the heck…sure I'll take it." When she "scratched" the ticket, she was in shock to learn she had won a lottery prize of $1,000! Uranus was in her 2nd House.

Since this House concerns the money you earn from the work you do, you may experience finding a job that pays you more money than you've ever earned, or find your salary gone because you were fired, unexpectedly. Surprise, surprise! Welcome to transiting Uranus in your 2nd House.

It Brings the Unexpected

Marty was totally focused on earning money and holding onto the security of his six-figure, marketing job. He had been with his firm for 21 years and was well thought of by many of the company executives, so his job seemed to be virtually guaranteed. When Uranus went through his 2nd House, Marty was totally unprepared when his boss of 14 years was immediately transferred to another division. Within 48 hours, Marty received both a new boss and the news that his company was being downsized. Fortunately, Marty would receive a severance package, yet none of that changed the fact that he had unexpectedly lost his job.

Paula had climbed the ladder to a supervisor's position in her company, eating lunch at her desk and working 60-hour workweeks. She was tired of the everyday grind of her job and looking forward to two weeks off. However, Paula's vacation changed her life when she flew to Israel and visited a Kibbutz (a collective community that is traditionally based on agriculture). She was totally excited about the whole concept of people working together in a united way – with no emphasis on making money, instead being in cooperative relationship with each other for a common good. Paula could hardly wait to say "yes," when she was invited to stay and live in Israel through a government-sponsored program. Within 60 days she had quit her job, leased her apartment to someone else, sold her belongings, and was living on a commune in Israel.

A Time to Be Shocked

Remember: the influences of Uranus can be shocking, unexpected and always unpredictable – both *positively* and *negatively* as it impacts your 2nd House. For example, if you make money through real estate, you might have the fortunate experience of finding a "below-market" investment property drop unexpectedly into your lap. Alternatively, you might find that the property you thought you owned free and clear is now encumbered because of liens you never knew existed.

You may find possessions are suddenly obtained or extracted out of your life. Take Phil, for example. His material belongings were the most important things to him in his life – from the new wardrobe he bought every year, to the latest entertainment systems and computers, to the Rolex watches he owned. These objects gave him personal pleasure and great status in public. One weekend, when Phil left town, burglars cased his home, disabled the alarm, broke into his house, and carted off everything valuable he owned. With a Uranus transit: "expect the unexpected."

On a positive note, the sudden and surprising changes that Uranus brings into your life will be a source of excitement and challenge. No matter what, while Uranus is transiting your 2nd House for seven years, you can expect your values, resources, wealth and material goods to change significantly during that period. Equally important, you'll notice that your relationship to each of these areas will be changed so that you can continue to grow, discover, liberate yourself and enjoy new freedom because of Uranus' influence. Remain open to these changes and new opportunities that come into your life and you'll benefit from Uranus' influence in this House.

Considerations, Actions, Decisions During Uranus in 2nd House

What the Hell Is Going On in My Life?

1. What changes in your work would excite and liberate you?
2. Do you have any exciting talents you'd like to pursue?
3. Are your possessions and assets secure?
4. Are there any technologically advanced gifts you'd like to buy?
5. Is there any way that you'd like to radically change your values
6. Do you have any innovative ideas that might make you money?
7. Be alert for an exciting investment opportunity.
8. Would you like to start a technology business?
9. Is there anyone you'd like to surprise with a gift?

NEPTUNE In Your 2nd House of Values & Resources

A Time To Develop New Ideals and Values

During the next fourteen years as Neptune transits this House, you'll undergo a total shift in your attitudes toward your material possessions and your overall values. Neptune's influence causes you to be selfless and concerned with higher ideals and values instead of just gratifying your own ego needs in the material world. You could say its effect is to "dissolve" your ego so that you're no longer motivated just to satisfy your material wants and needs.

No matter how much you might like money or material possessions, imagine that suddenly they are far less important to you. Instead you find yourself pondering what values would really bring you happiness and contentment. Neptune's effect is to give you a new orientation toward your values and possessions during this period of your life. One client thought it was so important to give back to others that he established a scholarship fund at his old school. Another client found a spiritual teacher located in India and spent a summer living there and studying with him.

The way Neptune energies work is to minimize your ego needs, allowing you to feel a sense of detachment from whatever you've been *"attached"* to. For example, you may say, "I used to care about wearing the latest fashions and buying a new car every year." Neptune's influence has a mysterious ability to cause your interest in material things to disappear. You may find yourself saying, "I like the idea of living a simpler life. My old jeans are just fine and I'm glad I sold my big gas-guzzler." For instance, if you've always been attached to the notion that what was really important in life was being popular, living in a mansion, and driving a Rolls Royce, you may find yourself no longer subscribing to those values. You become *"detached"* from their previous importance. Conversely, if you've been attached to the idea that beauty is only skin deep, living in a rented apartment is perfect, and driving an older model car serves you well, you may alter those values, too. Neptune's influence can cause you to re-evaluate and change your mind.

Be Careful of Confusion, Delusion & Loss

Neptune's passage through your 2nd House can affect you in another way. It can cause you to be confused, even unsure about your ideas, values, and attitudes toward money and material goods, especially if you've based your self-worth on your possessions. As a result, you might find yourself saying, "I was so sure that once I had a high-paying job, a big house, and an expensive car I'd be happy." Thus, you may find yourself re-thinking and re-orienting your views.

You may have a bigger challenge if you're so materialistic that your main identification in life is based on what you have, instead of *who you are*. If that's the case, Neptune is likely to teach you a lesson about making the material aspects of your life less important, causing you re-evaluate your values. You may even learn this lesson through the loss of your possessions at this time.

Neptune's influence in this House is not about *literally* losing all your possessions or resources. However, psychologically or emotionally, you may find yourself losing interest in them to the point where they become unimportant. As you go through a re-orientation of your values and possessions, you may experience a lack of clarity in matters of the 2nd House. What you may notice is that the pursuit of material gain doesn't have as much importance to you. You're mentally and emotionally distracted as you consider your real values. Therefore, Neptune's transit through your 2nd House is a time to be careful how you invest your money and resources. You're not seeing these matters with the same crisp clarity that you normally do because you don't attach the same level of importance to them. Thus, these aren't the ideal conditions upon which to make an important investment.

For example, if you buy property this is a time to do a thorough analysis of your purchase. Neptune energy can cause you to be unrealistic and unclear about reality, to the point where you can't tell the difference between what's true and what's not. Matthew came to me to discuss some real estate he was excited about acquiring, after talking extensively to property owners and other developers in the area. He was told that the city was making big development plans in the area where the property he was interested in – was located. One person confided that a new airport was being considered nearby and another person revealed a major sports team was considering building their stadium there. Matthew was sure this was a fabulous investment that could not lose.

Because Neptune was in his 2nd House, I counseled him to wait longer and continue his investigation and due diligence, before considering his purchase. I pointed out that during this transit, he would be unable to clearly see this property's future and he couldn't trust the perceptions of others. What he had heard might only be "smoke and mirrors," or the illusion of a great opportunity. Under Matthew's Neptune transit, he was vulnerable to being deceived and victimized. Alternatively, he might be guilty of his own self-deception where what he thought was true, was not the real truth of the matter. Matthew politely listened to my cautionary advice, but then, replied, "I've done my research and I can't wait on this. It's a fabulous opportunity and someone else will buy it – if I don't."

Matthew made the investment and seven years have now passed since he acquired that property. During this time, all the rumors concerning his property's location have died down. The airport and stadium were never built near his property or anywhere in the city. He has paid a small fortune in property taxes and has a great deal of his net worth invested in a property that no longer seems ripe for development.

Neptune is the most *mystical* of the planets, so it's hard to understand and sometimes even harder to fully explain to clients. Especially those who are totally bottom-line focused, placing their greatest value on making money and acquiring material possessions. The ethereal nature of Neptune just doesn't make sense to them. Ironically, it's these same people who often experience the harshest lessons of loss when Neptune goes through their 2nd House. I think it's Neptune's way of pulling their attention away from their material possessions, in order to get them to consider other values.

Years ago, I remember having my home burglarized with all my worldly possessions carted off in a truck. At first, I was angry and depressed and then saddened at the lost of "all those things" that I had accumulated over so many years. It felt like my life had been stolen from me. Then, after a time as the pain of the loss subsided and perspective returned to me – I realized that I no longer needed to be attached to my worldly possessions. It was an epiphany. Those *things* were nowhere near as important as I had originally thought. In many ways, they were a weight on me because I was so materially attached to them. In contrast I've had known people who've had similar losses who were so disturbed by their possessions being taken from them that they immediately went out to the store seeking to replace all they had lost. A Neptune experience can help you discover what is really important and what is not.

Be Careful of Deception & Self-Deception

Another area to avoid during this transit is gambling with your money or possessions. Be very cautious about involving yourself in any risky or speculative investment opportunities. Charles was the CEO of his own private equity company and saw a tremendous opportunity to buy an undervalued company that appeared to be a steal. He was sure this company's huge growth potential would double the value of his company. Charles' birth chart indicated he placed a tremendous importance on material values in life: how much money he had, his many big toys and expensive possessions. Of course his acquisitive nature, no doubt, played a positive role in his success. But it also made him vulnerable to not seeing the "big picture" clearly, and the realty of certain situations. In addition, Neptune was transiting his 2nd House, so I counseled him to pass on the acquisition of this company until a time when his transits would be more favorable to him. He said, "No, there are three other bidders for this company that know it's a steal. My gut is telling me this is a great deal." He outbid the competition and bought the company.

About 18 months after the acquisition, problems occurred with his newly acquired company. EPA violations were reported and soon lawsuits began appearing. Charles considered costly litigation with the company's previous owner, but his attorneys told him it would be a losing strategy. The costs of maintaining the new company through these problems, was draining profits from his other company. He called me up, to say: "Larry, you were right. I should never have bought this company. Yet I was so sure. How could I have known about these problems?"

That's the exact point about Neptune's influence during the time it transits your birth chart: *You don't know.* Your thinking may be confused and unclear. You're subject to wearing rose-colored glasses, not seeing matters realistically. This can result in becoming the victim of deception by others; or result in self-deception as in Charles' case, where his fantasies of increasing his company's value by 50 percent, totally clouded his judgment.

It Brings Inspiration & Idealism

One very positive effect of Neptune transiting your 2nd House is it may cause you to start developing your own spiritual values. You may discover that in the past you've over-emphasized the importance of material wealth. Many of us have been raised to place high value on making

2nd House: Money & Values

a great deal of money, becoming rich, buying a status car or having the latest hi-tech toys. We're taught that we must work hard to attain wealth and possessions, so the struggle to achieve this goal leaves many of us focused solely on the material. Neptune's lesson is easier to learn if you embrace the truth: acquiring great material wealth does not bring you happiness and fulfillment. During Neptune's transit you may come to that realization.

Early in her life, Teresa inherited a great deal of money. She completed her education degree, found a job, and began teaching at a public high school. The job gave her a chance to work with young people and use her teaching skill. It was satisfying, but there was still something missing in her day-to-day life. We conducted her transit consultation during the time that Neptune transited her 2nd House and Teresa told me she was feeling as though her life didn't have any great purpose and that she'd fantasized doing more with her wealth than just teaching.

When I asked her if she felt that her ideals and values were changing, she said, "Absolutely." All she knew was that life seemed very empty and wanted to do something that expressed her compassionate nature and desire to make a difference in society. I asked her if she'd ever considered starting her own school for less privileged children or children with special needs. Her eyes lit up, she smiled and said, "That could be very exciting. I never thought of using my inheritance in that type of philanthropic way. That's a great idea, I'll look into it."

It turned out that Teresa never started her own school, but her research led her to a private school that was in need of financial assistance to better serve students. She became its executive director, transforming the facility into a modern special needs high school. Teresa donated a portion of her inheritance to endow the school, which was totally under-funded, so it could grow and expand within the community. It was Neptune's passage into her 2nd House that caused this value shift within Teresa, inspiring her to use her own resources to make a difference.

Be Careful of How You Spend Your Money

When Neptune transits here, it's especially important to be vigilant about the way you manage your resources, monetary possessions and the way you spend your money. Be wary of buying luxury items that appear important, because you'll probably find they won't be. Since this is a time when you could be confused or easily deceived, avoid risky investments because you're highly subject to being taken advantage of by others. That means – avoid propositions from telemarketers calling you at dinnertime, or an investment opportunity to buy shares in the Brooklyn Bridge, or to sell ice machines to Eskimos.

Positive Neptune transits are likely to help you make decisions that are consistent with your true values. You may want to find a helpful book, a trusted friend or an uplifting experience to help you figure out what your values are at this time in your life. Negative Neptune transits may bring very disappointing results, so avoid major decisions unless you've done some extra homework.

Considerations, Actions, Decisions During Uranus in 2nd House

1. What changes in your work would inspire you?
2. Have you noticed any change in what you value?
3. Are your possessions and assets of less importance?
4. Are your possessions and assets safe?
5. Are there any talents that you could use to make a contribution to society?
6. Are you interested in making a time or financial commitment to a charity?
7. Carefully evaluate any purchases you make.

PLUTO In Your 2nd House of Values & Resources

Look For Your Resources & Values to Be Transformed

Because of the sheer power and profound effect it exerts in your life over so many years, a Pluto transit is the "Mother of all planetary transits." It can bring sudden or gradual transformation of your values or material possessions. You may also experience Pluto's effect as a major shift on a deep, even profound psychological basis that you feel internally. For example, as you undergo a major change in your values you may realize you've been a "taker" all your life and now you want to be a "giver." Perhaps, the opposite maybe true, and you'll realize it's time for you to learn to receive from others.

A transformation is not a small change. It's a major "earthquake" shift where your life is radically altered. Since we're talking about the affairs of the 2nd House, you'll experience major changes in your financial circumstances, especially in the money that you make. You could go from "rags to riches!" Of course, transformation works both ways, so you could go from "riches to rags." When Pluto transited my 2nd House, my entire portfolio of stocks was decimated by the stock market crash of 1987 and I went from having great wealth to no wealth. The painful lesson I learned was to be more prudent in the way I invested my money.

The ultimate effect of a Pluto transit is to bring a total transformation to the area of life that it's transiting. Pluto's energies change you from the old you to a new you, in the same way that a caterpillar turns into a butterfly. That metamorphosis consists of a *death-rebirth* process that leads to something new being created that is better than what was there before. However, just like the mother who goes through a painful labor in delivering the birth of a child, Pluto can cause you to go through a painful birthing process before you come back out into the world in a new and transformed way.

The brilliant astrologer, Robert Hand talks about how Pluto's transformational process begins first with an unpleasant *"break-down"* phase where circumstances require you to make do and get along often, with less money and fewer resources. This phase is especially upsetting because it feels like you're constantly running into obstacles and barriers with no control over what's happening. In fact, you may feel powerless.

You May Be Going Through a "Breaking-Down" Phase

During this period, problems occur because resources you've depended upon, such as your income, are significantly reduced. This may be a time when your ability to make a loan is blocked; or you're burdened with unexpected expenses that tax your resources; or you encounter problems with your home that require you to invest money you didn't expect to, in repairs, remodeling or extensive renovation. Often during this *"break down"* phase your finances become reduced unexpectedly, where you can't count on your usual sources of income. Here is a typical example.

Margaret came to me feeling frustrated about her life, wanting me to look at her transits, to make sense out of what had happened in her life. She had received a fabulous opportunity to buy the home at a low price if she acted quickly to take advantage of this great deal. However, the seller wasn't willing to wait for a conventional mortgage closing, insisting on a cash sale as a condition of accepting her offer. So, she had purchased the home for cash. Margaret figured that wouldn't be a problem since she was sure she could quickly apply for a mortgage and pay back the money she'd borrowed from her retirement account. However, one bank unexpectedly declined because the appraisal showed the home to be overvalued. Another bank turned her down because her income level was not sufficient to justify the mortgage loan she was seeking. She was running into banks that would not offer her a mortgage or their offers were unfavorable, being far less than the funds she had borrowed from her retirement account.

To make matters worse, within 30 days of moving into her new home, she discovered major problems with the foundation that weren't found in the inspection report. The real estate purchase contract was written in such a way that she didn't have any re-course against the buyer. Litigation was an option, but was expensive and could take years to resolve. The whole experience was turning into a nightmare. Unfortunately, Pluto was transiting Margaret's 2nd House and producing a very unfavorable and negative transit to her birth chart. It was easy for me to understand why the timing of the purchase of her home would be fraught with problems – as it was. Margaret's upsetting experience, yet again, illustrates why it's to your advantage to use *favorable transits* to make important decisions.

2nd House: Money & Values

Brings a Breakdown & Transformation

During this break down phase, a Pluto transit can block your ambitions, bring adverse circumstances that seem beyond your control and create huge obstacles to the things you're trying to accomplish. Sometimes, this breakdown phase can cause something that you value – to die, so something better can be born in its place, which is what Jenny experienced when Pluto transited her 2nd House.

Jenny came to me to discuss closing down her business. She had spent the past six years building a small wholesale furniture business, working long hours for very little money. Her husband and her teen-age children complained they rarely saw her, except late in the evenings. In simple terms, her business had taken over her life. She realized it was tough for her to be successful because she was wearing too many hats and didn't have the time to build her company's sales.

She consulted with me to discuss her options, including whether she should close down her business. Jenny had a great deal of pride, never quitting any project until it was successful, so I reminded her there was a difference between quitting and letting go. One positive event that happened over the past year was she'd gotten to know one of her competitors while attending various trade shows. They talked about their respective businesses and she confided in him some of the difficulties she was having with her own business and he was extremely sympathetic and encouraging. He was so impressed with her tenacity and knowledge of their industry that he told Jenny if she ever wanted to make a change, he would love to hire her as the vice-president of his much larger furniture enterprise.

I discussed her transits and Pluto's breakdown phase in her 2nd House and explained that her transit was a call to end an old structure in her life, perhaps her business. Her opportunity to build a new structure might begin by becoming the vice-president of another company operating in the very industry she knew so well. Jenny was coming to the same conclusion. She began to appreciate the major change that was going on in her life and in her business. Her six years of experience in her own business helped her understand what was important to her. While she enjoyed her experience – her family and quality of life were her priority. As a result, Jenny ended up accepting the job offer to be the new vice president of marketing. As she found out, Pluto's message is often to let go of something that's no longer meant to be in your life, so something new and even better can then, come into your life.

However, the breakdown phase can work in another way with less positive results, as a client who owned a retail business found out. His business was declining during the time he had Pluto transiting his 2nd House, so he hoped renovating and modernizing his store would help attract more business. He was sure he had enough cash to do this. But he was shocked when he found out that the report showing the cash balance in his bank account was inaccurate. Upon closer scrutiny he discovered that his accountant had "cooked the books," and embezzled a great deal of money from his business. The business owner brought me his accountant's birth information, which showed that the accountant had Pluto going through his 2nd House, along with some very stressful transits adversely affecting his values and finances. Despite the accountant's many years of trustworthiness and integrity, his values had deteriorated to deceit and fraud, seeing embezzlement as the only way out of his own financial troubles. For the accountant, Pluto's breakdown phase would include jail as part of restoring his values.

Brings Opportunity To Re-Build

However, others — as Guy's story will attest, are fortunate enough to be further along in Pluto's re-building phase. Guy found a great job out of college working for a plastics molding company. He started out in accounting, but during his 12 years with the company he worked in all of its departments: production, finance, customer service, sales, and, marketing. He was a well-respected senior manager in the company, but his dream was to start his own business, so he came to see me to discuss the best time to do this.

Based on Pluto's transit to Guy's 2nd House, and other transits occurring in his birth chart, it was clear he would have obstacles requiring him to be extremely well capitalized in order to succeed. Despite his optimism, the difficulty of his transits indicated that building his company's sales might take 12 to 24 months longer than his business projections showed. The key to success would be having the financial staying power for longer than he had planned. To avoid great financial stress, Guy raised more capital from several investors who had great confidence in him. The additional cash reserve would insure he was well capitalized. It turned out that business growth was slower than he had anticipated in his first 24 months of operations. So, he hired a seasoned sales manager who soon had his company meeting its sales forecast by the 3rd year of operations. The business had turned the corner and was finally on successful footing.

The good news, as Guy experienced, is that as the *breakdown* phase ends and the *re-building* phase begins, you can once again transform the area of your life that you're striving to build and improve. However, the common problem for many people is that they will *resist* the breakdown phase, simply refusing to accept the need for total change. They will stubbornly hold onto assets, resources, possessions (e.g., job, business, property, values, talent or income) they're accustomed to – regardless of the genuine need to let them go out of their life.

This was the real issue and dilemma for Jenny. It would have been a big mistake for her if she had held onto her business despite the obvious limitations and lack of success she was experiencing in operating it. Her experiences in her business clearly fit the breakdown phase of her Pluto transit. If she had ignored its message, she would have only slowed down the process that required total change, thus delaying the re-building phase, which in her case was an excellent opportunity to begin a new career; and a chance to transform her relationship with her husband and children.

In baseball the old adage is, "You can't go to 2nd base until you take your foot off of 1st." That's often Pluto's message when it transits through each House of your birth chart. By the time Pluto has completed its transit of the 2nd House you'll have often developed a new, transformed attitude toward your values, possessions and resources. Pluto teaches you to exercise control and transform your inner values so they fit *who you are*. But you're likely to have problems if you allow your resources and possessions to control you.

Considerations, Actions, Decisions During Pluto in 2nd House

1. What plans can you make to build your wealth for the long-term?
2. Is there a need to make any radical changes in your wealth, assets, or property?
3. Is there a need to improve, reform or transform your values?
4. Is it time to let go of certain values or assets?

5. How could you transform your assets so that they have more value?
6. Do you have the ambition to find a better job or start a new business?
7. Are your finances or values in a breakdown or re-building phase?
8. Do you have any talents you want to transform?

Do I Need To Run My Life According To My Transits?

We've talked a great deal about picking favorable transits in order to make important decisions. So, you maybe thinking, "Is Larry saying that I should run my life based on my yearly transits?"

My answer is, "Yes, I do believe that it is a good idea to run your life by your yearly transits."

After all, why not know the *best times* and *the worst times,* before you make important decisions? That's the advantage of having advance knowledge of your transits. It gives you foresight, which is better than hindsight. It's prudent to review the annual transits operating in your life and to use them for your benefit.

This does not mean that you are forced to operate your life according to your transits. Never forget, your "free will" to do what you want – can always be brought to bear. Additionally, we all know that a part of life is making decisions, even at a bad time when we may not want to. However, using your astrological transits for planning and decision-making, gives you the highest likelihood that you'll (a) be aware of any challenging or negative transits that may affect your decision; (b) have the option to change or delay your decision to a better time for success. After all, some times the best decision you make is: The *decision you don't make,* because the timing is wrong. Making an important decision during the time a negative or difficult transit is operating in your life often results in frustration, failure, and disappointment that could have been avoided.

2nd House: Money & Values

Transits to Use for Successful 2nd House Decisions

You now understand the areas of life that are featured in your 2nd House. We've discussed how each of the five transiting planets exerts its unique influence on the affairs of this House. This will help you better understand the changes you are experiencing, moods you're feeling, and the events taking place. Your awareness of this information may prompt you to:

1. *ACCEPT* the way things are and be content with what is going on in your life.

2. *CONSIDER* that you'd like to make some change, in which case you may evaluate your options and further contemplate your situation.

3. *DECIDE* that you're ready to make a change, take action, and make a decision pertaining to the affairs of this House.

If you do need to make a decision, you'll want to learn how to pick the best transit to produce a successful outcome for it. Please know that the art of picking and interpreting transits requires very thorough analysis, normally done by a professional astrologer. Therefore, I've kept the discussion of selecting and using transits simple, for illustration purposes.

Keep in mind, that there are no *best* transits. Some transits are better than others for producing a particular successful outcome. However, just as beauty is in the eyes of the beholder, a favorable transit can also be in the eyes of the beholder. Let's use our picnic example to further illustrate how each planet can affect a simple decision: You want to plan an enjoyable picnic.

So, as your astrologer, suppose I said to you, "I have picked out a great day for you to have an enjoyable picnic. However, you can have a choice as to the kind of 'enjoyable' picnic it will be. Which of these choices would you prefer?" (Note: the planet used to produce a particular effect.)

- You can have a friendly, social picnic *(Jupiter Transit)*.

- A practical picnic where everything is organized well and goes smoothly *(Saturn Transit)*.

- An exciting picnic where you experience a "surprise," something different than you expected *(Uranus Transit)*.

- A romantic, sensuous, and ideal picnic that inspires you *(Neptune Transit)*.

- A profound, transformative picnic where you are very moved by the memorable experience you have *(Pluto Transit)*.

They are all positive outcomes. But your favorite choice might be based on how you feel that day and whom you'll be picnicking.

Remember: the effect and influence of each of the five planets, *Jupiter, Saturn, Uranus, Neptune* and *Pluto*, vary a great deal. For that reason, in the examples below, notice how successful 2nd House decisions turn out based on the transiting planet that was used.

Using a positive JUPITER Transit

DECISION: *I want to earn more money.*

Explanation: If you recall, Sara was a computer consultant who was having difficulties finding clients and making enough money to support her lifestyle. I've reprinted her Astro Action Plan so that you can more clearly how she used her Jupiter transit to earn a great deal of money and create great success in her career.

* * *

Sara's Astro Action Plan

1. Fill up my calendar up with opportunities to meet people who could lead me to consulting contracts.

2. Attend networking events, association shows and chamber of commerce events.

2nd House: Money & Values

3. Make a list of business friends, colleagues, past clients and clients who have said "no" to hiring me previously.

4. Re-approach and call each of them during this time to set up meetings, lunches and coffees to discuss using my consulting services.

5. Initiate a marketing effort of ads, correspondence, and e-mailing to promote my service.

6. Look for any opportunities to make one-on-one and group presentations selling my service.

* * *

Using a positive SATURN Transit

DECISION: *I want to make sure that I'm really happy with my art purchase.*

Explanation: If you recall Virginia was planning a major expenditure for a new piece of art to complete her home. We used an excellent transit which would provide Virginia with a clear vision of the type of art she would find pleasing, yet make her purchase a smart long-term investment. The influence of this transit would help her be prudent about staying within the budget she had set for herself and provide her confidence that she would be happy with her purchase.

* * *

Virginia's Astro Action Plan

1. Phone galleries and discuss the paintings and her budget.

2. Use the Internet to view paintings that might be of interest.

3. Visit galleries for viewings with a friend who is an art expert.

4. Ask myself if I truly love the painting in a deep way.

5. Consult with the art expert to get his recommendation.

6. Buy a painting during the time frame of the transit.

* * *

Using a positive URANUS Transit

DECISION: *I want to introduce my new invention to the world.*

Explanation: Priscilla is a gifted techno-geek with brilliant ideas. She has been working on an *iPhone* application she believes will be a big hit. She wants to market to a company in the mobile phone marketplace such as *Apple* at the best time for her invention to be approved.

This Uranus transit is fabulous for bringing anything new or innovative to the marketplace. It produces great excitement and can bring positive news and interesting encounters with others. It's a time when she will discover people who will help her advance her new application. Unexpected, yet positive surprises can come into her life. It's an ideal transit for her to promote a new invention.

* * *

Priscella's Astro Action Plan

1. Research on the web and elsewhere, how mobile phone applications are being marketed and find the most successful process to use to get my invention before decision makers.

2. Make a target list of company executives to send a proposal on my new mobile phone application.

3. Network and make contacts directly within companies that would be interested in my invention.

2nd House: Money & Values

4. Seek informational interviews with company employees. Ask them for referrals to the appropriate decision makers within their company.

5. Contact marketing organizations that sell applications to mobile phone users. I'll discuss my "app" idea with them as well as a joint-marketing effort.

6. Attend hi-tech and electronic trade shows to network and make contacts.

* * *

Using a positive NEPTUNE Transit

DECISION: *I want to explore the spiritual side of myself.*

Explanation: Ken wants to do more with his life than just work, come home, spend time with the family and sit in front of the TV set. He's finding himself drawn more to the spiritual dimensions of life, helping others and volunteering.

This transit will help Ken experience a dimension in his life where he finds himself empathetic and compassionate to the problems of others. The influences of this transit make it a perfect time to volunteer his time, especially to those less fortunate and experience the joy of being of service to others.

* * *

Ken's Astro Action Plan

1. Read books on the spiritual and metaphysical to learn more about topics of interest.

2. Go to lectures and attend classes in these areas.

3. Join a spiritual-based group or organization.

4. Take up yoga or meditation.

5. Interview charity and volunteer organizations to find one that I would enjoy volunteering.

* * *

Using a positive PLUTO Transit

DECISION: *I want to renovate my dream home.*

Explanation: Edward bought an old house in the country that was in ruins. He'd always dreamed that one day he'd totally renovate it. For years he's contemplated investing a sizeable amount of money to remodel it, but he's held off due to the horror stories he'd heard about the enormous time, energy, and expense involved in such a project. Edward wants to begin at the best time.

His Pluto Transit provided the perfect time for Edward to renovate his dream country home. He'll have tremendous physical energy to accomplish a major project. Since this transit lasts over a long duration, he'll be able to work long and hard over an extended period of time to accomplish his goal. The influences of Pluto are geared toward the rebirth process of letting the old die, so something new and better can be born in its place. Edward will benefit from Pluto's positive energies, which are ideal for rebuilding and restoring real estate like an old country home.

* * *

Edward's Astro Action Plan

1. Organize and begin this project during this transit.

2. Set up all a project team (i.e. architect, contractors) to agree by contract to complete this project during the 2-year period in which the transit occurs.

3. Commence ordering materials and supplies during best transit times.

4. Schedule project review meetings during best transit times.

5. Proceed with confidence and totally commit to renovating this project exactly as I have planned.

* * *

NOTE about Astro Action Plans: *We've discussed how to create Astro Action Plans in Part III. And you've seen examples of Astro Action Plans shown in the 1st House and 2nd House chapters. Astro Action Plans will no longer be shown at the end of each House chapter. Please use the past illustrations as a reference guide on how to create them.*

REMEMBER: You can use the FREE Transit Calculator that's discussed in Part IV of this book to go back in time to see which transits were occurring when a major event happened in your life. It might be a wonderful learning experience, especially since most transits repeat themselves over your lifetime. Also you can find out where your transits are today or in the future.

3rd House

Communications

- "She speaks so clearly and passionately."
- "His persuasive talk sure convinced me."
- "Her tone of voice is so aggressive."
- "She has the vocabulary of a very educated person."
- "He talks like he has marbles in his mouth."

What do people say after they've had a conversation with you? Your communications style can be your greatest asset. Of course, if you communicate poorly, it can be your worst liability. We are in awe of public speakers, politicians and theologians who speak powerfully and eloquently, but we're just as aware of people who talk to us abrasively, fearfully or indirectly. Your communication style will be noticed just as much as your physical appearance, maybe more.

Most people are not truly aware of their communication style. There are those who communicate assertively, in a direct, honest and appropriate manner, while some individuals communicate aggressively, with an emphasis on venting anger, upset, and humiliating others. At the other extreme are people who communicate non-assertively, in an indirect and subordinating manner, bending to the will of others.

The 3rd House of your Horoscope is known as the House of Communications and Intellect. As we discuss this area of your life, this is the perfect time to reflect on *your* communication style and how it impacts on your relationships, career, and the various activities you engage in. The way you communicate is the key to having satisfying relationships, achieving your goals and making successful decisions. When you express yourself, do others see you as thoughtful and intelligent, boring and uninspiring, *or* superficial and flighty?

3rd House: Communications

The 3rd House represents all types of communications: including telephone, letters, e-mail, computers, documents, and contracts you write. Which type of communicating do you prefer? There are those people who prefer face-to-face communications to the telephone, while others prefer a quick e-mail as a way of sharing thoughts. Some people "talk, talk, talk" – to the point where you want to hang their tongue in a delicatessen. Others hate talking on the phone and insist on writing an e-mail instead. For many, there's no time for those forms of communication, texting will do fine, thank you. What mode of communication is most effective and comfortable for you? Are you skilled in your use of it? Do you use it to your highest advantage? Could changing to other forms of communication make you a better and more versatile communicator?

This House concerns how you think, your unique manner of communicating, the special style in which you express ideas, and your day-to-day thinking. Let's face it: the way you talk can motivate and impress people or bore them so much they lose interest in what you're saying. There's a big difference when your thoughts are organized as opposed to scattered. Look here for insights as to whether your mental abilities are sharp – someone who catches on quickly to what's being said or someone whose intellect works more slowly so that ideas have to be repeated over and over. This House will give you some understanding about your intellectual interests. Some people never read. For them, a book is a decoration for a coffee table while others are voracious readers and love being a member of a book club that discusses the literary classics. (Note: If you're reading this book, clearly *you* are an intellectual giant! No worries.)

You may have a curious mental attitude because you're the type who's always researching anything you're interested in. This is where to look to comprehend – what is your learning style? After all, most people have their own unique way of learning. Some are more *auditory*, learning through listening and needing to hear what's being said to learn most easily. Those who are *visual*, learn from seeing, comprehending information, ideas and concepts when they're associated with pictures and images. There are those who are *kinesthetic* (or tactile) learning through experience, or carrying out a physical activity, rather than listening to a lecture or watching a presentation.

Do you remember my "hot stove" example in Part III? If you're an *auditory* learner, you heard your mother's advice about not touching the stove, believed the information she gave you, and never touched it. If you're a *visual* learner you watched your little sister touch the stove, and never made the mistake of touching it yourself. If you're a *kinesthetic* learner you touched the stove (but only once ☺).

This House is fascinating and complex because it rules ideas, thinking and communicating which are all inter-related. This is the area of your birth chart that indicates your unique mental acuity. You may have an analytical mind that requires spending time to sort out facts or an intuitive mind that grasps answers to problems as if they seeped through a crack in the wall into your head. You don't need an encyclopedia to tell you the answer, "ya...just know it."

Lastly, this is the place to learn about how well you express yourself – whether words just seem to roll off your tongue or whether they mumble out of your mouth. This House can indicate whether you're a born speaker who's likely to be a raconteur at the party, where audiences of admirers await your next story, or someone who's likely to be shy and introverted speaking in crowds.

If you want to see your penchant for being a researcher and how likely you are to search for knowledge, this House will offer you answers. It shows how you'll express your unique mental energy to the world. In case you fancy yourself as a writer or a public speaker this House can show your skills in writing, editing, researching, reading as well as the way you think and speak. It's an excellent place to understand your ability and desire to learn, which is a key indicator whether you'll be a good student or a poor student. It's also a good forecaster of whether you're someone who'll find ease or difficulty learning foreign languages; or, whether you'd enjoy a profession as a teacher.

This House will give insights into how you approach and analyze problems, which may give you skill in drafting agreements and contracts; or make you a brilliant investigator or attorney. It may also point to your talent in creating proposals and presentations used in sales, marketing, promotion and public relations.

If you want to know if you have a short or long attention span, look at this House. Yes, it can give indications of whether you're likely to have issues with some type of attention deficit disorder. It will reveal the likelihood of your perceptions and logic being clear, accurate, cloudy, or faulty. This can be useful information to help you understand how you can approach being a better student. This area of your birth chart may also be invaluable in helping you sort out what type of work or career you want to pursue.

This House rules your early environment and early learning in lower education from nursery school to 12th grade including your perception of your childhood experiences. Take a moment to remember whether learning was easy or hard when you were a young person. How did your family environment impact your ability to learn? Your answers may give you some insight into *what the hell is going on in your life* right now.

This area also represents your relationships with brothers and sisters, cousins, relatives and neighbors. This House can indicate whether you'll have a close relationship with your siblings or whether you'll likely argue and fight like cats and dogs!

It governs your day-to-day life, your comings and goings, short journeys that you make on a daily basis, all forms of local transportation, including cars; short distance trips and local travel. It's interesting to note that some people insist on driving everywhere while others look to take public transportation to get around with the least amount of stress. Some individuals have a life that they live, within a few miles of their home, while others are on a plane every week traveling somewhere. This House offers you insights and information about all these areas of your life.

Your Body in the 3rd House

This house rules speech, vocal chords, arms, hands, fingers, shoulders, lungs and nervous system. Since there is nothing more important than your health, pay special attention to these areas of your body whenever a planet transits this House. It may indicate a period of time when you'll experience health benefits, issues or even problems you should be aware of. If you observe anything unusual, you'll have the opportunity to consult with a medical doctor or a health care practitioner.

Your 3rd House Decisions

You now understand that the 3rd House of your birth chart concerns all the ways that you communicate, think and use your intellect. It also pertains to your early environment, siblings, and short-distance travel. As you read about the description of this house, it's time to ask yourself a few questions.

How well do you communicate? Do you play to your strengths by communicating in a way that is most comfortable and effective for you? Do you have an aggressive and domineering communications style that turns people off? Or, do people consider you timid, indirect and non-assertive in the way that you express yourself to others? Do you evoke confidence because others see you as someone who communicates honestly, directly in an assertive manner? Are there any ways that you could enhance your thinking and your intellect? Is it time to start reading more or taking a class to further your knowledge? Is your style of communication easy and non-threatening? Or, do people seem anxious and on-edge when you talk to them? Do people seem enthralled and totally mesmerized with your stories and overall conversation? Are you a "blow-hard" and conversation hog? Or, are you someone who is afraid to open up and speak your mind? What is the biggest change you'd like to make in the area of your communications and intellect?

These are all significant questions and your answers may lead you to make important decisions to change your life. Here are a few examples of decisions clients have made based on the activities and issues of the 3rd House.

Situation: Bonnie has a job at the local bank, but her passion is writing poetry. She dreams of writing a complete collection of poetry that might be published some day.

DECISION: *I want to take a vacation to write poetry during a period of time when I'll be inspired to write.*

*   *   *

Situation: Martin has a management job with the local union. He needs to prepare a new labor contract that competently addresses critical issues between his union and the company's management. This is an important task affecting the earnings and livelihoods of thousands of union members.

DECISION: *I want to find the best time to skillfully craft a new labor agreement.*

*   *   *

Situation: Francine is very practical when it comes to car purchasing. She tries to buy a car that will last her many years, but the last two cars she's bought have been "lemons," requiring lots of expensive maintenance. This year, she's excited about trading in her old car and buying a new one that won't be problematic.

DECISION: *I want to buy a dependable new car that I'll be happy with.*

* * *

Situation: Wayne has always been a shy and timid. At work, others see him as a non-assertive person, one who communicates indirectly, never looking anyone in the eye, afraid of any potential conflict, and forever subordinating his needs to others.

DECISION: *I want to find someone to help me communicate confidently.*

* * *

During the transits of *Jupiter, Saturn, Uranus, Neptune,* and *Pluto* – Bonnie, Martin, Francine, and Wayne will have many opportunities to implement their decisions at a favorable time to produce the outcome they want.

The Transiting Planets Reveal Your Past, Present & Future

Your main focus is using astrology to understand *what the hell is going on in your life.* Once you do – this book will show you the best time to make a decision to change it, should you have a desire to do so. As you read about the five planets transiting the 3rd House, notice the way each planet exerts its unique influence and effect, bringing specific opportunities, issues, problems, and events into this area of your life. But if you're curious as to how these planets are personally affecting YOU *today,* in your *past,* or in your *future,* you can find out where each transiting planet is in your birth chart by using the *FREE Transit Calculator* (see Part IV).

JUPITER in Your 3rd House of Communication & Thinking

A Time for Learning

Imagine that you just swallowed a "smart pill," and your mental faculties are cranked up in high gear; your cognitive abilities are sharp. That's how you're feeling during the period that Jupiter transits this House. You're a sponge seeking to absorb knowledge as a way of mentally growing and expanding your mind, assimilating information very easily. That's why this is an extraordinarily great time to be educating yourself, studying and learning through classes. You can expect to be so enthused that you'll be asking your employer to give you opportunities to participate in training programs or workshops. Perhaps, you'll decide to finally enroll in a course over at your local university. You're mentally stimulated and receptive to acquiring knowledge about a diverse range of subjects, so it will be easy to find a course that interests you.

Edwin was forever studying and taking classes in the evenings at the local community college. Over the years I'd known him, he talked about the excitement of going on an archaeological dig in Egypt, since he was fascinated with learning more about Egyptian history and the pharaohs of the 18th dynasty such as King Tutankhamun (aka King Tut). He yearned for the day when he might visit the great tombs where the pharaohs were buried. The year that Jupiter transited his 3rd House was the ideal time for him to join a special tour group traveling to Egypt because he'd be assured of a wonderfully stimulating adventure to a place he had only traveled in his mind.

A Time for Connecting with Siblings

This is a very favorable time to be making contacts with people in your personal world, which may include enjoying positive interactions with brothers, sisters and relatives. You can look forward to having very good relations where you'll enjoy their company and receive tangible benefits from your associations with them.

Becky was never close with her much older sister, Greta who was 12 years her senior. They were from a different generation and seemed to have little in common with each other. Their parents were no longer alive, so there were no family connections to bind them any longer. Eventually, they each moved far away from each other, with Greta accepting a job as the editor of small regional magazine on the East Coast and Becky working for a non-profit environmental organization on the West Coast. The sisters rarely had contact with each other and lost touch soon thereafter.

That changed when Jupiter transited Becky's 3rd House. She found herself nostalgically thinking about growing up as a little girl with her older sister, Greta. It saddened Becky to think they were each other's only family, yet so far apart. Despite feeling uncomfortable and unsure of herself, she spontaneously picked up the phone on a Sunday morning and called Greta. The conversation seemed almost surrealistic. Greta warmly received her phone call, ironically relating that she'd also been thinking of Becky lately. It was an emotional reunion for both of them as they talked for almost two hours about their childhoods and the different life paths they each had pursued. Both decided that they had found a perfect way to re-connect when Greta offered to do an article on "world hunger" to help her sister's environmental organization educate the public about places in the world where starvation still existed.

A Time for New Thinking

The important effect of Jupiter transiting your 3rd House is that it brings a maturing influence to your thought processes and overall consciousness. After all, as you grew up, much of what you learned was from adults, and the experiences you had during those years. Now you'll have the opportunity to broaden and expand the old ideas and attitudes you adopted when you were very young. Many of those ideas may have remained a part of your thinking as an adult. Whether you were raised in the North, South, East or West, they may even include prejudices you were exposed to, which you've adopted unconsciously or consciously. These ideas and attitudes may have narrowed your views and limited the way you think about certain people, activities and aspects of life.

During this formative time you'll find yourself becoming more open to learning and understanding new ideas, which will allow you to be more tolerant of the differences you notice in the people you interact with. You will now experience a major shift where you grow into a more mature, sophisticated person. Rather than base how you think and what you believe on your past experiences (and what other people told you), you'll now base what you believe on your own experiences.

Jesse had grown up in a small town with a grandpa who referred to African Americans in derogatory terms and uncles who used racial slurs. He was raised to think that was just the way you referred to Black people. As he advanced in age he learned it was an insulting way to speak about Black Americans. However, as he grew from being a small boy to a young man he still retained a prejudice that was part of his early upbringing.

Life got complicated when he went to a club and met Abby, a young Black woman he became totally fascinated with. They started out in casual conversation and the more they spoke the more excited he felt about having met her. He was further impressed to find out she had recently completed her M.D. degree and was now in residency at a local hospital. Abby explained that her father had been a doctor as well and that she'd enjoyed a very privileged upbringing and Ivy League education. She was bright, articulate and beautiful. He'd never really socialized with a black woman before and was enthralled and excited to know Abby better, hoping she might be interested in knowing him as well. All the prejudices he'd been raised with were playing in the background of his head as he and Abby continued chatting away. He realized when he first sat down and talked with Abby he had already formed a negative stereotype about her, even though she hadn't said a word. Rather than meeting her as someone new, he had greeted her with preconceived attitudes that had been instilled in him when he was a child. As he listened to Abby joke and laugh with him, he felt ashamed of himself and his family for years of their ignorant comments about Black people. He was angry at having been taught so much prejudice.

A light went on in his mind, as Abby captivated him with her intellect, character, and radiant smile. He was learning something first-hand about not pre-judging people, and it would profoundly change his thinking forever. He had Jupiter transiting his 3rd House.

Just like Jesse, you may see the world in a bigger more expansive manner without the limitations that were self-imposed because of old beliefs you learned that are now, no longer valid. This is a time when your self-discovery helps you take the blinders off so that you can see things clearly. Since you're comfortable expressing your ideas and thoughts, you'll communicate well, without the usual communication misunderstandings. Having this ability will make you more effective in planning necessary activities, projects and goals. You'll be inclined to openly and

3rd House: Communications

candidly discuss whatever you think or feel about your life as you experience it. It's wonderful to feel how mature and capable you are at managing your life.

A Time to Write

This is also an excellent time to write or engage in any publishing efforts. In fact, some people become voracious readers, fascinated with literature of all sorts as well as poetry. You're intellectually open and mentally bright, enjoying various forms of communication, whether it's having interesting political or philosophic discussions with friends, or just writing your thoughts in a personal journal.

Marne had dreamed of writing a screenplay, some day. She'd taken screenwriting classes in the past, but hadn't felt motivated to sit down and get her "hands dirty," writing. Then, on a very relaxed weekend, she wrote the outline of a screenplay plot she'd been thinking about. A week later she wrote much more detail. Within the next month she found herself using her evenings and weekends to write scenes until the entire screenplay was finished. Eventually, she met with her old screenwriting professor to seek his help and guidance. He enthusiastically gave her his opinions and opened her mind up to new ideas for improving her screenplay. He also suggested she join a group of other "would-be" playwrights, which led to someone mentoring her, and making valuable recommendations on the best agent to submit her screenplay. This all happened during the year that Jupiter transited her 3rd House.

Lastly, Jupiter in this House is a time when you'll learn more about the immediate area where you live through short trips and travel within your immediate surroundings. You'll enjoy pretending you're a tourist as you ride a tour bus visiting sites in your own city; or you may find it mentally stimulating to visit local art galleries and museums; or just take a nice drive to a special place you haven't been to in a long time. It's an ideal time to plan some of these outings with relatives and friends whose company you'll enjoy.

Considerations, Actions, Decisions During Jupiter in 3rd House

1. Do you want to learn anything new that will broaden your view of the world?
2. Do you want to communicate more effectively?
3. Explore anything that will stimulate your intellect.
4. Take a class, read a book, or go to a museum.
5. Do you want to change your mind, attitude or prejudice?
6. Do you have any ideas for an interesting project or new business?
7. Make fun plans with a sibling or relative.
8. Do you want to change your neighborhood?
9. Do you want to write or publish anything?
10. Do you want to buy a car?

3rd House: Communications

SATURN in Your 3rd House of Communication & Thinking

A Time to Examine Your Communications and Surroundings

When Saturn transits your 3rd House, you'll need to re-examine, and make refinements in your thinking, ideas, attitudes, habits, manner of speaking as well as the way you listen to others. For example, no matter how well you communicate, there are times when you're unclear and not easily understood. Or, perhaps, you have ideas that are incorrect because they're based on a faulty premise. Additionally, you'll have to ask yourself if your attitude is helpful or hurtful to your communication. For example, does your speech reflect an off-putting attitude of, "Do, I really need to do this?" versus a more inviting attitude of "I'd be happy to do that." After all, your attitude may vary a great deal depending on how you feel that moment or based on the person you're interacting with; or the situation you're encountering.

You may also want to evaluate your habits or manner of speaking to make sure they're effective and not distracting. Some people's speech irritates others because they mumble, talk too loudly, or too aggressively. How well do you listen? Poor listening skills can result in misunderstandings or mistakes. Thus, there are many facets to your thinking and communication style that are in need of re-examination and re-adjustment if you want to be effective in your interactions with others.

Saturn's influence will also concern your communications and contacts with those in your more personal social circle such as relatives or neighbors. You may decide to re-evaluate some of those relationships, perhaps a brother you never spend much time with or an aunt who was kind to you when you were growing up. Saturn in this House also affects your short-distance travel, including travel by car, bus or plane. Are you ready to buy a smaller more economical car to replace that expensive "gas guzzler?" Will a heavy rush hour commute cause you to re-think that public transportation is a better choice than freeway driving?

During Saturn's transit here you're more serious in your exchange of ideas and opinions and overall communication with others. You may find that people will challenge your ideas and the way you think. It seems like the people you interact with are being stubborn. Ironically, they find you fixed and rigid in your thinking as well. It may even seem like your best ideas are being blocked. For that reason this can be a time when your efforts to communicate with others can be frustrating and even depressing.

New Ways of Reacting

As you reflect on the ways you've previously communicated, you may realize that your past methods of self-expression have been totally ineffective. In fact, they may have failed you. If that's the case, now is the time to stop using them and try new communication approaches that will be more successful in producing positive results in your interactions with others.

Walter grew up talking to people in an angry and aggressive fashion. When Saturn transited his 3rd House, his inappropriate way of speaking to others came to a head with incidents that forced him to address his offensive communications style. He was in a movie theatre sitting next to someone who was talking on his cell phone, so he barked at them, "Shut up!" This resulted in a yelling match, and he was ordered to leave the theatre. On another occasion, he was at a restaurant on a first date with a woman he'd recently met. Someone at the table next to him was talking very loudly. He started feeling upset as their loud banter interrupted his conversation with her. Instead of kindly walking over to the person at the other table and calmly asking them to speak more quietly, Walter loudly screamed a humiliating comment that everyone at the restaurant heard: "Hey, man, keep it down, I don't want to hear all about your love life!"

The first incident resulted in a verbal fight and got him thrown out of the theatre and the second one caused an embarrassing disturbance; and not surprisingly, no second date. Saturn's influence was bringing Walter these small crises and forcing him to re-examine his communications style and the problems they were causing him.

A Time for Serious Results

When Saturn transits the 3rd House, you become interested in how you can use knowledge in a practical way to improve your life. For example, you might enjoy buying a do-it-yourself book that teaches you how to re-tile your bathroom or research how to obtain grants and scholarships on the Internet. This is a time when your attention is focused on new sources of knowledge and information that will help you achieve your goals and live life more successfully. If your employer informs you that a special class would qualify you for a promotion, you're "all ears." The most obvious places you'll look may include schools, career-training programs, advanced educational courses or seminars.

You're motivated to examine your life, gravitating toward experiences from the outer world that will satisfy your hunger for a fresh perspective and feed your thirst for knowledge. You may be seriously interested and involved in research, analysis or other investigative projects. If you are – you'll do an excellent job writing your doctoral thesis or a major report for work. This is a period when you develop profound insights that will benefit you in your career and all aspects of your life.

Tanya was a brilliant research scientist working on break-through research on gluten-free, diets. She was excited about the article she was preparing for publication in a food industry scientific journal because it was sure to bring her the recognition she so richly deserved. Saturn transiting her 3rd House was the ideal time to present her original research findings.

Facing the Family "Music"

Just like clothes that get old and musty, hanging in a closet for a long time, so can the thinking, attitudes, ideas and opinions you've had for a long time. So, this is the perfect time to refine and re-examine them. What's happening is you're in the process of finding new ways of communicating with others to genuinely reflect your views and ideals. In effect, you're getting clear on what you think by re-examining your mental processes and how you want to express yourself to others in a way that authentically fits your beliefs.

As a result, you may find that people in your immediate environment such as siblings, relatives, neighbors, who are used to your old ways of thinking and communicating may become uncomfortable with the way you're now expressing yourself. The fact that you're sounding and thinking differently may be threatening to them to the point that they totally resist your ideas and new ways of thinking. As you try to communicate with them, their responses may cause you to feel inhibited and restricted.

Suddenly, the warm rapport you shared with these people is gone. Further communication with them may produce troublesome conflicts, which may be discouraging and even depressing. Remember: Saturn's influence is there to encourage you to express your ideas and thoughts according to your own ideals, even if they're different from those of others; and even if they produce a disagreement.

This was the dilemma Jessie faced. If you recall, he'd grown up in a small town in a family environment of relatives who were extremely prejudiced and racist. The night he met Abby changed his stereotypical attitudes and made him confront his own prejudices towards Black people. After six months of dating Abby, he was seriously in love with her and had decided to take her home to meet his family. They nervously joked about the conversation he would be having with his parents: "Hey, Mom and Dad – guess who's coming for dinner?" But the truth was, Jessie was very nervous when he finally spoke on the phone to his parents. He told them he'd just gotten engaged to a wonderful, woman, he was madly in love with. They were happy for him and eager to meet her, so a trip was planned for a family re-union to celebrate the occasion.

However, Jessie was dreading it. In fact, he was feeling depressed over his fears of a confrontation. His anxieties mounted as he worried about having to face a family that would embarrass him. Worse – he expected that he'd encounter arguments, insults and even ugly comments from family members. Upon arrival at the local airport of his hometown, he and Abby checked into a nearby hotel. His plan was to meet with his family, privately before introducing them to Abby.

When he arrived at his parent's home, his mom, dad, grandfather, and uncles were all having drinks in the living room. After greeting them all with hugs and hellos, he sat down on the couch to speak to everyone. He explained that before they met his fiancé, he wanted to have a heart to heart talk, and an open discussion with them. Jessie asked that they hear him out before making any comments. The first two sentences that came out of his mouth put a shock on everyone's face: "I have fallen in love with a wonderful woman who I'm going to marry. And, she's Black."

Jessie went on to say that since he'd moved away from his home and family, he had re-examined many of the ideas, attitudes and prejudices he'd been exposed to while growing up. He confessed to having many uneducated stereotypes and racist ideas about Black people. Jessie told them that his relationship with Abby, and her friends, had made him realize how ignorant his thinking had been. He announced he was no longer going to live his life bound by such antiquated ideas and prejudice.

Jessie said, "I understand you all have your own attitudes and opinions about people of color. I know it might be surprising and even disconcerting to have a Black person as a member of our family. Out of respect for all of you, I wanted to tell you about Abby and my plans to marry her, before I introduced her to you. If you're not open to receiving her into our family, she and I will fly out of town tonight. "My first hope is that you'll love Abby and respect her as I do. If so, that'll make us comfortable to visit and spend time at family get-togethers. However, if some of you cannot make the adjustment of treating her warmly and enthusiastically, as a new member of our family, it'll just mean we won't be able to visit or spend much time together. I hope you'll keep and open mind because I want us all to enjoy being a family together."

There were plenty of stares and nervous looks around the living room as Jessie talked. After Jessie was done speaking, everyone aired their feelings. The conversation started out calmly and soon became heated but after a lengthy discussion, ultimately his family came to a consensus that his father articulated on behalf of almost everyone, "Jessie, we love you. And, we want to support your happiness and marriage. If any family member can't do that, they can make their own decision to not participate when we have a family event. There's no doubt, this is a bit of a shock and some of us may need time to adjust, but we're open to trying. Please bring Abby over for dinner tonight so we can meet her."

The discussion hadn't been pleasant for him, but he felt authentic – like a man of integrity; and he felt good inside for expressing his true beliefs and taking responsibility for them. While the lessons of Saturn are often, not pleasurable, they are "character-building."

Be Serious, But Have Fun

Saturn's transit in the 3rd House is a time when you may have focused so much on seeking the truth, acquiring knowledge and re-evaluating your thoughts and ideas, that you haven't had time to socialize. So, you may desire to share what you've learned with others. If so, pick up the phone and call a friend or a colleague to talk about what you've learned. If you aren't in the mood for a personal discussion, consider writing an e-mail or letter. You're likely to feel a sense of importance and purpose about what you're expressing at this time, so communicating with others can be an excellent outlet for you.

On the other hand, Saturn's presence in this House can be a serious and somber time as well, causing you to feel lonely and isolated. So, don't be surprised if you feel a bit depressed, because your life is so focused on serious intellectual matters of the mind as well as new ways of thinking and communicating. To help counter all this laborious mental activity, consider recreational pursuits, hobbies and fun events that take you away from your more serious day-to-day life. Since you may not be drawn to fun and laughing it up during this period of your life, make plans to enjoy some activities that give your serious side a well deserved break.

Maintain Your Car & Check Out the Neighborhood

The 3rd House also rules neighbors, short journeys, daily transportation, and travel within your country. You may encounter conflicts with neighbors you share your environment with. This could be the noisy neighbor who, apparently wears heavy lead boots when he walks through his apartment; or the tenant across the hall, who thinks you're a 24-hour convenience store, perpetually asking to borrow food items from you.

Guy moved into his new apartment in a neighborhood he wasn't familiar with, but that fit his budget. At first, it seemed cozy; unfortunately, he didn't count on his upstairs neighbor playing music all night long or the next-door tenant being an insomniac who listened to movies into the wee hours of the morning. It wouldn't have been so bad were it not for the fact that the walls of his apartment seemed paper-thin. Lastly, he didn't realize that his assigned parking spot was so narrow he was now forced to take extra time threading his new car into his space to avoid scraping the doors. He was ready to pull his hair out, as he thought about all the limitations and adjustments living in this building would require.

During this Saturn transit, you may encounter transportation and travel problems because you haven't maintained your car. For example, you neglect to pay attention to the flashing red light on your car dashboard. Now you have to deal with costly repairs as well as finding some other transportation to get to work. Any inattention to your mechanical possessions will often lead to breakdowns. This may also be true of communications equipment, telephones, computers, appliances, and other machinery you rely on every day in your immediate environment. Therefore, consider taking preventative measures before problems occur in these areas. Consider buying a warranty for any equipment you purchase during this two and a half year period of your life.

These are the types of challenges that may come up for you while Saturn transits your 3rd House. When this transit is over, you'll have improved your rational mind and refined your thinking. You'll be much smarter, using the knowledge you've learned in more practical ways to solve problems; and you'll have re-evaluated some of your old ideas, which may have been incorrect. By replacing ineffective ways of communicating with methods that produce better results, you'll be more effective in the outer world.

Considerations, Actions, Decisions During Saturn in 3rd House

1. If you're depressed, make sure you get plenty of exercise, Join a gym and use it.
2. See a life coach or therapist to talk over your goals and feelings.
3. Join a public speaking group and practice your communication skills by making speeches.
4. Schedule some fun activities with friends, even if you don't feel like going out.
5. Make a list of all the challenges you face and the long-term benefits you'll receive if you stick with them.
6. Replace a bad habit with a more beneficial habit.
7. Make any needed repairs to your car, computer or other equipment.
8. Take a class in something practical and useful to your life.
9. Go back to school and commit to a course that will benefit you long-term.
10. Work on a hobby that brings you joy, even if it has no practical usefulness.

URANUS in Your 3rd House of Communication & Thinking

Surprising Communication

During the time that Uranus transits your 3rd House your everyday encounters with people, especially friends, relatives and neighbors; and even your business dealings, will be unreliable or unpredictable. You may find that an argument abruptly ends a friendship or a neighbor you've always relied on suddenly moves. This is a time when you may experience radical change in your mental attitudes, ideas and habits. You used to hate talking about politics, now it's a stimulating topic of discussion. You were never a morning person, now you can hardly wait to grab the newspaper and meet a friend for some coffee. You'll experience life in new ways that are different from before. You may also communicate with others in very different and unusual ways as Claude found out.

Claude grew up with a hearing impaired brother. While in his early teens, the whole family learned sign language in order to communicate with him. After college, his brother moved out of the United States and many years passed without using his sign language skills. Claude went on to become a professor at a local college. One day he saw an ad in the local newspaper looking for volunteer teachers with knowledge of sign language to teach a once a week adult education class for the deaf. Carl smiled to himself – recalling that he'd just told his wife he wanted to find some way to volunteer and help others. Right in front of him was an "out of the blue" opportunity to be of service that he hadn't thought of before.

If you're intellectually inclined, you'll be excited about your ability to see and understand the inner workings of your life in ways that you were never aware of before. All of sudden you're interested in stopping off at the public library. The signs in the windows of the retail shops look interesting. It seems like a great idea to buy a special "app" that shows the real-time schedule of local buses running through your neighborhood. Using technology is exciting.

3rd House: Communications

Uranus' influence brings you new attitudes, habits and ways of thinking to replace old ones that are in need of updating, or no longer appropriate. In the past, it was a hassle to drive to nearby neighborhoods. Now you're curious to check out some of the new ethnic restaurants in the area. You'll find yourself open to new ideas, knowledge and interests during this time. Checking the newspaper or the Internet is fun because you want to find out which club has a great musical act or where can you attend an interesting lecture. It's a fascinating period of your life to learn new things and advance your knowledge whether through reading books or friendships with people who stimulate your mind.

When Uranus transits your 3rd House your intellect is piqued and you may have a break-through in the way that you think. It's a time you feel very receptive to new learning that's creative, original and even unconventional. Astrology always sounded weird, now you're ready to set an appointment to have an astrologer analyze your birth chart. Your mind is invigorated and seems to function with great dexterity and unusual flexibility. Today, you decide to do your first crossword puzzle because you're mind needs stimulation.

These seven years are a period of time when you extremely aware as you experience new insights and realizations. You aren't likely to care whether other people have the same beliefs or opinions as you do because you're inspired to think for yourself, make your own interpretations and discoveries, arriving at your own conclusions. You decide to finally share some of your radical ideas with a group of friends, not caring about the old saw "that you shouldn't talk politics or religion," because you're feeling free to discuss both. You find yourself getting rid of old habits, seeing things in new ways, with your mental instincts sharp, as you rely more on your intuition. You're enjoying a mental freedom that is invigorating.

Since your mind is operating with a keen awareness, you may feel mentally impatient or restless, with your temperament willful, even rebellious. It's suddenly fun to make outrageous comments at the dinner table to get a rise out of people and express your ideas. Recognize that you're undergoing some radical change in your thinking that will give you the opportunity to learn, and see your day-to-day world in a new way, while changing your ideas and view of life. You're tired of having superficial conversations and look forward to having more discussions with intellectually open people. During this time you're excited to seek the truth and make discoveries. For that reason it's an excellent time to learn, take classes, seminars or any advanced training to bring you new knowledge. You'll feel a sense of intellectual detachment and objectivity as you learn about the world around you. Since you won't cling to your old beliefs for egotistical or emotional reasons, this is an excellent time to analyze, research or investigate any areas or topics that interest you.

Time to Write or Be a Public Speaker

It's an ideal time to write and creatively express your ideas and beliefs especially about anything unique or original. It's an especially prolific time to write a book if you have ever fantasized doing so. Your mind and your intuition are "super-charged," as you experience epiphany after epiphany. You can even use the exciting energies of Uranus to further your interest in being a professional speaker.

Malcolm had written a science fiction fantasy novel a year ago. It was well reviewed, but owing to very little promotion and publicity by the publisher, his book sold very few copies. This bothered him because he was proud of his book and sure that if more people new about it, they'd buy it. As Uranus transited his 3rd House, the idea came to him to organize a local speaking tour where he would visit all the book stores in a 100 mile radius and approach them about letting him present a one hour book lecture on his sci-fi book. He planned to bring extra copies of his book in order to autograph them at the end of his lecture.

After just 60 days of doing lectures at local bookstores, he was amazed to discover that he had sold nearly a 1,000 copies. Malcolm had become skilled at delivering a very unique and interesting lecture that excited his audience and motivated them to buy his book after his talk. He was now ready to expand his promotional efforts by offering lectures at bookstores throughout the state.

Time to Do Something Different

Since you're not concerned or influenced by conventional thought, during this transit, it's an excellent time to make discoveries, whether it's an actual invention or creating a new food recipe. During Uranus' transit through the 3rd House, you may want to explore such non-traditional interests as astrology, tarot, palmistry, feng shui, yoga, or any mystical or psychic activities; or even an unconventional exercise regimen like Maggie.

3rd House: Communications

Maggie chose to join a "pole dancing" class. She had always been a real jock in school and still managed to stay very physically fit. She totally shocked her friends when she said that her next vigorous exercise activity would be pole dancing. At first, she was the butt of many jokes: "Hey, Maggie, since you graduated Phi Beta Kappa, you'll be the smartest stripper to ever slide down a pole." Then, there were the lewd jokes from her men friends, wanting to know what time her class was, so they could come by and watch her perform. Maggie didn't care in the least what her friends thought.

She'd found out about the class in a totally unexpected way when she was casually walking through her neighborhood and saw a large sign that said: "Have Fun and Exercise with Pole Dancing." She walked into the studio and sat down with the teacher who made it clear that this was not a class to train nightclub strippers. It was a strenuous exercise-fitness class. The instructor explained that the class was based on a performing art combining dance and gymnastics, with students performing acrobatic tricks with a vertical pole. Maggie learned that it was great way of exercising and staying fit. That was all she needed to hear to sign up for the class.

You'll notice exciting and unusual changes in your daily communications with others, such as your face-to-face conversations, phone calls, e-mails, texts and letters. Since the 3rd House rules short distance trips and routine travel like driving your car or taking the bus, you may encounter unexpected events in this area as well. As you travel through your community you'll enjoy the diversity of your immediate surroundings and the positive interactions you have with friends, relatives and neighbors. You're absorbed in making contacts with others, communicating, sharing your insights, opinions and any new information you learn. You'll find your daily life moving more quickly, the tempo of events, and everyday communication, all having a sense of urgency and importance beyond the usual. What's happening is that your *consciousness* is being revolutionized by even the small changes you observe occurring in your life. It seems as if you can't rely on many of the things you've been use to, after all: The energies of Uranus demand change. Be warned that if you find yourself resisting or being afraid of change, you may discover these changes happen anyway but in a far more upsetting and disruptive way. This may also be true if your need to change is obstructed by others. Being aware of this dynamic of Uranus will help you better understand *what the hell is going on in your life*.

Make Sure Not to Suppress the Need for Change

Uranus' influence is a call for you to allow something *new* to occur in your world. Sometimes, people go to great lengths to prevent change from coming into a certain area of their life. When they do this, they're blocking a natural flow of energy from occurring in the same way a dike stops a river from flowing. If you prevent this needed change from manifesting, you may experience an accident, as an expression of your blocking a change that should be allowed to come into your life.

Ronnie was a sophomore in college, majoring in accounting and he hated it. What he really wanted to do was study art, so it made him angry when he thought about how he'd allowed his father to pressure him to pursue an accounting career, just so he could make a good living. Ronnie's fantasy was to be an artist with his own studio where he could be free to create, paint, draw and express himself.

Discussion of his interest in being an artist caused big arguments around the dinner table, usually resulting in his father screaming, "Ronnie, I am not going to pay for you to go to college to become a starving artist! You're good with numbers. Be an accountant like your Uncle Wally. He makes a great living, especially around tax-time." That was all Ronnie could think of as got into his car, slammed the door, and drove out of the parking lot. Fantasizing an imaginary conversation with his father, Ronnie started pounding on the steering wheel, yelling at him, and calling him names. In his violent upset, he was so distracted he ran the stop sign at the intersection. In order to avoid another car, he swerved into a telephone pole. When he woke up in the hospital his parents were at his bedside.

It's dangerous emotionally and physically to obstruct the energies of Uranus from manifesting. What can happen illustrates the "law of unintended consequences," where an intended solution, for example, "You should be an accountant not an artist," causes a worse problem: a horrible accident that brings attention to the need for change. The positive way to embrace Uranus' energies is to be open to the discovery and adventure of change. In Ronnie's case, unfortunately, a well-meaning father blocked him from doing that. But, it was up to Ronnie to find a way out of the restriction he felt by standing up to his father or perhaps, by finding a way to pay for his college classes himself. If you (or others, who interfere) are not willing to adapt to a needed change, your psyche will be disturbed, creating a great deal of stress, and maybe even a serious accident. That was precisely the chain of events that occurred for Ronnie.

3rd House: Communications

However, if you're flexible and accept change, you'll find that what's happening in your life will be stimulating and liberating.

Use the transit of Uranus through your 3rd House to re-create yourself and the way you communicate in your immediate environment. This is a time when you'll be energized to reorient your mental processes as well as your contacts with your day-to-day environment. Allow change to come into your life. Consider it as an opportunity to experience something new, freeing and exciting about yourself and the world you live in.

Considerations, Actions, Decisions During Uranus in 3rd House

1. Do you want to communicate in new ways?
2. Do you want to move to a more exciting and interesting neighborhood?
3. Are you feeling stimulated to write or publish anything?
4. Do you want to buy a unique car that expresses your individuality?
5. Be open to new ideas, such as reading books about unusual subjects, attending talks, or joining a discussion group.
6. Take day trips to explore nearby places you've never been to before.
7. Initiate conversations with people who seem totally different from you.
8. Talk to your siblings about things you've never discussed.
9. Make an appointment with an astrologer to interpret your birth chart and transits.
10. Explore non-traditional areas such as astrology, herbology, palmistry, feng shui, yoga or mystical practices.
11. Go to a performance of music, dance, or theatre that is radically different from your usual tastes.

NEPTUNE in Your 3rd House of Communication & Intellect

Be Aware of Your Mental State & Your Communications

Neptune's influence can connect you to your spirituality, but at the detriment of not paying attention to the more practical concerns and details of life. As a result you find yourself operating in your day-to-day activities without your usual mental objectivity and sense of discrimination. In fact, you may find yourself daydreaming, finding it hard to concentrate and becoming absent-minded about tasks or matters that you're normally very vigilant about. Therefore, pay special attention to your day-to-day interactions because Neptune's transit of your 3rd House may bring a lack of clarity in your communications with others.

This can lead to misunderstandings in your personal life with friends, relatives and neighbors. It's a good practice to go out of your way to make sure you and the other person really understand each other. Consider putting important agreements in writing because this is the wrong time to take for granted that everyone understands each other perfectly. You should err on the side of caution by carefully reviewing all your communication with others.

Under Neptune's influence you may have dealings with people who deliberately misrepresent or even attempt to deceive you. For this reason, during this period of your life, if you enter any contracts or agreements proceed with extreme care. Carefully scrutinize any investments you're considering in order to avoid serious problems or even financial losses. Above all, make sure to carefully review all details for accuracy before taking actions or making any decisions. Lastly, consider getting others (i.e., family members, trusted associates) to assist you in any important dealings or before you sign any important documents.

Be Careful of Misrepresentations

Wilson couldn't believe his good fortune when his wife started her new job with a real estate investment company. She was involved in the mortgage lending side of the business and came home every night with great stories that her new bosses shared about the exciting returns that investors were getting. Wilson became more curious about how big the returns were. She reminded him that she was still new to their business but said that she would check with her bosses. The next day her boss, Raphael, called Wilson up and said, "I heard you might be interested in investing in one of our real estate deals." He proceeded to tell Wilson about a big shopping center deal that offered an "almost" guaranteed 25 percent return. By the time Raphael explained how many other people were interested in making an investment in this deal to get the 25 percent annual return, Wilson felt like he was the luckiest guy in the world to hear about this opportunity. He started fantasizing about where he'd spend the $100,000 profit he would receive on his $400,000 investment.

His wife wasn't as sure about the investment, reminding Wilson that while her employers seemed honest, she didn't really know them that well. Wilson made the investment anyway. A month later, after not receiving his promised return, he sensed there might be a problem. Indeed, there was with Neptune transiting his 3rd House, Wilson had deluded himself. This wasn't a safe time to have faith in this investment or the people involved in it. Within one year, this real estate project went bankrupt and Wilson lost his entire investment. With a Neptune transit, if something sounds like it's too good to be true, it usually is.

Because of the potential for miscommunication and deception during Neptune's transit here, make sure to evaluate all your decisions very carefully. Then after you've done so, ask someone you trust to do a separate evaluation before you make your commitment.

A Time of Enlightenment

However, Neptune transiting your 3rd House is likely to have a powerfully *transformative* effect on you mentally. Neptune's influence will connect you to your spiritual or metaphysical self. For example, this may be when you discover there's more to life than the acquisition of material goods, leading you to seek some form of enlightenment that soothes and nurtures your psyche. You may be curious about the mysteries of life and the more mystical, giving you the desire to learn about karma, reincarnation, yoga, mysticism, or astrology. The connection you feel to your spirituality arouses your interest in the deeper meaning of life and how you can apply this knowledge personally.

Randle worked as a nurse in a hospice and enjoyed being of service to the patients he cared for. Since he was on the geriatric floor he had many patients who were grappling with illness and old age infirmities that would soon end their lives. He became close to many, seeking to give them solace about the life they had lived, and even re-assurance that they would come back to live another life. Since he believed in reincarnation, this was the perfect time for him to learn more about it. He found a metaphysical learning center in his community and decided to take a course there on reincarnation, where he could learn more and pass on what he discovered to those patients who might be interested.

Your Intuition Can Protect You

When Neptune transits your third House, you perceive and analyze your everyday world using your intuition as well as your feelings – not just your rational intellect. Your mind is open and adaptable and you become more aware of your creative side, as you realize that your capacity for imagination and fantasy are greatly enhanced. If you're an artist, designer or writer this can be a very exciting time where your artistic talents are expanded and you have creative visions you've never had before. You're in touch with a part of you that's idealistic and inspired to achieve something extra-ordinary, instead of the usual.

Because Neptune's influences can bring both deception and self-deception into your life, take extra care that your heightened imagination doesn't interfere with your ability to see reality. Other Neptunian influences you may experience are confusion, uncertainty, self-doubt and fear. Therefore, this is a time when it may be difficult to see the truth in many life situations you're confronted with – unless you have the ability to access your intuitive side, which warns you of potential problems. It's the innate psychic part of you that can discern truth and reality, amidst subtle and sometimes, sinister Neptunian influences.

Neptune rules the psychic-intuitive mind which aids you in perceiving beyond the rational. If you tap into and develop the intuitive capacity within your psyche, you're blessed with the gift of having your own "human-radar" device available at all times. It protects you from the dishonesty and deception most people are never aware of, either because they haven't developed that capacity, or because their conventional and rational way of looking at life makes it impossible for them to access their intuitive side. Worse, they may even be skeptical that one exists.

3rd House: Communications

Ironically, this is the part of your being that's actually capable of picking up subtle insights and "vibes" that alert and protect you from the deception of others, by acting as your lie-detector.

If you're the type of person who's connected to your spiritual and psychic-intuitive side, you've probably learned to trust your intuition, one of Neptune's most positive influences. You know that your psychic perceptions can *pick up* on subtle insights, ideas and even the behavior of others – allowing you to understand and *know* on the level that the rational mind might not comprehend. This can help you discern when miscommunication, misrepresentation or even deception are occurring, so that you can clear up the matter or protect yourself from being a victim of it, as Marina discovered.

Martina sat at the bar of a trendy club. She saved a seat and waited for her friend to meet her for a drink. Just as she sat down, her cell phone rang and it was her friend apologizing for not being able to meet her tonight. They said their goodnights and made plans to meet another evening. As she clicked off her phone, a good-looking man with wavy black hair, dressed in a stylish sports coat gave her a big smile and said, "Sounds like your friend has stood you up. My name is Mitchell. Do you mind if I join you?" She said sure and took her coat off the seat she had reserved for her girlfriend.

As she looked at this handsome man, all she could think about was that something didn't "feel right." It was as if he was a predator, lying in wait for her. It seemed crazy, but her intuition told her to be on guard. Despite his charm and good looks she sensed that there was something sinister about him. Just as he offered to buy her a drink there was a commotion. A young woman, with two policemen in tow, rushed up to Mitchell.

The young woman yelled loudly at Mitchell: "That's him...that's him!" The policemen came up to him, and asked to see his ID. After confirming his identify, they told Mitchell he was under arrest, cuffed him and took him away. Martina quickly got up and ran after the woman.

Martina asked her, "What was that all about? The woman replied, "Girlfriend, you're lucky! That man drugged my drink and attempted to take me out of this bar, where I was likely to be 'date-raped.' Fortunately, for me, my girlfriend saw me leaving the bar with him, took one look at me, and knew something was wrong. She stopped him from taking me away, once she saw that I was 'out of it,' and immediately took me to an ER clinic. After a blood test, the doctor said that my drink was spiked with Rohypnol, which is a potent tranquilizer (aka "Roofies"). The bartender is a friend of mine and when he spotted Mitchell coming in tonight, he called me. I contacted the police. Then, we came here." Martina's experience is an example of how important it is to trust your intuition. I encourage you to cultivate its use in your daily life. And as you do – you'll find yourself relying on it more and more to help and protect you.

Your Psychic Ability

Neptune's energy promotes spiritual and psychic abilities within a person. Of course, not everyone has developed or even accepted that this dimension exists in most people. Neptune's influence stimulates psychic capability and keen perceptual skills within a person who is open to receiving such guidance as in Martina's experience. But if a person is not open to it because, for example they think it is "hokey" and weird, they are more likely to experience Neptune's effect as confusion.

During this period of your life, you're extremely sensitive to the feelings of others, experiencing a high level of intuition and psychic connection in your relationships with people. For this reason, Neptune's transit through the 3rd House can be an excellent time to study psychology or any healing services.

Considerations, Actions, Decisions During Neptune in 3rd House

---

1. Do you have any ideas that are inspiring you?
2. Forgive a sibling or relative.
3. Be open to new areas of spirituality and learn about astrology, mysticism, meditation, reincarnation, yoga, or religions and spiritual practices.
4. Volunteer at a non-profit charity, environmental organization, or other group that reflects your beliefs and desire to help others.
5. Explore an artistic pursuit, such as taking classes in drawing, painting, photography, pottery, music or any other creative endeavor.

6. Write a short story, article or even a book about fantasy, idealism, compassion or service to others.
7. Join a group or class to expand your intuitive and psychic ability.
8. Talk about your ideals, hopes, dreams and aspirations with others.
9. Carefully evaluate any documentation requiring your signature and get advice from trusted friends or an attorney.

PLUTO in Your 3rd House of Communication & Intellect

Your Communications Are More Intense

Pluto's transit through the 3rd House is a time when your mind and communication abilities are transformed. This may occur because you've just finished high school or college; or you've obtained a professional degree, making you more authoritative. Perhaps your last work experience filled you with the confidence to really know what you're talking about.

You begin to discover the power of your intellectual expression, which may manifest in your day-to-day communication with others or even your talent in research or investigation. You may realize that your influencing skills make you a natural sales person. This is a time when you seek to discover truth and the deeper meaning of your day-to-day world. You were once content to watch flowers bloom in the springtime, now you want to dig them up and plant a whole new garden.

You're able to focus your intellect and concentrate on solving problems as well as finding solutions in any area of your life be it at home, school or in your job. Your perceptions are keen and your creative potential is powerful. You have a strong willpower and a great ability to achieve the goals you've mentally set for yourself. This is the perfect time to begin something important: your education, a job, a business, or tackling any project.

During Pluto's transit through your 3rd House, daily communications are more serious and intense, whether they're face-to-face conversations, phone calls, or even e-mails. Your connections with friends, relatives, and neighbors; and your everyday business and routine activities, seem to be more significant. They're no longer just casual. You're undergoing a profound psychological change and inner transformation as you examine many of the beliefs, ideas, and views of the world that you previously accepted at face value. A radical change is occurring, where your life circumstances force you to re-examine how you're living it. For example, you may have been living with situations that have been stressful or produced tensions. Now they may reach a crisis point, where you'll take

3rd House: Communications

action to resolve them. Problems that have existed in your day-to-day life may now have to be confronted.

Perhaps, you've been living with a situation or relationship that you've accepted at face value. Now you are going through a lengthy period where you're more aware of your life, questioning what's working, what's not, and what must be changed in your immediate environment. Changes you make as a result of this awareness will help you grow and be happier, although some of them may be quite upsetting, as well.

Carl had lived all of his life in the same city with his family and relatives. They were a close-knit family with European roots. Quite often all the relatives, grandparents, aunts, uncles, as well as his mom, dad and brothers would all enjoy a large family dinner at one of their homes. In addition to delicious old world cooking, there was always plenty of conversation, often resulting in heated discussions and arguments. Carl began to realize that members of his family actually enjoyed arguing and criticizing one another. There seemed to be no boundaries. Everyone's life was up for discussion, review and subject to group opinion as to how to improve it and live it better. If a relative made a comment that was insulting or hurtful, well – so? What was the big thing? Their response was always: "We're family. We are only making suggestions to help you live your life better."

He wasn't sure what to make of all this as a teen-ager. However, Carl often left a family gathering feeling criticized and disapproved of, with his feelings hurt. As an adult he started to understand that this was his family's dysfunctional way of relating to each other. They didn't understand or care that most people had personal boundaries to be respected. Instead, they'd lived their lives communicating in this opinionated, argumentative manner, so it seemed normal to them. But it wasn't normal to Carl because he was tired of being criticized, arguing and defending himself. When Pluto transited his 3rd House he was ready to make a major change in his life, deciding it would be better for him if he moved away from his family.

When family members heard he was moving across the country, they all agreed it was a big mistake Carl would regret. After all, why would anyone move away from their family? They criticized him for his bad judgment and let him know they were upset he was moving. No one wished him good luck. In fact, a few of them tried to make him feel guilty about moving so far away from his mother with remarks such as, "Think about how much she'll miss you. It will be very upsetting for her, if you're so far away." Their critical reactions made Carl even surer that moving to a new environment would be a very positive psychological change in his life.

Transformation Can Happen in Your Neighborhood

Another area where you may experience profound change is in local travel and short-distance trips in your immediate environment. You may have experiences in your own neighborhood that transform your life.

The worst thing about Danielle's old job was the long drive in heavy rush-hour traffic every day, so she was excited about her new one for many reasons. One of the best things about it was she no longer needed her car to get to her job; instead, she took a commuter train from her home to work each day. However, that was only one of the major changes that took place in her life as Pluto transited her 3rd House. Over the many months she commuted, she enjoyed lots of stimulating conversations, meeting many interesting people and making several really great friends. Then, one day she met a stockbroker who so impressed her that she let him manage her 401-k. Within one year he had increased the value of her account by more than 30 percent.

But the biggest surprise was a romantic one. For weeks on her daily commute, Danielle saw a very cute guy hop on the morning train, carrying a cup of coffee, newspaper and his laptop. First they smiled at each. Eventually they said "good morning." Then, one day they spoke to each other. The next day they went out on a date. The week after, they went out almost every night. That was six months ago. Today he's the love of her life. A change in transportation brought transformation to her life in ways she'd never imagined.

Intense Relationships with Relatives

When Pluto transits this House, your relationship with siblings, relatives and neighbors are more important to your life. You feel a more powerful and even intense connection with them. This is a positive time when you can enjoy a deeper and more satisfying emotional relationship with them as long as you avoid any attempt to control or dominate them, which would only result in a power struggle or confrontation.

Clark never knew his cousin Jeremy well. They had seen each other at family functions for years but never beyond that. At their grandparent's

40th Anniversary party, they found themselves really enjoying their conversation, the books and movies they shared in common. Soon after, they agreed to meet for dinner. Within the year they were more than distant cousins. They'd become close friends and talked about starting a business together.

Great Time to Engage in Powerful Communication & Learning

Pluto's influence in the 3rd House gives you a penetrating mind which makes it a fortunate time for those engaged in research, investigation, teaching, psychology and counseling. This is also a very beneficial time for writers, lecturers and public speakers since this transit gives them the capacity for intense, profound and powerful communication through both the spoken and written word.

You're likely to be very interested in your own personal psychology as well as others. As you find yourself thinking more deeply about the way you function in your immediate environment, this becomes an ideal time to explore psychotherapy or other personal growth activities that help you know yourself better. You'll find yourself having a more serious perspective on your life. By purging yourself of old beliefs and attitudes that no longer seem relevant or helpful to accomplishing your goals, you're able to make your life work more effectively. Because you're geared toward self-improvement, take advantage of any urge to enroll in an educational class, or some sort of advanced training; or even to go back to school.

Pluto's long transit here is an opportunity for you to transform your intellect, ideas, beliefs, attitudes, and opinions. It's the perfect time to improve your communications skills so that you're able to resolve problems and conflicts that have psychologically troubled you for years. You have the capacity to understand your world from a deeper perspective through your experiences and contacts in your immediate environment.

Considerations, Actions, Decisions During Pluto in 3rd House

1. Do you want to become a more powerful speaker?
2. Study psychology, personal growth or any area of transformation.

3. Join a writing group and write a mystery, screenplay or even a book with characters who have hidden secrets.
4. Do healing work or therapy to uncover deeply buried issues in your psyche.
5. Step into your power and take on a leadership position in your job or in an organization in which you're a member.
6. Do investigative research in any topic that interests you deeply.
7. Set new goals and commit to achieving them.
8. Are there any changes you want to make so that your life will work better?
9. Confront and resolve any power struggles you've had with others.
10. Socialize with your siblings to see if you'd enjoy an even deeper connection with them.

3rd House: Communications

Transits to Use for Successful 3rd House Decisions

You now understand the areas of life that are featured in your 3rd House. We've discussed how each of the five transiting planets exerts its unique influence on the affairs of this House. This will help you better understand the changes you are experiencing, moods you're feeling, and the events taking place. Your awareness of this information may prompt you to:

1. *ACCEPT* the way things are and be content with what is going on in your life.

2. *CONSIDER* that you'd like to make some change, in which case you may evaluate your options and further contemplate your situation.

3. *DECIDE* that you're ready to make a change, take action, and make a decision pertaining to the affairs of this House.

If you make a decision, you'll want to learn how to pick the best transit to produce a successful outcome for it. Please know that the art of picking and interpreting transits requires very thorough analysis, normally done by a professional astrologer. Therefore, I've kept the discussion of selecting and using transits simple, for illustration purposes.

The key is to remember that each planet has the ability to bring a *different* positive quality of success to your decision. For example, *Jupiter's* effect may provide opportunities to expand and grow; *Saturn's* effect is more practical; *Uranus'* effect is sudden and exciting; *Neptune's* influence may bring you inspiration and idealism; *Pluto* may bring an intense and transformative effect for major change. This knowledge will help you understand how your decisions are affected by these planetary influences.

In the examples below, I chose a planetary transit to produce a favorable result for each individual's particular decision. This will help you see the many possibilities available to create the right outcome and make your 3rd House decisions more successful.

Using a positive JUPITER Transit

DECISION: *I want to find someone to help me communicate confidently.*

Explanation: We discussed earlier in the chapter how Wayne has always been a shy, timid and non-assertive person. He wants to confidently communicate honestly and directly with others at work. He joined a speaker's organization during an excellent Jupiter transit. The energies of Jupiter will be ideal for his self-improvement, confidence and ability to learn during this period of his life. Jupiter's energies further assure that he will have the assistance of helpful and supportive people who can teach him how to speak confidently in front of others.

* * *

Using a positive SATURN Transit

DECISION: *I need to create a new labor agreement.*

Explanation: We discussed Martin's need to prepare a new labor contract for his negotiation between the union and management of a company. We used a Saturn aspect, which favors work that requires mental discipline and hard work. This transit favors planning, organization, and is helpful to putting ideas into practice for long-term planning. The energies of Saturn under this transit gave him the unusual ability to see all the intricate details and issues pertaining to the agreement while crafting an agreement with integrity and fairness to all.

* * *

3rd House: Communications

Using a positive URANUS Transit

DECISION: *I want to buy a car that will bring me excitement and express my new identity.*

Explanation: Matt has always been conservative. He's ready to change his life on many levels. One of the ways he wants to bring excitement into his life is by buying a car that will make a statement about himself as a unique individual. He hopes his car will bring him new experiences meeting people he might not otherwise meet.

Matt began doing research on some of the sporty, unique, exciting cars on the market. He decided to buy a car during his Uranus transit, which would be excellent for making a big change from his former conservative tastes.

* * *

Using a positive NEPTUNE Transit

DECISION: *I want to heal my relationships with my brother.*

Explanation: Myron and Phil always had an up and down relationship as brothers. As they got older they seemed competitive with each other and one day they got into a big fight that seem to dredge up all the upsets from their past. They decided not to speak to each other. That was 10 years ago. Myron decided that it was time to approach his brother and see if they could repair their relationship and forgive each other for their differences.

This Neptune transit brought love, compassion and forgiveness to Myron's personality. It was a time where he could ask for forgiveness in his attempt to re-establish a relationship and offer forgiveness to his brother. Neptune energies allowed him to detach himself from his own ego and focus on being sensitive and compassionate to the pain his brother must have felt from their estrangement. It was the perfect transit to use for a successful reconciliation with his older brother.

* * *

Using a positive PLUTO Transit

DECISION: *I want to write a deeply moving screenplay about divorce.*

Explanation: Sylvia was a trained psychologist and marriage counselor. She was deeply motivated to write a screenplay based on her many years of counseling couples who had gone though divorce. She wanted to take several months out of her counseling practice to do this.

A Pluto transit gave her the ability to do very profound, transformational writing. The influence of Pluto would give her the ability to write about the psychological motivations of her characters with great depth and intensity. She could use her creativity and writing talents to reveal the hidden aspects of her characters, making her overall story compelling in a way that would capture her audience's interest.

* * *

REMEMBER: You can use the FREE Transit Calculator that's discussed in Part IV of this book to go back in time to see which transits were occurring when a major event happened in your life. It might be a wonderful learning experience, especially since most transits repeat themselves over your lifetime. Also you can find out where your transits are today or in the future.

4th House
Family & Home

How often have you heard a person explain their life with the familiar phrase, "That's just the way I was raised." You may have fabulous parents who prepared you for life, building up your confidence and supporting you in every way. Or, perhaps, your parents were too busy making a living to spend adequate time with you. As a result, you grew up in a hurry, forced to accept responsibility at a much younger age. Whether because of divorce or some other reason, many of you were raised by a single parent. Regardless of what kind of parents or family you were born into, your formative years growing up shaped you into the person you are today.

The 4th House is extremely important because that's where it all began for you. This House rules your home, family, heritage, your domestic affairs and early environment. It gives you a clear understanding of the domestic conditions you were raised in. You can tell a great deal about person's emotional makeup by seeing the type of home they create for themselves.

Interestingly, this is the area of your birth chart that describes the type of home environment that will make you emotionally comfortable. You've noticed some people love the idea of living in an old rustic, traditional home, while others find psychic comfort living in a modern or even minimally furnished place. This House gives insight into a person's domestic preferences, such as whether or not it's important for them to live in a clean, well-organized home. It will tell you if they're more likely to be OCD (i.e., obsessive-compulsive disorder) in their housekeeping or be comfortable living like a slob. Sometimes, the condition of a person's home is based on their emotional reaction to the way their home was kept when they were growing up. For example, I had one friend who grew up in a messy, disheveled home, always reminding me how emotionally uncomfortable he was with the way his mother kept their home. As an adult he vowed never to live that way, so his home was always spotlessly clean, organized with everything in its place. Another friend grew up in an unruly, disorganized home and that's just the way his home was as an adult. That domestic environment made him emotionally comfortable.

This House can indicate whether or not your home life was easy and relaxed. Did you grow up with parents whose requests were understanding and lenient, such as, "If you're going to be a little late, please call us" or with more demanding, strict parents who may have warned, "If you're home after 10 p.m. you'll be grounded!" Interestingly, this House represents the parent that most nurtured and influenced you, and who was at home the most as you grew up (usually the mother). Finally, this House gives insight and understanding as to how well you got along with your parents and family. It shows the likelihood that you were closer with your mother than your father or vice versa.

The 4th House represents your personal experience growing up as a child, how safe and secure you felt; and the very roots of your emotional being. This House is profoundly important because it's your foundation in life and concerns your connections to the past, the end of life and endings in general.

This is where to look to see whether you'll be homeowner or a land baron because this House rules land, residences, property and real estate. For most people a home is extremely important and serves as the foundation for their internal security. For others, it's a burden and they prefer not to own a home so they can be free to live, unencumbered in a rental, or in many homes in the course of their life.

Your Body in the 4th House

This House rules the breasts, stomach, digestive system, uterus and womb. Since there is nothing more important than your health, pay special attention to these areas of your body whenever a planet transits this House. It may indicate a period of time when you'll experience health benefits, issues or even problems you should be aware of. If you observe anything unusual, you'll have the opportunity to consult with a medical doctor or a health care practitioner.

Your 4th House Decisions

You now understand that the 4th House of your birth chart concerns your emotional foundation of safety and security; your home, family, domestic affairs; and real estate you own.

4th House : Family & Home

As you read about the description of this house, it's time to ask yourself a few questions. How did your home life affect you? What kind of relationship did you have with your parents? Was there only one parent to help and guide you? Was the other parent never around and too busy to take time out for you? Did you grow up in a happy family? How will you create your family to be different from the one you grew up in? Are there any issues related to your upbringing that have helped or hurt your ability to have close relationships, or even your own family?

Do you want your own family? If you have family, is it a satisfying experience for you? Are you happy with the relationship you have with your parents? How could it be improved? What kind of home do you want? Do you feel emotionally secure where you live, and the way that you live? Would you like to move and change residences? Would a sunnier climate elevate your mood instead of living where you do now? What are your attitudes towards real estate? Some people grow up loving the idea owning and renting property for income; others don't want the responsibility of being a landlord. What's the biggest change you'd like to make to the area of family, home, and real estate?

These are all significant questions and your answers may lead you to make important decisions to change your life. Here are a few examples of decisions clients have made based on the activities and issues of the 4th House.

Situation: Lee has been saving his money for the past two years, all-the-while looking for a home to buy.

DECISION: *I want to buy a home that will give me joy, satisfaction and security.*

* * *

Situation: Roxanne realizes that having a family is a big responsibility. She wants to be ready emotionally and financially before she takes this important step.

DECISION: *I want to find the best time to start a family, have my first child and be a great mother.*

* * *

Situation: Growing up Mickey never got along with his parents. Eventually, he moved far away and hasn't seen them in years. He feels great sadness about not having any relationship with them.

DECISION: *I want to find the best time to visit my parents where I can establish an emotional connection with them; and heal our relationship.*

* * *

Situation: Frederica wants to take advantage of the low interest rates and favorable real estate market to buy some income property.

DECISION: *I want to find the best time to make a prudent investment in income property.*

* * *

During the transits of *Jupiter, Saturn, Uranus, Neptune,* and *Pluto* – Lee, Roxanne, Mickey, and Frederica will have many opportunities to implement their decisions at a favorable time to produce the outcome they want.

The Transiting Planets Reveal Your Past, Present & Future

Your main focus is using astrology to understand *what the hell is going on in your life*. Once you do – this book will show you the best time to make a decision to change it, should you have a desire to do so. As you read about the five planets transiting the 4th House, notice the way each planet exerts its unique influence and effect, bringing specific opportunities, issues, problems, and events into this area of your life. But if you're curious as to how these planets are personally affecting YOU *today*, in your *past*, or in your *future*, you can find out where each transiting planet is in your birth chart by using the *FREE Transit Calculator* (see Part IV).

JUPITER In Your 4th House of Family & Home

Home Sweet Home or A Great Time to Move

When you think of Jupiter transiting through this House, think of the sign that says, "Home Sweet Home." No matter how tough life can be in the outside world, Jupiter's transit here brings a sense of optimism, joy and faith to matters of the 4th House. Under Jupiter's influence you seek inner peace, joy and security and you'll find your home to be a very comforting place for you. Jupiter's transit through this House is a fortunate time when you feel very secure and appreciative of your family and personal life because your family provides emotional support that's very soothing. This is the perfect transit to host family events whether it's a barbeque in the backyard or a large sit down meal for everyone at Thanksgiving.

It's also an ideal time to move to a new residence or even a new city and put down "new roots," because Jupiter's influence brings your new home good fortune and blessings. Your home nurtures you, giving you a feeling of belonging as well as a sense you're part of a family and even a community. This transit brings inner security and emotional comfort into your domestic life.

Martin just completed his sentence in a federal penitentiary for a drug crime. It was a horrible experience, but he tried to make the most of it, taking on-line courses to become a car mechanic. He still had many friends in his hometown involved in the drug trade, so it was clear that if he wanted to stay out of prison he needed to get away from them and the environment where he grew up dealing drugs. The prison counselor was extremely helpful, plugging him into job networks that connected him to work opportunities. Above all, it was agreed he should find a totally different environment to live where he wouldn't run into anyone from his past. Jupiter transiting his 4th House was the perfect time to move to a new city where he would receive the necessary emotional support to begin his new life.

Great Time to Find a New Home

Jupiter's transit her brings an influence that favors your domestic life where you have the warm feeling of being in homey surroundings that are perfectly suited to your needs and comfort. You're happy where you live. This is also a favorable time for any home improvement projects such as decorating, a simple re-modeling job, or an extensive renovation.

In fact, this is an auspicious time to purchase a home, land, or other real estate, since your home and property symbolize your desire to bring emotional stability into your life. It's a lucky time period in which to make real estate investments that can provide long-term security for your future. One of my clients used a positive transit to this House to buy new properties. He would save for years and then, during a Jupiter, Uranus, or Pluto transit, buy some type of property that he could fix up and then rent for income. Over 30 years, he accumulated 10 very successful properties.

Coleen and Weldon both grew up in rural areas of the Midwest. After college, they each moved to the city where they eventually met and married. During their married years they enjoyed the fun, excitement and cultural activities that city life offered, but after 20 years, they were ready for a major change in their lifestyle. In fact, they decided they wanted to move to a small farm in a rural county where they could enjoy the simpler living and more self-sufficient lifestyle. They used the year that Jupiter transited Weldon's 4th House to search for and buy a charming, picturesque farm they could live in for years to come.

Great Time to Heal Family Problems

You'll find that under Jupiter's positive influence family members are likely to be of great help and benefit if you need assistance. Your relationship with your parents is very harmonious. The warmth of Jupiter's energies makes this an excellent time to socialize and enjoy the comfort of family. This is a time when families come together and help each other out of genuine love and kindness. For this reason, Jupiter's transit is an ideal time to resolve any family problems or disagreements. As you enjoy the pleasures and healthy feelings of satisfying family connections, you're no longer likely to endure unhealthy or dysfunctional relationships that may have existed in the past. The 4th House represents a time of endings, so if you have unsuccessfully tried to heal past family wounds, you'll accept that you have done all you can and let them go. Or, you may use the healing influence of this Jupiter transit to try one more time to resolve differences – as Monica did.

Monica had never been close with her mother, enjoying a much more loving relationship with her father. He'd spoiled her, always so affectionate, constantly doting over her. As an adult, Monica came to realize that during her childhood and adolescent years, her mother had competed with her for her father's attention. The truth was that her mother felt threatened and insecure about the relationship she'd had with her father. Monica hadn't thought about this for a long time. But, after talking to a friend about her relationship with each of her parents, she realized this was the very reason why she and her mother were never close.

One day, her father called with distressing news that her mother was very sick, insisting that Monica fly home to see her. Monica had tears in her eyes as her memories took her back to her childhood and the many times she wished she could have been closer to her mom. When she finally went to her mother's bedside, they both felt a wellspring of love and compassion for each other. There was so much that Monica wanted to tell her mother in the hopes they would have time to heal their relationship.

Considerations, Actions, Decisions During Jupiter in 4th House

1. Move to a comfortable new residence that is even larger than you imagined.
2. Buy a home that you'll feel pampered in.
3. Move to a new city, state or country.
4. Start your own family.
5. Resolve family problems or disagreements.
6. Buy real estate for an investment.
7. Sell real estate.
8. Get financial help or other assistance from your parents.
9. Avoid any over-optimistic expansion.

SATURN In Your 4th House of Family & Home

Brings Responsibilities

As Saturn transits your 4th House, you'll be concerned with re-defining and re-structuring your home, family, domestic and emotional needs, so that they provide you with more security. That may mean that it's more economical to re-model your kitchen instead of spending a lot of money on a new house. It could result in your converting the basement into another bedroom for the birth of a new family member. Under this transit, you may find yourself moving back into your parent's home or having them move into yours. You may also re-define your relationship with your mother. For example, one client set some boundaries with her mother since her mother was overly critical, constantly giving her opinions on how to raise her children.

During these two and a half years, you'll build a foundation for your life that makes you feel more emotionally secure and safe. You may realize that it's time to become more economical and finally get serious about saving money for a rainy day. However, this is when you can expect to feel some sense of restriction that prevents you from achieving goals and receiving material rewards in the outer world. For example, there may not be enough money improve your home in the way that you want. Or, you may find that the money you had planned to use for other investments has to be used to pay for costly home improvements, repairs, remodeling or unexpected maintenance you hadn't planned

It's a time when you may feel isolated and alone even if you have family members around you. You may find yourself feeling rather introverted, looking for ways to nurture yourself and those around you. However, it's an excellent time to plan, organize and save money in order to feel more emotionally secure. It's a wonderful time to make plans to build your material foundation, such as buying your own home in the future; or making plans to buy investment property that can provide you with future income.

Brings Responsibilities and Obstacles

You'll find that you're engaged in a process of learning about responsibilities associated with your home and living situation. The maintenance to run a home may be way beyond what you had expected. Unless you must do so out of some necessity, typically, this is not a good time to move into a new residence or buy a home because there's likely to be a special burden, responsibility, or duty associated with your doing so. You may realize that the costs of moving are way beyond your budget or that a favorable mortgage is impossible to obtain. If you're moving to a rental apartment, you may even find that you'll have to spend more money decorating it than you had originally anticipated.

But if you feel it gives you a greater sense of security upon which to build a foundation for the future, you may consider moving to a new residence or buying a new home. However, when buying a home under this Saturn transit make sure you have sufficient funds for your purchase and any unexpected improvements that may be required.

If you do find it necessary to make a change in your domestic situation, the key is to be prepared for some challenges. Be mindful of the fact that Saturn's energies are restrictive (unlike Jupiter's which are expansive). They block your ability to achieve prosperity and create abundance. Saturn's influence can bring burdensome responsibilities related to your home where you may encounter difficulties and problems related to your residence or living conditions.

Marie was a first time homebuyer and sure that she could qualify for a mortgage to buy a one-bedroom condo. However, during the time that Saturn transited her 4th House, it seemed like every bank she approached, placed unreasonable demands and restrictions on her in order to qualify. Eventually, one bank said they would only give mortgage approval if her parents were willing to co-sign on her loan. That's what she ended up having to do to buy her new home. By the way, Marie's experience is a typical example of the kind of restriction you may encounter when Saturn transits your 4th House.

Because of personal limitations in your domestic life you may find yourself dissatisfied by your living arrangement with a family member or a spouse. Perhaps, you've been feeling this way for years, but haven't confronted or resolved the underlying problem. As a result you may find yourself reevaluating where you want to live or even consider changing your domestic environment.

Saturn's influence can bring additional responsibility into your life, because your mother, parents or family place additional demands on you. In some cases, this is a time when you may find yourself taking on parental responsibility for someone else's child or find someone acting as a parent to you. During this transit a client of mine, and her husband made the decision to adopt a child, since they couldn't have any children of their own.

Saturn's influence is one of accepting responsibility, so you may gladly take on additional responsibilities for your parents or other family members. One of my clients decided to have his elderly mother live in his home. She was a spry and independent woman who asked her son if she could live with him instead of at a seniors' assisted living facility. He knew it would be an adjustment, but was happy to accept the responsibility to have his mother live in his home.

A Time to Address Emotional Wounds

Saturn's transit to your 4th House is a perfect opportunity to re-evaluate your family and domestic life, and if necessary, consciously *let go* of any relationships that aren't positive and productive. You'll seek to improve any upsetting family interactions you've lived with for a long time. For example, if you've accepted a dysfunctional relationship with family members you'll confront them at this time. If there have been disagreements or problems with family members, you'll now seek to resolve them. If family members limit or restrict your efforts toward resolution you'll find yourself locked in a confrontation with them.

This two and a half year period is an opportunity for you to clean up any unfinished business in your family or domestic life that has been unresolved. Saturn's influence encourages you to bring any problematic situations to a completion so that you can begin to build a new, even better foundation in this area of your life. You may decide to sort out an upset with a family member by meeting for a cup of coffee to finally air your differences; or call a family gathering to bring closure to any upsetting matters. By doing this you'll begin the next phase of your life with stronger family relationships and a more solid domestic environment.

Since this House concerns your early childhood conditioning, this is when you may dig into the emotional roots of your being where you'll focus on memories of your early childhood and growing up with one or both parents. On an emotional level you may become profoundly aware of the ways your parents and family life have affected your personality and psyche. You'll remember what you learned from them as a child and how it has shaped and influenced your behavior and relationships with others. This transit caused one client to recall the pain she felt as a child from the years her family called her "fat." Another client remembered the way his father made fun of his lack of athleticism. This is an important opportunity to become aware of any deep hurt your parents caused you so you can heal yourself.

If you had a childhood or family life that left you with bad feelings, even deep emotional wounds, and behavioral problems that have been an outgrowth of that period in your life, this will be when you can responsibly confront these issues and resolve them. If you wish, you can now effectively heal your deepest hurts through some form of psychotherapy or counseling. As an adult, you can no longer blame your parents for the pain you feel they caused you. Saturn's transit here is a call for you to take responsibility for the emotional upsets you experienced growing up in you family and their impact on your life.

Helena was the youngest child and only daughter of five children. Her four older brothers and parents never seemed to want to acknowledge that she'd grown up. They saw her as this short, petite "cupie doll" sister even though she was 26 years old and a recent graduate of the FBI Training Academy in Quantico, Virginia, soon to be in the field on dangerous assignments. Helena was embarrassed by the way they treated her like a teen-ager at family events. It was disrespectful and hurt her feelings deeply. At the next gathering, she decided to let them know she'd no longer tolerate their behavior. If it didn't change, she wouldn't fly in for family events.

A Time to Explore Your Past Memories

You may find yourself recalling past memories as you grew up. Even normally, unconscious behavior that was a part of your personality is now awakened. You're able to make insightful, deeply personal and psychological discoveries at this time which is why this is a wonderful opportunity to explore your own psychological journey with a loved one, a friend or a counselor.

Let me share a personal story from my own life. When Saturn transited through my 4th House, I remember listening to a PBS show that featured the psychologist, John Bradshaw who hosted a television series on the "The Dysfunctional Family." Bradshaw discussed the ways that "family systems" and parental behavior affect our personality development as adults. During that two and a half year period of Saturn's transit, I learned a lot about my family system – the good, bad and the ugly. I was able to make some profound discoveries about how my childhood and family experience influenced my attitudes and close personal relationships. It was a very healing time for me, finally understanding so much about the origins of my behavior and how they had affected me as an adult.

This House represents the emotional foundation for your life, not just the physical home you live in. This is an ideal time to tap deep into your inner self, so that, maybe for the first time, you NOW understand – how "a man like you, got to be a man like you." Or, how "a woman like you, got to be a woman like you." This is a profound transformational period in your life that allows you to drill into the core of your emotional being as you've never done before. You have the ability to heal psychic wounds that will produce tangible, lasting effects as you build a more secure foundation in your world and move forward to achieve your ambitions in life.

Considerations, Actions, Decisions During Saturn in 4th House

1. Evaluate whether this is a good time to move to a new residence.
2. Save your money and make plans for the best time to buy a home.
3. Decorate, repair or remodel your home.
4. Evaluate whether this is a good time to move to a new city or state.
5. Evaluate if you are ready for the responsibilities and expenses of starting your own family.
6. Resolve family problems or disagreements.
7. Carefully evaluate if this is the time to buy or sell real estate.
8. Evaluate if this is a realistic time to get help from parents or others.

URANUS in Your 4th House of Family & Home

Brings Surprising & Shocking Change

During the time Uranus transits your 4th House, sudden, even shocking change will occur in the most personal aspects of your life, especially in your home, domestic life, as well as your relationships with your parents and other family members. For example, someone in your family who seems happily married suddenly files for divorce or a family member becomes pregnant, while another dies.

You may also experience a radical change in your living arrangement or a complete change in your residence, causing you to move unexpectedly. For instance, you may receive an amazing promotion but it requires you to move to a new city; or you suddenly fall in love and move in with the other person; or you receive an eviction notice for violating your lease. Uranus brings needed change and reform into your life, which often results in disruptions and upsets. However, these experiences will ultimately give you a sense of freedom and liberation from your past.

This House rules the emotional foundation of your being. For that reason, you may look at your family, home and domestic life as the part of you that makes you feel secure and anchors you, because you trust it will never change. So, when change does occur in this area of your life it can be quite disturbing. The influence of Uranus demands that you become adaptable as well as flexible when you encounter change in your personal and home life. Uranus challenges the structures in your personal world that may seem secure, and in the process brings you a sense of freedom and new experiences in those areas where you allow change and liberation.

The influence of Uranus is known for disturbing the deepest and most personal elements of your life causing them to become unreliable and subject to sudden change. During Uranus' transit in this House, changes may occur in your family, threatening its normal security as Arthur found out.

Arthur hung up the telephone but couldn't believe the news that his father had just died of a heart attack. There was so much he had wanted to say to him before he passed away. But before he could even properly grieve, his mother brought him back to reality when she asked, "Arthur, who'll take over your father's business?" She was right to be concerned because there was no one left but Arthur, to take over the family business, which employed more than 100 people in their town. Arthur knew the business well, having worked there part-time during his high school years and full-time during his summers off from college. It was intended for Arthur to inherit the business one day, but father and son agreed that Arthur should first work elsewhere for a few years to get a different perspective. Arthur was shocked to inherit the family business so soon and in such a sad tragic way. He had looked forward to working along side his father before ever taking the business over.

Independent & Free At Last

You're not concerned with security and stability at this time, because you're so excited about changing the core of your inner being. The 4th House rules *"endings,"* with Uranus' influence bringing change and reform to the areas of your life that have been rigid and fixed. Since this House concerns your domestic life, home, family and parents (especially your mother), you may experience tension and problems in these areas. Uranus transiting here is a period in your life when you want to break free from you parents and your family environment. You're not concerned with emotional security. This is a time when you'll feel like you can live in the moment, assert your independence and take control over your life. You're in the process of becoming your own person and ready to learn, experiment and find your own way.

Tricia was the youngest of five in her family. Her brothers and sisters had moved out of their parent's house years ago. But at 21, her parents continued to pressure her to live with them, constantly reminding her how unsafe it was for a pretty single woman to be out on her own. They were forever trying to scare her by showing her news stories of young women who had been robbed, raped or killed out in the world. It seemed like at every turn they took the opportunity to undermine her confidence and point out how unprepared she was to live on her own.

When Uranus transited this House Tricia suddenly felt rebellious, independent and ready to break-free of her parents. She was surprised that she felt no fear about leaving, only a sense of freedom, liberation and limitless potential. Tricia was determined to take control of her life, so she enlisted a friend's help to look for an apartment in the city. After looking only a short time, Tricia fell in love with a small, cute studio rental. The next day, once her credit check was complete, she signed a one-year lease. She was as free as a bird. The only people more surprised than her would be her parents.

Unexpected Change in Your Home

Expect that problems you've chosen to ignore will now surface. They may be based on your relationships with people in your personal life, family members or parents. Or, you may experience problems with your home such as the need for unexpected repairs. It's also possible that if your home or living arrangement has been a source of tension or dissatisfaction, you'll change it during this transit. In all likelihood, if you do change your residence or domestic situation, you'll find the changes you make will eventually bring you a freedom that will benefit you.

Here's another experience that occurred in my life when Uranus transited my 4th House. It brought me an unexpected opportunity I would never have imagined. I was renting in San Francisco and decided I was ready to buy a new home. Home prices were high and I wasn't finding a home I liked for a price that fit my budget. After a frustrating day of looking at many properties and seeing none that I liked, I decided to stop for lunch at a restaurant on Fillmore Street. Sitting at another table nearby was an old friend, Ray. He and his friend were having lunch. When he saw me, Ray invited me to join them.

I accepted, sat down and met his friend Ernie. Our pleasant conversation began with Ray asking me what was happening in my life. I explained that I had spent the last month unsuccessfully looking for a home to buy. I said, "So far – no luck." His friend Ernie, sporting a big smile, said, "Well, your luck is about to change. I'm a developer, and I've just completed a project of nine condos on Sutter and Pierce Streets. They're new, beautifully done and reasonably priced. Go take a look." I did, and I was so impressed, I bought one of his homes and lived there for almost 10 years. I am still friends with both of them, and Ernie is still a successful developer.

That story is a perfect illustration of the kind of unexpected and surprising event that can change your home and domestic life when Uranus transits this House.

Considerations, Actions, Decisions During Uranus in 4th House

1. Would a change in your residence or domestic situation bring you more freedom?
2. Is there any remodeling work in your home that would make it a more exciting place to live?
3. Look for an exciting opportunity to buy or sell real estate.
4. Plan a unique and unusual family gathering such as a luau.
5. Do you feel restricted by your family?
6. What changes would make your family life more exciting and interesting?
7. Do you want to be free of any emotional upsets your family has caused you?
8. Are you excited about having a family?

NEPTUNE in Your 4th House of Family & Home

Creating the Ideal Home

Neptune represents the "ideal" and when it transits the 4th House of your home, you may find yourself wanting to improve your home so that it will fit your image of perfection – a place of beauty. I had a client who hired a feng shui consultant to decorate and create a vibrant feeling of joy and harmony in her home, making sure to arrange furniture in a way that would provide the best energy to support the specific activity intended for each room.

During this transit you may even want to move to a home that's more suited for your needs. I had one client who bought a modest home early in his marriage, became wealthy and when Neptune transited this House he hired an architect to design his fantasy home with water falls, beautiful garden landscaping, including a koi pond. Of course, make sure that your need to achieve the ideal of a perfect home is both realistic and achievable so that when this Neptune transit is over you don't have regrets.

A Time to Explore the Roots of your Past Behavior

Since Neptune rules the spiritual and the mystical, you may find yourself interested in exploring your inner spirituality. Now you're ready to psychologically explore the roots of your past behavior by delving into your subconscious to discover the essence of who you are. You'll find yourself becoming exceptionally aware of your feelings and your emotional nature. This may be when many of your repressed childhood memories come to your conscious mind which is why this is an excellent time for introspection, exploring a personal growth workshop or psychological counseling to know yourself better.

Kent was adopted at the age of 10 from a foreign adoption service. He seemed shy and introverted, so his new parents merely accepted that cultural differences might account for his timid behavior. However, by the age of 12, Kent's behavior was noticeably inconsistent and strange. His parents began to worry about what they should do to bring their child out of his shell.

When Kent's mother, Caryn, asked me to review his birth chart, it seemed clear that he had experienced some type of childhood emotional trauma. Kent had Neptune transiting his 4th, which made it a propitious time for him to enter professional counseling. His therapy revealed that as a very young child, he was severely beaten by his birth father and Kent remained deathly afraid of being abused again. The therapist explained that Kent had talked openly about his traumatic experience and released some of his repressed emotions about it. Now, it would be much easier for Caryn and her husband to make him feel safe and earn his trust through patient love and nurturing.

Be Aware of Strange Problems in Your Home & Family

Sometimes Neptune's influence can result in strange problems occurring in your home such as a gas or water leak that presents itself out of nowhere. I had a friend who moved into a new home and started having respiratory and asthma-like symptoms during the time Neptune was transiting her 4th House. It turned out her home had horrible allergenic mold and mildew problems, which could only be resolved by a remediation service and ozone treatments.

Neptune's influence can also reveal some neurosis or secret behavior that has been in hidden within your family or domestic life. For example I know a mother who found out that her daughter was anorexic during her Neptune transit. Neptunian related problems can also manifest with family members acting oddly or even suffering from problems of addiction to alcohol or drugs. It's a good time to be extra sensitive to your family and domestic surroundings in the event that you can help a family member in need or crisis.

As she experienced this transit, a client began to question whether a parent's prodding was based on his being helpful, or controlling and manipulating. Whether or not your perceptions are accurate or not at this time, your reality is that you're feeling these emotions. This is symptomatic of a profound change that's taking place within your psyche, which is being reflected in your interactions with your family and parents. Under Neptune's influences you're picking up something on your "psychic" radar. You are trying to sort out what is real versus imagined.

4th House : Family & Home

One effect of this transit is that your feelings of internal security are being disturbed. You may feel a sense of anxiety, fear or doubt that makes you uneasy. This may come from difficulties you're having with your family or even with one of your parents. Another outcome of this transit is that you may be called to care for an aging parent or a family member who is in ill health. In fact, you may encounter strange or peculiar problems with a parent, especially your mother (or primary caretaker) as Beth discovered.

Beth had a close relationship with her mother over the years. They lived a few miles apart and saw each other regularly. One day her mother made a strange request, asking Beth to drive her to the nearby church for Sunday mass. This was surprising since her mother stopped going to church 34 years ago. The last time her mother had been inside of a church was to attend Beth's wedding. However, Beth was happy to oblige and dropped her off. Soon her mother was not only going to Sunday mass but also the daily service throughout the week. She became a devout follower, never without her prayer book. The Bible was now beside her bed, often in her hands when she fell asleep. One day, Beth asked her, "Mother what's going on in your life? Lately, it seems like you've become the 'church lady.'"

Her mother proceeded to tell her the strangest story she could have imagined. She said, "Beth, before I married your father, I regularly attended Sunday mass. Over the years, I fell in love with a priest. I tried to get him to reconsider his vows and marry me but he wouldn't. He told me he was already married to the church. I was so distraught and broken-hearted that I could never bring myself to see him again. In fact, whenever I thought about going to church it brought back painful memories that emotionally upset me. I never went back to that church or attended any church services, until your wedding. Two months ago, the priest I fell in love with died. It made me realize how sad it was that I gave up my faith because of my own pride. I did some soul-searching. I realized it was time for me to heal myself and renew my faith. And, I have."

Neptune's passage through your 4th House is a time to explore the psychology of what makes you tick, come to grips with it and achieve an inner peace. It's also a time when you can use your creativity and imagination to create your ideal home and family life.

Considerations, Actions, Decisions During Neptune in 4th House

1. Is your intuition revealing any insights into your family relationships?
2. Are you interested in exploring your past behavior?
3. Are there any childhood experiences that are a source of upset to you?
4. Have you noticed any strange problems around your home
5. Are any of your family members acting strangely?
6. Do you want to confront any family problems?
7. Are there any family addiction problems?
8. Are you interested in decorating your home so that's more beautiful?
9. Are you interested in buying a more ideal home?

4th House : Family & Home

PLUTO in Your 4ᵗʰ House of Family & Home

A Time to Examine Your Behavior

At this time, you'll turn your attention to transforming your emotional foundation. You're engaged in examining old conditioning, perceptions and habit patterns that were learned during your childhood in order to decide if they're still appropriate. As an adult, have you ever had someone scold you by saying, "You're acting like a child." Well, maybe you were. During this period of your life, your focus will be on re-examining the behavior you learned as your grew up. Out of early habit patterns, you may have adopted much of what you've learned. Now, you have the opportunity to more consciously eliminate habits and behaviors that require change and will better fit you as an adult.

Ray had issues around money. His mother called him frugal; his friends called him thrifty; and the women he dated called him cheap. There was something in his personality that made him watch pennies and only spend money reluctantly. He would clip coupons and take his dates to restaurants that offered "2 for 1 Dinner Specials." A pained look would cross his face when he calculated the minimum tip and paid the bill.

Ray's mother raised her son to be very careful, even fearful about spending money, and he practiced this same behavior as an adult. The previous week he'd had a rather upsetting experience when he took a woman he really liked out for dinner. When she attempted to order steak for her entree, Ray told her that the steak at this restaurant was "way over-priced." He suggested she order the hamburger, instead. So, he was shocked when she jumped out of her seat, grabbed her coat, and left the restaurant calling him a "cheapskate!" Ray was so upset he asked his close friend Simon to help him understand why situations like this happened to him. Simon replied, "Ray, you're a very successful professional guy and you make a good living. You don't have to limit yourself to only going to restaurants that offer discounts. I think you have a weird compulsion about spending money, and it's gone way past being thrifty. In fact, your need to "avoid" spending money, sounds like an obsession."

Simon continued saying, "Women you've dated are turned off by your extreme tightwad behavior. And, when you tell them to order a less expensive item on the menu, they think you're being cheap. You're sabotaging the possibility of women getting to know your many good qualities. I'm your friend, so I wanted to tell you what I see happening." Of course, Ray was shocked and hurt to hear Simon say this to him. But he couldn't deny that he didn't have many repeat dates. Maybe it was time for him to take a new look at his behavior.

Simon encouraged him to call up a few of his previous dates and talk openly about their experience of going out with him. He also recommended that Ray talk to a therapist about his behavior and get to the bottom of why he felt such an all-encompassing need to restrict how he spent his money.

A Time to Transform Yourself

The transit of Pluto brings tremendous psychological changes in your intimate personal and family relationships. This may be a period when you become aware of psychological issues or psychic wounds that originated in your childhood. You may have been told you were "stupid...or fat...or ugly." Perhaps, you were emotionally or physically abused, left alone a lot, or felt abandoned. As an adult, you're now able to see how these deep hurts have affected your adult life as well as the consequences they've produced. If you become aware of your own wound, you're ready to confront and resolve it, in order to create a permanent change within you.

This is a period of time when you may also confront obsessive, impulsive or irrational behavior that may have been a part of your childhood but is no longer appropriate as an adult. An overweight client of mine still feels compelled to eat the entire pint of ice cream after growing up with siblings who never left her a fair share. With Pluto transiting her 4th House, she's finally ready to confront her obsessive behavior, making deep changes in the foundation of her being.

Ginnie's wound began when her father abandoned her as a child, leaving town one day and never coming back. Her mother could not take the pressure and responsibility of raising her alone, so at age five, Ginnie was dropped off at her grandmother's house where she grew up. She decided at a very early age that her parents didn't love her and she couldn't depend on anyone other than herself.

Even though Ginnie was very attractive to men, she grew up avoiding intimate relationships. When she went out with a group of friends to a party or club, she had plenty of excuses to discourage men. Whenever girlfriends brought up the subject of men and relationships, she became uncomfortable and moved the discussion to other topics.

Ginnie was now working on her doctoral dissertation and was researching at the university library every day. She couldn't help noticing a tall, attractive man with blond hair who always seemed to be smiling at her whenever she looked up. Despite his obvious interest, she ignored him. Finally, one day she confronted him. "I've seen you here at the library for weeks. You always seem to sit near me and just smile at me. Then you get up to search for books when I do. Is it my imagination or are you following me?"

His face turned red from embarrassment and he sheepishly replied, "Well, yes, I plead guilty. I have to admit that I was too shy to approach you directly. When I first saw you, I was very attracted to you and wanted to meet you but didn't know how. My name is Anthony. Would you take a break and maybe have a cup of coffee with me?" Now it was Ginnie's turn to become embarrassed, but she liked the sound of his voice, which was friendly and re-assuring. She was so disarmed by his honesty and charm that she said yes. Soon they were having coffee every day, and that led to their first dinner date and many more.

Ginnie did a lot of thinking about why she was so afraid to trust a man and allow him to get close. It didn't take much soul-searching for her to realize how she'd grown up feeling abandoned and needing to protect herself. Since she'd met Anthony, it was time to confront the demons of her childhood so she could allow herself to be close to someone and have an intimate relationship. This is how Pluto transiting her 4th House brought transformation into her life.

A Time When Your Domestic Life Changes

You may notice tremendous changes in your living situation or move to a new home. I went from years of renting to buying my first home during this transit. If you own a home, this may be a time when you'll have to make a major repair or remodel it. A friend of mine bought an old fixer-upper and totally gutted and rehabbed it during Pluto's transit in his 4th House. You may also experience a big change in your family because a member of the family goes through the upheaval of divorce or separation; or perhaps a loved one dies.

During this period of time you're likely to find that the nature of your family relationships will change, especially with your parents. If you've been dependent on them, you may decide you want to break free from them by finally getting a place of your own. If you've been independent of them for years perhaps you'll need to take care of them in their old age.

A Time to Transform Your Family Relationship

Pluto's transit through your 4th House is a time when power struggles with your family may happen. If your parents are controlling and for example, not ready to let you have the freedom you need, you may be involved in some sort of power struggle with them. (Note: if you're controlling and not willing to let your kids have enough freedom, you may also experience power struggles and conflict with them.)

However, most of the likely changes that will occur in your family and in your relations with your parents will not, necessarily be problematic or negative. I've had many clients who have developed an intense and loving bond with their children during this transit. But, what is likely is that Pluto's influence will bring profound change and even a total transformation into this area of your life as Felix discovered.

Felix enjoyed the comfort and security of living with other people his whole life. First he'd lived with his family and at college he lived with a roommate in a dormitory. Then, after college he moved in with three college buddies. One by one, his friends found relationships and spent more and more time with their girlfriends. Felix was spending a lot of time alone and at first, it depressed him because he didn't like being on his own. Eventually, he got use to it. With Pluto transiting this House he was experiencing a major change in the way he lived. Eventually, two of his roommates told him when the lease was up, they'd be moving in with their girlfriends. His other roommate was going to find a smaller apartment. So, Felix realized that it was time for him to find a place where he could live on his own and experience what it was like. This Pluto transit is not only transforming Felix's living situation but also his emotional maturity so that he can continue to grow and evolve as an adult.

At the end of Pluto's transit of your 4th House you'll have explored and resolved many of psychological issues that grew out of your childhood conditioning. You'll have eliminated behaviors and emotional responses that no longer serve you as an adult. You'll have secured your inner emotional foundation, emerging as your own person, more mature and able to stand up for yourself in a healthy way.

Considerations, Actions, Decisions During Pluto in 4th House

1. Is there anything about your family relationship you would like to transform?
2. Are there any psychic wounds that you want to heal?
3. Are you ready to leave your parent's home and go off on your own?
4. Move to a new residence that you're passionate about living in.
5. Repair or renovate your current home.
6. Buy a home you can improve or re-model.
7. Move to a new city that's a major change from the one you grew up.
8. Start your own family or expand it.
9. Resolve family problems or disagreements.

Transits to Use for Successful 4th House Decisions

You now understand the areas of life that are featured in your 4th House. We've discussed how each of the five transiting planets exerts its unique influence on the affairs of this House. This will help you better understand the changes you are experiencing, moods you're feeling, and the events taking place. Your awareness of this information may prompt you to:

1. *ACCEPT* the way things are and be content with what is going on in your life.

2. *CONSIDER* that you'd like to make some change, in which case you may evaluate your options and further contemplate your situation.

3. *DECIDE* that you're ready to make a change, take action, and make a decision pertaining to the affairs of this House.

If you make a decision, you'll want to learn how to pick the best transit to produce a successful outcome for it. Please know that the art of picking and interpreting transits requires very thorough analysis, normally done by a professional astrologer. Therefore, I've kept the discussion of selecting and using transits simple, for illustration purposes.

The key is to remember that each planet has the ability to bring a *different* positive quality of success to your decision. For example, *Jupiter's* effect may provide opportunities to expand and grow; *Saturn's* effect is more practical; *Uranus'* effect is sudden and exciting; *Neptune's* influence may bring you inspiration and idealism; *Pluto* may bring an intense and transformative effect for major change. This knowledge will help you understand how your decisions are affected by these planetary influences.

In the examples below, I chose a planetary transit to produce a favorable result for each individual's particular decision. This will help you see the many possibilities available to create the right outcome and make your 4th House decisions more successful.

4th House : Family & Home

Using a positive JUPITER Transit

DECISION: *I need additional money for a down payment in order to buy a home.*

Explanation: Linda wants to buy her first home and will need some financial assistance to be able to afford it.

As we discussed Jupiter in 4th House is an excellent time to experience good fortune in your efforts to buy a home. We chose a transit from Jupiter to a planet in her birth chart that would bring her luck in finding a home that would be affordable. Jupiter transiting her 4th House is also an ideal time to approach her parents (and family members) about a loan to assist her in qualifying for this purchase.

* * *

Using a positive SATURN Transit

DECISION: *Our goal is to eventually own our own home.*

Situation: Joe and Deb had lived in an apartment for a number of years and decided that it was time they bought their own home. They'd saved up money toward a purchase, but were worried that it would not be enough. Since Saturn was transiting his 4th House, it was not an ideal time to buy a home unless Joe was willing to bear the huge responsibilities of a mortgage and the upkeep of a home. He decided that might be too much of a strain. So, we chose a positive Saturn transit for making the commitment toward a purchase, knowing it would provide Joe and Deb the discipline to economize so they could save even more. An important part of this decision was waiting until Saturn had completed its two and a half year transit through Joe's 4th House.

* * *

Using a positive URANUS Transit

DECISION: *I want to sell my home and move abroad.*

Explanation: Roxanne had always wanted to live abroad. After her fun vacation in Paris she was even sure of it. We used a Uranus transit through her 4th House as the perfect time for her to make an exciting change in her home life. She understood she'd be experiencing many surprises along the way. This transit gave her the courage and sense of freedom to discover a new home and life in a foreign country where she could enjoy a totally new perspective.

* * *

Using a positive NEPTUNE Transit

DECISION: *I want my brother's children to live with us.*

Explanation: Samuel's brother and sister-in-law died unexpectedly in an auto accident. Since their deaths, their two young boys had been living with their elderly grandparents. Samuel knows it's too difficult for his father and mother to take care of them. Even though it will be a strain on Samuel's finances, he and his wife would like to raise his two nephews and have them live with their family. We chose a Neptune transit to Samuel's 4th House because it brought energies of compassion, sacrifice and love to his decision to parent them.

* * *

4th House : Family & Home

Using a positive PLUTO Transit

DECISION: *I want to find the best time to remodel my home.*

Explanation: Harriet hated the idea of going through a remodel of her kitchen and bathroom. She had heard so many horror stories of people who had bad experiences with contractors. Pluto transiting her 4th House was the perfect time to transform and remodel her home, creating a brand new kitchen where she would enjoy cooking; and a bathroom where she would enjoy pampering herself. Because it was a favorable transit from Pluto, she would be able to trust the expertise of the contractor as someone who had the experience and resources to do an excellent job of remodeling her home.

* * *

REMEMBER: You can use the FREE Transit Calculator that's discussed in Part IV of this book to go back in time to see which transits were occurring when a major event happened in your life. It might be a wonderful learning experience, especially since most transits repeat themselves over your lifetime. Also you can find out where your transits are today or in the future.

5th House
Love Life & Creativity

The 5th House of your birth chart rules several very important areas of your life: creation, procreation and recreation. It's known as the house of creativity, passion and pleasure, whether it is the creation of a child, a love relationship or art. This House rules love, romance, dating, fun, amusement, hobbies, inner satisfaction and self-expression, as well as children.

Whether you're a single person looking for romance or married and wondering how to make your relationship more romantic, this is an extremely meaningful House for you. Whether or not you're content with the affairs of this House will tell you a great deal about *what the hell is going on in your life*.

As you read this chapter, ask yourself what activities bring you pleasure and satisfaction. How you express yourself creatively in the world will give you clues to those questions. Is there anything unique about you that you'd like to flaunt, celebrate or be acknowledged for? What gives you a sense of pride? Is it your artistic creations or your talent in acting, music, singing, dancing, writing, painting, craftsmanship, fashion, home decorating or athleticism? Your popularity and fame may come from how well you express your creative energies. The 5th House is where you convey a sense of drama in your persona that can make you a larger than life person who is memorable and attractive to others. This area shows your penchant for leadership as well as your ability to inspire confidence and respect from others.

This House expresses a great deal about your social and romantic life, even your popularity, revealing your passion and what stirs it. This area of your birth chart speaks volumes about who you'd find attractive to date and have a love affair. First, and foremost, this House is about LOVE: who you love and what you love to do. If you're looking for a

5th House: Love Life & Creativity

love relationship, this House will reveal the romantic times in your life when sparks will fly, romance will blossom and total commitment will seem just right around the corner. Romance and love begin here, hopefully turning into a full-blown relationship. When that happens your romance becomes a "commitment" causing it to fall under the domain of the 7th House of Partnership. (Note: If you've recently made a commitment from romance to partnership then please read the 7th House chapter on *Relationships, Marriage & Partnerships* for a new perspective on what you can expect.)

This area of your birth chart rules all aspects of love relationships, those times in your life when you are enthralled with romance, dating, courtship, love affairs, and sexuality for fun (and for procreation). This House describes the lover you're likely to be and the kind of lover you might be attracted to. You might be a very sensuous, romantic lover who insists on lighting candles and putting on mood music before making love. Or, you might be described as a more practical, earthy lover who doesn't need any pomp and circumstance to commence having sex. Who knows, you might considered a "wham, bam, thank you ma'am," type. Or maybe you're a bit of a freak, enjoying sex toys, whips, chains and an unconventional romp in the hay.

This House shows how you express your joy for living, the fun you have at parties, the trips to amusement parks and all the other social activities you partake in. From this vantage point you can see where you get your spontaneous enjoyment in life, including the kind of leisure games, sports, recreation, hobbies and pleasures you'll choose to enjoy. Any activity that brings you a sense of fulfillment, joy, bliss, even self-indulgence is featured here. Who knows, your enjoyment might even manifest in your being a flashy and dramatic decorator who likes to buy new furnishings to show off your home. Or, you may love showing off your singing voice at the local pub on karaoke night.

This is the special area of your birth chart that rules children, the source of pleasure they are to you, and how you relate to them as parents. After all, you may be a doting parent who can't spend enough time with your child or someone who finds the responsibility of taking care of them stressful and demanding. This House can be a mirror for you to see the forms of pleasure you'll share with your children, such as sports, science, literature, art, music, dance and theater. This area reveals how you'll play with them for pleasure and emotional enrichment, whether it's throwing the baseball back in forth or doing a science project together.

This House will give insights as to how willing you'll be to take a risk on love, money or elsewhere in life. This part of your birth chart is known as the House of gambling, prizes, games of chance and card playing. This gambling can also include financial risk-taking and speculation, such as in stocks and other investments.

Your Body in the 5th House

This house rules the heart, spine, sides, and upper back. Since there is nothing more important than your health, pay special attention to these areas of your body whenever a planet transits this House. It may indicate a period of time when you'll experience health benefits, issues or even problems you should be aware of. If you observe anything unusual, you'll have the opportunity to consult with a medical doctor or a health care practitioner.

Your 5th House Decisions

You now understand that the 5th House of your birth chart concerns your creativity and self-expression, including your artistic expression. It also concerns your love life, affairs of the heart, children, amusement, and gambling.

As you read about the description of this house, it's time to ask yourself a few questions. Are you using your creative energies in life or are you bored because you aren't? Do have special artistic talents you have longed to cultivate? What kind of love life do you have? If you're dating, do you meet eligible people that could turn into marriage partners? Or, do you continually go out with commitment-phobic types or abusive losers? How is your sex life? Do you enjoy it? Or is it a source of frustration because you don't have a sex life? Are you sexually inhibited? Is sex reserved only as an intimate activity in a committed relationship or do you enjoy sex even in the most casual of relationships?

If you have children, are you a fun parent who does activities with them? If you have no children, do you want any? Are you interested in having more leisure and recreation in your life? Do you like to gamble? Are you lucky or not? Should you avoid speculation?

These are all significant questions and your answers may lead you to make important decisions to change your life. Here are a few examples of decisions clients have made based on the activities and issues of the 5th House.

5th House: Love Life & Creativity

Situation: Hank enjoys vacationing in places that give him the opportunity to gamble. So, twice a year he plans trips where he can enjoy the thrill of playing cards and slot machines. Sometimes he wins, but most of the time he loses.

DECISION: *I want to go gambling when I am lucky and likely to win.*

* * *

Situation: When she was younger, Rosalind loved acting in her high school plays and she misses the creativity and camaraderie she experienced then.

DECISION: *I want to study acting again so I can audition for plays that are presented at the local community theatre.*

* * *

Situation: Stan works hard most of the year and doesn't spend enough time enjoying recreational activities with his three children. The last several family vacations have been routine and not much fun.

DECISION: *I want to pick the ideal time to take a fun family vacation that everyone will enjoy.*

* * *

Situation: After a 20-year marriage, then a difficult divorce, Angela has taken time off to recover and reconnect with herself.

DECISION: *I want to pick the best time to date again and find someone special.*

* * *

During the transits of *Jupiter, Saturn, Uranus, Neptune,* and *Pluto* – Hank, Rosalind, Stan and Angela will have many opportunities to implement their decisions at a favorable time to produce the outcome they want.

The Transiting Planets Reveal Your Past, Present & Future

Your main focus is using astrology to understand *what the hell is going on in your life*. Once you do – this book will show you the best time to make a decision to change it, should you have a desire to do so. As you read about the five planets transiting the 5th House, notice the way each planet exerts its unique influence and effect, bringing specific opportunities, issues, problems, and events into this area of your life. But if you're curious as to how these planets are personally affecting YOU *today*, in your *past*, or in your *future*, you can find out where each transiting planet is in your birth chart by using the *FREE Transit Calculator* (see Part IV).

JUPITER in Your 5th House of Love & Creativity

Great Year to Be Out Socializing for Fun & Romance

Jupiter transiting your 5th House is a time when your creativity and self-expression grow to new heights. You feel confident, having the courage to express yourself in a natural and easy manner. All your relationships benefit because you project yourself in a warm and friendly way to others. You have a positive and optimistic demeanor, which is attractive to others and makes it easy for you to have honest and open (and even sexual) relationships. In fact, when you have Jupiter transiting your 5th House, you have been given a gift you can use to achieve good fortune in all the areas that have been mentioned.

Jupiter's influence brings a special potential for enjoying love and romance in your social relationships. You'll enjoy and delight over any romance you encounter because it's likely to be a love affair that's exciting and passionate. You may even be attracted to someone of a different social or ethnic background. One of the features of your relationships right now is that they have the capacity to teach and help you expand your worldview so that you're more sophisticated than before this transit took effect.

When Jupiter transits this House, it's a wonderful time to socialize in order to meet people who will introduce you to all kinds of fun and pleasurable activities you'll enjoy for years to come. If you're single and want to meet someone for a satisfying relationship that could lead to commitment, this is your year because you'll have many opportunities. You can take advantage of this good fortune by busying your social calendar with many activities, parties and events where you can meet people.

Shelley was an introvert and even though she was very attractive and bright, she didn't feel comfortable out in public. She'd rather be curled up in bed with a good book, taking her dog Sadie out for a walk or even catching a movie alone. As her girlfriends developed relationships, with some of them getting married, Shelley began to think about how nice it would be to find a love of her own. She fantasized about making a gourmet dinner for someone special, or holding hands at a romantic movie, or enjoying a fun weekend out of town together.

Shelley felt awkward going to parties and the clubs her girlfriends frequented seemed like "meat markets." She mused, "If only I had a different attitude about socializing with total strangers." Fortunately for her, Jupiter was transiting her 5th House when she came for a consultation.

This was Shelley's year to have a great romance. Sure enough, with her Jupiter transit, she started feeling more confident and adventurous about socializing. She made a list of cultural activities she would enjoy attending, such as a lecture or the ballet. She also joined an Internet matchmaking site, filled out her profile, and started to meet men through the service. Shelly also called up all her friends and told them about the qualities she admired in a man, and asked to be fixed up with single men they knew. In the course of the year, Shelley had dozens of dates, and a number of short-term dating relationships. Then, one day she met Peter at a symphony black-tie event. He was handsome, sweet and shy. They felt comfortable with each other immediately, became serious and decided to date each other exclusively. Shelley used the good luck of Jupiter to find romance.

A Fortunate Time to Have a Child

The 5th House rules children, so if you have kids, it's an excellent time to be a parent and participate in activities alongside your child. You're likely to be especially proud of their accomplishments. Regardless of your closeness, Jupiter's influence will enhance and improve your relationship with them. You'll find yourself feeling a special sense of kindness, friendliness and ability to teach them as well. Jupiter in this House favors all activities with children, including the possibility of becoming pregnant and having a child.

Marybeth and her husband had wanted to have children for years, but had been unable to conceive despite their vigorous efforts to try to become pregnant. After they each underwent complete medical check-ups, they were told there was no reason they couldn't become pregnant. Despite that clean bill of health, Marybeth was 35 and becoming nervous and worried it would never happen. Desperate to have a child, the couple was willing to use their savings to pay for the services of a well known fertility clinic that specialized in helping couples get pregnant through the latest in vitro fertilization techniques. However, since each attempt to get pregnant would be very costly, they decided to begin their pregnancy efforts at the most favorable time for Marybeth to conceive. That's why they began their fertility procedures when Jupiter transited her 5th House. Their first attempt was so successful they had twins during that exact time period.

A Time to Show Your Talent

Jupiter's influence expands your creative talents to express yourself. Therefore, if you have any artistic or theatrical abilities, this is a favorable time to develop and feature them in the public for special recognition. If you work in this professional area, this may be the year when you'll find fame and fortune, making more money than usual through the work you do in your art or craft.

Lyle was tired of his telemarketing job at the call center where he worked. What he really wanted to do was to be an actor. Acting was his passion. He kept up with all the periodicals and services that featured "call-ups" as well as going on auditions. He made sure he was the first to arrive and ready to read for any part. Everyone told Lyle how much talent he had, so it was a mystery why he felt so blocked and frustrated each time he missed getting a great part. However, it wasn't a mystery to me. When Lyle first came to talk to me about his career, he had Saturn transiting his 5th House, which (as you'll learn in the next section of this chapter) was a time when his talents met with obstacles, restrictions and limitations. Understandably, he was so discouraged by his failures and inability to win acting parts he told me he was seriously considering giving up acting completely.

I explained to Lyle that Saturn would soon be moving out of his the 5th House. Best of all, Jupiter would be entering his 5th House (which rules "acting"). The beneficent energies of Jupiter would bring him luck and good fortune during most of the year. This would be his time to be successful. All he had to do was to stay positive and persevere. In fact, I counseled Lyle to put out more energy and effort than ever before. Besides going out on casting calls, he needed to call agents and drama coaches, and anyone who might know of acting opportunities or contacts he should be making. Within the first three months, he had secured several small parts and felt confident a big, meaty one would soon be offered.

Please note: Lyle's success wasn't based on doing the obvious things that any aspiring actor would do, such as going on casting calls, auditions and calling agents. Every wanna-be actor does that. His success came from working hard and doing those things *during the time* that Jupiter was transiting his 5th House when he was more likely to have luck and good fortune bring him results. Without the *right timing*, you can do all the right things, but still never have success.

A Time to Have Fun and Play

Jupiter's transit here is a time when your creativity, imagination and self-expression are very much favored. You're able to let your hair down and be a kid once again. The idea of going on the roller coaster brings a smile to your face and a chance to play miniature golf sparks your enthusiasm. You take pleasure in fun and recreation, enjoying life in a way you haven't before, because you're free of the usual burdens of responsibility. There's nothing more satisfying than your leisure time alone or with family and friends.

It's also likely to be a very social time where you enjoy parties, celebrations, amusing events and all types of entertainment. You have a special joy going to someone's costume party or a friend's Super Bowl party. You're excited as if you were a child again when your wife throws you a surprise birthday party. You may stop off at the sporting good store because you're excited to buy a badminton set to use in the backyard. This may also be a year when you have lots of fun participating in sports and competitive games such as running, cycling or skiing. You may have just as much enjoyment seeing a great movie or reading an interesting book if that's your pleasure.

You're feeling great self-confidence, finding your social interactions with others successful and well received. Everyone congratulates you for putting together a bowling team for company employees. You may also receive special recognition for your work in the outer world. Other parents thank you for coaching the soccer team at the recreation center. Depending on the rest of your horoscope, you may be extremely lucky in gambling and other forms of speculation such as investing. You're excited to plan a vacation to Las Vegas just so you can have fun at the casinos. This is a period when you have the opportunity to learn, grow, and feel a wonderful freedom of self-expression and self-assurance as you enjoy life, having fun. Take advantage of this joyful time in your life.

5th House: Love Life & Creativity

Considerations, Actions, Decisions During Jupiter in 5th House

1. Do you want to develop an artistic skill?
2. Do you want to plan a fun activity or vacation?
3. This is a great year to join an organized sports team.
4. Do you want to find a lucky time to speculate or gamble?
5. Do you want children?
6. Do you want to enjoy fun activities with your children?
7. Do you want to find romance or a love affair?
8. Do you want to enjoy sex more?

SATURN in Your 5th House of Love & Creativity

More Responsibility, Less Fun

During these two and a half years, you may experience obstacles, restrictions or limitations in such areas as your self-expression, creativity, love, romance, sex, children, speculation and gambling. You may feel a sense of frustration that you can't seem to make things work out the way you want. For example, even though, you're normally very eloquent, you deliver a speech, stumbling on your words. Or, when you go out with friends to the clubs, you rarely meet anyone you're interested in. In fact, it seems as if people aren't interested in meeting you. Perhaps, your kids are going through some period of growth where they're misbehaving at home, requiring you to be a disciplinarian. Almost every week, you "lose your shirt" at the Friday night poker game. You may be asking, "What the hell is going on in my life?"

While these encounters may not be pleasant, their ultimate purpose is to help you grow and improve yourself by examining your actions and making necessary adjustments so you'll ultimately have more successful results. The reason Saturn is not fun and games when it transits this House is because you have to go through some difficult restrictions as you learn the lessons of how to be more responsible – as Rickey found out.

Rickey was always joking and kidding about any topic that friends or family would discuss with him, never taking any subject too seriously. He'd been that way all his life, avoiding serious discussions because he just wanted to have fun and enjoy himself. He figured there would be plenty of time for that kind of talk when he was older, like his parents. Even though he was 18, he didn't want to spend time concerned about the responsibilities of being an adult.

Whenever his parents tried to discuss important questions such as: "What are you going to do after you graduate college?" "What are your plans for work?" or "What do you see yourself doing with your life?" – Rickey would make jokes and avoid deeper discussion. However, life was about to get more serious for Ricky because unbeknownst to him, Saturn was transiting his 5th House. He began to notice that hanging out with friends and playing video games or going to a ballgame was no longer as much fun. His buddies all seemed too busy to just hang out. Instead, they were finding jobs to pay for college, their first apartment or the car they were planning to buy. He had to admit that even he was feeling the need to get more serious about organizing his life lately. Suddenly, his father got laid off from his job and Rickey realized he'd have to find a part-time job to afford college. He was feeling a lot less like joking and kidding these days. Saturn's call is for you to accept responsibility in whatever area of your life it's transiting.

Time Re-Evaluate What's Fun?

Normally this House concerns fun, recreation and amusing times in your life. However, Saturn in this House isn't known for bringing you a lot of fun. Right now you may feel like you aren't enjoying certain activities like you use to. You may be trying to figure why you aren't experiencing pleasure in many of the ways you have in the past. Perhaps, you're redefining what fun is for you as you realize your tastes have changed. For example, you no longer find golf enjoyable since 3-4 hours for a round of golf is too much of a time commitment. Maybe reading a book on self-improvement is your "new" fun.

Another manifestation of Saturn's transit here is that you may get "serious" about your fun. One client who raced Formula One cars for fun, decided to put together a racing team and professionally race.

During this transit you're critically evaluating how you express yourself, what you do to be creative, the activities you engage in to have fun and all matters of the 5th House. In contrast to feeling the light, relaxed and carefree energies of Jupiter, you're feeling the weighty, somber energies of Saturn.

A Time to Evaluate Your Romance

Saturn's transit here is a serious time when, through introspection and self-analysis, you'll examine how you express yourself when you socialize or date. Do you establish rapport with people or do they find you off-putting for some reason? In this period of your life you'll learn more about how you engage others in your social interactions. You may focus on ways to have a more fulfilling romantic life that will lead to a meaningful dating relationship. If you're tired of dating the same type of people, perhaps you need to be more creative in your efforts to meet different types. If you don't have much of a romantic life, you may be giving thought as to why that's the case. Is it because you need to find new places to socialize? Or, is it because you enjoy your freedom and aren't all that interested? You may be going through a process of re-defining and re-structuring the best way to approach your romantic life.

This is also a time when romantic relationships can be challenging, demanding or even difficult. Your love life can seem more complicated or have a different flavor to it. For example, you may find yourself having a love affair with an older person who plays a parental role in your relationship. Or, the reverse may hold true, where you play a parental role to your partner. You may also find yourself feeling inhibited in your sex life, either because your needs aren't being met or perhaps you aren't meeting the needs of the other person. This may be a result of a demanding work schedule that causes you to be tired and less available for intimacy. Then again, it's always possible the best seller you're reading is more engrossing than your current lover.

This can be a serious time when you'll contemplate your love life and examine any romantic relationship you're engaged in. Be aware that Saturn's energies can make you feel discouraged or depressed causing you to question whether you're worthy and deserve to be loved. In fact, you may lack the confidence to find a love relationship during this period of your life. These are all possibilities to consider as you evaluate what may be going on in your life.

Bettina started dating just as Saturn transited her 5th House and predictably, she was finding the process frustrating. She'd have lots of first dates and then not be asked out a second time. Or, when she did go out with a guy a few times, the relationship never seemed to go anywhere. Bettina was losing confidence in her ability to be attractive to men and started questioning if there was something wrong with her. She wondered if she was loveable and deserved to find a great relationship.

Bart had been dating Tess for almost a year. They enjoyed doing things together but he wanted to spend more time with her and have a serious relationship. He was feeling a deep desire to find his soul mate, settle down and build a life together. When Bart asked Tess about their future, she explained she really enjoyed seeing him once during the week and on the weekends, but otherwise, she was really busy with her career. That was her priority. The reality was clear to Bart that they both wanted different things. Saturn transiting Bart's 5th House revealed it was time

5th House: Love Life & Creativity

to end his relationship and find someone who had the same partnership goals as he did.

Both Bettina and Bart used their Saturn experience to take a serious look at the kind of love relationships they were experiencing. This transit gives you the opportunity to critically evaluate your love life and make the appropriate adjustments so that a romantic relationship can become a reality.

A Time to be Responsible for Your Children & Your Sex Life

Be aware that children may be a source of restriction, difficulty or burden during this transit. While having children is a blessing, raising them and meeting their needs carries with it great responsibility. During these two and a half years you may find that children will make heavy demands on you that require you to accept even more than the usual responsibilities for their care.

Since the 5th House concerns both the sex that you may enjoy in a romantic (or committed) relationship AND children, please note that Saturn's transit here forces you to be responsible in your sex life or face the consequences. Not being sexually responsible can result in an unwanted pregnancy occurring during this transit. Therefore, if Saturn is transiting here and you have adolescent children, make sure to discuss the topic of responsible sex with them. If you're single and involved in a sexual relationship – with no desire to have children, make sure to use contraception during this period of your life.

Saturn demands you be accountable and bring you tests and lessons to teach you responsibility as Bill found out. Bill wanted to be a good father to his two young children now that he was divorced from their mother. The truth was his former wife had always taken responsibility for spending time with their children while he worked late at the office or played golf with his buddies. Now that he was spending time with his kids as a single dad, he realized how little he knew about taking care of children and entertaining them. It was obvious to him that he'd been a selfish parent, focusing only on his life – not theirs. He loved his kids and was ready to accept the responsibility of being an attentive father. Driving his car, he stopped off at a bookstore and picked up a book on parenting. Next week, he would make an appointment to meet with his children's teachers at their school. There was no question his efforts to be a more responsible parent would mean he'd have to change his lifestyle. But he was finally ready to be more of a father to his children.

A Bad Time for Gambling

Speculating and gambling are usually not favored when Saturn transits your 5th House, since Saturn's influence demands you be cautious, conservative and very prudent. Saturn's energies are about working hard and getting paid for your labors. Thus, the idea of trying to make money the "easy way," by dropping money in a slot machine or going to the $20 window at the race track isn't consistent with the principles of Saturn. When Saturn transits this House, it's a time be careful with your money and not take risks, because Saturn's energies will restrict or limit your ability to win. In fact, your success is usually minimal and you may even lose.

A client, who loved gambling, joined a big gambling junket traveling to Macau. Unfortunately, it was during the time when Saturn was transiting his 5th House. He was normally very lucky. However, during the seven days of his gambling vacation, he was extremely frustrated and angry, because no matter whether he played poker, roulette or the slot machines, he lost a great deal of money each day.

Success in life is all about good timing and making the right choices. The singer-songwriter, Jim Croce said it perfectly in the lyrics of one of his songs where he sang about some things in life – you shouldn't do. He said, *"You don't tug on Superman's cape. You don't spit into the wind. You don't pull the mask off the ol' Lone Ranger."* And, let me add: You don't gamble when Saturn transits your 5th House.

A Time to Get Real with Yourself

Saturn's purpose is to force you to assess and re-evaluate critical areas of your life. When things in your life aren't working out the way you want, it's time to take an objective look to see if there's a better way to achieve what you desire. Saturn helps you do this by bringing you into confrontation with your goals, your relationships, and the activities you're involved in. It may even cause a crisis in your life to make you finally come to terms with something you need to face and resolve. If your old approaches don't work, it's time to find new ones that will. You may also have to face reality and "let go," of something that doesn't work, instead of wanting something that "can't be." Saturn's energies force you to "weed the garden" of those elements of your life that no longer serve you.

A female client of mine was 40, still single and depressed about not having found a marriage partner after so many years of dating. She never seemed to meet a man that met her critical expectations. When she met a man who was interesting, it didn't seem to work out. She discussed this recurring problem with her therapist and finally admitted that she was afraid of commitment because of her fears that a man would be too possessive and inhibit her freedom.

Saturn's message as it transits your 5th House is to re-examine and re-evaluate your actions in all matters related to this area of your life. Ask yourself if the way you express yourself creatively is effective or even satisfying. Are you interested in finding new ways to have fun and amuse yourself? Would you enjoy meeting someone different for a meaningful romance? Is a time to acknowledge that the romance you're involved in is just not going to lead to a serious commitment? Does your child need more attention, help or discipline? Do you need to change your approach to speculating and gambling? If you truly know what you want and are willing to work hard to get it, Saturn will make it real, so that it can manifest in your life.

Considerations, Actions, Decisions During Saturn in 5th House

1. Do you want to develop or refine an artistic skill that takes discipline?
2. Are there any activities you want add or remove from your life?
3. Are you avoiding gambling or speculating during this time?
4. Are you in a romance that will lead to commitment?
5. Are you a romance that you should end?
6. Are there any restrictions blocking your ability to have a romance?
7. How are you feeling about your responsibilities towards your children?
8. Are you teaching your children lessons about responsibility?
9. Are you feeling sexually restricted?
10. Are you being sexually responsible?

URANUS in Your 5th House of Love & Creativity

A Time for Exciting Romance

When Uranus is in this House it's an exciting period of life to seek out new ways of self-expression and creativity. You're feeling free to experiment and have experiences you've never had before. If you do this, Uranus will bring you liberation, freedom and newness into your life, especially in the area of love and romance. So, if you've been telling a friend, "I would love an exciting romance to come into my life," – well, you're going to enjoy Uranus transiting your 5th House. It's likely to bring you an unusual love relationship. A romance you experience at this time will force you to break from any conventional tendencies you might have, to ones that are more flexible and adaptable. That's precisely what will make it exciting for you. Be prepared to experience romances that are passionate, exciting, volatile, but not necessarily long-lasting. They may turn into "on/off, on/off," relationships that are quite unstable.

Another feature of romantic relations during this Uranus transit is that you may encounter an unusual relationship with someone you would normally not have a romance, such as someone of a different social class, ethnicity, or of very different age than you. You may find yourself saying, "I can't believe I'm going out with a man so rich!" or "I can't believe I'm going out with a woman from that part of the world," or "I can't believe I'm going out with someone so young!"

Since Uranus brings the influence of volatility to romances, you may find you attract many exciting romances that suddenly start as passionate affairs, yet end just as quickly. Or, a love affair may suddenly come into your life, causing an end to a relationship that had existed in your life for some time.

Joan had been in a safe but rather boring relationship with Stan for the last six months. They did interesting and fun things together, but there was no spark or exciting sexual chemistry. She considered Stan a "placeholder." He seemed to be "Mr. Right – for now," not "Mr. Right – forever." Her life took an amazing turn one day as she was riding up the elevator to work. A good-looking, well-dressed young man, with a dark

5th House: Love Life & Creativity

tan, stepped in the elevator. He had to be at least 12 to 15 years younger than she. She stared at him, as a risqué thought crossed her mind, *I wonder what he would be like in bed?* Their eyes met as they stared at each other, and finally he introduced himself. He said he was new to the office building and suggested they have a drink to get acquainted. She surprised herself by accepting.

They experienced an amazing chemistry as they talked over cocktails, which led to a wild evening back at his apartment. From there, they saw each other every day enjoying fun activities and a hot romance she'd never had before. In order to make time for her new love, Joan told Stan that it was over between them. Meanwhile, she felt liberated from the prim and proper woman she'd been in the past, free to be a woman who was enjoying the most exciting affair of her life.

Uranus energies bring great instability to a relationship at this time. But they're *sooooooo* exciting because they take you away from the more routine, predictable relationships you've had in the past. In fact, if such a relationship eventually becomes too stable and routine, you may no longer remain interested because you'll be bored. After all, it's the very instability of the relationship that keeps you fascinated and excited to keep it going. Such is the nature of Uranus' influence on romance as it transits your 5th House.

Uranus energies demand freedom! So, even if you do find yourself enjoying the excitement and passion of new romance, you'll resent any attempt by the other person to tie you down and take away your freedom. In other words, you will not tolerate a new love interest becoming possessive of you. Therefore, you should enjoy dating and short-term relationships, even if they don't last a long time. Actually, you may find yourself purposely, "playing the field," avoiding long-term commitments at this time, since they may restrict you socially. You may want to be free as a bird during this transit.

A Time for Sexual Freedom

This is a very sexually exciting time because Uranus' influence brings out your unconventional nature. Are you ready to "get ur freak on?" If you've been wanting to let your hair down and be crazy like your friend, who makes you blush, telling you about the wild places she and her husband make love, this is a period in your life when you could get your wish. Uranus' energies remove your inhibitions and give you a sense of freedom to experiment in your sex life, if you're so inclined. If you're married, this may be the time when you re-energize sex in your marriage, making it exciting once again. Also, know that it can be a time when a married person might be tempted to engage in extramarital affairs.

Certainly, whether you're in an intimate relationship or single, you may be very sexually stimulated and feel free of the restrictions that have tempered your sexual freedom in the past. There's nothing holding you back from doing whatever you please! It's as if a big weight has been lifted off your shoulders. You're feeling independent, in a unique frame of mind to seek adventure, experiment, and be sexually liberated in ways you've never been before – as David discovered.

David was raised with very Christian values that included remaining a virgin and saving himself for marriage. Being abstinent had been a way of life for him for many years. Quite frankly, it was a challenge to remain a virgin amidst so many friends who felt free to enjoy sex before marriage. He felt envious at times when his college friends would come home from dates and tell him about their sexual experiences at some wild frat party. The truth was he lived vicariously through his roommate Jim who had regular sex with his girlfriend. However, David remained steadfast and committed to being abstinent until marriage.

That changed when Uranus transited his 5th House and he began having wild and rebellious thoughts, asking himself why he was so committed to not having sex before marriage. What was the point? Growing up he'd succumbed to both parental and religious pressure but now he was free to make his own decisions and live his life as he thought best. He felt an urgent need to assert his independence and enjoy the forbidden fruit of pre-marital sex.

One evening he went to a get-together at a friend's house where he bumped into Jessie, a very attractive girl he'd met at several other parties. She seemed very interested in him. As they chatted, she was easy to talk to, asking lots of questions about his life and social background. He was open in discussing his religious upbringing and limited experience in relationships. She surprised him by confiding her own dilemma about saving herself for marriage, after being raised by a strict, church-going father. Then she excited him by telling him about the first time she had sex, how much she loved it and the freedom it brought her.

She talked about her experience in such a natural and inviting way that he found himself aroused and attracted as if he'd finally found his liberator. Reading his mind, she leaned over mischievously whispered in his ear, grabbed his hand, walked with him into a bedroom and locked the door. When he came out, he felt like a new man. That's how quickly and spontaneously Uranus can bring you an experience that will change your life.

Your Children May Surprise You

This House rules children; so if you have any, don't be surprised if you notice sudden changes in their behavior that may be a source of amazement or upset to you. This is an important time to pay attention to their growth and development because you may face challenges that require you to find new ways to parent them successfully. Perhaps, a compliant son turns into a rebellious teenager or a shy young daughter blossoms into a world-class swimming champion.

The positive manifestation of Uranus' effect is that your children will be a source of fun and stimulating experiences, which will bring joy and excitement into your life. To your delight your children may distinguish themselves by doing something unique or original that will fill you with pride. One client had an eight-year-old daughter with an incredible intellect and amazing memory, and the child became a contestant at a state spelling bee championship. Another client, a proud father and baseball fanatic, took great pride going to a semi-pro baseball game and watching his son pitch, throwing a fastball in the high 90s. The father's pride turned to shock when a major league baseball scout called to make an appointment to discuss signing his son to a contract.

The negative manifestation of Uranus is that your child's behavior may become willful, rebellious and difficult for you to handle. It's possible that during this period of your children's life, they'll experience upsetting events, such as accidents, illnesses or problematic behavior that requires immediate attention. If you have a child who tends to be free-spirited, thrill-seeking, or perhaps engages in behavior or activities that would put him at risk, make sure to give him extra supervision and attention during this transit.

I had a client who was in shock when police came to the family's home to arrest his teen-age son as a drug dealer. The police produced a warrant to search their house, eventually finding a huge supply of drugs in their son's bedroom. The father was mortified.

What the Hell Is Going On in My Life?

A Time of Creative Excitement and Willfulness

Because you'll find yourself being innovative, discovering new ideas and ways to express your unique individuality, this is an exciting time to be creative. If you're involved in the arts, theatre, design or any other artistic pursuit, you'll find yourself developing original approaches and new forms of creative expression in the work you're doing. You're filled with a risk-taking spirit, ready to enjoy fun, recreation and new activities. Your energy is so high, it's like someone plugged you into a 220-volt electrical socket. You're in the mood to be stimulated and to experiment in order to enjoy life to its fullest.

However, avoid letting your enthusiasm for fun and amusement cause you to act imprudently or carelessly. You may find yourself feeling so self-confident that others see you as being strong-willed, egotistical, or just stubborn. In fact, quite often this is a period in life when you may find yourself acting in a rebellious manner against any form of authority whether it's a boss or a parent. Try to refrain from making blunt statements such as, "You can take this job and shove it!" or, "I don't care if you're my father, I'm an adult and I can do what I want." They're not the best ways to get what you want, especially with those in authority.

Be careful, because in the process of exerting your own free will, you may throw caution to the wind, totally lacking in discretion or good judgment. When you're in the clutches of a Uranus' influence, you "do what the hell you want!" You won't likely be open to thoughtful reflection and calm reasoning. (Remember what that one vulture sitting on a branch, said to the other? That's you – at this time.)

TIP: If you find yourself feeling very angry, rebellious, with a great urge for freedom, discuss your upset with a loved one or friend who can advise you to keep your head about you and help come up with some constructive options.

When it comes to speculating and gambling, it's important to be prudent because the influences of Uranus are unpredictable. You can't rely on them, even though you're likely to be excited, enthused and filled with confidence. Just be aware that taking risks can have consequences that can either be exciting or upsetting in their result.

Considerations, Actions, Decisions During Uranus in 5th House

5th House: Love Life & Creativity

1. Do you want to develop an exciting artistic skill?
2. Are you interested in developing new ways of being creative?
3. Are there any fun activities, sports or events that would be exciting to try?
4. Be aware of surprising outcomes if you gamble or speculate.
5. Are you interested in an unconventional new romance?
6. Do you want to make your current relationship more exciting?
7. Use your intuition to better understand your children's behavior and needs.
8. Are you looking for more sexual freedom in your relationships?

NEPTUNE in Your 5th House of Love & Creativity

It Brings an Ideal Romance

Neptune's transit through your 5th House is likely to manifest in several ways. From the standpoint of your social life and love nature, you're likely to be attracted to a highly romantic relationship that meets your ideal. You derive a special joy from reading *Romeo and Juliet*, seeing a romantic movie, receiving flowers or a greeting card from a lover. Your interest in a love affair is based on wanting a real spiritual connection, not just a physical one based on sexual chemistry.

Neptune's influence has the effect of dissolving or reducing the demands of your ego, making your wants unimportant, thus allowing you to put the needs of someone else ahead of your own. It pleases you to give of yourself in a very charitable way. It's not too much trouble to spend the day preparing a candlelight dinner that might please your lover. You'll gladly hold his hand as he tells you how depressed he is at not receiving the promotion he really wanted. He, on the other hand, happily cancels his golf date, because you're under the weather, not feeling well. Therefore, if you're in a romantic relationship you'll find yourself sacrificing your needs in favor of the other person. Neptune's influence bestows a quality in you, giving you the capacity to see that person in a very loving, compassionate, ideal light.

A client shared her many experiences dating men who were just "not romantic." One date would come over to her apartment dressed in a sloppy manner, never thinking to bring flowers, and often taking her to some casual hamburger joint. Then, she'd go on a date with another man who took her to a classy restaurant, but had no manners, behaving like a "dog in heat." The moment an attractive young woman walked into the restaurant, his attention switched from their conversation to stopping mid-sentence, staring, and ogling the woman up and down. (*TIP:* if anyone does this to you, *stop talking*. Only begin talking again when you have their full attention.)

Happily, her dating experience changed when Neptune transited her 5th House. She met a man who was the ideal romantic suitor, bringing her flowers on their first date, taking her to a quaint, intimate place to have some wine and pasta. It was so refreshing and captivating to talk with him at the restaurant, noticing his eyes never moving from hers, despite the many sexy, beautifully dressed women who walked by their table. She'd found a man who was a throwback to a different era: polite, charming and attentive. That's the romantic experience that may await you when Neptune transits your 5th House of Love and Romance.

Be Careful of Illusion and Fantasy

Neptune's influence can be magical, bringing illusion and fantasy to your love life. This can be the perfect time to find an ideal romance as long as you don't let your idealism cause you to have unrealistic expectations or put someone on a pedestal they will fall from. Therefore, it's important to make sure your romantic relationships are grounded in reality and not some fantasy you saw in a movie or read in a book. During this transit it's easy to believe in fairy tales and romantic myths. While your heart may be wide open for love, which is wonderful, it's not a time to ignore reality. If you meet someone you're romantically attracted to, avoid over-idealizing that person. If you do, when they show their human side, you'll be disappointed and you may even feel deceived.

Also, be especially aware that during this time, love affairs are often not what they seem. You may find yourself falling in love with someone's image rather than who they really are. For example, during this transit, you may fall in love with someone who's not available, whether it's because they're already married, or because of some strange, unusual, or even mysterious circumstance.

In consultations, many clients express a deep desire to find a fulfilling love relationship. So, let me share three different romantic experiences that occurred when Neptune transited their 5th House.

Kathy had seen an attractive stranger on her commuter train for weeks. A friendly conversation turned into a cup of coffee, which turned into a dinner date, which turned into this deep romantic connection. One day, her new love interest confessed that he was married with 2 children and not available for anything more than an affair.

Brad couldn't believe his luck meeting such a charming young woman at a party. The whole evening was spent talking to each other as if no one else were there. She had a vivacious personality, crazy and fun to be with.

He invited her back to his place where they talked for a few more hours, eventually making love and finally going to sleep. He woke in the morning to find a note on his nightstand saying, "Brad, I had a great evening. Sorry to have to tell you this: I'm serving time at the state prison where I'm incarcerated. Don't worry – I didn't kill anyone, it was a drug-related sentence. But for good behavior, I was given an overnight pass as part of a special work-release program. I'm sure this all sounds weird but I really enjoyed meeting you. Thanks for a fun time."

Barbara was head over heels over a gorgeous man she met at a career networking party. After three of the most fun dates she'd ever had, he confessed he was bisexual and he explained to her that if she wanted to continue their relationship, she'd have to accept his lifestyle.

Stay Away from Unhealthy Relationships

Also, be careful of becoming involved in dependent relationships, where either you or your partner, view each other as a savior. For example, be wary of a romantic relationship with someone who has an addiction to drugs, alcohol or any other addiction such as gambling, food, work, shopping, television, religion or pornography. Neptune can heighten your sense of compassion, causing you to want to "save" them. Make sure you put your energies in healthy relationships with an equal partner during this period of your life. Don't make the mistake of falling in love with someone's "potential."

When it comes to love and romance, one of the dangers of Neptune's influence is that it can cause you to deceive yourself about the person you're in love with or the nature of your relationship. Neptune's transit through your 5th House can be especially disappointing for people who have a predisposition to "subconsciously" attract unhealthy relationships. Such people seem to have a magnetic compass that draws them to abusive or codependent relationships. For example, one person (or both), in an unhealthy way, is psychologically dependent on the other person who might be addicted to drugs or other self-destructive behaviors.

Unfortunately, more and more people find themselves in these harmful types and destructive relationships. This issue comes up frequently with clients who'll tell me they repeatedly have love relationships with a person who later turns out to be abusive or addictive in some way. One client said she frequently meets men who are initially exciting and interesting, only to find out later they are "drunks, liars or cheaters."

Another client said he continually dates women who are "gold-diggers," only interested in his wealth.

In analyzing the personality and birth chart of someone who has a history of these bad relationship experiences, I often see where their problem originates. They're pre-disposed to attracting unsavory characters who they're destined to have unhealthy relationship. I call this pre-disposition: the "bad-boy" or "bad-girl" syndrome.

One way this syndrome manifests is in the chart of the woman who comes from the "right side of the tracks" – a good family and moral upbringing. But, unfortunately, she finds most "nice" men (that her parents would approve) uninteresting, boring, and "too white bread." Instead, she's excited and fascinated by a man who comes from the "wrong side of the tracks." He appears fascinating and mysterious. Some women are even more bewitched if the man seems dangerous. There's something forbidden about his character that makes him very captivating. Perhaps, he dropped out of school, had some trouble with the law, is a member of a gang or drives a motorcycle. He may have an exciting sexual charisma or just appears a bit freaky. In some way, he's a "bad boy."

In addition, he may be intriguing because he lives a carefree life, unconcerned about society's approval. The woman admires this "bad boy" for his rebellious ways and his: "to hell with everyone else, I do what I want" attitude. (And, if her parents would disapprove, so much the better.)

Likewise, men with a history of being attracted to unhealthy relationships with women, have a similar syndrome. For example, I mentioned the male client who felt abused by women because they were only interested in his money. His chart showed he was predisposed to being solely interested in women who were beautiful, shallow and materialistic. It was no wonder they were interested in his wealth since that's what they valued most. Then, another male client, in his 50s, with a history of disappointing relationships, only wanted to date women in there 20s and early 30s. He complained that he felt used when these young women eventually left him for a relationship with a man closer to their age, with whom they had more in common.

Another way this syndrome causes unsatisfying romances is when someone is primarily attracted to romantic partners they "can't have." It's as if their romantic interest comes alive because the other person isn't available or interested in them. One female client spent two years going out with a man whose behavior clearly showed he wasn't that "into" their relationship. Her low self-esteem made her feel she didn't deserve more. Neptune's placement in her birth chart gave her a propensity to deceive herself, so she ignored the many signs of this man's lack of serious interest in her. Her Neptunian delusion prevented her from seeing the reality that she was only having a one-sided relationship with this man. This negative Neptune influence can keep a person in a self-defeating behavior pattern resulting in their repeatedly experiencing disappointing relationships.

Tips for Avoiding Unhealthy Relationships

Neptune's transit through your 5th House can be a fabulous time to heal yourself so you can enjoy the love of a healthy romantic relationship but you have to be willing to set boundaries. You also have to be very conscious and try to "ground yourself" in reality even though you'd prefer "to stay in the clouds."

Here's some helpful advice I give clients who want to stop attracting abusive and unsatisfying relationships into their lives:

1. Recognize that when it comes to romantic relationships, you are prone to fantasy, delusion and self-deception (and the deception of others).

2. Be conscious that this makes you vulnerable to attracting unhealthy relationships.

3. Make a list of qualities that you will not tolerate in your next relationship.

4. Make a list of the positive qualities you must have in your next relationship.

5. The next time you meet a romantic prospect who interests you, make sure to discuss with them the positive qualities you're looking for in a healthy relationship. Pay attention to their response to what you've said.

6. Make sure to discuss the qualities that you consider unhealthy. Pay attention to their response to what you've said.

7. Trust your intuition; if you meet a "bad boy," or "bad girl," don't waste your time — move on because you can't change them. As a healthy person, recognize it's not your job to do so.

8. If you're not sure whether it's a healthy relationship for you, go slow in dating and really get to know the person.

9. It's not necessary to "vomit" on them about all your past relationship disappointments. It only makes you sound like a "loser!"

10. To stop the pattern: Don't play the victim. You are always responsible for the people you decide to have relationships with.

11. Admit that you've made some bad choices. Today is a new day. You won't be making these bad choices again.

12. If early warning signs tell you this person is wrong for you, exit the relationship, immediately. No more contact.

13. Then after you've done this, look in your mirror so that you can see what a healthy person looks like. *You* are that healthy person!

You can break your pattern of having unsuccessful relationships if you commit yourself to these simple tips.

Pay Attention to Your Children

Since this House rules children as well, be careful not to over-idealize them, which may result in incorrectly perceiving their true behavior. When Neptune transits through a parent's 5th House, they feel so much for love for their children that they may not perceive their personalities accurately. If you have children, don't be surprised if you find their behavior strange and their actions confusing. Make sure your antennae are "up," sensitive to any unusual behavior your child exhibits, especially their use of drugs, alcohol or other addictions. Spend time together and make sure to promote good communication between you and your child, having open discussions and clearing up any misunderstandings that occur.

Ira was a very supportive and generous father, helping his struggling son Bruce, who was trying to find a job as a comedy writer in Los Angeles. For months he paid Bruce's rent, sent a living allowance, and paid for writing classes. Bruce assured his father he was working at a part-time job to help pay expenses and was spending his nights writing comedy.

Each week when Ira called to get the latest news, Bruce told him things were looking promising and that it was just a matter of time when he'd land a writing job. The following week, Ira was on business in San Francisco, so he decided to catch a quick flight to L.A. and surprise Bruce. When he walked into Bruce's apartment mid-day, Ira was the one who got the surprise. The door to Bruce's apartment was wide open. The place looked like a pigsty with empty bottles and pizza boxes scattered all over, reeking of the smell of marijuana. Lying on the couch were two half-dressed women in a deep sleep. Lying on the reclining chair was Bruce, face down and totally naked. It looked like the remains of a party where people had gotten "wasted" on drugs and alcohol. Clearly there was a lot Ira didn't know about what was going on in his son's life.

Be Careful of Drugs, Alcohol & Gambling

During Neptune's transit to your 5th House be careful of any tendency toward extreme pleasure seeking or any excess that may lead you to the use of drugs. This goes "triple" for those people who have addictive personalities that may already be troubling them. This transit may further amplify these tendencies. I have known parents who've had to endure the tragedy of a child's downward spiral into alcoholism or death through drug overdose.

Note also that the negative influence of Neptune relates to toxic substances and poisons. During this period of your life pay special attention to what you put into your body, making sure it's wholesome and healthy. This is an ideal time to take stock of your eating habits and make any necessary changes.

Since Neptune's influence can bring fantasy, delusion and self-deception, you should avoid speculation, gambling and any risky investments. Since the effect of Neptune is to keep important information hidden from your view, you may not be aware of a vital detail that could affect your investment decisions. Therefore, this isn't a dependable time to invest because you can easily be deceived or the victim of fraud. Even worse, you may be subject to delusion during this time where you have great faith you can't lose. As long as Neptune transits your 5th House, you're in danger of losing, so check, double-check and triple-check your investments and research and evaluate them carefully.

The influence of Neptune is likely to give you excellent intuition, and heighten your imagination and creativity. It's an excellent time to develop your talents in the arts, music, theatre, media or any artistic pursuit.

Considerations, Actions, Decisions During Neptune in 5th House

1. Do you want to develop an artistic skill or musical talent?
2. Is there any activity that would inspire you?
3. Avoid gambling or speculation.
4. Are you in a healthy romance?
5. Is there anything unusual going on in your children's behavior?
6. Do you want to have a very romantic love relationship?
7. Are you in a co-dependent versus healthy relationship?
8. Do you want to confront any of your addictions?

PLUTO in Your 5th House of Love and Creativity

Guide Your Child

Pluto's influence can profoundly affect your relationship with your children, producing powerful and long-lasting effects in their life for years to come. A child's personality development certainly begins right after birth, however, a significant portion of that development occurs between the ages of three to 12 years old. By the time a child finishes his adolescence at 18 years of age, he has more clearly developed his personality, character, identity and morals. That means, as a parent, you have only a certain number of years to make an impact on your child's development.

For that reason, Pluto's transit of your 5th House is a gift to you as a parent because it's when your parenting skills can have a profound and positive effect on your children's development. You'll have the opportunity to influence them through the counseling you give them and the time and activities you share with them as my client Sam experienced.

Sam was in the military during the years his son Randall was a little boy. His son idolized his father with pictures of Sam in his Army uniform wearing his metals, prominently displayed throughout Randall's room. Sam decided not to re-enlist and was honorably discharged and heading home for good. When I spoke with Sam about his relationship with Randall, I explained that with Pluto transiting Sam's 5th House he could have a life-changing influence on his son. Sam told me he was totally committed to spending a great deal of time with his son.

After a few days of family celebration, Sam sat down on the couch with Randall and let him know he'd planned lots of events and fun activities for him to do with Randall – just the two of them together. Randall was so excited. Sam told me that his son spent hours asking questions, wanting to learn from him. Sam's focused effort to make his son feel mentored is a good example of a parent bringing resources, ambition and intention to actively shape their child's behavior in a positive way.

The intense energies of Pluto on the other hand can produce a more negative effect where tensions build up between you and your children as you seek to convince them to make choices you believe are right for them. After all, as adults and loving parents, most of us want to firmly guide our children to take the right actions and make the best decisions. The key question for you as a parent is: How do you convince your child to follow your instructions?

In counseling parents who are having disciplinary problems with a child, I compare both of their birth charts. What I often find during Pluto's passage through the parent's 5th House is that the parent is often using tactics such as manipulation, pressure and force to compel their child to make choices the parent thinks best. That is the wrong strategy to employ because most often the result is a clashing of wills and power struggles between the parent and child. Worse, such parental behavior may result in programming (or imprinting) the child to use those manipulation tactics on the parent (and others) as well. It's more effective to have open, direct discussions where you can positively motivate your child to make decisions that are in their best interest.

If you're hoping to be a parent, Pluto's transit through your 5th House is a powerful sexual and procreative period in your life. Many clients have successfully used this transit as a favorable time to start a family. If you have a child during this time, you'll likely form a deep, intense bond with them. Birthing a child during this transit often explains why, over the years, your relationship with them turned out to be so powerfully close.

Enjoy a Passionate Romance

Since the 5th House also rules love affairs, it can signify the beginning of an intense romantic relationship between you and another person that will be based upon strong emotional feelings as well as deep sexual passions. Think of any true love story and you'll capture the intensity of Pluto's transit here. Romantic relationships that occur at this time may seem profound and even fated. You may feel all consumed or obsessed in ways you haven't been in your previous love affairs. There is something about the other person that attracts you like an insect to a spider's web (and sometime just as dangerously).

If you're already dating someone, or in a well-established love relationship, you'll find Pluto's transit here, making your romance even more intense. One client casually dated a man for a few months. Then, several months later, she found herself deeply captivated by him, wanting to spend every day in his company. Their relationship changed or "transformed" into a far more serious one that led to a more committed partnership.

However, Pluto in the 5th House can be bad news for you if you're in a troubled or unhealthy romance. This is because Pluto's influence has the capacity to bring upheaval destroying your relationship and causing it to end. But if a relationship is really meant to be, even if it has been interrupted, Pluto's energies can resurrect it to life as this couple found out.

Barry and Laura grew up as teenage sweethearts dating until their sophomore year of high school. Barry never tired of looking at Laura's beautiful long red hair. She melted whenever she saw him flashing his big smile. It all suddenly ended when Laura's father received a promotion and moved the family to the West Coast. Barry and Laura were devastated at the news, and while they vowed to never forget each other, inevitably they lost touch.

Once college was over, Laura accepted her first job in Chicago where she lived, enjoying the singles life. Barry accepted a job as sale rep job in Milwaukee. He was so successful that he was going to be honored this year at the company's annual awards banquet in Chicago.

Barry arrived in the Windy City late on a Thursday night, and met a bunch of the other sales reps for a drink at a club on Rush Street. Barry was raising his glass for a toast when, out of the corner of his eye, he saw a woman with a pretty face and long red hair looking in his direction. She looked like she had seen a ghost. Barry was sure he was looking at one, too. His eyes must be playing tricks on him as he looked again. He thought, *No...it couldn't be. It looks like Laura!* The redhead's eyes locked on his once again. He could see tears streaming down her cheeks. For a moment Barry couldn't speak and was stunned at what he was seeing. It *was* Laura. They couldn't believe how fate had drawn them together after so many years. After hugging and kissing each other, they finally sat down and spoke non-stop for the next two hours about their lives. The spark and the chemistry were obviously still there. All they knew for sure was they had to see each other again.

Obsessive Love

When Pluto transits your 5th House, you may find yourself romantically obsessed with someone who's not a good person to be in a relationship. You may notice yourself having an irrational urge to be with this person even though you know they're not right for you. You can't explain why, but like a moth to a flame, you're drawn to them. All you know is that your feelings are so intense you want to possess the person. The opposite is possible as well, where someone who's not right for you, nevertheless, is obsessed with wanting a relationship with you.

This unhealthy obsession played out with a new client, Douglas. He came for a consultation and said, "I finally got rid of an ex-girlfriend who has been hounding me. When I first started dating her, she gave me a copy of her astrology chart. I'd love to understand why she behaved as she did." He then proceeded to tell me the story of his relationship with her.

Douglas dated this woman for over a year, thinking that the relationship was getting serious. One night he proposed and his long time girlfriend politely said no. When he asked why, she explained that it was about money: she was wealthy and he wasn't. She told him it was fine to have a dating romance, but she had no intention of marrying a man who made so little money that one day, she feared, she'd have to support. Douglas felt deeply hurt to hear her words, but her response made him realize she was the wrong person for him to ever consider marrying. He quickly ended their relationship.

Four months later, he met the sweetest, most down-to-earth woman he had ever known. They were both crazy about each other from the start, sharing many of the same values, and both wanting to find a permanent relationship. His ex-girlfriend heard through a mutual friend that Douglas was now in a new relationship. She immediately contacted him, wanting to resume their relationship even suggesting she'd now consider marrying him. He said no and wished her well.

A few months later, when she heard that Douglas was getting married, she started calling him, leaving messages, pleading again for him to come back. In her last message she offered him one million dollars to return to their relationship.

After reviewing his ex-girlfriend's birth chart and her transits, I explained to Douglas that she was a very calculating and controlling person, only wanting a relationship with him on her terms. It was also clear she was highly manipulative, with her birth chart indicating she was especially possessive when it came to her money. Interestingly, her obsessive nature was magnified during the time they dated, because she also had Pluto transiting her 5th House.

Enjoy the Intensity

This house also rules self-expression, creativity, fun, amusement, leisure, recreation, theatre, and artistic pursuits. You may find this to be a wonderful time to be a self-confident performer who receives fame and recognition. Pluto's influence is likely to provide you with intense and powerful experiences in each of these areas. This is when you'll be attracted to deep, profound transformational experiences and activities, not superficial pursuits that scratch the surface of life.

Considerations, Actions, Decisions During Pluto in 5th House

1. Do you want to develop an artistic skill or talent you're passionate about?
2. What fun activities would provide you with a transformational experience?
3. Are there any obsessions in your life that block your self-expression or ability to enjoy a romance?

4. Do you want to have a deeply profound romantic relationship?
5. Do you want to have intense sex or a passionate love affair?
6. Do you use manipulation tactics to get your child to follow your directions?
7. Do you want to positively mold your child's behavior?

Transits to Use for Successful 5th House Decisions

You now understand the areas of life that are featured in your 5th House. We've discussed how each of the five transiting planets exerts its unique influence on the affairs of this House. This will help you better understand the changes you are experiencing, moods you're feeling, and the events taking place. Your awareness of this information may prompt you to:

> 1. *ACCEPT* the way things are and be content with what is going on in your life.
>
> 2. *CONSIDER* that you'd like to make some change, in which case you may evaluate your options and further contemplate your situation.
>
> 3. *DECIDE* that you're ready to make a change, take action, and make a decision pertaining to the affairs of this House.

If you make a decision, you'll want to learn how to pick the best transit to produce a successful outcome for it. Please know that the art of picking and interpreting transits requires very thorough analysis, normally done by a professional astrologer. Therefore, I've kept the discussion of selecting and using transits simple, for illustration purposes.

The key is to remember that each planet has the ability to bring a *different* positive quality of success to your decision. For example, *Jupiter's* effect may provide opportunities to expand and grow; *Saturn's* effect is more practical; *Uranus'* effect is sudden and exciting; *Neptune's* influence may bring you inspiration and idealism; *Pluto* may bring an intense and transformative effect for major change. This knowledge will help you understand how your decisions are affected by these planetary influences.

In the examples below, I chose a planetary transit to produce a favorable result for each individual's particular decision. This will help you see the many possibilities available to create the right outcome and make your 5th House decisions more successful.

Using a positive JUPITER Transit

DECISION: *I want to go gambling when I'm lucky and likely to win.*

Explanation: As we discussed earlier in the chapter, Hank wanted to go on gambling vacation when he would have good luck and win. We chose a transit from Jupiter to a planet in his birth chart that would bring good fortune to his week of gambling. Because his overall birth chart was not lucky for gambling, I urged him to be moderate and not try to break the casino bank.

* * *

Using a positive SATURN Transit

DECISION: *I want to find out why I have so much difficulty finding a romantic relationship.*

Explanation: We discussed earlier in the chapter Bettina's frustration at having so many experiences of short-term relationships that never seemed to work out. We used a Saturn transit in order for her to re-examine and re-evaluate whether or not her behavior or appearance restricted her ability to attract romance into her life. She agreed to attend a relationship workshop where she could meet with a large group of single people and discuss her dating experiences, attitudes and the issues that might be blocking her ability to attract a romance into her life. The Saturn transit would give her the ability to be realistic about herself, do a critical evaluation of her strengths and weaknesses, make changes where needed and bring them into reality.

* * *

Using a positive URANUS Transit

DECISION: *I'm divorced and finally ready to date again.*

Explanation: We discussed that after a 20-year marriage and a difficult divorce, Angela was ready to date again. We chose a Uranus transit because it would likely bring her exciting, liberating social experiences that would free her from old patterns she experienced in her prior relationship. It would likely give her the courage to be out and about, meeting men who were different from the one she had married.

* * *

Using a positive NEPTUNE Transit

DECISION: *I am excited about taking an acting class.*

Explanation: We discussed earlier in the chapter how Rosalind was ready to take acting lessons in the hopes of pursuing an acting role at a community theatre. We chose an excellent Neptune transit since it would be a great influence in helping her tap into her creative and artistic talents. The Neptunian energies of illusion and mystery would give her the ability to be a charming and beguiling actress who could assume the roles of different characters.

* * *

Using a positive PLUTO Transit

DECISION: *I want to take a tantric sex workshop with my wife that will transform our ability to be intimate.*

Explanation: We chose a Pluto transit because it brings energies that are profound and intense to the sexual union of two people.

Pluto's influence would allow for a merging of their spiritual and sexual energies. It would arouse their passions on a very intimate level, so that the workshop experience had the promise of deeply transforming their intimate relationship.

* * *

REMEMBER: You can use the FREE Transit Calculator that's discussed in Part IV of this book to go back in time to see which transits were occurring when a major event happened in your life. It might be a wonderful learning experience, especially since most transits repeat themselves over your lifetime. Also you can find out where your transits are today or in the future.

6th House

Health & Work

The 6th House of your birth chart rules your health, your working environment, and pets. If you want to know *what the hell is going on in your life*, all you have to do is look at the quality of health you're enjoying and the amount of happiness you experience at work. One more thing, do you have a pet in your life to love?

One of the greatest riches you can possess is great health. There's no better asset to have. Most people would agree that without good health, life can be miserable, a constant struggle where each day is filled with pain and discomfort. No amount of money or wealth can compensate for being in bad health, so please pay attention to this important House and its effect on you. Many of us grow up paying far too little attention to our diet and exercise regimen until it causes a problem, and by then, it may be too late. Have you ever said, "I'm so busy that I only had time to pick up a hamburger and fries at the local fast-food joint." Or, "It's hard to find time for exercise because I work such long hours."

There are people who find excuses for why they don't pay proper attention to their health. This House will give you clues as to why you're lucky enough to enjoy good health and physical wellness. Or, it may help you understand why your health is at risk, facing the potential for chronic problems. This area of your birth chart also concerns the protective measures you take to secure your health, such as diet and exercise. Look here to see if you're someone who's likely to be concerned about hygiene and the proper care of your body's health in order to accomplish your goals in life. This House gives insights as to whether you're the fastidious type who's likely to take two showers a day, insuring that you smell fresh and clean everywhere; or, if you're the type of person who's not concerned with personal hygiene, occasionally showers, considers deodorant optional, and uses cologne only for special occasions. Perhaps, you just enjoy just being *au natural*.

The 6th House also rules clothing, showing your penchant for neatness and a well-groomed appearance (or, lack of it). In this House you'll no doubt, see many opportunities to make important decisions for improving your health and sense of well-being.

Work is the other main domain of this House, which includes your day-to-day job, the people you work with, employment conditions, and your relations with your employer. Clearly, each of these elements can greatly affect your mental and physical health.

If you have employees working for you, whether in a corporation setting or as an entrepreneur, you can look to this House to see your affect on them as well as their affect on your health and well-being. This House also concerns dependents and anyone who provides service to you, from the person who cleans your house, to the service that mows your lawn, to the hairstylist whom you see every month.

Whereas the 10th House concerns your career, the 6th House focuses on your *job*. This area of your chart indicates a great deal about your attitude toward work and service. Look here to understand if you require a job that will put you in the spotlight or if you require an environment where you have low visibility, working in the background. Consult this area to learn whether you're likely to volunteer your time and service to others.

This House also rules domestic pets, small animals, and your attitude about them. It will indicate if you're a animal lover and likely to be a pet owner; and it will even suggest whether you'd be an ideal volunteer to work at an animal shelter or well suited to a career as a veterinarian.

Your Body in the 6th House

This house rules the bowels, colon, intestines, solar plexus and abdomen. Since there is nothing more important than your health, pay special attention to these areas of your body whenever a planet transits this House. It may indicate a period of time when you'll experience health benefits, issues or even problems you should be aware of. If you observe anything unusual, you'll have the opportunity to consult with a medical doctor or a health care practitioner.

What the Hell Is Going On in My Life?

Your 6th House Decisions

You now understand that the 6th House of your birth chart concerns your health, your day-to-day job, the people you work with, your employment conditions, and your relations with your employer; service providers and pets.

As you read about the description of this house, it's time to ask yourself a few questions. How is your health? Do you eat and exercise properly? If you don't, why don't you? Are you interested in having better health and making decisions that will help you achieve this? Do you like your job and the work you do? Do you like your co-workers and your employer? Does your job satisfy your need to be of service to others? If you're an employer, how do your employees feel about you? Are you happy about the working atmosphere you've created?

These are all significant questions and your answers may lead you to make important decisions to change your life. Here are a few examples of decisions clients have made based on the activities and issues of the 6th House.

Situation: Neil is having health problems because he's over-weight. Diabetes runs in his family and soon he'll have to take insulin unless he radically changes his diet and loses 40 to 50 lbs.

DECISION: *I want to find the best time to manage my diabetes, change my eating habits and lose weight.*

* * *

Situation: Ross enjoys his job but can't stand the company politics or the attitudes of the people in his department. His discontent is starting to affect his work, so he knows he needs to do something about his situation.

DECISION: *I want to find the best time to change my working environment.*

* * *

Situation: Betty has wanted a dog for years, but she knows that being a pet owner is a big responsibility.

6th House : Health & Work

DECISION: *I want to pick the best time to buy a dog that I'll enjoy having as a pet.*

* * *

Situation: Harriet has built her business into a large company. But she's concerned because there's no longer a spirit of cooperation among her employees, instead there seems to be a great deal of unhealthy competition and apathy. To grow her company to the next level, the work atmosphere must improve.

DECISION: *I want to find the best time to make employee changes that will create a productive atmosphere of teamwork in my company.*

* * *

During the transits of *Jupiter, Saturn, Uranus, Neptune,* and *Pluto* – Neil, Ross, Betty, and Harriet will have many opportunities to implement their decisions at a favorable time to produce the outcome they want.

The Transiting Planets Reveal Your Past, Present & Future

Your main focus is using astrology to understand *what the hell is going on in your life.* Once you do – this book will show you the best time to make a decision to change it, should you have a desire to do so. As you read about the five planets transiting the 6th House, notice the way each planet exerts its unique influence and effect, bringing specific opportunities, issues, problems, and events into this area of your life. But if you're curious as to how these planets are personally affecting YOU *today,* in your *past,* or in your *future,* you can find out where each transiting planet is in your birth chart by using the *FREE Transit Calculator* (see Part IV).

JUPITER in Your 6th House of Health & Work

Excellent Time for Healthcare

The 6th House rules your health. Jupiter's influence brings strength and vitality to your body, which makes this an excellent time for good health as well as improving your body's overall physical fitness through diet and some type of exercise regime. You can make use of this transit by signing up with a personal trainer to get special attention and set goals to get into better shape. It's also the ideal time to join some sort of exercise group whether it's a cyclist club or a yoga studio.

If you have bad eating habits or want to change your diet, this is the time to consult a dietician. For example, one client began feeling much better shortly after switching to a gluten-free diet. One cautionary note: Jupiter's influence can also produce weight gain, so it's important to pay attention to your diet and not over-indulge during this transit. So, if weight gain is an issue for you, you'll want to be especially vigilant this year.

If you have other habits that may adversely affect your health such as smoking, you can use this transit to successfully quit, once and for all. I encourage you to take advantage of this gift that can make you even healthier than you already are. If there's anything you've thought of doing to improve your health, now is the perfect time to do it. You can use this year to your advantage by discovering new ways to promote health for the rest of your life, not just for the year.

If you require medical care or advice, this is when you're likely to find highly skilled physicians and other health care professionals to provide beneficial assistance. Because Jupiter has a re-vitalizing and healing influence on the body, it's an excellent time to recover from an illness or to rehabilitate from an injury. For example, if you're planning elective surgery, use Jupiter's transit through your 6th House as the time to get it done.

This is why Joe decided to have his knee surgery during this time. He'd played football in college and injured his knee many times. Now he was in his 60s and his doctor said he needed a knee replacement, which made it important for him to find a specialist who could do a first class job. Joe's primary doctor referred him to an orthopedic surgeon who specialized in sports injuries and traumas, and performed surgeries for the players on many of the local sports teams. Joe met with this specialist and was confident he was in good hands. The doctor explained that Joe would be out of work for a period of time, but with physical therapy, his ability to walk, exercise, and even play golf would be greatly improved. Joe chose the year of this Jupiter transit to do his knee surgery. This is, yet, another practical example of how you can use astrology in your life to your benefit.

Great Time to Work

You'll find that work provides an enormous source of satisfaction because it gives you a sense of purpose and structure in your life. This is a time when you enthusiastically thrive on work and are interested in improving your performance. If someone in your company can show you how to be more technically competent on your computer or some other task, you'll seek that person out to help you. You're so jazzed you come to work early and leave late if that's what's necessary to produce results. You enjoy your working environment, achieving success in your job, while experiencing very little stress. Day-to-day responsibilities provide you with opportunities for growth and personal development. You're looking for new ways to advance in your job that could lead to greater responsibility or even a promotion.

This is the House of Fulfillment of Duty, so Jupiter's energies here give you a special desire to be of service to others. You may find yourself getting an urge to volunteer for a company fund-raising event in the community. You're ready to help other people because it makes you feel good to do so.

Great Time for a Promotion

It's possible you'll need advanced training or even be required to travel more to accomplish your tasks, which will make your work more gratifying. As you're driven to work to high standards of excellence, you'll notice how much more satisfying work becomes; and others will notice the great job you're doing as well. This is when someone at work taps you on the shoulder and says, "With your talent, we want you to manage this project for the company." This could be when you get a promotion with more challenging responsibilities, a salary increase, or just a general improvement in your working conditions as Glenda experienced.

Glenda joined a start-up company and was employee "No. 7." At that time her responsibilities were mostly administrative and at times secretarial. She did her work from a small cubicle, answering phones, typing reports, and often eating lunch at her desk. That was seven years ago. Since then, the company has gone public, and a prosperous future retirement has been assured, thanks to the many stock options she has been given over the years.

She now has a corner office at her company's headquarters, with a magnificent view overlooking a lake and the park. Glenda has been promoted frequently, each time to a more responsible executive position. In fact, during Jupiter's transit through her 6th House, Glenda received another promotion and a company car. She's extremely excited about the opportunity to manage the sales performance for six of the company's field offices.

Great Time to Find a Job or Hire People

With this Jupiter transit, you'll find yourself getting along with your co-workers, superiors and employees. You have a can-do attitude where you willingly cooperate with the people you work with, happy to assist them. Everyone seems to appreciate and acknowledge you for the excellent work you do. If you're job searching, it's a favorable time to seek new employment because Jupiter's positive influences bring you opportunity and recognition.

If you're a business owner or a supervisor at a company, this may be a time when you'll expand your operations and hire others to work for you. You'll accomplish this objective by seeking co-workers who operate at high standards of performance because you're interested in building a team of employees who can work effectively in a cooperative environment.

Fine Time to Choose a Pet

The 6th House also rules pets, which makes this an ideal time to acquire a pet if you've always wanted one. Or, if you have a pet, it's a good time to expand your activities with your pet. For example, my friend Lorna decided to enroll her puppy in an obedience training school. This is also an advantageous time for animals to be bred for positive results.

However, my favorite pet story for successfully using Jupiter's transit of the 6th House concerns the love of my life, Leslie. During a time I was extensively traveling, she asked if we could adopt a cat to keep her company. Since it was going to be her cat, I looked at her transit chart. I told her that her transits weren't favorable at that exact moment for finding a cat she'd be happy with. But, if she waited about two months, she'd have a very favorable transit to find the ideal cat she would love. She said great. Then, a few days later she said, "Why don't we just go to the San Francisco animal shelter and just look." I said that was fine with me as long as we only looked. We drove over to the facility to see all the cats that were available for adoption. Of course, we petted and played with lots of cats. Then, the inevitable happened. Leslie saw one that she really liked and said, "Larry, I just love this little kitty. Her name is Minnie. She seems timid and shy, but so lovely. I want her for my cat." I looked at her and said, "Before you make your final decision, I want to remind you that according to your personal transits, it's a bad time to choose a cat. But, of course, if you really want that cat, we'll get it." She said that she didn't care about the transits. So, we adopted Minnie.

Over the next 3 weeks, Minnie proceeded to hide under the bed and everywhere else. The cat wasn't just timid; she appeared to be very frightened. Minnie was not the least bit social, outgoing, or interested in being around us, despite all of Leslie's loving care and patience. Finally, with tears in her eyes, Leslie said, "It's been almost 3 weeks. I'm sorry, but I am not enjoying having this cat as my pet. I am the wrong owner for a cat with this personality. Can we, please take her back?" When we returned Minnie, the people at the animal shelter were very understanding, telling us that she hadn't been properly socialized prior to adoption, and should have been gone to a family with multiple cats.

We waited another 30 days for Leslie's positive transit to occur. On that anointed day, we drove to the animal shelter and looked at a number of cats. One caught my eye, a large, furry, friendly *Maine Coon* named Rocky. I showed him to Leslie and she fell in love with him immediately. We played with him for a while, seeing that he was outgoing, curious and unafraid. He really enjoyed being touched and petted. Each time Leslie put him down he jumped right back onto her lap to be petted some more. It was clear: he was the right cat at the "right time." We've had Rocky for seven years. He's a totally sweet, affectionate, people-cat. If it ever comes down to Rocky or me I could be playing second fiddle J.

TIP: Use a positive transit to your 6th House when picking the best time to choose a pet. Both you and your pet will be happy you did.

Considerations, Actions, Decisions During Jupiter in 6th House

1. Do you want to improve your health or complete an elective surgery?
2. Do you want to make healthy changes in your diet?
3. Do you want to begin a regular exercise program?
4. Are you interested in taking on more responsibilities in your work that would help you grow and develop your skills?
5. Let your employer know you'd like to be considered for promotion.
6. Establish more cooperation by becoming friendlier with your co-workers.
7. Do you want to change your working environment where there's more opportunity?
8. Do you want to upgrade and find even better service providers?
9. Are you interested in volunteering where you can be of service to others?
10. Do you want to buy a pet that you'll love?

6th House : Health & Work

SATURN in Your 6th House of Health & Work

Time to Evaluate Your Health

Saturn's influence in the 6th House requires you to pay serious attention to your health because during this period of your life, you'll be especially accountable and responsible for your health and appearance. I've had friends as well as clients who will talk about their sincere interest in addressing their health issues. They'll earnestly say, "Yes, I know I have to lose weight; quit smoking; stop drinking so much; have the doctor perform that operation; see the dentist about my teeth; or begin some daily exercise." Unfortunately, they may make those same statements year after year, never doing anything about them. Saturn brings "Judgment Day" to your health. When Saturn transits this House, any health issues you've ignored or not properly resolved can reach a crisis point where you may experience a breakdown or further deterioration of your body's functions.

The influence of Saturn is often a time of a health crisis, making you face problems you've ignored. It can also be a time when you'll discover a hidden health issue. Saturn's purpose is to put you in a position where you're forced to confront these health issues and resolve them or pay the consequences of not doing so.

Big Al worked as a waiter in an Italian restaurant. Over recent years, he paid little attention to his eating habits, slowly gaining weight. He was now 60 pounds overweight. Obesity ran in the family with his father and older brother also very large, both dying of a heart attack while in their late 40s. Big Al was now 47. At his annual physical check-up, his doctor informed him if he didn't lose weight through a healthy diet and exercise, he would likely suffer a heart attack like his father and brother, and be known as "Dead Al." With Saturn in his 6th House, he decided that now was the time to finally confront his unhealthy life style before it was too late.

It should be stressed that when Saturn transits your 6th House you may not encounter a *major* health crisis – it might be just a minor one, but nevertheless important. When I was in my 20s I rarely saw the dentist other than for a major problem like a cavity. Like many people,

I hated the experience of visiting the dentist. One day a friend pointed out that my teeth were stained. That poke at my vanity was all it took for me see the dentist and begin a program of coming in for regular exams and teeth-cleaning twice a year. My Saturn transit brought me a test (a friend who kindly pointed out a health problem) allowing me to "re-evaluate" what I was going to do about it? I realized that it was time for me to accept the responsibility for giving my teeth better care. Keep in mind, I could have "failed" the test by ignoring my friend's comment. That's how Saturn *tests* you, giving you the opportunity to resolve a problem for your benefit. By the way: 40 years later, thanks to my commitment to dental health, I've been blessed with healthy teeth.

If you do experience health problems, make sure to re-evaluate your life style, diet and exercise regimen. Next, make necessary changes that will help you become a healthier person in the years ahead. The good news is: if you do strive to improve your health during Saturn's transit through your 6th House, you have the opportunity to rehabilitate and transform your physical well-being. Fortunately, Saturn brings you the pay-off you deserve, so if you work hard to improve your health, you'll be rewarded.

Test and Lessons at Work

Saturn's transit here will affect you in your work life, too. This will be a time of tests and lessons in your daily job, where you may feel overwhelmed with considerable responsibility. No matter how much energy you expend, it doesn't seem to be enough. Expect that Saturn's influence will result in your having to work harder than normal, requiring you to be more organized and find more efficient methods to accomplish your goals. "Necessity is the mother of invention." So, if you have much to do, Saturn's message is to come up with more innovative ways of accomplishing your tasks.

There Are Heavy Demands at Work

Another source of difficulty under this transit may be that your employer makes heavy demands on you; and when you work hard to meet these demands, you may find you're not recognized, appreciated or even paid for your extra efforts.

This was the dilemma Gwendolyn faced in her company. The company was in bad financial shape and fighting to stay solvent. Sales were way down and her employer had laid off a number of factory workers and office staff. Now, the remaining supervisors, like her, were being asked to work longer hours for no additional pay. The president told Gwendolyn that the company was in survival mode. He went on to say that all supervisors and management would have to take a 15 percent pay cut, effective that week. Even though she was grateful to still have a job, it was depressing news to hear. This happened in her life as Saturn transited her 6th House.

There May Be Restrictions at Work

You may also find that your work is restrictive and unfulfilling, which may result in your wanting to quit in order to find work that is more satisfying. To understand *what the hell is happening in your work life*, you must accept that Saturn's influence is here to teach you something even though the lesson may not be pleasant. During these two and a half years your abilities at work will be tested. How good are you at your job? Have you gotten into a rut or routine? Have you stopped learning or being creative? Are you as well organized, as you should be? Or, have you taken on too much responsibility? These are the questions you must answer for yourself.

You may realize that you need to refine your skills and talents, and re-evaluate the way you do your job. You may find that your job is difficult because you aren't prepared, lack a necessary skill, or the right plan. Use this time to critically review your work and ability to do it well. Make sure you're prepared, should you be tested during this time. This transit is imploring you to improve your abilities, let go of any unproductive work methods, make any necessary changes that will help you improve, and perform your job more effectively.

Take Dan's experience. He used to have lots of freedom to do home alarm installations for his company until a new manager, Tim, took over the department. Tim is a perfectionist and thinks the installation work can be done better. He insists on checking every one of Dan's installations. This frustrates Dan, slows down his workday and makes it even longer. As a result, Dan is feeling angry and restricted by Tim's constant scrutiny.

Don't try to avoid these lessons by quitting a challenging job and taking another, because you may find yourself experiencing the same limitations and restrictions in your new one. Saturn's influence does not bring immediate gratification for your efforts. However, if you stick it out over the long run, your hard work will be acknowledged and rewarded in some beneficial way such as a promotion, higher compensation, or both.

Think of Saturn as the strict disciplined teacher you once had in school. You didn't always appreciate her methods at the time, but as you grew up – you were always grateful she was your teacher. Remember: "the teacher can only teach, when the student is ready to listen." Saturn's transit through the 6th House brings you tests and lessons in your health and work. If you learn them well, it's good to know that your hard work and efforts to improve yourself will bring you rewards for years to come.

Considerations, Actions, Decisions During Saturn in 6th House

1. Are you experiencing any health problems that are threatening your health or limiting you in some way?
2. Do you want to make a long-term commitment to improve your health?
3. Do you want to change your diet to one that's much healthier?
4. Do you want to do more rigorous exercise?
5. Are you experiencing any restrictions or limitations at work?
6. Do you want to make any constructive changes in your working environment?
7. Would learning a new skill or taking a class make you more effective in your job?
8. Are you ready to make a serious commitment to volunteering?

URANUS in Your 6th House of Health & Work

Revolutionize Your Health

When Uranus transits your 6th House of health it brings with it the same unpredictability it does in other Houses. The negative manifestation of Uranus' energies occur if you consciously ignore any tension or upset that's happening in your life when it transits here. In that case, you may experience a health problem such as a nervous condition, depression, a sudden accident, or problems with some part of your body, such as your heart.

However, Uranus energies can also positively benefit your health by causing you to be interested in experimenting with a new exercise regimen that will lead to greater physical fitness. Or, you may make the discovery that eating healthier foods and making dietary changes will improve your overall health. This is a time when you may gain many valuable insights on how to rejuvenate your body that you'll be excited to try. Uranus' influence makes you receptive to all sorts of new and unconventional approaches to health and exercise.

Here are some new health regimens that clients have tried during the Uranus' transit: Going on a seven-day juice fast to rid the body of toxins; joining a weight loss center to stop insulin dependency for diabetes; enjoying the aerobic benefits of belly dancing; adopting a no carb diet; joining a kick-box class to improve stamina; changing to a gluten free diet to help manage celiac disease; and getting a colonic for colon health.

Free Your Self From Normal Routines – Try Something New

Uranus in the 6th House brings newness and excitement to the work you're doing. It's a perfect time if you've ever said, "I'm ready for a new challenge. Give me something to do I've never done before." You're totally receptive to taking risks and stepping out of any conventional box you've been in. You start sensing all the potential possibilities for improving yourself at work. This may lead you to discover new ideas and create innovative methods to make your work more exciting. You may have a brilliant idea or a new solution and now you're ready to bring it forward at work and show others what you've discovered. A big part of your motivation is that you want to free yourself from the normal, routine way of doing things. You're seeking to eliminate those parts of your job that you consider to be dull or boring, which will inspire you to try innovative approaches rather than continuing with the traditional ways you've always done your work.

You may find yourself rebelling against having to follow conventional methods. Uranus' influence gives you a desire for freedom, independence, and radical change as well as a disdain for regulations, restrictions or any kind of limitation. Your very soul is crying out: "Please, free me from my normal day to day work!"

Recognize that this is a period in your work life when you want to be creative, excited and stimulated in the way you do your work. This feeling is so strong in you that if you're not getting this need met, you may find yourself becoming irritated and even defiant. The less you're able to create liberating changes for yourself at work, the more likely you'll feel upset and tense. No matter how successful you've been at accepting the status quo, you won't be able to any longer. If you start feeling restless and discontented in your job, you are feeling Uranus' influence at work in your life.

Be warned you may have such a deep need for change that your frustration and dissatisfaction may motivate you to seek work opportunities that bring you freedom from any situation that has been too restrictive. As a result, you may just quit a job that has made excessive demands on you or that you've found to be totally unfulfilling.

Uranus' energies at this time tend to be upsetting and disruptive. So, expect to feel tension and anxiousness during this transit. It may feel like some "powerful force" has taken hold of you. Even though you may not be happy about having to make a change, you'll feel compelled to do so. Under this transit I've known people who, one day, packed up the things from their office, walked out and never returned to their job again. What's happening is that you're now ready to make a radical change and seek work that offers you freedom from your previous responsibilities and obligations.

One client had been a sales rep, selling medical supplies for the past 10 years. She was tired of traveling every week, hopping on a plane, renting a car, and visiting customers in a 12 state region. The job used to be fun and exciting, especially since she was highly paid and lived a first class life on the road. But for the past year she'd grown to hate the same grind and routine. It was getting difficult to wake up, get dressed, drive to the airport and spend so much of her life away from her home. She was so ready to quit that she wrote her letter of resignation on a Friday and had an overnight courier deliver it Monday morning to her company. There was no question in her mind she had to leave her job.

Take This Job and "Shove It!"

The energy of Uranus can be upsetting to the point where you want revolt and make an immediate change from the work you're doing or the job itself. Nevertheless, your desire to rebel and make a sudden change may not be in your best interest. So, if you start feeling like you can no longer tolerate your current situation, don't make an impulsive change. Instead, make a constructive plan to look for a new job that brings you the freedom and excitement you desire.

However, the worse thing you can do when a Uranus transit comes into your life is to repress the tension and upset you're feeling. You may find yourself doing just that if you feel trapped in your current work situation, with no way to escape and make a necessary change. It's best not to deny how upset you are, continuing as if everything is normal – when it isn't. When Uranus' energies are ignored on a conscious level, they manifest on a physical level, often causing a problem that "forces" you to change your work routine, duties, or even change your job. In other words, if you *don't* make the required changes to your life, something unexpected is likely to happen, compelling you to make needed changes. Uranus' energies can express themselves in your life by an unforeseen event occurring – a sudden health problem, accident, or just verbally "exploding."

Chris' boss Gene was bigot, constantly making racist statements and using racial slurs. Chris just turned away when these tirades began and tried to ignore what he was hearing. But he felt guilty about not protesting when Gene made his foul comments and wondered if his silence made Gene think he felt the same way about minorities. Maybe that was the reason why Gene gave him the most favorable work assignments, always addressing Chris in a familiar way, "Hey Chris, buddy."

After two years of hearing Gene rant about how the entire country was going to hell because of all those "free-loading" immigrants and the rest of "them bastards," Chris had enough. Just as Gene started to complain, Chris cut him off and said, "Gene...just shut your big mouth! I can't stand working for you any more. I don't care how much money you pay me. I can't work for you anymore. I quit!" With that, he stormed out of Gene's office for good.

If Chris had not bottled up his anger and exploded in the heat of the moment, he might have been able to sit down with Gene and calmly explained why he was uncomfortable with Gene's remarks about minorities, asking him not to make them in his presence, perhaps saving his job. Unfortunately, with Uranian energy, often an explosion creates an abrupt break. This is another reason not to ignore the tensions and upsets you're experiencing, foolishly believing you can control them, because you may not be able to.

TIP: When you feel the effects of Uranus try to react like a pressure cooker with a *gauge* that lets out the steam to prevent an explosion – rather than a stick of dynamite with a short fuse.

The lesson of Uranus transiting your 6th House is to bring revolution and liberating change to your health and your work. Now you can free yourself from routines and patterns that have become dull or boring that have restricted or even oppressed you. Allow yourself to find new ways of experiencing the work you do. If you've been doing the same work for many years and wanting to break out and do something totally different, heed Uranus' invitation to make a change.

This transit is also a fabulous opportunity to make exciting and innovative changes in your health and diet. At this time, you'll be open to new ways of becoming a healthier person.

Considerations, Actions, Decisions During Jupiter in 6th House

1. Are you ready to experiment and try some new ways to improve your health?
2. Do you want to revolutionize your diet by removing foods that are unhealthy?
3. What type of exercise would you find exciting to engage in?
4. Do you need a more stimulating working environment?
5. Do you want to find a new job that will be more exciting?

6. Do you have any ideas for innovative projects that would be more exciting to do at work?
7. Is there some new way you can be service to others?
8. Do you want to buy an exciting and unique pet?

NEPTUNE in Your 6th House of Health & Work

A Time to Find Work Where You're of Service

Your ambitions are altruistic and not motivated just to profit yourself or your business. No matter how driven you were to work for your own personal gain, now you want work that will allow you to make a difference in people's lives, otherwise, you'll feel frustrated, discouraged and unrewarded for your efforts. In order to accomplish your goals it's important for you to balance your desire for selfless service with the practical need to remain grounded and produce results in your work.

The energies of Neptune may cause you to discover that the real purpose of your work is to serve others. Doing so may be a labor of love that will bring you joy and contentment you've never felt before. During this transit, I've had clients realize that working in the corporate world was too materialistic and unfulfilling. They preferred a job in social service or working for a non-profit organization where their efforts could be focused on applying what they'd learned in the past for the benefit of the community or society. Some people express their need to be of service by volunteering their time outside of their regular job.

Your Work Attitude & Motivation May Change

When Neptune transits your 6th House you may notice a difference in your attitude toward the type of work you want to do. You're extremely intuitive and perceptive, having the ability to make your creative visions a reality. If your goal is to improve yourself and others by diligently acting on your vision, this can be a time of great accomplishment. If your work supports your ideals, you'll labor unselfishly and relentlessly to achieve your ambition. What you do for work matters at this time; it has to really inspire you. Neptune's influence is selfless, altruistic and geared toward working to help others.

It's an excellent time for achievement if you're working in service of others, which means the harder you work to help others, the more success you receive from your effort. But it's not a time geared toward self-focused or egotistical drives where you work solely for you own advancement. In fact, Neptune's energies are focused on benefitting the masses, not the individual. Remember, "It's no longer just about you – it's now about others." For that reason this may not be the best time to advance your own career aspirations if your goals are focused only on your own personal interests.

Brenda was working for a tech company as a creative software developer where she made lots of money creating her award-winning video games for kids. It was a fun job, but she noticed that so many of the games she was asked to design were centered on the theme of young kids embroiled in on-screen video battles, "killing the opposition." She started feeling guilty, wondering if she was wasting her talents, to no benefit to society, other than increasing her company's quarterly profits.

Then one day, a friend of hers, Lou Ann who worked for a children's non-profit organization, asked her if she would volunteer to design a fun educational game to improve the reading skills of children. Brenda told Lou Ann she'd try to come up with some creative ideas. Over the weekend, Brenda fantasized creating an amazing game that would make it fun for kids to learn. She was totally inspired and came up with a unique game idea that would engage children's reading ability, while increasing their comprehension skills.

Within 90 days, using her spare time, along with the help of a few volunteers from her company, she came up with a prototype of a brilliant game concept that might excite kids to want to read. Over the next six months, Brenda used her weekends, working diligently on the implementation of her reading video game. She was so excited about the opportunity to do something worthwhile with her talents that she didn't think twice, when Lou Ann said, "The executive director of our non-profit wants to meet with you to see if you'll come over here and work full-time with us. Of course, we can't match your salary, but we can pay you in a lot of satisfaction." That's how Brenda decided to make a difference with her work. Her experience is a perfect example of how Neptune's transit here, can bring a person creative work that allows them to be of service.

Be Aware of Deception

The negative manifestation of Neptune can result in misunderstandings, confusion and even the deception with others. During its transit through your 6th House of work, be careful how you communicate with co-workers, employers or employees because you may encounter unusual difficulties and even deception in your interactions with them. Odd circumstances or conditions may occur that lead to your dissatisfaction or disappointment. For example, you may find that a promotional opportunity you deserve is being withheld for no apparent reason. Ultimately, it could be because you have a hidden enemy who's working against your interests, even though you have no idea who it is – as was the case for Phil.

Phil wanted to return to his old company where he'd been their No. #1 salesman. In fact, he was told if he ever wanted to return, there would always be a place for a "top-producer" like him. Despite leaving the company on good terms two years ago, he can't understand why they won't re-hire him now. He may never know that one of the company's new board members worked with Phil years ago and has a petty grudge against him. As a result, the board member has blocked his return to the company. The person Phil has been in contact with would love to hire him back, but has been told to give Phil the excuse that "right now, we aren't hiring any new sales people."

One of the best ways of countering any of the negative influences of Neptune in the 6th House is to be sensitive to your work environment and trust your intuition. If something does not seem right in your work experiences or relationships, dig deeper to discover any unusual problems that might be blocking your ambitions. In Phil's case, had he done more research, he would have found out that the executive board now included an adversary of his. That might have helped him understand why his re-hiring was blocked. He could have even arranged for a meeting with his adversary to see if their relationship could be repaired.

Neptune rules deceit and deception as discussed in Phil's experience. Most often, you'll have to be sensitive that others aren't deceiving you. However, be careful during this transit not to deceive others, even inadvertently. Make sure that the work you're doing is totally honest and scrupulous, with no dishonest practices going on at work that you may be unaware of. Also, remember, Neptune influences are most positive if the work you're doing is of genuine service to others with the focus on what you can do for them – not what they can do for you.

Pay Attention to What You Put into Your Body

This is a time when you must be very careful of your health, since your body is more apt to contract illness or infections than usual. Of course, if

6th House : Health & Work

your health is normally good, you're less likely to suffer from this influence of Neptune. However, you should still be especially careful of diseases caused by germs, viruses, toxins and poisons. The strange way they may come into your life was illustrated in Jenny's case.

Jenny was a nurse at a hospital, normally very careful when giving injections to patients and disposing the syringes in the sharps container. However, she was feeling tired and overworked at the end of her shift. After giving an HIV patient an injection, she fumbled the syringe and got a needle-stick in her forearm, puncturing the skin. Jennifer panicked as she realized she'd have to undergo testing and continual monitoring to determine if she contracted the virus and needed subsequent treatment.

During Neptune's transit here, your body may be vulnerable to mysterious and unusual health problems that you wouldn't normally encounter. I found this out first hand when I was a graduate student and contracted a mysterious virus that forced me to be hospitalized. I was sick for three weeks with symptoms much like malaria, even though I had never been in a jungle or any of the locales where one typically contracted malaria. The doctors were puzzled and despite many tests and prognostications, the medical staff in the hospital could not diagnose my virus. Eventually, I got better, even though no one was sure why, and was discharged. I'll never forget that strange health experience when Neptune transited through my 6th House.

Under the influence of this transit, be vigilant about your health, aware that illnesses can develop slowly and be difficult to diagnose as in my experience. Avoid the stress and strain of over-working, because it's easy to lower your immune system when you feel fatigued. Be careful also of a fad or strange diet concerning your nutrition during this time. Some people have such disdain and distrust of modern medicine that they're quick to accept treatments that sound holistic, often endorsed only by individuals without licensed medical credentials. When it comes to your health and your body, before accepting any unusual treatments, drugs or supplements, research and consult with licensed medical authorities.

While you may find a new diet can be helpful, it's just as likely that you'll find one that will cause ill effects that will not be of benefit to your body. Drugs and alcohol have a very bad effect on your body during these years; therefore, be moderate or avoid their use altogether.

During the time that Neptune transits here, your work and health will strongly be affected. In its positive manifestation this is period in your life when you'll feel inspired, idealistic, with your sense of imagination and vision heightened. You'll have the potential to tap into your imagination and fantasy as if you were in a wonderful Disney movie.

Considerations, Actions, Decisions During Neptune In 6th House

1. Are you inspired to improve you overall health?
2. Check out any illnesses that seem odd and cannot be easily diagnosed.
3. Do you want to remove any unhealthy or toxic foods from your diet?
4. Are you interested in meditation or yoga?
5. Do you want to do work where you can be of greater service to others?
6. Are their any hidden enemies you should be aware of?
7. Is their anything strange going on at work that suggests a problem for you?

PLUTO in Your 6th House of Health & Work

Transform Your Career

Pluto transiting your 6th House brings great changes to your work, perhaps a job or even a career change. At the very least, you may find that your responsibilities or duties radically change during this period. Keep in mind that with the long length of a Pluto transit, change may actually occur over many years. But when the transit is complete you'll realize you've experienced a major shift in the work you're doing. This is an excellent time for you to develop your organizational abilities, be involved in work where you research, analyze and investigate; or have a job working on projects where you improve or actually re-build something.

Marcy had been a paralegal secretary for 10 years and enjoyed many aspects of her job. The attorneys she worked for had been extremely impressed with her writing skills, grasp of legal proceedings and research abilities. As a result they continued to give her more and more responsibilities, as she prepared the filings and legal briefs for their review and editing. That gave her the idea of how she might turn herself from a moth to a butterfly – by going from a paralegal to becoming an attorney. All the attorneys at her firm thought she'd make an excellent lawyer and totally supported her decision. So, six years ago, as Pluto transited her 6th House, she enrolled in night school to get her law degree and become an attorney. She recently completed law school and obtained her JD degree. She's now enrolled in a bar study course, preparing to take the bar exam and officially become an attorney.

Be Aware of Power Struggles

During this time, whether by choice or circumstances, your work and your relationships with others become more intense and serious. You may be deeply engrossed in whatever you're doing, as if you were a dedicated scientist obsessed with finding the cure for a dreaded disease that will save humanity from great suffering. You bring a high level of concentration and focus to the work you're engaged in. Pluto's influence can give you penetrating insights as well as the ability to make critical judgments about people you work with. You feel plugged into people's psyches and motivations. This can be a great asset for you as long as you are tactful when sharing your observations. If you're diplomatic in sharing your views, people will be astounded by your insights. However, if your tendency is to be blunt and insensitive, you'll create tensions in your relationships at work, especially with those in authority. We all know people who make rude or hurtful remarks, excusing themselves by saying, "Well, I was just being honest." Thus, they create conflict and upset in their working environment because they didn't tell their "truth" in a sensitive or kind way.

Be mindful of the fact that Pluto's influence may cause you to be compulsive or controlling in your working environment. So, it's important to be aware of potential strains in relationships between you and others that may escalate into ego clashes or power struggles, especially with your boss. If you're locked in such relationships, you may find it necessary to change jobs or others may decide for you.

Marshall was a brilliant scientist who did a great deal of cutting-edge research. However, he was egotistical and thoughtless in the way he communicated with many of his colleagues and superiors, constantly embroiled in arguments. As a result, his boss, Theo ended up having to mend wounds and apologize to co-workers for Marshall's aggressive communications style – often to Theo's annoyance. Marshall's relationship with Theo had always been strained, as they'd never gotten along very well. The only reason Theo tolerated Marshall was because he was such a brilliant scientist. However, there was a limit to how long Theo was willing to put up with Marshall's inappropriate and alienating behavior.

The last straw occurred at their departmental meeting when all the scientists met to discuss their research findings and budget requests for the next year. Marshall continually interrupted and contradicted Theo, often embarrassing him in front of the group. When the meeting was over Theo decided to meet with Marshall to explain he would no longer tolerate his insubordinate behavior. Either Marshall changed his behavior immediately or he would be terminated.

Great Time for Transformation

Pluto's energies pertain to work that involves regeneration, restoration and transformation, which makes it a helpful influence for you if you've a job

6th House : Health & Work

where you fix, repair and restore physical objects; or do work that involves transforming the mind, such as psychology or some form of psychotherapy; or even repair broken down buildings that need total restoration.

A client, Douglas bought an old farm with many old and unused sheds that were used to harvest, process and store crops. He's often thought that if he renovated them he could expand his business and secure new contracts with local processing plants. After looking at his transits, we agreed that the perfect time to do that work was occurring when Pluto transited his 6th House.

Transform Your Health

When Pluto transits your 6th House, you have to be very careful of any health or physical problems you encounter during this period of your life. There's the potential of your having new problems you'll discover at this time, as well as having to confront chronic health problems you've lived with for years. During this Pluto transit, you'll no longer be able to ignore these issues. If you do ignore your health needs at this time, you're in danger of having a complete physical breakdown. Even if your health has been, generally very good, use this time to gain greater control over your body by adopting a healthy life style through preventative medical attention and check-ups.

On the positive side, Pluto's transit here is an opportunity to transform your health. By paying attention and addressing any health problems, you can physically regenerate and rejuvenate your body to a healthy state, thus avoiding a physical breakdown. Consider starting an exercise or diet program to re-build your body and restore physical fitness, no matter what condition you're in. This is the perfect time to improve and transform all elements involved with increasing your body's vitality and health. The transformational power of Pluto in this House has helped people who weighed 300 pounds lose 100 pounds; become vegetarians; wean themselves off of insulin required by their diabetes; or go from drug-user to drug-free.

Claudia has myopia and has had trouble seeing for years. She has been putting off laser eye surgery to correct her shortsightedness, for years. Her doctor has recommended she have a LASIK procedure done to correct this problem. Pluto's transit through this House gives her the perfect opportunity to undergo a successful surgery and correct her eyesight once and for all.

Considerations, Actions, Decisions During Pluto in 6th House

1. Do you want to transform your health by making major changes?
2. Do you want to undergo a surgery that will restore your body?
3. Do you want to make a major change to your diet and eating habits?
4. Do you want to begin a restorative exercise program?
5. Are you interested in changing your working environment?
6. Do you want to make a significant change in your job or career?
7. Do you need to change your behavior towards co-workers in any way?
8. Do you want to volunteer for a service that will help transform and heal others?

6th House : Health & Work

Transits to Use for Successful 6th House Decisions

You now understand the areas of life that are featured in your 6th House. We've discussed how each of the five transiting planets exerts its unique influence on the affairs of this House. This will help you better understand the changes you are experiencing, moods you're feeling, and the events taking place. Your awareness of this information may prompt you to:

1. *ACCEPT* the way things are and be content with what is going on in your life.

2. *CONSIDER* that you'd like to make some change, in which case you may evaluate your options and further contemplate your situation.

3. *DECIDE* that you're ready to make a change, take action, and make a decision pertaining to the affairs of this House.

If you make a decision, you'll want to learn how to pick the best transit to produce a successful outcome for it. Please know that the art of picking and interpreting transits requires very thorough analysis, normally done by a professional astrologer. Therefore, I've kept the discussion of selecting and using transits simple, for illustration purposes.

The key is to remember that each planet has the ability to bring a *different* positive quality of success to your decision. For example, *Jupiter's* effect may provide opportunities to expand and grow; *Saturn's* effect is more practical; *Uranus'* effect is sudden and exciting; *Neptune's* influence may bring you inspiration and idealism; *Pluto* may bring an intense and transformative effect for major change. This knowledge will help you understand how your decisions are affected by these planetary influences.

In the examples below, I chose a planetary transit to produce a favorable result for each individual's particular decision. This will help you see the many possibilities available to create the right outcome and make your 6th House decisions more successful.

Using a positive JUPITER Transit

DECISION: *I want to buy a dog that I will enjoy having as a pet.*

Explanation: Betty wanted to pick the best time to buy a dog that she'd enjoy having as a pet-owner. We chose a transit from Jupiter to a planet in her birth chart that would bring her good fortune in finding a loving and affectionate dog. The benefits of Jupiter would likely result in this dog being smart and friendly. This would also be a favorable time to trust that she was making a good decision for the future.

* * *

Using a positive SATURN Transit

DECISION: *I want to choose the best time to manage my diabetic health problem.*

Explanation: We discussed that Neil was having health problems because he was almost 50 pounds over-weight. His weight issue needed to be addressed so he could more effectively manage his diabetes, so we chose a Saturn transit because it brought seriousness to his goal. He planned to go to a weight-reduction clinic that specialized in working with diabetics, and also providing a full medical analysis on how to improve his condition. This transit provided him with discipline and a sense of commitment. It was also a favorable time to re-shape and re-structure his body for long-term health improvement.

* * *

6th House : Health & Work

Using a positive URANUS Transit

DECISION: *I want to find the best time for me to change my working environment.*

Explanation: As we discuss earlier in the Chapter, Ross couldn't stand the company politics or the attitudes of the people in his department. He knew he needed to make a change because his dissatisfaction was starting to affect his work. We used a Uranus transit for him to look for a new job that was innovative and very different from the routine work he'd been doing. The influence of Uranus would likely bring him a non-traditional work environment where people were independent and free of organizational politics that had bogged him down. His new work would be exciting and liberating.

* * *

Using a positive NEPTUNE Transit

DECISION: *I want to make employee changes that will create a productive atmosphere of teamwork in my company.*

Explanation: We discussed Harriet's interest in growing her company in an atmosphere of positive teamwork where everyone worked together for a common goal. She wanted to hire people and make employee changes during a time when this atmosphere could be created. We chose a Neptune transit, since under this influence she would be effective at creating an environment where employees worked for the common good of all – not just for their own personal benefit. The energies of Neptune would help her instill qualities of idealism, compassion, inspiration and faith – all helpful to her employees working harmoniously in a team atmosphere.

Using a positive PLUTO Transit

DECISION: *I want to pick the best time to have cosmetic surgery.*

Explanation: Rosalind had bad acne scars on her face, left over from her teen years, which made her feel self-conscious. We used a Pluto transit since it was ideal for doing a surgery that would transform and re-make her body on a deep, profound level. Another influence of the transit would be to enhance the beauty of her face and skin in a restorative manner. It was also a time favored for her surgeon to produce skillful results in her procedure.

* * *

REMEMBER: You can use the FREE Transit Calculator that's discussed in Part IV of this book to go back in time to see which transits were occurring when a major event happened in your life. It might be a wonderful learning experience, especially since most transits repeat themselves over your lifetime. Also you can find out where your transits are today or in the future.

7th House

Relationships, Marriage & Partnerships

In my 35 years as an astrologer, the question I am asked most often is, "Larry, when will I meet someone for marriage?" Look no further – this is the House that holds the answer to that question. It may also hold the answer to, "How long will I stay married?" This is the House of intimate partnerships such as marriage, where there's a deep commitment of love between two people.

Understandably, most everyone is curious about knowing more about their partner (or who you might be their ideal partner). When I do a personality analysis for clients who are single, they'll often ask, "Can you describe the characteristics of the man (or woman), I would want to marry?" Well, this is the house of your birth chart that will answer that question and give you insights as to the needs you'll have within that relationship. Often a person is attracted to someone who just does not satisfy their needs. Have you ever heard a friend say, "He's so brilliant, but I need someone who wants to have more fun," or "She's gorgeous, but I am so bored in her company. I need someone more intellectual," or "I like so many of his qualities, but I really need someone who can express what he's feeling inside, emotionally." So, it's important to get a firm fix on not only the qualities that are attractive to you, but also the ones you *need* in a partner. They may not be the same.

This House foretells the unique "identity" of your relationship, based on the merging of your personality and character with the other person's, to produce a new entity known as a partnership. As in: The two of you "make wonderful music together." You've probably heard someone exclaim, "They make a lovely couple." That person is noticing the special qualities two people exude when they're together as a couple. Let's face it – your partner can have a dramatic affect on you, for better or worse. Thus, this House raises a serious question: Who do you *become* when you're in close partnership? After all, there are partners who bring out our best and our worst sides. This House will raise serious questions about you and your relationship (or lack of one) and shed a bright light on *what the hell is going on in your life?*

The seventh House of your Horoscope is known as the House of relationships, marriage as well as divorce. It also pertains to other partnerships such as business, legal, personal, as well as contractual relationships (e.g., attorneys, accountants, doctors and professional consultants). This is the place to look if you've ever asked yourself if you were the type of person who's well suited for business partnership; or wondered if you were better off working alone and independently.

This area of your chart rules contracts, business agreements, lawsuits, court trials, open enemies, war and peace. This House gives you a better understanding of your behavior in close personal relationships with people in the public.

On a broader basis, this area of your chart indicates how you'll express yourself in relationships, especially in committed relationships. Will you become more assertive, aggressive or timid; or, perhaps, you'll become more confident and forthright because your relationship makes you so secure.

This House can show the kind of business partner you're likely to be and the unique qualities you'll seek in a business or professional partnership. Do you need to be the "alpha dog," desiring a partner you can dominate? Or, do you need a thoughtful, cautious partner who can restrain your impulsive tendencies? This area of your birth chart can provide you with an understanding of whether or not being in partnership is compatible with your needs.

Why Do Partnerships Fail?

KEY POINT: *Personality incompatibility* is one of the main reasons that marriage partnerships (or business partnerships) fail. Prospective partners have different personalities, values and needs, and when they clash it can lead to failure. Before entering a serious partnership two people must analyze if they are truly compatible for a long-term relationship. They must avoid the crucial mistake of underestimating their relationships needs.

7th House : Relationships, Marriage & Partnerships

Let's face it, when you're 22, you have simpler and less "re-fined" needs than you have at 32, 42, 52, or 62. As you mature and accept more responsibilities your relationship needs grow and change as well. That means that the qualities that attracted you to a partner at 22 might not be satisfying enough for you 10 or 20 years later. So, it becomes necessary to dig under the facade of each person's personality to see if there's true compatibility. After all, every couple starts out saying the same words: "We love each other." However, can they live with each other? As the great soul singer, Tina Turner exclaimed in her poignant song: *"What's love got to do with it?"*

We've come a long way in the evolution of how marriage partners are matched for long-term relationships. It wasn't that many generations ago when parents arranged a marriage based on religious, social, economic, or political considerations. (Obviously, it's still done that way in certain countries.) For many years, parents preached that marriage success was based on two people having, for example, religion in common, "Have I got a nice Jewish girl for you!" or social compatibility, "Where do his people come from?" or, financial status, "Darling, this young man you want to marry has no wealth to take care of you." Eventually, most people started making their own decisions about whom they wanted to marry (or live with), independent of parental pressure

Here we are today, with relationship connections being made in many unorthodox ways. You can look for a mate "online" by joining a whole variety of Internet dating web sites. You can even find a mail-order bride by looking at pictorial ads of available mates, then flying to a foreign country to meet your future spouse. Additionally, there are the many services offering to match you with a *love connection*, using personality profiles and compatible tests, which they say will improve your odds of finding an ideal partner for a long-term relationship.

The Secret to Finding a Compatible Relationship

Using astrology for *matchmaking* is an extremely accurate analysis technique for determining long-term relationship compatibility. If you're seriously considering marriage – comparing your birth chart with a potential partner helps determine whether you're likely to have a successful relationship (or business partnership). It reveals the likelihood of your relationship being a harmonious, day-to-day living experience. It shows how well you'll communicate, feel an emotional connection, find domestic living comfortable or stressful, have similar financial goals, enjoy sexual compatibility, or share spiritual values. Oh, and did I mention whether or not you'll have great sex together?

This analysis can reveal if you'll be close friends or competitive. It can show whether one of you will be the teacher and other the willing student. Or, will the wiser partner who tries to teach, be resisted by the other, causing personality clashes and friction? Will there be power and control issues between you? Through this analysis, you'll learn what areas you and your partner complement each other, so that you can play to each other's strengths and support each other; or whether you'll become codependent through your mutual weaknesses. It will reveal in what areas of life you'll have to compromise and where you're likely be challenged.

If you're single, dating, and interested in a committed relationship, you should ask the question: "Is he (or she) the right one?" Single people often spend months and even years dating each other or living together, only to find out in the end they are basically incompatible. That can be a painful way of discovering reality and the truth. So, before you invest a great deal of time together, why not find out whether you are mutually compatible for a long-term relationship? The solution is to have an astrologer compare your birth charts to see if you are *really* compatible by doing a "chart compatibility analysis."

A compatibility analysis reveals your individual strengths, weaknesses and compatibilities, thus allowing you to fully understand the dynamics of your partnership. You can then decide if the qualities that make up your relationship will be a positive complement to the partnership you envision, likely resulting in a successful marriage together. Additionally, you can decide if you can live with the personality differences that may cause you and your partner friction and disagreement. By the way: We are not talking about looking for the *perfect* partner – just one you can love, grow with and enjoy a satisfying life. My old astrology teacher, Hannibal used to say, "Everyone is a little crazy. The key is to find someone whose 'crazy' works for you."

This same process should be used to decide whether you would be compatible with a potential business partner in a joint venture – before you invest your life savings, and months or years of hard work in a partnership. Incompatibility between partners can cause even a great business to fail, resulting in the kind of upset and discord that leads to lawsuits – all because you partnered up with someone you thought you knew, but really didn't.

When you choose a business partner, one of your criteria may be to choose someone with a complementary area of expertise to you. Maybe they're technical and detail oriented and you're not; or maybe you're big picture-oriented with expansive vision and they're not. However, there are many other vital areas of compatibility you must also pay attention to if you're going to have a successful and cooperative partnership. Do you make decisions well *together*? Is one of you ultra conservative while the other is ultra liberal? What is your attitude towards money? Is one a "saver" while the other is a "spender"?

When two partners have differing approaches they tend to complement each other by bringing a different perspective to problem solving. However, be careful because while polar opposites may attract each other, they tend to make each other crazy. At first blush, you may think these opposite approaches may balance a relationship. The reality is they usually polarize partners and result in arguments and stalemates. These differences can stop a business (or marriage) from growing and even cause it to decline. Many people are attracted to their opposites and imagine that two halves make a whole. The truth is: two wholes make a whole.

By contrast, if your overall compatibility suggests you'll make decisions well, with one of you being a long-term planner, while the other a short-term planner, this may be the ideal compatibility for your business venture together. It may be a complementary dynamic between you if, for example, you're both comfortable spending money in your business, with one of you being quick to invest in expansion, while the other requires more analysis before committing funds to it. Successful partnerships usually thrive when each partner has a sphere of influence and responsibility, with both partners keeping each other informed, and always being open to compromise.

Your Body in the 7th House

This house rules the ovaries, lower back, buttocks, kidneys, and veins. Since there is nothing more important than your health, pay special attention to these areas of your body whenever a planet transits this House. It may indicate a period of time when you'll experience health benefits, issues or even problems you should be aware of. If you observe anything unusual, you'll have the opportunity to consult with a medical doctor or a health care practitioner.

Your 7th House Decisions

You now understand that 7th House of your birth chart concerns your partnerships and relationships. As you read about the description of this house, it's time to ask yourself a few questions about these areas of your life.

If you're in a marriage relationship (or in any other type of committed partnership), is it a loving, happy relationship? If you're in a very satisfying partnership – what are the qualities about it that make it work so well? What would make your relationship even better? If you're not happy, how can you make your partnership more satisfying? What are the problems in your relationship? Do you want to end your relationship or divorce based on irreconcilable differences?

For people who aren't in a significant love relationship, the question often becomes: "when am I going to find a partner?" Here are other questions you may have pondered: Why am I having so much trouble finding the right partner? Why do I seem to attract inappropriate partners? Why do I attract angry and abusive types? Why do I meet lovers who are commitment-phobic? Why do I find it so difficult to get along with someone when I'm in a one-on-one relationship? Am I meant to be alone?

When it comes to your relationship, or your lack of one, are there any changes you want to make in the way you behave in your close personal relationships? Are you happy and fulfilled with the one you are in? Are you interested in finding a satisfying love relationship that is perfectly suited to your needs: emotionally, mentally, spiritually, financially and sexually?

Does your business partnership function in a cohesive way where you work cooperatively toward the goals you've set? Do your strengths and weaknesses compliment each other? Do you each have a skill-set that brings depth and expertise towards achieving the results you are working to accomplish? Or, is there a clashing of egos and opposing operating philosophies? The right partnership is heaven. The wrong one is hell. The ones you're likely to enjoy here on earth are usually a little bit of both. But by knowing whether you are fundamentally compatible, you're more likely to have a relationship that is successful.

These are all significant questions and your answers may lead you to make important decisions to change your life. Here are a few examples of decisions clients have made based on the activities and issues of the 7th House.

7th House : Relationships, Marriage & Partnerships

Situation: Roberta has dated many men and had lots of enjoyable short-term relationships. Now she's ready to settle down.

DECISION: *I am committed to socializing and meeting a partner for a long-term, relationship. In other words: I'm ready to meet Mr. Right for Marriage.*

* * *

Situation: Albert is an inventor. Unfortunately, another company has infringed on his patent.

DECISION: *I want to commence a winning lawsuit that will accomplish my objective of protecting my patent.*

* * *

Situation: Bella wants to start a new business with a partner. She knows her talent is in the production side of the business. She wants to find the right partner with sales and marketing skills that will complement her. She just met Mark, who might be an ideal partner.

DECISION: *I want to find the answer as to whether Mark and I would be compatible business partners.*

* * *

Situation: Terry has endured an abusive marriage for too long. His efforts to resolve his problems in counseling have failed miserably and he realizes he's married to someone he's just not compatible. However, he has two wonderful children, he must also consider.

DECISION: *I am ready to divorce at a time that is beneficial to me, and my children.*

* * *

During the transits of *Jupiter, Saturn, Uranus, Neptune,* and *Pluto* – Roberta, Albert, Bella, and Terry will have many opportunities to implement their decisions at a favorable time to produce the outcome they want.

The Transiting Planets Reveal Your Past, Present & Future

Your main focus is using astrology to understand *what the hell is going on in your life.* Once you do – this book will show you the best time to make a decision to change it, should you have a desire to do so. As you read about the five planets transiting the 7th House, notice the way each planet exerts its unique influence and effect, bringing specific opportunities, issues, problems, and events into this area of your life. But if you're curious as to how these planets are personally affecting YOU *today,* in your *past,* or in your *future*, you can find out where each transiting planet is in your birth chart by using the *FREE Transit Calculator* (see Part IV).

JUPITER in Your 7th House of Relationships & Partnerships

Lucky Time for Marriage

Jupiter transiting the seventh House gives you the opportunity for favorable partnerships and love relationships. If you're single and want to find a wonderful loving relationship, then you've received a valuable gift when Jupiter transits your 7th House. It's an incredibly lucky time to find a partner. If you've just said to a friend, "When will I ever meet my prince (or princess)?" – the universe has answer for you. This could be the year!

What's great about this time is that you are an expansive state of mind where you're genuinely open to a relationship. You're likely to feel sociable, generous, affectionate, loving and very capable of intimacy with others. Perhaps in the past you've enjoyed the excitement of being single, dating around and having fabulous romantic experiences. You now realize your happiness comes from sharing your life with another person and learning about yourself in the process. You'll have many fortuitous opportunities to socialize and meet desirable "potential" mates for a long-term committed relationship. I remind my clients that what's so great about Jupiter transiting the 7th House is that, unlike other times when you may have met unsuitable partners, now you'll meet ones for the long-term who may be "marriageable."

Don't squander this gift by sitting at home or working your usual long day at the office. This is your year to be out in the public, networking, socializing, asking to be "fixed-up," and pro-actively meeting potential mates.

If you're already in a committed relationship, Jupiter's transit here can provide you with positive assistance to improve your partnership and make it even better. You may discover during this year you love and enjoy your partner even more than you did when you first married.

Brings Joy & Friendship

Jupiter's beneficial influence on marriage may result in meeting a partner at this time whom you greatly respect and enjoy as a friend. It may be someone who is mature, experienced and established in the world. If you're fortunate enough to meet the person you want to marry (or commit to), you're likely to have a successful long-term marriage.

This was the case for Margaret, who for years worked at a research institute with many brilliant and dedicated people. She developed a friendship with an older gentleman named Morris who was a distinguished scientist and a widower. Her friendship with him grew over the years and continued to blossom. They lunched together almost every day, talking about everything from work, to discussions about life, books, movies, and their dreams for the future. Then, Morris started asking her to share dinner together, take a walk and go to a movie. Eventually, they found themselves spending a good deal of time together outside the lab. It was clear to Margaret that Morris was open to having their relationship be more than just friends. As time went by, she found herself growing more and more fond of him, all the while realizing he was growing in his affection for her as well.

When Margaret met with me for her annual transit consultation, she told me about her scientist friend Morris. She admitted that her affection for him was turning into love. Jupiter was transiting her 7th House of partnership, so her loving feelings and desire for partnership made total sense. I told her this was an excellent year to pursue a long-term romantic relationship and perhaps even marriage, if she was so inclined. She admitted that was exactly what she was thinking about, so I encouraged her to follow her feelings of love and have a heart-to-heart discussion with Morris about how she felt. This would give him the freedom, in return, to be honest about how he felt about her. It might be the catalyst to formally take them down the road to a long-term love relationship.

Brings the Opportunity to Improve

If you're already in a relationship, you'll find that it's an especially joyful and satisfying time in your partnership. Since Jupiter's influence is oriented toward self-improvement, even difficult relationships can improve during this time, whether it's through couples counseling, attending a relationship workshop, taking a class together, or just a fun vacation that might bring you closer together. One client took advantage of the self-improvement benefits of Jupiter by taking a weekend skills workshop with her husband to find better ways to communicate. They both ended up having a fabulously enriching experience, making their marital relationship even better.

This is a period where your intimate one-to-one relationships can teach you a great deal about yourself and the world you live in. One client never cared about learning history and geography in school, but she fell in love with a man who was a world traveler and became fascinated with his experiences living in foreign countries. You'll find that people you attract into your life at this time can be fortunate and helpful to you in many ways. Another client who was a talented artist met a love interest who was an artist and gallery owner, and besides a love relationship, he provided her a special mentorship, helping her perfect her craft.

You're very motivated to pursue activities with others instead of alone, because you recognize their company can provide you great enjoyment without threatening your sense of individuality. This is a fabulous time for socializing whether it's throwing a brunch for a bunch of friends or joining a literary book club. Jupiter's influence often brings foreign travel and people of other cultures into your life that can result in a close relationship or partnership. I had a client who had great fun going to international gatherings and cultural events, such as ethnic food celebrations and lectures at the foreign council on international relations. She had a special interest in socializing with people of other cultures, which is where she eventually met her husband.

Another outcome of Jupiter's influence is that you might find yourself in a relationship with someone whose background is so different from yours, economically or spiritually, that it causes you to expand your philosophy of life. Jupiter's effect is to broaden your worldview and sophisticate you. Someone at this time can teach you a lot and change your mind.

Brings Courage, Wisdom & a New Philosophy

It should be noted that Jupiter transiting this House may also be a time where a relationship ends or a divorce occurs, which may actually be fortunate for one or both parties. Sometimes, it's good fortune that allows a person to escape an unhappy relationship in order to be free and available for one that's much more satisfying. Since Jupiter brings you wisdom and the opportunity to grow in your relationships, if you've endured an abusive or dysfunctional relationship, with no improvement in sight, then you're likely to see that you deserve better. You'll have the courage, capacity and vision to realize you should no longer be in your relationship.

When Margo had Jupiter transiting her 7th House she started to think more and more about ending her marriage. After 22 years of living with her emotionally abusive partnership, she had enough. Margo had felt this way for a long time, but always lacked the courage to break free from her marriage before now. Recently, through a volunteer program in her community she met a gentleman named Hal. While he seemed to be a very nice, all she knew about him was that he was very spiritual, practiced Buddhism, and was happily married. They'd developed a relaxed friendship, which made it easy for them to chat and have a cup of coffee together at the end of their volunteer shift. Margo was fascinated as Hal spoke about Buddhist teachings, which gave her the opportunity to learn more about his religion and spirituality. She'd never known anyone who practiced Buddhism, which led to her asking more questions about his experience and his personal journey.

When Hal asked about her life, Margo felt comfortable confiding in him about the deep upset and anguish she felt in her unhappy marriage. As she told him details of her relationship with her husband, she broke down in tears since it was painful to recount how miserable she felt. When Margo asked for Hal's feedback about her situation, he gave it to her in a compassionate, non-judgmental, accepting manner. It was sage-like advice that resonated, giving her the courage and clarity to see the truth of her situation in a way she hadn't seen before. Margo eventually divorced, but always credited Hal with helping her through her difficult time with his wise counsel.

Trusted Advisors, Courts & Law Suits

The 7th House rules all kinds of close relationships with trusted advisors, so this is an excellent time to seek the professional assistance of lawyers, accountants, doctors, public relations professionals, or any consultants who have an expertise you may require. I've had clients complain that their lawyer lost a major case; or their accountant forgot to take an important deduction; or they weren't happy with their doctor's service. For that reason, this Jupiter transit is a fabulous opportunity to improve the services you receive from new professionals who'll do a better job to your liking. You'll obtain good counsel and have fortunate associations with those you consult with at this time.

Since Jupiter in this House governs lawsuits, if you have any legal matters that must be dealt with, this is an especially lucky and fortunate time to be in court to instigate or to resolve a lawsuit. However, avoid being greedy or over-confident, overlooking important details or overestimating the benefits you may gain from winning your case or settlement.

Jupiter's influence is likely to make it important for you to be in relationship with people you can respect because of their high principles of character, honesty and integrity. Take stock of the friends, associates and professionals who are in your life. If anyone you know doesn't operate according to your standards, be honest, and let them know or consider making a change in your relationship. This is a time in your life when you'll operate with a sense of fairness in your dealings with people and won't tolerate injustice.

This is a wonderful time to meet friends who will make an important contribution to your life. I have met a lot of brilliant, helpful friends and professionals during Jupiter's transit through my 7th House. Many of them became mentors and lifelong friends. I'll never forget a dear, departed friend of mine named Morty. He and I used to have lunch regularly and take long walks together along the ocean where he listened to my problems and my dreams, always giving me great counsel and useful suggestions that made my life work better. If you're open to such relationships, you'll find them during this time. They'll be very special, teaching you a great deal and allowing you to grow as a person.

Great Time for Education & Publishing

This is also a very advantageous time for the pursuit of higher education, which may take the form of working towards an advanced degree or just going back to school to increase your knowledge in a particular area. If you've been thinking, "I'd like to finish my degree," I suggest you locate where Jupiter is transiting in your chart to assist you in picking a successful time to complete your education. Using a Jupiter transit is, yet another example of how you can use your personal transits to your benefit.

If you're writing, this is an auspicious time to pursue any interest you may have in publishing. I wrote my first book when Jupiter was in my 7th House. I also had a client who had taken several writing classes at her community college and started writing the novel she'd always dreamed of publishing. She completed her manuscript and her book proposal. Now, all she needed was to find a literary agent to sell her book to a publisher.

Her Jupiter transit provided a very fortunate time for her to find a trusted advisor, such as a literary agent. She went to a writer's conference and in the course of talking to different people had a wonderful connection with an agent who specialized in her fiction genre. He was immediately enthused about her book's potential. Additionally, he turned out to be a very positive influence, giving her constructive feedback to improve her book, and working on her behalf to find the right publisher.

The best advice I can give you is to use the year that Jupiter transits your 7th House to create many favorable relationships that will help enhance your life and your goals. If you have a great marriage you can make it even better. If you want to find a mate for marriage put your social life on "steroids" meeting eligible partners. For many people this will be the year when you'll be married or find the perfect business partner.

Considerations, Actions, Decisions During Jupiter in 7th House

1. Find an enjoyable romantic relationship.
2. Find an honest, principled business partner who will be lucky for you.
3. Go back to school for your degree or enroll in an educational course.
4. Get married to that special person.
5. Improve your current relationship so that it's even more satisfying.
6. Get divorced from someone who is not right for you.
7. Take a trip to a foreign country for a learning experience.
8. Write and publish something.
9. Go on a spiritual journey that will bring you inner growth.
10. Hire a doctor, lawyer, accountant, or other trusted advisor

SATURN in Your 7th House of Relationships & Partnerships

A Time to Evaluate Your Love Relationship

This is when you'll evaluate your love life, your marriage, or any committed relationship you're in and take responsibility for whatever it has become. For example, a woman had causally dated a man for years and her partner had grown impatient and finally said to her, "Either let's commit to each other and get married, or end our relationship." Another client didn't spend much time in his relationship, always working or playing golf with his buddies. Now that his wife was very ill, he needed to accept greater responsibility for taking care of her.

Saturn's transit through your 7th House requires you to make some adjustments in your relationship. You'll experience growth by re-defining and re-structuring the essential needs you have in your love life. The client who was not ready to commit after years of a dating relationship may have to make an adjustment to being single again or accept the responsibility of making a marriage commitment. The man who spent so much time away from his wife will be required to restructure his work and time golfing in order to accept the responsibility of taking care of his wife. The responsibility that you must accept requires you to re-define your needs and re-consider your priorities.

You'll learn lessons and be tested in terms of how flexible and compromising you can be with your partner. Have you ever heard someone say, "It's not easy being married." These are the lyrics to the song that Saturn will sing to you, if you're in a committed relationship. Close relationships like marriage or business partnerships become demanding and difficult, requiring a great deal of effort on your part to maintain. Saturn will constantly test them. What's happening is that you're put in a position where added responsibilities burden your relationship, requiring you to give more, not less. You're called to unselfishly sacrifice some of your freedom and even make some adjustment that may not be comfortable.

Saturn's influence in this House can produce tensions, frustrations, and pressures in marriage as well as in business partnerships. These energies inevitably lead to confrontations that force you to examine your relationship so you can determine whether it satisfies your mutual needs and expectations. You may have been staying in an unhappy relationship out of convenience, however, now the status quo cannot be maintained. You must face the music. For this reason, many relationships end because they demand more attention and effort than both partners believe the relationship is worth. This Saturn's transit will test the mettle of any relationship, no matter how happy it has been. This is why transiting Saturn in the 7th House is often a time when marriages may break up and end in divorce.

Be aware that even if your marriage is solid and going well, you may still have to confront flaws or issues in your relationship. However, this can actually be a very positive "wake-up" call allowing you to make needed changes that will stabilize your relationship so that it thrives and is much stronger than before. One marriage partner decided it was time to stop being a workaholic in order to spend more time with a spouse. Another partner realized she was no longer in love and must try to adjust to that reality. Yet another spouse was caught being unfaithful and must chose between marriage counseling or divorce.

Saturn's influence requires you to re-define, re-structure and even re-evaluate your current relationship. If this is done in a positive way – where both partner's concerns are addressed then a good relationship will be even better. Perhaps a compromise is reached such as, "We're agreed, from now on – I'll make sure to be home from work by 6 p.m." or "Let's agree to go to couples counseling and work on saving our marriage." The partner who came to the realization that she's "no longer in love," must decide if the practical benefits she enjoys from her marriage are enough. If a necessary adjustment cannot be made or a resolution can't be achieved, then it may be best to let go of the relationship. The cuckolded partner may say, "I'm sorry, I am no longer willing to tolerate your infidelities. I want a divorce."

Makes You Responsible

Saturn represents *karmic* law. Or, expressed in other ways: What you sow, you shall reap; what goes around comes around; what you put into something is what you get out of it. Sir Isaac Newton (another astrologer, by the way) states in his *Third Law of Motion:* "For every action there is an equal and opposite reaction." Or, as stated by Larry Schwimmer: "Payback is a bitch!"

So, if you've behaved badly in your relationship, this will be the time when you'll be held accountable and responsible for your actions, even if your past behavior was not noticed or challenged by your partner. For example a dissatisfied partner may be confrontative and say, "You're no longer thoughtful and romantic. You use to buy me flowers and remember my birthday;" or "You use to care enough to listen and show interest in my feelings."

During this time you'll find that limitations or shortcomings that have caused you to be less than an ideal partner will be revealed either by your partner or, even by circumstances that compel you to improve your behavior. Here are some examples, "You never tell me you love me any more," or "I've just been diagnosed with cancer," or "I'm calling to inform you that your spouse has been in a bad accident."

Unfortunately, you may not even be aware of behaving inappropriately in your relationship. Saturn in the 7th House gives you the opportunity to change your ways because it often brings a crisis into your relationship where you're forced to face the problem that exists. Hopefully, your sense of responsibility towards your spouse or partner will bring with it a deep desire to bring resolution to the upset that has occurred. Of course, some partners aren't responsible or willing to change inappropriate conduct in their relationship. Saturn has a way of bringing their behavior to the light of day. Often, a partner who's engaged in improper behavior will be exposed during Saturn's pass through their 7th House.

This transit has coincided with many an unfaithful spouse getting caught cheating. They were *outed* when their spouse saw evidence of their infidelity such as lipstick on their handkerchief, intimate and personal text messages on their phone, or unusual hotel charges on their monthly credit card statement. These are examples of how Saturn brings about circumstances that can lead to upsetting confrontations in a person's relationship. The ultimate purpose is to cause a re-examination of the relationship in order to either resolve the root problem or let the relationship go, if the partners can't come to terms with it.

Relationship Endings & New Beginnings

Shirley and Pete had been dating for about a little over a year. Pete started out being a very considerate boyfriend, but once he'd won Shirley's affection, he began taking her for granted. He no longer put any effort into making her feel special as he had during the first few months of their relationship. He also went from being a thoughtful lover, planning a special evening for Valentine's Day, to being a dolt and totally forgetting her birthday. Despite Shirley telling him how his behavior was hurtful, Pete continued to be insensitive, inconsiderate, and thoughtless.

One day, Shirley was surprised to receive a phone call from her old boyfriend, Danny. He was in town and asked if she'd be open to having a cup of coffee because he had something important to discuss. It had been almost two years since she had last seen him. Shirley and Danny had some fun, exciting times together in the six months they had dated. Then he broke off their relationship when his company promoted and transferred him to another state. As disappointing as it was to hear, Danny had been honest with Shirley and told her he couldn't handle the demands of his new job responsibility while having a long distance relationship. This really broke Shirley's heart, even though she accepted it at the time. But there was no denying she had loved Danny and remembered him for the great boyfriend he'd been. Danny made her feel special with his thoughtfulness and his ability to just listen to her problems without trying to fix them.

Talking over a cup of coffee, Danny confessed to her that he had made a mistake in ending their relationship when he did. He explained some of the personal reasons that caused him to do this and told her how much he missed her. He confessed he was in love with her and wanted to plan a future together – if she was open to it.

Ironically, both Shirley and Pete had Saturn transiting their 7th House at the same time. For Pete, the lesson of Saturn was that his thoughtless and insensitive behavior toward Shirley was now clearly exposed. He was being called to task. His inconsiderate behavior had created upset and tension that brought their relationship up for re-evaluation. For Shirley, her Saturn transit was about re-examining whether being a relationship with Pete was really right for her. The return of her old love Danny was the catalyst that brought it all to a head.

Upon Shirley's own introspection, she realized the tension she'd been feeling was based on an inner awareness that she needed to end her relationship with Pete. She'd been unhappy with him for a long time, because the truth was their relationship didn't emotionally satisfy her needs. He was the wrong partner for her.

Shirley met with Pete and told him about her decision. At first he tried to talk her out of it, but reluctantly accepted it. She decided she'd take some time out before making a decision about going back into a relationship with Danny. She and Danny agreed they would stay in touch; and she'd let him know when she was ready to talk about their relationship and their future together. Under Saturn's influence Shirley realized the need to maturely reflect on her past relationship with Peter and cautiously evaluate how she felt about resuming her old relationship with Danny.

A Time of Testing

Saturn's influence is a time of testing that will determine whether your relationship will deepen and become real or impermanent in your life. During its transit through your 7th House, you're able to perceive your relationship clearly and realistically for what it is. For example, if you've been in a love relationship for some time, and it's what you want and need, you will decide to make a firm commitment to it. If you realize that after months or years, it's *not* going to work out despite all your efforts, maybe the relationship must end. Saturn's energy brings forth real tension and pressure in your relationship so that you feel responsible to re-examine it and make a conscious decision as to its importance in your life. Shirley's experience was a very typical example of how Saturn's transit through the 7th House can manifest and affect a person's relationship by bringing a crisis to it.

During this Saturn transit be sure you and your partner communicate openly and objectively about any issues that exist. If necessary, get a mediator or a counselor to help you clear the air so that you can have an open discussion. The tensions between you will only grow deeper, creating greater upset, if you don't resolve them now. Express your expectations of each other to avoid any future disappointments. This is when you air your "dirty laundry," and release all your "withholds," (those ill feelings you haven't told your partner for the sake of peace and harmony). If you choose to be 100 percent honest, you'll have the opportunity to come to a new understanding and re-structure your relationship in a way that works to everyone's satisfaction.

Remember that Saturn's influence requires you to assume responsibility for your relationship whether it's good, bad or somewhere in-between. The dynamics and personalities of two partners may indicate that two people are willing to live in an unhappy partnership for a whole host of reasons and rationalizations. Some people are willingly stay in a long-term relationship where they feel frustrated and trapped, hoping that their partner will change. Ironically, the only person who can change is *you* – even if your partner doesn't. Saturn's message may be that it's time to stop blaming your partner and take responsibility for the relationship "as it is," knowing that if you decide to remain in it – that is *your* decision. When you make yourself accountable without criticizing your partner, you may find they will change on their own accord.

A Time to Re-Define Your Relationship

Glenda and George had been happily married for six years. However, their relationship changed last year when George accepted a new job that required some traveling. Eventually, he was asked to travel more and more and was now away for two weeks per month. At first, Glenda was understanding because George liked his job and made an excellent salary.

But as she started feeling lonelier and more resentful about his absence, she and George began fighting during the time he was home. Because of anger and dissatisfaction, she was even tempted to have an affair when he was away. Their relationship had reached a crisis point because it was not the kind of marriage she wanted. To Glenda, marriage included sharing an intimate day-to-day domestic life with her husband, sleeping each night in the same bed with him. As Saturn went through her 7th House of partnership, her discontent came to a head and she sat down with George and explained how she felt. George was empathetic, confessing he too, had been unhappy about the extra travel that kept him away from Glenda, but rationalized it was necessary to make more money. They debated their options and eventually agreed that no amount of money was worth adversely affecting their relationship. Either his travel requirements had to be reduced or he had to change his job.

After George explained the situation to his manager he was offered a transfer to an administrative position that wouldn't require travel, but at a 20 percent salary reduction. When George talked over the new position with Glenda, they weren't happy about the economic sacrifices they were going to have to make based on his pay cut. However, they agreed that it was worth it to restore their marriage back to the day-to-day intimacy they both valued.

This Saturn transit produced a test for Glenda and George's marriage, bringing them a relationship crisis that required a re-evaluation of what they both wanted, along with the need to make a financial sacrifice to achieve it. As their story illustrates, Saturn's energies are not about happy, warm endings; rather, they are about working through difficulty and hardship, and being practical and realistic in order to resolve a problem.

Brings a Need to Re-Structure

As Saturn transits here it brings you tests and lessons in all close relationships. The challenges you face may create immense pressures for you to be accountable for the state they are in. While this is especially the case in your love relationships, it can also extend to your business partnerships. For people, especially those who aren't married, a business partnership can feel like a marriage and suffer from some of the same tensions and upsets during Saturn's transit through the 7th House.

Keith and Alex had been in business for 18 years and had a successful business partnership. Together they took their small business from a storefront to a bustling operation that supplied linens to the hotel industry. But over the last few years Alex began having health problems and was sick so often that he was no longer able to contribute very much to the day-to-day operations of the business. Keith had the entire responsibility for running the business. Initially, Keith was understanding and compassionate toward Alex's health problems, but soon he started feeling resentful at having to put in so much extra time to compensate for Alex's inability to share the workload fairly. Keith knew that it was time to re-examine their partnership.

Saturn transiting Keith's 7th House created tensions and pressures in his

partnership, requiring him to find a way to change it. As he evaluated all his options, he realized the time had come to buy out his partner. However, rather than take advantage of Alex's ill health, Keith wanted to be fair and responsible. They met to discuss Alex's retirement and the best way for Keith to buy out his shares in the company. Alex had been feeling guilty, knowing full well his ill health was putting a great burden on Keith to run their business. So, Alex was agreeable to working out a partnership buy-out. This was the perfect way to alleviate the tension and strain that Alex's illness had caused, yet allow Alex to retire with enough money for him to live comfortably. The high standards of Saturn demand that a person operate with integrity and character just as Keith did in his fair treatment of his partner.

Relationships & Loneliness

Ironically, this transit can also bring a sense of loneliness, even if you're presently in a relationship. For example, if your needs aren't being met by your partner, you may feel a sense of aloneness, despite sleeping in the same bed each night. If this is the case, Saturn's lesson is to try to get you in touch with the limitations and restrictions you may be feeling in your relationship. Something may be missing or not working, so now is the time to ask yourself what it might be. You may have to recognize the inadequate ways your partner is treating you or the fact you're emotional needs aren't being met. Now is the time to have an honest, open discussion to review, re-establish, and rebuild your relationship so that it's more fulfilling, and working better for both of you.

If you're single, you may be feeling lonely because you don't have a love relationship in your life. Saturn energies can make you depressed about being alone. I remind clients that if they feel a bit down when Saturn transits their 7th House, to remember that it's only temporary. Saturn's presence is there to help you re-evaluate any changes you can make that would bring a love relationship into your life. If you spend too much time by yourself, perhaps it's time to get out of the house and socialize with others. If you're so critical that no one seems interesting, maybe it's time a meet different people or reevaluate your standards. Or, maybe it's time to come to terms with whether you actually want a romantic partner in your life. Saturn is there to encourage some change that will help you get what you want.

If you're single and have been dating someone exclusively, seeking a long-term relationship, this can be a serious and intense time of deciding to have a committed love relationship in the form of marriage or living together. Or, it maybe time to be realistic and recognize that you are not in a relationship that will lead to the long-run commitment you want. Saturn's message: Review and re-evaluate your relationships (or lack of).

Being Single & Looking for the "Perfect Mate"

In my astrological consultations I meet with lots of single people who sincerely want to find a wonderful, love relationship, get married, and build a life with someone. Many of them are frustrated that after dating so long and having numerous relationships, they still haven't found the "right one." In fact, I frequently get asked: "How come it's so hard for me to find the right guy (or gal)?" Of course, their personal birth chart usually reveals the answer. I explain to them, "Saturn transiting through your 7th House may provide you with an answer to that question and with some important insights to consider." Saturn brings realism and practicality to the affairs of your heart. If you've been frustrated in your attempt to find a special love relationship, you need to make an honest assessment of yourself and your attitude towards the romantic prospects you're meeting. One question to ask yourself is: "Are you too picky and critical when it comes to selecting a potential mate?"

If your answer is yes – then it may be time to be more accepting of yourself and your own imperfections. By doing so, you'll be more likely to not seek perfection in another person. This will allow you to make an adjustment from what may be unrealistic standards to ones that are more reasonable and attainable. You'll suddenly open up the field of relationship possibilities and find it far easier to meet partners who are compatible and potential mates.

When I was single, I remember periods of endless dating, never finding the right woman for me. Part of my problem was that I was "stuck" on my list of criteria I insisted a woman meet before I would consider her for a relationship. Many of my *wants* were important, but many were not. I had a specific "picture" of how the perfect woman had to be. I came to realize that picture guaranteed I would be a lonely bachelor forever. Eventually, I changed my picture and the most amazing love relationship I've could have ever imagined came into my life.

I ask you: Is it time for you to let go of certain relationship requirements that in the past were fixed, in order to make it possible to achieve the goal of having a close relationship? If you genuinely do this, you'll allow marriage to be a distinct possibility that might not have been possible before Saturn transited your 7th House.

You may know a single person who has unrealistically high standards and who's always critical of the people they date. Often, their critical behavior is based on deep-rooted psychological issues, which may require therapy and counseling to help them resolve their issues. But for others, they may need to adjust their standards from perfection to human. Ironically, such a person may attract a relationship into their life that they find totally exciting and captivating. In fact, they're sure they have finally found the perfect soul mate – their ideal marriage partner – only to ultimately find that the other person was unsuitable and not really a good match for them. They're disappointed that the person didn't measure up to their expectations, yet they failed to realize that it was their *expectations* that caused their dissatisfaction – not the other person. You can change your expectations but you can't change the other person.

If you've had this experience, especially during Saturn's transit to your 7th House, it's an opportunity for you to take responsibility for your inability to find a suitable partner. Never forget: when you have a relationship with someone who ends up not meeting your standards, the common denominator is *YOU!* Therefore, it's time to re-examine your approach to love relationships, your criteria and expectations. The energies of Saturn will help you become realistic and find a new approach to bringing a love relationship into your life.

A Call to Be Realistic

As Saturn went through Arnie's 7th House, he was at a crossroads in his life, as far as love relationships were concerned. He was 47, never been married and still on the hunt for the perfect woman whom he described, "as being a tall, thin, blonde, and at least 20 years younger" than he. He ignored the fact that he was short, balding and 30 lbs. overweight. He thought his wealth would act as compensation for all of his physical shortcomings. So far, years of unsuccessful dating suggested that Arnie was incorrect in his assumption. His wealth was not a trade-off or sufficient compensation to the many women he had one or two dates with that never worked out.

Arnie was even more discouraged after his most recent experience. He was enthralled with a woman very junior to him who he described as a real babe. Arnie was sure he'd finally found the young goddess he was looking for. He rationalized to himself, so what if her vocabulary seemed to be mostly confined to one-syllable words and constant exclamations of "Oh my God...Oh my God!" Within a month it was clear she was more interested in Arnie's wealth than in Arnie.

Arnie and I discussed his birth chart and why he was having no luck meeting the future Mrs. Arnie. Saturn in the 7th House is a call to get serious, be realistic and to re-define what you want in a relationship. I candidly explained to Arnie that his birth chart showed him to be someone who was superficial and unrealistic in the area of romance. Worse yet, he had the natal chart of someone whose orientation toward women was extremely critical and perfectionistic. In simple terms, it was clear: no woman was ever good enough for him because he wanted perfection. He found a convenient way to sabotage his relationships and delude himself by saying that he *wanted* to get married, despite having a dysfunctional mindset that assured he never would.

I was totally frank with him and counseled, "Arnie, you can continue your life with the same inappropriate behavior and unrealistic attitudes towards women, for another 20 years if you desire. Or you could face reality and accept that your criteria for choosing a woman for a romantic relationship must change and become more mature and realistic. It's time for you to be honest with yourself and decide *if* you really want to have a long-term relationship in your life." Arnie said he would seriously think about what he wanted to do.

Having a Mature Relationship

Transiting Saturn in your 7th House has the capability of bringing into your life a karmic relationship that seems predestined. It may be with someone whom you feel a strong connection with, who while not fitting your exact pictures, satisfies all the practical needs you've wanted in a life partner. You may also find yourself in a love relationship with a much older person who's there to teach you how to have a loving partnership. In that case, you might find yourself being tested in ways that help you grow and mature like never before. I've had clients who've had a history of behaving childishly in their relationships. Then, they meet someone who's cultured, sophisticated and authoritative whom they greatly respect who helps them grow up. This older person is able to mentor them, making them feel secure, teaching them and broadening their worldview. For that reason, it's probably not surprising that many May-December romances, where two people are of considerable age difference, occur during Saturn's transit of the 7th House.

Finding a Solution to Relationship Issues

Whenever I meet with couples who are going through relationship issues, and one of the partners has Saturn going through their 7th House – I remind them that they have fabulous opportunity to help their relationship by entering couples counseling or individual therapy. During this Saturn transit you can learn important lessons about how your love relationship can work to satisfy both partner's needs. If you or your partner has brought some "emotional baggage" to your relationship that chronically causes upsets and problems, your current crisis might be a golden opportunity to bring resolution to the discord you're experiencing.

If you've grown up feeling unloved or unaccepted by your family, with low self-esteem and feelings of inferiority, especially in your love relationships, this is a useful time to explore those feelings and issues with a therapist. You can re-structure your beliefs about yourself and learn that you're loveable and worthy of a fulfilling love partnership.

For someone like Arnie, therapy might also be an option, if he sincerely wants to create a change within himself so an appropriate relationship can come into his life. Unfortunately, like many people, Arnie doesn't appear to be ready to take responsibility for the results he's receives from his life experiences. He's more committed to the problem than devoted to its solution.

Saturn's energies make you serious and ready to look at the issues that have adversely affected your ability to have a satisfying relationship. You then have the opportunity to make any necessary adjustments. Are there any changes you want to make in your relationships and partnerships?

Considerations, Actions, Decisions During Saturn in 7th House

1. What changes can you make that will help you find a serious love relationship?
2. Make a firm commitment to a romantic or business relationship.
3. Are you experiencing any crises in your relationships?
4. Re-structure or re-adjust your relationship so that it works better for both partners.
5. Seek therapy or counseling for yourself or your relationship.
6. End any close relationships that are not working.
7. Find a partnership that fulfills your needs on a practical basis.
8. Re-evaluate and re-structure a business partnership so it's more effective.

URANUS in Your 7th House of Relationships & Partnerships

A Time to Breathe New Life into Your Relationships

This is a period in your life when you'll likely experience a breakthrough in your marriage or partnership. You may be saying, "Hallelujah, I need one!" This is your chance to breathe new life, new adventure and fresh air into your relationship, especially if it's gotten dull and routine. You may find yourself eliminating and breaking free of your old, traditional ways of relating with those you have a close relationship. Perhaps, you haven't been affectionate, now you feel like hugging and kissing more. Maybe discussing certain subjects was off limits before, but now you find talking about controversial topics stimulating and interesting.

The influences of this Uranus transit can bring you a sense of freedom, excitement, and even new insight in your relationships, making them fresher and more alive. You'll find yourself wanting to break old patterns and try new things. Now you want to get out of the house with your partner and go on a bike ride instead of taking the car; or, instead of always eating at home, you'll plan a fun picnic together where you can have a glass of champagne as you sit on a mountain top. You're spontaneous and ready to experiment even if you're normally staid and conservative. It's an ideal time to be innovative and experimental in discovering how you can fulfill your needs and desires in your relationship. You're likely to see your partner in a new light and will look for new ways to bring excitement into your marriage. This is when you surprise your husband as he comes home late from work, by opening the door in a sexy negligee you haven't worn in years. Or, you may find yourself shocked when your husband tells you to pack an overnight bag because he's planned a romantic weekend at a five star resort hotel and spa.

If you're single, you're likely to be very excited about dating, courtship and having a romantic relationship during this time. You're enthralled because there's something edgy and kinky about the new woman you've been dating. The man you've been seeing over the past few months is always surprising you by taking you to fun places like a train ride through the mountains, the zoo or a roller coaster ride – things you haven't done since you were kid.

If you're someone who needs to break free from a bad marriage or partnership, Uranus will greatly affect you during this period of your life. Its energies will bring upset and disruption into your relationship to jolt you out of any sense of complacency you've been in, so that you change your situation. The purpose of this Uranus Transit is to liberate and free you from an intolerable relationship you've remained in because of reasons that are no longer valid or compelling. Some examples might be, "I have to stay together because of the kids," or "How will I support myself if I leave?" or "He'll stalk me if I break up with him," or "She'll threaten to commit suicide if I end our relationship."

In order to foster a needed change this transit brings stress and tension to your relationship, especially if it's not working out well. Over the years, you may have forced yourself to stay in a relationship that was unsatisfying for the sake of your own emotional needs, the other person's, because of children, or even financial dependency. Therefore, Uranus' passage through your 7th House creates enormous tensions in your relationship that fill you with an urgent need to break-free and even rebel against it. I've had many clients who, thanks to Uranus, got up the nerve and the gumption to finally liberate themselves from untenable relationships by either changing them or leaving them.

Free at Last . . . Free at Last!

Remember, Uranus' energy, is there to liberate you from old habit patterns, so that you can learn new ways of expressing yourself as well as to teach you something new that will help you grow in the area of relationship. Problems occur when you try to avoid making a needed change, perhaps because you're comfortable with the old and familiar. It's possible that your resistance to making necessary alterations brings about a major disruption in your life, forcing those changes to happen anyway. This is often the dynamic at work when a person suddenly decides to break up their marriage through separation, or even divorce. It can also be a time when an unsatisfactory business partnership ends as well.

Nancy realized that if she stayed in her marriage any longer, she was going to have a nervous breakdown. She'd tolerated the stress of an unhappy marriage for many years while trying to bury herself in her job as an investment banker for a large mergers and acquisitions firm. If that weren't enough, she was busy the rest of the time as a homemaker, as well as being available for her children's activities such as soccer and ballet. She'd stayed in her unfulfilling marriage for years out of guilt, a sense of responsibility, and the fear of disapproval from others. Nancy also had concerns about striking out of her own and for the welfare of her children. The kids were now teenagers, but they still needed her. Yet for the past year she'd had an urgent need to be free of her husband and their unhappy marriage.

Uranus' transit of her 7th House provided her with the big shot of adrenaline she needed. It gave her a sense of detachment, the courage to do something she'd not been able to do for years, and a compelling drive to break free from her marriage, right away. She immediately made plans to leave as soon as possible. Before anyone tried to stop her and before the first tremors of shock were ever felt, she got in her car and started her drive out West to begin a new life. Naturally, her family and friends thought she'd gone crazy. Her husband begged her to come back with the same empty promises he'd made many times before. Her children were surprised, emotionally upset, and even felt abandoned. None of that mattered to Nancy since she needed to be free, no matter what.

This story is an example of the powerful effect of a Uranus transit, one that compels a person to make a life change they would otherwise not make under normal circumstances. Uranus' influence has the ability to "rock your world" with shock and surprise, harnessing the most explosive energies you can imagine. Its purpose is to bring freedom, liberation and new discovery into your life by either a positive or negative manifestation. Let's continue to explore its influences and effects.

Uranus' energy requires you be authentic, demanding a new level of honest communication that often requires you act with courage and integrity, letting your partner know how you're feeling about your relationship. You're in an important period of your life, which calls for you to eliminate rigid and obsolete ways of behaving in your relationship. Now it must provide you with greater freedom, creativity and originality in the way it works. This transit has the ability to transform the way you relate to others. You'll find that whether you *begin*, *continue*, or *end* a relationship, it will never function in the same way.

Even if you're in a secure partnership, you'll still experience important change, but you will likely remain together. However, now you'll insist that your relationship offers you more freedom and excitement then it has in the past. Either way, it's a time when you'll have a need to make significant changes in your relationship to escape the boredom and routine that may have developed over time.

Brings Excitement & Liberation

For some people, especially those who are already in a relationship, this may be a time when you may be drawn to a new relationship as a way of escaping the dull routine of your old one. There's something exciting about a new person who comes into your life. A new love relationship or an exciting affair can be a very appealing and thrilling way of escaping from your present relationship. Suddenly, the man who just started coming to your yoga class looks very intriguing. The exotic-looking woman who just moved into your apartment building and gave you a big smile and a warm hello seems so inviting.

Be aware that one of the manifestations of Uranus' transit through the 7th House is that you may have a wild, unusual and unstable love affair that is often erratic and unreliable. One client enjoyed the excitement of his on-and-off relationship with a flight attendant who he'd see frequently during her 10-day furlough and then not again for two weeks while she was flying. Another client was enthralled with her affair with a foreign exchange student here on a six-month internship, but anxious about what would happen to their relationship when he returned to his country.

Just be prepared that if you do fall in love, this is a time when the romance you attract is likely to be exciting, improbable, and rather free-spirited. It may very well be with someone who's very different then you, either in ethnicity, age or background. But no matter what, you're likely to find the relationship exciting and liberating. However, be on notice that relationships that begin during this time often end just as suddenly.

One female client had been faithful her entire 18 year marriage, never thinking of looking at another man. However, here she was: 42 years old and bored with a workaholic husband she hadn't had sex with in months. Still, she was shocked at herself, flirting with a young man in his late 20s at her gym. But she couldn't deny that for the first time in her life – the idea of a thrilling sexual affair was exciting. What was happening to her?

Another client became aware of his true sexual nature during his Uranus transit. He enjoyed dating women, even though he once experimented by having a brief sexual relationship with a man. Otherwise, his dating was exclusively with women. He shared with me that for some time, he'd been feeling that dating women seemed boring and unfulfilling. Something was missing for him because he felt so inauthentic and couldn't deny the attraction he felt for men. He became aware that instead of being bi-sexual, he was really gay. The time had come for him to enjoy the freedom and excitement that only a relationship with a man would offer him.

But one of my favorite stories of the unexpected surprise that Uranus can bring happened to a female client of mine. Ironically, while she was quite an adventurous sort, always open to trying anything "once," she was unprepared for her Uranian moment. Her husband told her to get dressed up because he was taking her to a surprise party at a big mansion. When she got to the party, she saw a bunch of couples she'd never met before. The women were all dressed in very alluring, sexy outfits and lots of see-through tops. After using the powder room, her first surprise came when she walked by a big bedroom and heard what sounded like moans of passion. She rejoined her husband for a drink, smiling and remarking to him, "They sure are a friendly bunch of people." Her second surprise was when her smiling husband replied, "They should be – this is a Swinger's Party! Would you like to know the rules of engagement?"

All these clients had Uranus transiting their 7th House. Its influence provided each of them the opportunity to break free of their normal way of having a relationship, in favor of the freedom to experiment and create a new more liberating type of relationship.

Surprises & Enemies

Also, be aware that the 7th House is known also as the House of open enemies. That means there may be someone you know (or may not know), whom you've had a relationship or done business, who may lash out and take some sort of action against you. So, be aware this may be a period of time where you'll experience tensions, problems and conflicts in your relationships with others. I've had clients call me to tell me that they're in a relationship with "the most exciting person they've ever met," only to call me the next month and tell me the relationship is over because a horrible argument ended it; or they discovered that the person was certifiably "crazy."

For this reason, you need to be prepared to resolve some unusual and unexpected problems that may come up. I had a woman friend who had an intense and volatile on-off relationship with a man. One day she suddenly broke it off because she could no longer stand his uncouth and aggressive behavior. Within a few weeks, she realized this man was stalking her. She ended up having to file a restraining order against him.

Since this House rules lawsuits, you may experience upsetting and disruptive legal problems with others. One client found it necessary to file a mal-practice suit because her cosmetic surgery was done incorrectly by her plastic surgeon. Another client dated a very promiscuous woman a few times and then never again. Soon after, he received a call from her saying, "I'm pregnant and you're the father."

Brings Unusual Business Partners

When Uranus transits your 7th House, any partnerships you're in may be subject to radical change. Uranus' influence will affect your business partnership in ways similar to its effects on intimate personal relationships like marriage. If you're having any issues or difficulties in your professional or business relationships, you'll find that the discussions in this chapter will apply similarly to your current business partnership.

The need for newness, change and freedom cause many business partnerships to end during Uranus' transit through the 7th House. One client finally ended his partnership with a partner who wasn't doing his fair share in their business venture; another ended his partnership because he realized he was bored and un-stimulated after being in the same business for 30 years. In a positive vein, if you're looking for a business partnership during this time, Uranus may bring an unusual or exciting partner or association into your life. I've had clients meet the most brilliant people for business collaborations and partnerships under this transit. You'll find that people who are geniuses or just intriguing and unusual "come out of the woodwork" during this period of time. All you have to do is go to social gatherings, meetings, and organizations where you'll meet potential partners for projects you're interested in. For example, this could a time when you might discover a rather unconventional partner (such as an inventor, scientist or astrologer) who could lead you to new discoveries.

Brings Recognition

Uranus governs people and groups who are dedicated to humanitarian or progressive ideals. So if you're doing work that benefits others, during the time of this Uranus transit, you may receive some special recognition from society. A client who was a retired physician had written a unique medical self-help book that discussed wellness and the use of alternative treatments for chronic pain conditions. His book made people aware of his innovative methods so they could lead healthier, pain-free lives. This transit presented him with the ideal time to work with an agent and public relations firm in finding a publisher and eventually achieving public recognition for his work.

It's one thing to do something that's beneficial for the masses, but it's another to find the right time to launch your project when it will receive acclaim for its value to society. If you've discovered or created something that you think would be of great benefit to society, this transit may provide you the opportunity you've been looking for.

Brings Radical Change

Uranus in the 7th House causes many a relationship to undergo a radical change to make it fresher and more alive. If this isn't possible, Uranus' energies can lead to a breakup or divorce. If you have this transit, it will explain a great deal about what is going on in your life.

Uranus' influence is there to prevent you from falling into rigid patterns that may be detrimental to your personal relationships. I call it the "boredom-preventer." Let's face it: If you've been in a relationship with someone for years, you may need to bring new life and vitality to it. Your relationship may have gotten predictable, dull and routine. It may need a "blood transfusion," to keep it exciting and alive. So, Uranus' energies are there to promote change that will bring greater freedom and excitement to your marriage, partnership or other close relationships. If you find that your relationships have become disruptive and upsetting, it may be an indication that you're dissatisfied with them. This is an important time to ask yourself if your relationship still excites and interests you, or is boring.

Realize that if you're unhappy and want to break free of a partner, be aware that the person you're in relationship with may consciously or unconsciously *pick up on* and respond to the adversarial signals you're sending. Their reactions may produce conflicts and troublesome upsets. For that reason if you're intuition tells you that you or your partner are discontent, be sure to talk about your feelings openly in order to seek some resolution before a big blowout occurs.

Overall, these seven years will be a time when you experience feeling more independent, enjoy a greater sense of individual freedom, make exciting discoveries, and find yourself being more assertive in your self-expression in your partnerships and relationships.

Considerations, Actions, Decisions During Uranus in 7th House

1. Make your current relationship more spontaneous and interesting.
2. Find a new relationship that will be exciting and liberating.
3. Break free of a restrictive, unsatisfying relationship.
4. Find a unique business partnership.
5. Consider having an unconventional relationship with someone.
6. Consider a separation or divorce from your partner if no satisfactory resolution can be found.
7. Are there any open enemies you should be aware of?
8. Are there any lawsuit or litigation issues you should be aware of?

NEPTUNE in Your 7th House of Relationships & Partnerships

Beware of Illusion

This transit affects all your one-to-one relationships in life, which may include marriage, living with someone, or business partnerships. It may also concern your relations with people that you consult with such as doctors, accountants, attorneys, and other trusted advisors. In all these relationships this is a long period of time, in which you should be aware of potential conflicts that can occur because of poor communications, misunderstandings, deceptions and outright misrepresentations.

During the coming years, make sure that you have your antennae up and alert, sensitive to any behavior or situations that indicate that there is a problem in any of your close relationships. For example, in your marriage you or your partner may be keeping your feelings hidden from each other or acting deceptively in different ways. It may be too painful or too scary to openly discuss differences that exist. Ultimately, when the truth comes to the surface, it may bring problems of resentment and upset.

Neptune's influence also brings the likelihood that one of you will over-idealize your relationship. You may love your partner so much that you create a fantasy about your relationship, and not see it realistically, to the point where you think things are going well when they really aren't. Another possibility is that at this time you don't truly understand your partner's motivations and intentions. They maybe hiding their true feelings or not even aware of what they are. So during this time, you're susceptible to self-deception where you may see your partnership, as you'd *like it to be*, instead of the way *it really is*. Here are some surprising statements that you or your partner may say during your Neptune's transit, "She said that she's no longer in love with me," or "I can't believe he's been unfaithful all these years," or "I thought we were happily married, so I'm shocked she's asked for a separation."

For this reason, it's especially important to have an open and honest dialogue with your partner to make sure you clearly understand what's really happening in your relationship. This will give you the opportunity to freely discuss any problems that may exist between you.

Beware of Delusion

Another manifestation of Neptune's influence is that it can cause a person to feel such a deep sense of love that they'll sacrifice themselves for the benefit of their partner. We all know people who wait hand and foot on their partner, only finding joy in serving, never receiving. The danger here is that the person who does the "sacrificing" loses their identity in serving the other person. Often out of their own low self-esteem, they sacrifice their needs as if their needs were unimportant. Ultimately, the "sacrificing" person sets themselves up for disappointment and disillusionment in their romantic relationship, whether it's in their marriage or another type of committed partnership.

This was the case for John. He was 18 and in love with Brenda whom he'd met during his senior year of high school. He was sure that she was "the one" to marry, have children, and grow old together. During the first few months of their relationship, Brenda was also smitten and listened to his ideas and plans for their future. She tried to explain to him that while she thought he was a terrific guy, she was still young, and wanted to enjoy being single and having no responsibilities. However, John didn't seem to hear her words. He was totally entranced by Brenda's beauty and how ideal of a partner she'd make for the life he envisioned. After two more months of dating, it was clear to Brenda that they had totally different goals. When she told John she was ending their relationship, it left him feeling heartbroken, betrayed, disillusioned and in shock. With Neptune transiting his 7th House, he had deluded himself, creating a total illusion that was not based on reality.

Gives You the Ability to Experience Love & Sacrifice

The positive influence of Neptune transiting your 7th House is that you're able to experience a love relationship in an ideal way that comes from your heart, not your mind. It may give you the capacity to see the person's inner beauty, unconcerned with their outer beauty because you recognize that beauty is "only skin deep." Or, under a Neptune transit, you may also find someone's physical beauty so entrancing (as John did with Brenda) that you fall under a spell that bewitches you regardless of their inner beauty. Either way, it's as if Cupid shot an arrow into your heart, because you feel inspired to love someone in a very magical, romantic way.

You'll feel a real spiritual connection that brings with it an ability to love the other person unconditionally, generously giving to your partner. I remember a client who for years, was very superficially focused on finding a beautiful woman to marry. Yet, a few years later, when I met his new wife, she was very plain looking and overweight. But when he spoke about her, he said that no woman had ever made him feel so loved. He saw her inner beauty through her many acts of kindness to him, his family members and her friends. When I looked at his transit chart, I saw that he'd gotten married when Neptune began its transit of his 7th House, a period in his life when he could see her true beauty and experience a spiritual love.

One manifestation of Neptune's passage through this House is that you may be required to care for a sick partner or someone who requires regular attention. You have a very compassionate nature at this time and are willing to put aside your needs to help your partner. If you've been through any major upsets in your relationship that require understanding and forgiveness, you'll now have the capacity to do this for each other. This transit helped one couple forgive each other for their infidelities, instead of splitting apart; and it enabled another to give each other healing support when the death of their child occurred.

Beware of Deception

Since the 7th House concerns partnerships, Neptune's influence requires that you be careful when forming partnerships of any kind because you may be taken advantage of in some way, either by someone who's playing to your sympathies, or someone who's trying to scam or swindle you. I counsel clients who are considering business partnerships to be especially careful.

When Henry had this Neptune transit, he was besieged with opportunities to invest in all kinds of partnerships. Someone from his health club approached him about putting money into a "gold recovery and recycling" business because of all the money to be made from rising gold prices. His new neighbor knocked on Henry's door to talk about a great location he had found to open a "state-of-the-art" carwash where he could triple his investment within two years! Everyone thought Henry (and his money) would make a fabulous partner for their business opportunity.

When I met with Henry, I cautioned him that because of the huge potential for deception and illusion to occur at this time, he needed to carefully scrutinize all partnership investment opportunities. I advised that he wait until a time when a favorable transit was occurring before committing to any partnership.

I caution clients who are in love to make sure that they've been realistic in appraising their partner. This is a time when miscommunications can create problems in your partnerships, so for that reason it's important to communicate clearly and make sure you have important agreements put into writing to avoid any misunderstandings. Under this transit it's also easy to be in a mental "fog," where you just don't see things as clearly as you normally do. I advised one client, who was getting married and in a total state of romantic bliss, to consider a prenuptial agreement so that he and his future partner would have a written record of their financial arrangements.

Another client, a wealthy widow met a man 25 years her junior. She told me that he seemed enthralled with her, courting her over the past three months with phone calls three times a day and invitations to go out for various activities, and regularly sharing dinners together. At first she was very flattered, then charmed, and soon convinced that she and this man were very much in love with each other. They started exchanging "I love yous," with discussions about how wonderful it would be to share their lives with each other.

At her transit consultation I explained that because Neptune was in her 7th House (and making other stressful aspects in her chart) she might be deluding herself about this relationship. When I analyzed the natal and transit chart of her new boyfriend, it was clear to me he was a very deceptive fellow with ulterior motives. Aside from their age difference, and the fact that she was 40 lbs. overweight while he had movie star looks, the chart comparison indicated to me that she was in great danger of being deceived and disappointed by this relationship. Three months later, when she refused to loan him money he ended the relationship. He was a con artist and she had Neptune transiting her 7th House.

Choose Advisers Carefully & Avoid Litigation

The 7th House concerns trusted advisors, courts, lawsuits and attorneys. Since this transit lasts for many years, the reality is that you may require professional assistance during this time, and may even be involved in legal matters. So, take special care in choosing professionals to assist you, ask for references when possible, and rely on recommendations of trusted friends and associates.

I advise clients to avoid trying to resolve legal issues during this Neptune transit. The problem is that there's likely to be confusion, an inability to discover the truth, and the possibility that some manner of deception will cause them to be a victim in the outcome. For that reason, this isn't a good time for resolving your legal problems. If this is not possible make sure to get trusted friends and associates to assist you in legal matters to lessen the likelihood of missing or misunderstanding some important detail.

Considerations, Actions, Decisions During Neptune in 7th House

1. Be careful of over-idealizing your romantic partnerships.
2. Be careful of misunderstandings in your relationships.
3. Be careful of deception in your relationships.
4. Be careful of investing in business partnerships.
5. Be careful of over-idealizing the other person in your professional relationships.
6. Enjoy volunteering and taking care of others.
7. Avoid sacrificing yourself in a relationship to the point that you ignore your own needs.
8. Avoid being in a co-dependent relationship.
9. Carefully scrutinize all details if you engage in a lawsuit.

PLUTO in Your 7th House of Relationships & Partnerships

Get Ready for Transformational Relationships

When Pluto transits the 7th House, your marriage or business partnership is transformed forever. During this time your partnerships and all your close relationships will go through a radical change. In simple terms, that means that whatever state they're in today will be profoundly different over the years that Pluto transits through your 7th House.

It's also possible your life will be transformed through a very personal and close relationship with another person. You may meet your soul mate who will become the love of your life; a business partner whose idea makes you rich; or a doctor who saves you from near death. Their presence in your life will change it forever. You can expect that all your relationships will be affected such as your marriage, a committed love partnership, a business partnership (even enemies), as well as those you have consulting relationships, such as doctors, lawyers, accountants, public relations professionals, and any other trusted advisors.

It's a time when your love life becomes intense and powerful in its depth of feeling. If you're married, you feel closer then ever, as if your personalities are now merged into one. You'll realize this is the person you were meant to be with.

If you're single, it's a period in which you'll have passionate romantic relationship encounters. You feel that destiny has brought you and the other person together for a deep connection unlike any you've ever had. You seem to be able to talk with them for hours about your deepest thoughts, as if you've known each other for years. You'll find that superficial relationships will be boring and unsatisfying because you're not interested in "weather talk"; instead, you want to know what's in a person's psyche and heart. You may explore such deep questions such as, "What is your purpose in life?" or "Why did fate bring us together?"

If you're already in a marriage or committed love relationship, it's likely to undergo dramatic change and transformation as well. The status quo is no longer acceptable, which means that whatever needs to be fixed in your relationship can't just be repaired. It will now require a something brand new to be in its place.

In its more glorious manifestation, you'll share an intense soul mate, love relationship with the other person. However, Pluto's energies may also bring a crisis into your partnership that will require a major change in the nature of how it operates. That crisis may come in many colors, shapes and sizes. It may center on such matters as the loss of one of the partner's job, retirement, financial difficulties, sexual incompatibility, menopause, infidelity, alcohol or drug addiction, an affair that threatens the break-up of your marriage, or even the death of a loved one. Some times, the source of the discord in the partnership is based on deep psychological issues such as incompatible values or destructive behavior that has damaged the relationship.

As a result, long-hidden tensions or chronic problems that have plagued your relationship will surface to be dealt with and resolved if your relationship is to continue. I remind clients who are going through the "breakdown" phase of this Pluto transit: "You're beyond *crisis*, you're now engaged in a process of *survival* which will result in the death of your current relationship as it is or the re-birth of a new relationship between you." I explain further, "Pluto's energies provide you with the prospect of transforming your partnership to something far better than it was before. The choice is up to you. If you're unable to make major changes in your relationship (or business partnership), it will likely end."

If you're in an inappropriate relationship, Pluto's influence may bring a crisis or difficult circumstances that will require you and your partner to radically change your relationship. If you're in a destructive relationship that's emotionally or physically abusive, or in an addictive or co-dependent relationship with someone who's unhealthy, this will be when it will die or be transformed to a healthy state. If you're already in a healthy partnership it may still undergo a difficult crisis that will transform it into an even deeper love relationship as Norm found out.

Brings Transformative Love

When Norm met Rebecca, he had Pluto transiting his 7th House. It was a prime time for him to finally create a deep, passionate and intense romantic connection with someone as special as Rebecca. From the very first week they met, they saw each other regularly with increasing frequency, and within six months they had decided to live together. It was a relationship that had changed Norm's bachelor lifestyle to a committed one-on-one, deep love relationship.

Over the next few months they both talked about their dreams and goals for the future and they were amazed how much they both wanted the same things. Everything between them seemed so perfect. That changed one day when Rebecca came home from her doctor's appointment to tell Norm she had Stage 2 breast cancer. Fortunately, her doctor had said it was treatable with chemotherapy and regular follow-ups thereafter. Rebecca tearfully told Norm that while she was very happy to be in a loving relationship with him, she reminded him, "You didn't sign-up for a relationship where you have to take care of someone just diagnosed with cancer." She felt bad for both of them and felt it only fair to release him from any sense of obligation to continue their relationship. Out of her genuine love for Norm, she wanted to be fair to him, and not take advantage in any way.

At first, he was in shock, but there was never a question of leaving her. He felt a deep, profound love for Rebecca. Despite having lived a selfish single lifestyle in the past, he was ready for a permanent relationship commitment with her. If that included being Rebecca's partner in her fight to beat her cancer, then he was ready to stand by her side. Pluto transiting his 7th House had brought a difficult circumstance into his life but it had also brought a love that had transformed him forever. His love for her was all that mattered.

Brings Power Struggles & Enemies

If you decide to marry (or start a business partnership at this time), it's likely to be an absorbing, emotionally intense, and even compulsive relationship. Imagine meeting someone and becoming so enthralled with their presence that you go from seeing them once a week to every day. It just happens. All you know is that your day is not complete unless that person is in it.

Your encounters with people in your close relationships are likely to have a significant impact on you and be a catalyst for transforming you. You sense you're meant to work through important personal issues together. For this reason, this can be an excellent time to engage in some form of therapy or couples counseling, in order to better understand yourself and how you operate in relationships.

7th House : Relationships, Marriage & Partnerships

However, one of the challenges that can occur when Pluto transits your 7th House is you're susceptible to power struggles with others, especially any enemies you might have. I tell clients this is a period in your life when you can have personal battles with people where they'll use all forms of manipulation from guilt to intimidation to fight you. Interactions with such adversaries can be extremely unpleasant and even destructive, especially if you're unaccustomed to them as Wayne discovered.

Wayne and Roger were 50/50 partners and had operated their business partnership for the past 10 years. Wayne was the hard worker, who showed up every day at 7 a.m. and left at 7 p.m. Roger had started out that way during the first few years of working their business together, but once they'd built it into a reasonably successful operation, he started sloughing off. Many days he'd come into work at 9 or 10 a.m., take two-hour lunches, and come back a little sloshed from drinking. The tensions of their poor working relationship had been building for a long time. Wayne had many discussions trying to explain to Roger that not doing his fair share of work was putting way too much pressure and responsibility on Wayne. The discussions they were having lately quickly deteriorated into arguments and yelling.

Pretty soon the upset between them started to negatively affect their business. Bad feelings were evident and threats were made. Eventually, they each contacted their own attorney and within 30 days filed lawsuits against each other. Roger had tried to punish Wayne by staying home, making phone calls to customers he had personal relationships, and telling them what a jerk and unfair partner Wayne was. Roger even made up a number of lies to get customers to sympathize with him. His dislike and hatred for Wayne made him feel justified in sabotaging both Wayne and the business, even though he had a 50 percent interest in it. All he seemed to care about was being vindictive toward Wayne.

Roger had Pluto transiting his 7th House of partnership and had experienced the long-hidden tensions that were brewing in their relationship. He was engaged in a destructive power struggle, which he eventually lost when the judge who heard their case ruled in favor of Wayne. The judge's ruling cited Roger for penalties and damages for sabotaging their business. The further result was that the partnership was terminated, with Roger being given a settlement that had been worked out by the two attorneys. Now the business was solely Wayne's. This was an example of the "fight-to-the-death" conflict that can occur under Pluto's influence.

Considerations, Actions, Decisions During Pluto in 7th House

1. Are you interested in an intense romantic relationship?
2. Make a life commitment to a marriage or partnership.
3. Start a new business with an empowering business partner.
4. Are you involved in any partnerships that need to be transformed?
5. Are you involved in any toxic or destructive relationships that should die?
6. Enter therapy or counseling to transform your relationship.
7. Avoid engaging in battle with enemies.
8. Seek out professional relationships that have the power to transform you.

Transits to Use for Successful 7th House Decisions

You now understand the areas of life that are featured in your 7th House. We've discussed how each of the five transiting planets exerts its unique influence on the affairs of this House. This will help you better understand the changes you are experiencing, moods you're feeling, and the events taking place. Your awareness of this information may prompt you to:

1. *ACCEPT* the way things are and be content with what is going on in your life.

2. *CONSIDER* that you'd like to make some change, in which case you may evaluate your options and further contemplate your situation.

3. *DECIDE* that you're ready to make a change, take action, and make a decision pertaining to the affairs of this House.

If you make a decision, you'll want to learn how to pick the best transit to produce a successful outcome for it. Please know that the art of picking and interpreting transits requires very thorough analysis, normally done by a professional astrologer. Therefore, I've kept the discussion of selecting and using transits simple, for illustration purposes.

The key is to remember that each planet has the ability to bring a *different* positive quality of success to your decision. For example, *Jupiter's* effect may provide opportunities to expand and grow; *Saturn's* effect is more practical; *Uranus'* effect is sudden and exciting; *Neptune's* influence may bring you inspiration and idealism; *Pluto* may bring an intense and transformative effect for major change. This knowledge will help you understand how your decisions are affected by these planetary influences.

In the examples below, I chose a planetary transit to produce a favorable result for each individual's particular decision. This will help you

What the Hell Is Going On in My Life?

see the many possibilities available to create the right outcome and make your 7th House decisions more successful.

(**Note:** *I've included Astro Action Plans with these examples, since so many of my clients and readers were interested in seeing how they were used with the decisions that concerned marriage and partnerships.*)

Using a positive JUPITER Transit

DECISION: *I want to get married.*

Explanation: Loretta is a single female who has become a very successful executive at a technology firm. Now at the age of 31 she has said to herself, "I want to settle down and find the right man to marry."

With Jupiter transiting her 7th House of partnership, I suggested this would be a fortunate time to meet someone for long-term relationship who would have such qualities as being fun, intelligent, loving, kind and generous. She agreed that her number one priority this year was to be out socializing in the public throughout the year, especially when her Jupiter transits were most intense.

* * *

Loretta's Astro Action Plan

1. Plan a social calendar of events that I can participate in during the evenings and weekends. Schedule them during the three months when my transit will be most intense.

2. Plan to go on singles weekend retreats.

3. Join a matchmaking Internet dating service.

7th House : Relationships, Marriage & Partnerships

4. Agree to attend events that I've not tried before, such as dances, parties, being fixed up by friends.

5. Commit to socializing (not work) during this period of her life.

* * *

Using a positive Saturn Transit

DECISION: *I want to find a business partner.*

Explanation: Bart had worked with two colleagues, Maxine and Walter. He thought they each would make excellent partners for a new business he wanted to start. Maxine was a real creative genius. Walter was a brilliant accounting "numbers guy." Both of them expressed a sincere interest in becoming Bart's partner and being in business for themselves. Now, the immediate question was: *who was the best partner for him to choose?*

The Saturn transit we chose was perfect for him to work on his long-range goal in life which was starting a business and choosing a business partner that would help him accomplish that goal. His instincts for accomplishing his objectives were very sharp. It was a favorable time to use his good judgment to find a business partner who would act with honesty, integrity, and discipline. This period of time favored starting his business, being realistic, and practical about choosing the right business partner.

* * *

Bart's Astro Action Plan

1. Have an astrologer do a chart compatibility analysis of each potential partner.

2. Compare the chart comparison of Maxine and Walt my birth chart. Assess their strengths and weaknesses and how each chart complements mine.

3. Discuss results with my astrologer to evaluate my best partner option.

4. Evaluate the information we discussed to really make sure that I am excited about my choice for my business partner on an emotional, and even spiritual level, not just on an intellectual and practical level.

5. Make a decision on the best partner for me to choose.

* * *

Using a positive Uranus Transit

DECISION: *I want to take a vacation from my marriage and take a three-month trip far away.*

Explanation: Veronica got married when she 18. She married her high school boyfriend, Jacob. They've been married for 22 years and now she is bored with her life and their relationship. Veronica decided that she was no longer willing to be in a stifling marriage that limited her freedom to enjoy new activities, new people, and even foreign travel. Her marriage was either going to change or she was going to leave it. After talking with her husband, he said he wasn't interested in traveling and she should feel free to go on her own.

So, she made a decision that she would take three months off and separate from her husband and enjoy traveling on her own. She had a perfect transit to break free, be impulsive and even experimental. This transit would be ideal to use for foreign travel, meeting fascinating people of other cultures, have interesting adventures, including an exciting affair if she so chose. Best of all Veronica could feel a sense of freedom, liberation and self-discovery that she had never enjoyed. Veronica was not concerned with her marriage. She was ready to be free and independent.

* * *

Veronica's Astro Action Plan

1. Meet with my travel agent to discuss various travel itineraries to visit foreign countries I am interested.

2. Book my trip.

3. Make plans to leave my house with a sufficient amount of savings to fund my trip.

4. Research travel ideas at the library.

5. Met with some fellow travelers to get suggestions and ideas for my itinerary.

6. Leave for a long vacation adventure.

* * *

Using a positive Neptune Transit

DECISION: *I want to start a volunteer program with my husband.*

Explanation: Sandy and Carl were both artists who'd built a small art supply business together. They'd talked about teaching inner city kids a basic art class with the idea that they'd contribute their time and the necessary art supplies.

Sandy was wondering when would be the ideal time to launch a successful volunteer project with Carl. With Neptune transiting her 7th House, we found an excellent transit that would assist her in making her volunteer vision a reality. She'd be able to help organize and present her project idea in a way that conveyed its originality, creativity and practical benefit to the authorities that had the power to approve her volunteer program.

* * *

Sandy's Astro Action Plan

1. Write a plan detailing our volunteer project idea and all the details of how the program would work for those participating.

2. Set up face-to-face meeting with school officials to discuss our credentials and the volunteer project idea.

3. Ask for the opportunity to do a "pilot program" so that we can show school officials the effectiveness of the program in the hopes they would expand to allow other artists to participate in it.

4. Make presentations during the time that our favorable transit is in effect.

* * *

Using a positive Pluto Transit

DECISION: *I want to find someone for a passionate, intense romance.*

Explanation: Leonard had been married once as a young man and then divorced within a year. He's been a bachelor for many years since then. Superficial relationships did not fulfill him and he longed for a deeper, more intense emotional

7th House : Relationships, Marriage & Partnerships

connection with a woman. He hadn't dated for a long time, but recently he was feeling a more compelling need to meet someone whom he could enjoy an intimate relationship.

With Pluto going through his 7th House, he was yearning for a very special transformational relationship that would affect him on a profound level. The transit we picked would bring him the opportunity to find a woman he could share a passionate connection. This transit would also draw out his magnetic, intense personality that would be attractive to the kind of woman he desired. Best of all, this transit was ideal to bring him the kind of love relationship that would transform his ability to love as well.

* * *

Leonard's Astro Action Plan

1. Make a list of places where I am more likely to meet women who are interested in a deep relationship connection.

2. Also, make a list of places that might seem to be filled with superficial women but that I will keep an open mind and visit.

3. Spend time socializing at all of the places on my list.

4. Attend various personal growth workshops.

5. Sign up with a spiritual Internet dating web site.

6. Ask friends to introduce me to a woman who is interested in a serious relationship.

* * *

> *REMEMBER:* You can use the FREE Transit Calculator that's discussed in Part IV of this book to go back in time to see which transits were occurring when a major event happened in your life. It might be a wonderful learning experience, especially since most transits repeat themselves over your lifetime. Also you can find out where your transits are today or in the future.

8th House

Sex Life, Investments & Transformation

The 8th House rules death, sex, taxes, investments and transformation. You may be thinking: "Am I going to die rich with a smile on my face?" To find the answer, please read on.

Prepare to learn about one of the deepest, most intense areas of your life since this House governs your darkest secrets, anything intense and taboo. Let's begin with transformation. Transformation deals with changing from the *old* person you once were, to a *new* and much more evolved person who has successfully altered his behavior. Have you ever had a major realization in life that you had to change your ways? It may have been an epiphany that came to you one day. Here are frequently heard statements made *prior* transformation.

Statements Made…Just Before Transformation:

- "I promise, I'll never be unfaithful again."
- "My kid turned to drugs and I was too busy working to be a parent."
- "She said she'd leave me, if I didn't stop my abusive behavior"
- "I'm sorry, please give me one more chance to change."
- "I've lost everything, I'm ready to stop gambling"
- "The doctor says I'm a candidate for a heart attack!"

Maybe there was a special moment that caused you to "really… really" want to change, behave differently, and be a new person. Was it that Sunday at church after confessing your sins to the parish priest? Or, was it that morning your child said, "Dad, all my friends have their dads at the soccer games – but you're never there." Or, was it when your spouse said, "I will no longer live with an alcoholic like you. Quit drinking and get help or I'm leaving our marriage!"

Then, you made a commitment to change your life, once and for all. You began the radical shift in your behavior that allowed you to change in order to truly behave like a genuinely new person. Well, that's how the *transformation* process occurs.

For some readers, those may seem like extreme examples but they are from real clients who've had a deep need to transform themselves. In essence, these people realized that some aspect of their personality, behavior, or ego had to die for *real change* to occur.

Baby Face Nelson & The Pain of Transformation

The kind of major change that we're talking about doesn't occur *automatically* when a person finally declares he must change. The true transformational process that occurs in the 8th House, usually involves some sort of sacrifice, which may be painful. After all, you're getting rid of something bad in order for something better to be re-born and take its place. Be prepared to know that while a beneficial change is taking place within your life, you may not realize it's happening for 1 or 2 years. I liken the process to "watching a pot of water boil." Nothing seems to be happening for all the time you spend looking at that pot, however in time, the water finally starts to boil.

During this transformational process you may even feel shame and humiliation as you finally comprehend the true significance of your past behavior and its affect on you and others. Just imagine a criminal who gets caught for a crime, is convicted, goes through sentencing, and is sincerely contrite for his crime. Quite often, he's ready to change his ways immediately. Of course, the courtroom judge is happy the criminal "sees the light," and wants to reform his behavior. Unfortunately, as part of his transformation process, the criminal will have to go through a long and painful incarceration where he can be properly rehabilitated. So, whether you're an addict, adulterer, absent parent, abuser of other people or just your own body; or someone who needs to strongly modify her behavior, the process of transformation is usually unpleasant and very long.

After all, what's happening is that one aspect of your life is ending and just like the criminal serving jail time, you're going through your own rehabilitation process, leading you to a true metamorphosis. It's a lengthy period of time that requires your sincere commitment and perseverance.

8th House: Sex Life, Investments & Transformation

Now that I've explained the process: Is there anything about your personality or behavior that *has to change* and be transformed?

The tremendous power of the 8th House of your birth chart provides you the opportunity to transform whatever isn't working in your life. But before the re-building process can begin – your inappropriate behavior must be eliminated. In essence you must take your *psychic garbage* out to the trash bin. Purging undesirable aspects of yourself allows a part of you to undergo a symbolic death, thus in a spiritual way, you die and are resurrected as a better person. This is why the 8th House is known as the house of renewal and transformation and is often symbolized by the phoenix rising up from the ashes to be re-born once again.

Of course, there are many less dramatic examples where you may want to create a change from who you are – to the new person you want to be. Hopefully, you'll be motivated because you realize that personal transformation will improve the quality of your life, your relationship with loved ones and friends, and benefit your career.

Even if you resist, perhaps you'll find someone who will know how to motivate you to go down the road to transformation. I am reminded of a famous quotation by a great influencer and motivator, the 1930s gangster, Baby Face Nelson, who once said, "You can get a lot more with a 'kind word and a gun,' than you can with just a kind word."

Just as Baby Face stuck a gun in your face to take your money, a Pluto transit can force you to hand over a prized position of great importance you'd rather not give up such as: "I really enjoy drinking alcohol," or "My favorite thing is to get high," or "I can't help it, I love to eat," or "I have to put in extra long hours to be successful." However, unlike Baby Face, Pluto has your best interests at heart, with the goal of making you a better person. But some times Pluto has to hurt you – to help you.

Other 8th House Matters

If you recall, the 2nd House concerned your individual earnings and resources, while the 8th House rules your spouse or partner's resources and wealth. This area of your chart concerns the money and assets of your marriage or business partner. In also relates to inheritance where both parties in a marriage or business partnership benefit if one of them passes on and leaves money or other assets to the estate. This House gives insights into the way you share and bond with others, whether you make commitments and if you're likely to keep them.

This important area of your chart governs your investments and the assets you have accumulated such as money, stocks and bonds. It also rules all practical matters that have to do with death, including wills, gifts and legacies. If you were hoping to receive a great big inheritance from generous old Aunt Bessie, this would be the House to consult. It also rules, alimony, child support, insurance and taxes.

The 8th House, quite importantly, governs sex, one's behavior and attitude towards sex, sexual desires and sexual drive. Whereas sex in the 5th House of your birth chart is where you might experience pro-creational or recreational sex, the 8th House is concerned with even more *intimate sex*. It's the special "gift of sex," where you give yourself to the other person as your lover and soul mate. This isn't to say that sex that is experienced in the 5th House is not intimate or personal, because it is. It's just that the sexual connection that occurs in the 8th House is distinguished by being very deep, profound and intense.

This House rules your secrets, the occult, spiritual transformation, and psychological and physical regeneration, including healing and surgery, where transformation can occur in your heart, mind, spirit, soul and physical body.

Your Body in the 8th House

This house rules the bladder, genitals, sex organs, reproductive system, muscular system, hernias, rectum, hemorrhoids, prostate and anus. Since there is nothing more important than your health, pay special attention to these areas of your body whenever a planet transits this House. It may indicate a period of time when you'll experience health benefits, issues or even problems you should be aware of. If you observe anything unusual, you'll have the opportunity to consult with a medical doctor or a health care practitioner.

Your 8th House Decisions

You now understand that the 8th House of your birth chart concerns your personal transformation, shared resources, investments, sex, death and taxes.

As you read about the description of this house, it's time to ask yourself a few questions. What areas of your life are ripe for major change and transformation? Are there any psychic wounds that need to be healed? Are there any secrets that burden you and need to be released? How do you feel about your sex life? What would your partner say about it? Have you thought about your own death and what you've accomplished in your life?

How are you at sharing your resources? Are you lucky or unlucky in your investments? Are there any practical issues around taxes, insurance, trust, wills and your estate, which you should be attending to? Is there anyone you hope to receive an inheritance; or leave an inheritance?

These are all significant questions and your answers may lead you to make important decisions to change your life. Here are a few examples of decisions clients have made based on the activities and issues of the 8th House.

Situation: Will believes he has met a woman who is his soul mate.

DECISION: *I want to pick the best day to get married for a long-lasting and intimate partnership.*

* * *

Situation: Marianne enjoys investing. Sometimes she seems lucky, other times, not so much.

DECISION: *I want to make a large investment in the stock market that will be profitable.*

* * *

Situation: Quinton is in his retirement years. He's accumulated a great deal of wealth in his life and has five children who haven't gotten along well. He wants to leave his estate in good order, but he's afraid that after he dies there will be fighting among his children.

DECISION: *I want to make an estate plan to leave my wealth to my heirs at a favorable time when my decisions will not be subject to dispute.*

* * *

Situation: Eric has emotionally abused his wife for a long time. But for the first time, he physically abused her. She threatened she wouldn't give him a second chance if he ever hit her again.

DECISION: *I am a "rageaholic" and need help to change my life.*

* * *

During the transits of *Jupiter, Saturn, Uranus, Neptune,* and *Pluto* – Will, Marianne, Quinton, and Eric will have many opportunities to implement their decisions at a favorable time to produce the outcome they want.

The Transiting Planets Reveal Your Past, Present & Future

Your main focus is using astrology to understand *what the hell is going on in your life*. Once you do – this book will show you the best time to make a decision to change it should you have a desire to do so. As you read about the five planets transiting the 8th House, notice the way each planet exerts its unique influence and effect, bringing specific opportunities, issues, problems, and events into this area of your life. But if you're curious as to how these planets are personally affecting YOU *today,* in your *past,* or in your *future,* you can find out where each transiting planet is in your birth chart by using the *FREE Transit Calculator* (see Part IV).

JUPITER in Your 8th House of Sex, Investments & Transformation

Great Time to Share Your Resources

When Jupiter transits your 8th House, you experience fortunate benefits from other people's resources. For that reason it's an excellent time to enter a relationship, such as a marriage or business partnership, in which you and the other person combine your resources together.

Darren and Julia were planning to marry, both having been in long-term marriages previously. Darren was divorced and Julia was a wealthy widow with three grown children. They had dated for two years and enjoyed each other's companionship and were planning their future together. Julia's deceased husband had accumulated a great deal of wealth during their marriage, so her only concern in marrying Darren was that she didn't want her new marriage to interfere with her children and grandchildren receiving their rightful inheritance. Fortunately, Jupiter's transit here afforded Julia some excellent times to put together a pre-nuptial agreement that would secure her assets for herself and her children, while being fair to her new husband Darren.

Excellent Time to Get Out of Debt

Your requests for financial assistance are very much favored during this time, so you should use this year to get any money or resources you need. This is the auspicious time you've been waiting for to borrow money from someone or to apply for a bank loan, whether to finance a car or secure a mortgage for the new home you'd like to buy. The friendly and beneficial influences of Jupiter make this a time when people are especially willing to help you and give you whatever you want, so put your banker on speed-dial and request a meeting to discuss an expansion loan for your business. Arrange to take a wealthy relative or friend out for a cup of coffee to ask them if they'd like to invest in your new venture. Or, call a supplier and ask them to give you more favorable credit terms.

It's a very fortuitous time to plan your estate, draw up your will, receive benefits from insurance companies, or even settle a tax matter with the IRS. If you've put off meeting with your financial planner to discuss your investment goals, or haven't been motivated to prepare your will, or have delayed meeting with your tax attorney to discuss the potential taxes on your estate – Jupiter transiting your 8th House is a very beneficial time to address these matters. You'll receive great benefit and favorable results from the actions you take. Remember: timing...timing...timing! Use Jupiter's transit here to your advantage.

My client Wilbur had tax issues with the Internal Revenue Service because several deductions he'd taken to lower his tax bill were disputed. To make matters worse, the IRS contacted him again to say they found evidence he hadn't reported all his earned income during the previous three years. Wilbur's former accountant acknowledged he had neglected to report all of Wilbur's income during two of the years when he had made a lot of money. Now Wilbur had the IRS claiming he owed more than $400,000 in back taxes, plus another $85,000 in penalties and interest.

Wilbur was very upset when he told me about his tax situation but with Jupiter soon heading into his 8th House, I recommended he ask the IRS to give him a few more months to come up with a payment plan, which he did. They agreed to his request. Then, once his Jupiter was in effect, his next step would be to hire a CPA who specialized in working with the IRS and negotiate Wilbur's tax bill to a lower rate. I explained that the influences of Jupiter would be lucky for him, likely resulting in a negotiation with the IRS that would work out to his benefit. He took my advice and within six months his $400,000 back taxes were negotiated down to $175,000, with all penalties and interest waived. Wilbur breathed a deep sigh of relief at his good fortune.

Great Time to Make a Fortune Through Investing & Inheritance

Jupiter's influence brings uncanny luck, which is why this is often an excellent time to invest your money and receive a great return on your investment (especially if other confirming transits occur during Jupiter's transit through your 8th House). You may also be rewarded with financial gain through inheritances, gifts or even lotteries.

I had a client who was having Jupiter transit her 8th House in August, so I told her that would be an extremely lucky time to invest, perhaps even to receive a lot of money from an unexpected source. I also recommended she invest in gold bullion. Within three weeks it was up almost 15 percent. Then, during the middle of August she went to her mailbox and discovered she'd received a totally unexpected $10,000 check from her father, something he had never done before. Since he was getting up in years, he wanted to give her a wonderful gift to enjoy while he was still alive.

TIP: If you're an investor pay careful attention to the time when Jupiter transits your 8th House as well as any dates when Jupiter makes favorable transits to this House. This is when you're lucky and your investments are likely to make you a handsome profit or even a fortune. (The FREE Transit Calculator will tell you when Jupiter transits your 8th House. *If you contact me, I can analyze your future transits and tell you the exact dates when you'll have great fortune making investments.)* This is another practical example of how you can use astrology to create a more prosperous and happier life for yourself.

A Time for Transformation

This is also a fortunate time for you in terms of developing a greater sense of self-understanding because you're able to make discoveries about your own psychological inner workings, enabling you to grow and mature as a person. In fact, if you have been through any kind of mental or emotional stress, or are presently going through a grieving process, this is a time when deep healing is possible.

Miriam's wonderful marriage of 30 years ended when her husband died of a sudden heart attack and she has remained in shock over his passing ever since. Even though it has been almost two years since he died, she refuses to discuss his death with anyone as she still remains in denial over the loss of her husband. Her children and friends encouraged her to enter grief counseling, but Miriam said she wasn't ready. During my consultation with Miriam, I suggested that when Jupiter transited her 8th House, it might be the ideal time to obtain a psychological release from her profound loss. Jupiter's energies would bring her healing, understanding and an opportunity to transform her grief from denial to acceptance. When Jupiter began its transit there, Miriam found herself finally ready to begin her grieving process.

Jupiter's influence brings wisdom, higher learning and self-discovery, which can make this an ideal period to deepen your religious convictions as well as further your spiritual development. Consider planning a spiritual outing or go on a yoga-meditation retreat because you'll be able to tap into a deep part of your being and learn much about yourself in the process.

Herb was a client who always analyzed his past mistakes, often wondering *why* he made the decisions he made, musing and speculating about *which* transits were going on in his life that influenced certain events to happen. I explained to him that if he looked back at the major events that occurred in his life, he'd see the corresponding transits going on at that time (Note: this is yet, another reason to use the FREE Transit calculator discussed in Part IV). Out of curiosity, Herb asked me to look back to the time of his 13th birthday when he had his Bar Mitzvah (a religious ceremony where a Jewish boy accepts the obligations of adulthood). Sure enough, his Bar Mitzvah occurred during the year Jupiter was going through his 8th House, a time of growth, maturity and transformation in the life of a young man.

A Time to Learn, Grow and Enjoy Sex

Jupiter's transit in your 8th House brings you the potential to learn about sex and experience it on a very intense soul mate level. As a result, you may find that a love relationship you have at this time brings you greater sexual enjoyment and pleasure than you've ever experienced before, because you're sharing sex with your partner in a deeply profound, intimate way. No matter how sexually experienced you are, Jupiter's influence makes it possible for you to enthusiastically learn, teach and grow in your sexual relationship. You and your partner are able to gain a deep understanding of how powerful a sexual connection can be when two people in love, merge their sexual energies into a single committed relationship – as May learned in the story below.

Steven and May married when she was 18 and still a virgin with very little sexual knowledge. They enjoyed a good marriage where he provided for her and was a kind and caring partner. Unfortunately, Steven wasn't an experienced or sexual man, so they had very little passion in their relationship. In fact, they rarely had sex and when they did it ended very quickly, with May receiving little satisfaction. After a few months of marriage, May discussed her sex life with an older friend who listened and then explained that her husband was the same way. Her friend confided she would just have to accept that men were "just like that," concerned mainly with their own pleasure. Since May had no other sexual experience to compare her relations with Steven, she accepted their sex life as the norm.

Tragically, Steven died in an accident at age 42 and May's life changed in many ways as she went through the grief and loneliness of being single again. Eventually, she met Randy at a social event at her church and she immediately felt a special chemistry with him that she'd never felt before. As they continued going out for a few months, their relationship deepened. Then one night Randy made love to May in a very passionate, tender way that was more powerful than anything she'd ever experienced. She was amazed at Randy's knowledge and skill as a lover, opening her up to a world of pleasure she never knew ever existed. The act of sex between them transformed May, making her realize both the deep intimacy and pleasure that was possible between a man and a woman

This story illustrates the joyful learning experience of sex through a deep love relationship. However, it should be noted: All the planetary transits through the 8th House make it possible for you to experience a passionate and intense sexual connection with another person even *without* love and commitment.

Considerations, Actions, Decisions During Jupiter in 8th House

1. Do you want to transform your behavior?
2. Begin therapy or some self-discovery process.
3. Do you want to heal a psychic wound?
4. Do you want to go on a religious or spiritual journey?
5. Do you want to have an intense sexual connection?
6. Do you want to buy insurance?
7. Do you want to settle a tax matter?
8. Do you want to apply for a loan?
9. Do you want to make a long-term investment?
10. Do you want to plan your estate or prepare your will?

SATURN in Your 8th House of Sex, Investments & Transformation

Bad Time to Rely on the Resources of Others

When Saturn transits your 8th House, you'll re-examine your personal transformation and sexuality so that you can be more accountable for how well these areas of your life have turned out. In addition, you may encounter challenges and even limitations in the areas of your finances and investments, as well as the assets you share with others. This may be a period of time when you'll have to take on more responsibility because you can't depend on the resources of others to assist you. The restrictions you may encounter are meant to teach you to be more independent of others.

You may find, perhaps through no fault of your own, circumstances occur where resources you need and depend on are no longer available to you. Perhaps, the financial support you've relied on is cut off or just not available. For example, the bank says no to your loan request; or your company has lost so much money this year there will not be a bonus; or perhaps a parent can no longer provide you with financial assistance as Marilyn learned.

Marilyn's father called her to explain that he just got laid off from his job, so he can no longer send her a monthly allowance during her freshman year at college. This is very disappointing news, since she'd planned to concentrate on her studies and use her free time to participate in the campus theatre club. Marilyn now has to find a part-time job to make enough money to cover her living expenses.

Vince has enough money for a down payment to buy a small condo in the city. However, several banks have declined his mortgage application, since his earnings aren't high enough to qualify him for a larger loan.

Pauline desperately needs money to expand her business. She was sure that even if the banks turned her down she could count on a Small Business Administration loan, but she doesn't qualify for that either.

8th House: Sex Life, Investments & Transformation

The experiences of Marilyn, Vince and Pauline illustrate they couldn't depend on financial resources being available, even ones they expected to be there. During the two and a half year period that Saturn transits your 8th House, you should plan on relying on your own finances and avoid being dependent on the resources of others as much as possible. If this isn't realistic, consider minimizing your reliance on others, just as Marilyn did by taking a part time job. In Vince's case, he'll have to find a less expensive condo he can obtain a mortgage. In Pauline's case, she may have to delay her plans to expand her business. Saturn's energies bring restrictions and limitations that will often delay or stop you from obtaining what you want to accomplish.

TIP: Since a Saturn transit brings responsibilities, limitations and restrictions, you should always know in what area of your life it's transiting. It will help you understand *what the hell is going on in your life*. On a practical level, it will also allow you to make any preparations you think necessary.

> *NOTE: The difficulties you may encounter as a result of this Saturn transit or any transit – illustrate the importance of finding out where your FUTURE transits are in your birth chart. It will also help you plan for a rainy day and make other important plans.*

Bad Time for Investing & Being in Debt

Take time out for soul-searching, so that you can truly assess your needs, your possessions, and the resources you share with others. The purpose of this transit is to help you evaluate what you have and what you're trying to achieve. Despite the limitations you face, you're mastering how to navigate your life, recognizing the reality that certain resources may not be available to you. In this process you'll learn valuable lessons about how to negotiate and cooperate with those you depend on. The lessons of Saturn help you become wiser and more mature.

Saturn's transit here is generally not a favorable time to make investments. The problem is that investments you make – somehow end up limiting you or becoming a burden or responsibility; or alternatively, they can bring an unanticipated restriction into your life that turns out to be inconvenient.

What the Hell Is Going On in My Life?

Sylvia was very careful with her money, always saving for a rainy day when she might need extra cash. When her friend told her about a hi-tech stock that would "double" over the next 12 months, she decided to throw caution to the wind and invest her savings in this stock. Within 60 days, the stock was down by 30 percent with her friend assuring her that it was nothing to worry about, as it would eventually go back up and continue to rise from there. However, he counseled her to be patient because it might take at least two years.

A week later Sylvia received a phone call from her younger sister asking for a temporary loan so she could pay for a surgery that her insurance didn't fully cover. In the past, when Sylvia had financial difficulties, her sister was there to help her, so now she felt duty-bound to do the same. Then, to make matters worse, the water pipe in Sylvia's home broke and flooded two of the rooms, ruining the carpeting and furniture. Now she needed money to repair and replace what was damaged. What was she going to do? Sylvia didn't want to sell her stock and take such a huge loss.

Sylvia's situation is a classic example of how Saturn's energies can come into your life bringing you unwanted responsibilities, restrictions and limitations as it transits this House. It's essential to be prudent, taking precautions during this period of time, being extremely conservative and resisting the temptation to over-expand.

In order to afford college, Jose took out a 10-year student loan. He hated being in debt, but it was the only means available to him. Working hard in school, he received his electrical engineering degree and was immediately hired by a local telecommunications company and in short time, his competence was recognized, with his company giving him more responsibility and a big raise. As a very conscientious, responsible young man, he was paying off his credit card debts and his college loan. In fact, he had only three years remaining on his school loan. With the extra money he was earning, he planned to buy some luxury items he had always wanted.

When I met Jose for his transit consultation, I explained that Saturn would be coming to his 8th House within two years. It would likely bring restrictions to his finances, especially if he needed any credit, so I recommended that instead of buying luxury items now, he use the extra money to pay off his credit card debt and any outstanding loans. That way, instead of having these debts looming in his life when his Saturn transit occurred, they'd be paid off in advance. That's what he did.

8th House: Sex Life, Investments & Transformation

A Time to Transform Your Behavior

Saturn's transit here gives you a remarkable capacity to transform yourself on a deep psychological basis, making profound discoveries about your own mortality, including investigating what death may mean to you. While your own death may be unlikely, this could be a time when it comes into your life, perhaps through the death of someone close to you. As a result, you may find yourself giving serious thought to your own feelings of mortality. It's a time when you gain wisdom and may even develop a spiritual interest in the process of dying. I had one client so intrigued with dying that he volunteered at a hospice in order to talk to people about how they felt being at the end of their lives. Another client was fascinated to explore a metaphysical class on reincarnation under this transit.

Years ago I participated in a personal growth workshop where I was asked to meditate, imagining: *What I would do with my life if I had only one year to live?*

This meditation gave me a profound perspective on how precious my life was to me, including the work I was doing, the friendships I had, and all the people that I loved and would miss when I was gone. It made me conscious of the importance of living in the moment and recognizing the "power of now." You can create an eye-opening experience for yourself, by just closing your eyes and thinking about that question.

When Saturn transits your 8th House, you find yourself re-evaluating both your desire nature and your use of power. You'll even re-examine the methods or habit patterns you use to achieve your objectives in these areas, whether it's through friendly persuasion or intimidation. For example, if your desire nature has caused you to manipulate others to get what you want or if you have a dominating nature and use coercion to get your way, you may decide to root out such behavior and make a change for the better. It's also possible that your improper behavior will be exposed by others, thus – forcing you to change it. This transit is often the undoing of abusers, bullies and sadists. These two and a half years are an opportunity for you to bring about psychological change that will transform you to be a healthier and more fully functioning person.

Hans had been brought up in an Eastern Bloc country and had immigrated to America as a young boy with his parents. He was raised by a very harsh, disciplinarian father, who punished Hans, beating him with a leather strap until he was bruised all over. As Hans grew up and started his own family, he exhibited the same disciplinarian, parenting behavior as his father. When his son Ronnie misbehaved, he pulled out a leather strap and gave him a whipping he wouldn't forget. Many of the beatings he gave his son were physically abusive, which made it understandable why Ronnie was very afraid of him. Han's wife, Anna Marie, had begged him to stop hitting the child in such an aggressive, abusive way. But he wouldn't listen and continued to mete out punishment to Ronnie whenever he perceived behavior that he disapproved. After all, Hans reasoned to Anna Marie, "My father treated me that way, and I turned out all right, didn't I?"

After watching her son receive one exceptionally bad beating, Anna Marie had enough of helplessly standing by and decided to get help. She went to her son's school and asked to speak with one the counselors, Mr. Meyers. She recounted, in specific detail, the beatings her husband had inflicted on Ronnie. Mr. Meyers was appalled and explained to Anna Marie that in order to protect Ronnie, he would immediately file a report with Child Protective Services, making them aware of Ronnie's physical abuse. Saturn was transiting Han's 8th House and it was time for Hans to be held accountable for his behavior and actions.

A Time to Be Sexually Responsible

Since the 8th House governs sex, this is when you may become aware of the power of your sexuality and its impact on your life. You'll likely learn lessons about the way sex functions in your relationships and regard sex in a more serious manner, whether you're having it or not. Also, if your relationship is sexually unsatisfying, you'll confront the underlying issues that cause it to be so. Saturn's energies demand that you be accountable for your sexual behavior or pay the consequences.

Brian was in his senior year of high school and like any teenager his testosterone levels were doing backflips. His new girlfriend Victoria was sweet and playful, but very naïve. They started going to parties and hanging out together, and they began to engage in kissing and heavy petting. Even though, Brian pushed Victoria to go further, she always stopped him, reminding him she was a virgin and wanted to stay that way.

One evening they came back to her house after a party, and her parents were already in bed. As they sat down on the couch and had some sodas, Brian complained that they needed to "spice up" their drinks. He was able to talk Victoria into raiding her parents' liquor cabinet and pouring some rum into their colas. Soon they were both drunk and they started kissing and touching and one thing led to another. The next thing they knew was they were having unprotected sex. It didn't take long for them sober up enough to realize what they had done. A month later a test showed that Victoria was pregnant. Saturn was transiting Brian's 8th House and he was soon to learn a lesson about being sexually irresponsible.

Be Conservative in All Estate Matters

It's also when you may experience limitations around estates matters such as wills, inheritance or insurance. For example, you may find out that your will wasn't properly drafted to minimize estate taxes; or you find out that you've been left out of an inheritance; or you may discover you were under-insured. It's generally not a favorable time to settle any tax matters, especially if you are guilty of evading taxes because the likelihood of receiving penalties and being punished is greater. In general, Saturn's energies demand that you be honest, prudent and conservative during these two and a half years, relying on your own financial resources.

Since Saturn's influence is a time when your finances may be restricted, settle any debts you have prior to this transit, if possible. Wean yourself from any reliance on credit cards and living beyond your means. Saturn's influence is to be responsible and very prudent before taking any financial risks, so be extra cautious in evaluating all investments before committing to them.

Considerations, Actions, Decisions During Saturn in 8th House

1. What practical benefit would you receive if you transformed yourself?
2. Begin therapy or some self-discovery process that will benefit you.
3. Do you want to heal a psychic wound?
4. Consider going on a religious or spiritual journey where you can contemplate your life.
5. Do you want to buy more insurance?
6. Be totally honest in all tax matters.
7. Avoid making loans at this time; or be very conservative if you do.
8. Be cautious in making any investments.
9. Do you want to conservatively plan your estate and draw up your will?
10. Are you being safe and responsible in your sex life?

URANUS in Your 8th House of Sex, Investments & Transformation

Look for Shocking Surprises

The 8th House rules joint finances, partnership assets that you share with someone else, other people's resources, as well as investments, inheritance, wills, loans, and taxes. When Uranus transits here, you'll experience revolutionary changes on a physical and even unconscious level in all matters of this House. Expect the influence of Uranus to bring you a shocking, *out of the blue* event that will be intense and even fateful. What happens is that a radical change suddenly occurs, upsetting the old order of your life, bringing in something totally new. But with Uranus you'll never know what to expect.

During this seven-year period, you may receive many surprises: You might be suddenly hired or unexpectedly fired; there may be a radical change in your partner's income (spouse or business partner) either positively or negatively. Perhaps, you and your partner abruptly go from "well off" to very rich or from wealthy to bankrupt. You may find out that an old investment is suddenly worth a fortune or is worthless; or a bank uncharacteristically calls a loan due.

Uranus may deliver the unexpected in many ways, such as you searching through your attic and finding Great Grandpa's old stock certificate worth pennies during the depression, but worth millions now. Maybe you receive a surprise inheritance from Aunt Martha leaving you a fortune or you may get a notice from the IRS that you have a large tax bill from your tax filing 2 years ago. Perhaps you go to a flea market and buy an old picture, take it home to re-frame it and discover that on the back of the picture are several rare stamps from the 1900s.

You may find your insurance company refuses to honor a claim, informing you that your policy doesn't cover your loss. Perhaps your lover becomes pregnant, even though you were careful and had protected sex; or someone who was close to you and connected to your past suddenly dies. You're likely to experience a great deal of instability in these

8th House: Sex Life, Investments & Transformation

areas during this period of your life, along with unexpected surprises you would have never imagined.

Uncle Milton was Cheryl's favorite uncle when she was a little girl, and she always remembered his big hearty laugh. He'd been a bachelor all his years, living a very modest life, working as a tailor in a men's clothing store. Cheryl was 13 when her family moved, so she rarely saw him any more. Years later they both attended a big family event after her graduation and had a wonderful talk about old times. He affectionately told her she was his favorite niece and that he was so proud of her.

With those memories in her mind, Cheryl was very saddened when her father told her Uncle Milton had a stroke and was not doing well. However, Milton had expressly asked that she fly up to see him, even arranging to pay her airfare. When Cheryl entered Milton's hospital room he said, "Sweetheart, thank you for coming and making your uncle so happy. Is there any wish you have, because long after I'm gone, I want to be sure all your dreams come true." Tearfully, Cheryl said, "Uncle Milton, I have everything I need. My only wish is that you recover and feel much better." The next day Uncle Milton died. A month later, the attorney for Milton's estate contacted Cheryl and said he'd left her $100,000 in his will to do with as she pleased.

Of course, the effects of Uranus may be less dramatic where you experience change, in a milder, yet still surprising form. For 12 years, one of my clients regularly received an annual bonus from his company. Each year the amount varied, but he always received one. With Uranus in his 8th House, he was surprised when he was told he would not receive a bonus this year.

Because of the instability of this period of life, it's best to avoid being dependent upon anyone else's financial assistance. This includes being very careful when taking out any loans or mortgages, making sure you can afford to pay them back without great imposition to your finances. The problem is that somehow in some way, these financial obligations may create upset and disruption in your life. Of course, with Uranus energies in play, you just don't know. Therefore, "an ounce of prevention is worth a pound of cure."

Be Aware of Partnership Upsets

Another manifestation of this transit is that you might suddenly become extremely upset about the partnership you're involved in. For example, if you share joint resources together, such as owning a property or sharing a mortgage, you may have a desire to break away from your partner and no longer be obligated to the person. A likely outcome might be a dispute, conflict, or big problem that disrupts your life and your partnership.

Lorraine, Cathy and Lucy bought a condo on the beach in Cabo San Lucas. They each own one-third of the investment, but Lucy has become increasingly upset with her two partners because of the irresponsible way they take care of the condo. Lorraine consistently leaves the place a mess and forgets to arrange maid service and every time Cathy uses the condo she throws wild parties that get out of control. The last party resulted in damaged rugs covered with red wine stains and broken furniture. Lucy has had enough of their partnership and wants out.

A Time for an Unusual Sexual Relationship or Adventure

The 8th House also rules sex, so Uranus' influence can often bring a new, exciting and unusual sexual relationship that's totally different than you've ever experienced before. It will likely be intense, unpredictable and unstable, and may end as quickly as it started. But the sexual excitement that Uranus brings can be intoxicating and liberating.

Tony and Penny were on their first ocean cruise enjoying a tropical vacation and meeting interesting people. Hand in hand, they walked into the ship's dining room and were seated at a table with a very stylish couple, Alec and Ursula. After ordering champagne, they talked about all the entertaining events on their cruise, and by the second bottle, everyone was feeling loose and relaxed. Penny commented about how cold Indianapolis was this time of the year and what a pleasure it was to wear so little clothing.

Alec agreed, and told them of their plans to visit their favorite nude beach club on the next shore excursion, sharing that he and Ursula found it so liberating to enjoy the freedom of being naked and uninhibited. Penny looked at Tony and finally said, "Tony and I are here celebrating our 18th anniversary and I have to admit that the folks back home would be shocked if we told them we went to a nude beach club!" Alec gave her a mischievous look and said, "Why don't you forget about telling them. Come with us tomorrow and spend the day at the club. It will give you a fun experience and an exciting memory of your 18th anniversary you'll never forget." Penny and Tony smiled and gave each other a look that said, "I'm game...if you are?" Finally Tony raised his glass and proposed a toast, "To a new friendship and new experience tomorrow!"

Brings Radical Psychological Changes

This is a period of radical psychological changes within your conscious and subconscious mind that will change old habit patterns within you. If you've grown up thinking you had to become wealthy, you may have an epiphany that makes you realize living modestly and enjoying what you have is quite satisfying or visa versa.

You'll find your intuition is strong, helping you make discoveries about yourself that free you from behaviors that are in your best interest to change. One client realized he'd grown up treating women like objects. By changing his perspective, he was now able to enjoy intimacy with a woman in a new way. Another client became aware of how "status-conscious" she was about the men she dated. She paid more attention to the clothes they wore and the kind of car they drove than their values and character.

If anyone has placed restrictions on you or if you've imposed restrictions on yourself, they'll become unbearable at this time. You'll find yourself rebelling and breaking away to obtain your freedom. A friend of mine had stayed in an unhappy marriage for years, just to avoid having the financial mess of splitting their assets. Uranus's influence caused him to no longer care about his wealth, only his freedom.

One of the surprises you may notice is a change in your attitudes, motivations and behavior. You're likely to assess your personal worth as an individual and become financially more independent. A client of mine, who lived off his family's wealth, rebelled and joined the Peace Corps as a way of renouncing money and his dependence on others. In the process he obtained his freedom from their expectations.

One of the triggers for this change in your attitude may be a result of the new people you meet and even situations you may never have expected to encounter. I tell clients who are struggling with issues relating to their own psychological transformation, sex, money, and materiality to talk to people who are rich and poor; talk to people about their investments; about what it's like to share resources in a marriage; about sexual matters; and about psychological experiences that were part of their personal transformation. There is so much to learn from other people about all these topics that will help you come to your own epiphanies and conclusions.

The liberating experiences you have during Uranus' transit through your 8th House may be a catalyst for major transformation in your finances, other people's resources, investments, sexuality, and in your own psychological behavior.

Considerations, Actions, Decisions During Uranus in 8th House

1. Are you ready to make a radical change in your personality or life?
2. Is there a religious or spiritual journey that you'd find liberating?
3. Are there any unusual or exciting investments you'd like to make?
4. Are you interested in surprising anyone by including them in your will?
5. Are you interested in trying a new or experimental therapy or self-discovery process?
6. Has your intuition made you aware of any psychic wounds that have occurred in your life? If so, would you like to heal them?
7. Do you want to have an unusual and exciting sexual encounter?

NEPTUNE in Your 8th House of Sex, Investments & Transformation

An Excellent Time to Explore Your Inner Self

When Neptune transits your 8th House, your attention turns to the hidden areas of your subconscious mind and you begin a process where you experience an internal change in your consciousness. You'll find yourself interested in the religious, spiritual and even psychic world. During this period of your life you may find yourself in a bookstore, suddenly drawn to the section that features spiritual, mystical, and metaphysical books. The idea of enrolling in a personal growth workshop or going on a meditation retreat may be intriguing to you; or perhaps, you'll decide to go with a friend to a lecture on Buddhism or take a Bible studies class. There is something very mystical going on in your life at this time.

This is a time when you are emotionally open and sensitive. You want to learn more about your own psychological drives so that you can understand the way your subconscious mind works. This exploration into the deepest aspects of your psyche will allow you to make necessary changes in your behavior they may not have been possible before. Your ability to better understand yourself offers the opportunity to free you from anxieties, fears and obsessions that have troubled you all your life. For that reason, it's an excellent time to delve into your inner self and heal any psychological problems that have limited you. This may be when you'll see a therapist or join a group that will help you make discoveries and find answers.

Patty continues to attract men who are selfish and uninterested in her needs and doesn't understand what aspects of her personality and behavior cause this to happen so often. Gordon has always been shy around women and doesn't know why meeting them has always been so uncomfortable for him. Gena is tired of having relationships with men who are commitment-phobic and wonders why she attracts those men into her life?

Neptune's influence may help these people find answers to their questions. The energies of Neptune allow you to detach your ego from yourself so that you can more objectively understand your psychological motivations and transform the deepest part of your inner being. You'll notice that you're able to make a connection to your creative and intuitive self. This may be a mystical time, where instead of focusing only on your personal desires, you're more concerned with the meaning of life and its mysteries.

Mary Ellen had always been drawn to the spiritual, so when her friend Samantha invited her to her yoga class she was very curious and excited to attend. After the class, the instructor invited everyone to stay for the meditation that followed, along with a brief question and answer discussion. The whole experience was invigorating for Mary Ellen physically and emotionally. She loved the exercise she had gotten from the yoga poses and the guided meditation helped her clear her mind, while her focused breathing allowed her to feel a real inner peace. Afterwards, everyone shared their experiences. The teacher was helpful, guiding the discussion and sharing insights on how to get the most out of meditating. Mary Ellen was amazed at how the entire class brought her a sense of peace and tranquility. It made her enthused about coming back and participating on a regular basis.

You may notice that your life is changing on a very subtle plane, either because you're changing; or perhaps, because some big change has occurred in your life, such as the death of someone close to you. When he was 10 years old, one of my clients had been close with his father, only to have him tragically die in a car accident. He described to me what it was like to be 16, playing football at his school, with all his friends' fathers watching them play, and feeling so strange and different as he realized his father wasn't there any longer to watch him. He felt a pain in his gut and deep loss in his heart, wondering when he might feel differently.

"Neither a Borrower Nor a Lender Be"

The 8th House concerns your personal investing and the joint finances you share with another person. Be aware that Neptune's influence in this House can bring you confusion, misunderstanding and misrepresentation with others over investments, property or money. In effect, you may be wearing blinders and not even know it. This means that you have to be especially careful of being deceived in these matters during this transit. The problem is often that something is being hidden that prevents you from knowing the full truth about what's really happening. Even worse, you may delude yourself into thinking that you've been quite thorough in your research or extremely cautious in your investment. Then, wham! You find out some information you didn't know previously and it totally boggles your mind. You look in the mirror and say to yourself, "How did I miss that?" That's when you may realize the answer: Neptune is transiting your 8th House. For this reason it's not a good time to loan or borrow money (or invest).

You may be safe arranging for a loan with a reputable bank where a strict, application process and business relationship exists. However, more casual transactions that occur when Neptune is transiting here are often done in a fog with a lack of clarity. It's an experience similar to waking up in the morning after a long night of partying and finding your vision blurry. For that reason, be careful if you pursue a personal arrangement to borrow or loan money from family or friends. This is a time when your dealings with them may leave you open to miscommunication, misunderstandings and problems – as Jerry found out.

Ira and Jerry had been close college buddies back when they were in school together. Jerry hadn't heard from Ira in many years, so he was surprised when one day he received a call from Ira saying he was in financial trouble and asking him for a temporary loan. It was odd because Ira said he wanted to borrow $5,000 for just one week. He told Jerry that in order to prove he was "good for it," he'd send him a post-dated check for $5,000 that Jerry could cash the following week. Because he totally trusted his old college buddy, Jerry was totally surprised the following week when his $5,000 check from Ira was returned by the bank, marked NSF (non-sufficient funds). When Jerry called Ira for an explanation, he was even more shocked to find that Ira had declared bankruptcy. Ira gave a quick apology and admitted to Jerry he had no money to pay him back.

Considerations, Actions, Decisions During Neptune in 8th House

1. Do you want to spiritually transform yourself?
2. Would going on a religious or spiritual journey inspire you?
3. Avoid borrowing or lending money unless you're extremely clear on the terms. Then, put it in writing.
4. Scrutinize any investments very carefully before making them.
5. Do you want to draw up a will and leave some of your wealth to a charity?
6. Begin therapy or some self-discovery process that might heal you.
7. Have you had any psychic visions or intuitions about your past?
8. Do you want to have a romantic, dreamy sexual connection?

PLUTO in Your 8th House of Sex, Investments & Transformation

A Great Time to Explore Your Self

When Pluto transits your 8th House, you experience personal growth and a deeper understanding of yourself, which can lead to your psychological transformation in all the affairs of this House. This is a time of profound change when you may find yourself letting go of values and personal attachments, which no longer fit who you are and may be inappropriate to your life. If your shared resources and investments must radically change, you'll begin the process of transforming them as well. If you need to make some major alteration in your sexuality, this may be when you begin. Now is when you can do deep work on yourself to become the person you've always wanted to be.

Get ready for your friends and family to remark how serious, intense and focused you are, because you're under this transit's influence. You may find yourself exploring your own psyche and be drawn to investigating the mysteries of life that in the past have never interested you; but now they do. You're connected to the psychic and spiritual part of your being, which may cause you to explore meditation, metaphysical teachings and even astrology.

Clients often make their first appointment to see me when Pluto is transiting their 8th House. They'll say, "I've never consulted with an astrologer before. This felt like the right time in order to learn more about myself." Their motivation was easy to understand because the 8th House rules the occult, which pertains to the taboo, mysterious and supernatural as well as psychic phenomena, mystical and magical beliefs. So, this Pluto transit often attracts people to search for *hidden* answers to their life they can't find from traditional sources. In fact, issues about themselves, as well as life and death become very significant to them during this transit.

Note: The truth is that astrology was never really considered *occult* since it was never hidden or secret. It was actually practiced openly in biblical times in many ancient civilizations such as Babylonia where it was used as a tool for understanding and forecasting. More recently astrology (although less openly) has been used throughout modern history by kings and presidents in the same ways. But to the average person astrology is a mysterious science (which hopefully this book will de-mystify).

This Pluto transit takes you on a long process encompassing a number of years where you can finally rid yourself of undesirable behavior once and for all. Your psychological energies at this time give you the resources to purge destructive behavioral patterns that must die in order for you to emerge as a truly transformed person. This is a period in your life when you're able to see they no longer serve you.

Rita grew up protecting herself from hurt and rejection by making sure to control her relationships with people. One of the ways she controlled others was through manipulation and even intimidation. Her behavior often resulted in verbal fights and power struggles with romantic partners and friends, frequently ending badly. After her last upsetting break-up, she spent time with a therapist who helped her see the destructive behavioral patterns that sabotaged many of her past relationships. This awareness gave her a deep motivation to stop behaving in these ways in order to have a more satisfying connection with others.

One of the catalysts for your own personal transformation may come through your experience of death. I'm not suggesting that your life is in danger or that you'll die, but Pluto's passage through your 8th House can often be a period in your life when people you've been close to may die. If this happens, their passing will have a profound effect on you. For example, the death of a parent may change your life circumstances in a major way or the death of a close friend may cause you to reflect on your own life and its meaning. It's a profound time where you become reflective and your concerns go very deep. I remind clients that while it's important to focus on the loss and grief that surrounds the death of a loved one, it's valuable to look at their death in a deeper way. Ask yourself, "What valuable lessons did your relationship teach you that have helped shape you into the person you are today?" You may want to ask, if that person's death makes you look at your own mortality? Your answers may give you a greater sense of closure and appreciation for their importance to your life.

In my own life, I reflect back to my father who taught me so much about kindness and understanding. I think of my first boss at the clothing store I worked at in Evanston, Illinois, who helped me get through my formative teen-age years teaching me to be a mature, responsible person. I remember a kindly uncle who took time out to teach me how to read a street map so that I could learn to navigate around the city in my car and find my way through life. Then, there was an employer who was a great mentor, teaching me about sales, marketing and how business worked; and the perseverance and dedication it would take to be successful. In my life there have been many wonderful friends who are gone now, but for many years they were there to guide me and support me. It's valuable to explore how someone's death has helped your transformation and growth as a person.

Barry and Rick were childhood friends and they went through grade school, high school and college together. As adults they'd known each other for 55 years and had a close relationship, taking walks and meeting for coffee at least once a week, sharing a deep emotional bond. When Barry died of a heart attack, Rick was in shock; all he could think about was all the years they'd been close friends and how much he would miss Barry. Barry's death was a reality check for Rick, waking him up to the fact that life was not forever. Rick was 66, and he felt himself becoming introspective, trying to examine what he'd accomplished in his life, knowing full well he wouldn't live forever. His friend's passing was a catalyst that forced Rick to confront his own life and the reality that one day he too, would face death.

A Time for Sexual Transformation

Since the 8th House rules sex in a deep and intimate way, you might experience more sexual passion than you have ever before with a lover because your sexual relationship feels so intense and transformational. There is a deep connection between you and your partner, arousing powerful and compulsive feelings of love, which unite you as soul mates.

While your sex life can be transformed in a very positive and profound way during this Pluto transit, such as those clients who were sexually awakened or who lost their virginity at this time, it's also possible to experience a radical change that results in the *death* of your old sex life.

Donald had always been a very sexual man from the time he was a teen-ager through his 20s. When he got married in his 30s, he continued to enjoy a wonderful and intense sexual connection with his wife. Their relationship continued this way for many years through his 50s, though he frequently used medical drugs, such as *Viagra*, to enhance his performance. Sex seemed a natural part of his life and the deep connection he shared with his wife. When he turned 60, however, he started noticing a

8th House: Sex Life, Investments & Transformation

shift in his interest in sex, sexual appetite and the frequency with which he had sex with his wife – and of course, she did, too.

Donald consulted his urologist, who explained that based on the normal aging process and decreasing testosterone levels, sexual appetites changed for men like him; otherwise Donald was very healthy. The doctor asked Donald how often he had sex with his wife. When he replied, "At least once a week," his doctor patted him on the back saying, "Congratulations, your sexual frequency puts you in the upper 1percent of all men at 60. Hey stud, quit your complaining."

While that news might have sounded good to his doctor, it was depressing to Donald. Of course, intellectually he knew a man's body changed as he aged; yet that answer wasn't very satisfying for him. He talked about sexual frequency with other men friends who had also slowed down and had less interest in sex, as well as those who talked of having sex more frequently than he did. What had changed him from a man, his wife often jokingly called a "sex-maniac," to a man with a waning sex drive, with less interest in making love than before?

Donald came to me for a transit consultation with this very question, "What the hell is going on in my sex life?" It was easy to understand the physical change he was experiencing because Pluto was making an important transit to his 8th House, transforming Donald's sexuality. This was creating a radical physiological change for him on one level and a major lifestyle change on another. The influences of his Pluto transit produced the "death" of his old sex life as it had been before.

I explained to Donald that he was now experiencing the re-birth of a new sexual life. This Pluto transit brought a sexual *right of passage* to his life. Yes, that might mean less frequent sex with his wife; however, he would still enjoy a deep, intimate and satisfying sexual connection with her. Perhaps, he would experience his "once a week" sex on a more profound level, putting even more loving energy into it because of its new significance to him.

Understanding this transit's transformational effect released a lot anxiety for Donald and helped him *accept* that his body had changed. He was no longer going to function like the young sexual man he was in the past years of his life.

I have witnessed clients who have tormented themselves wishing and hoping that something could be the way it once was. They may even give intellectual lip service (e.g.,"I know I've gotten older") to the fact that change has occurred, but emotionally they are still living in their past glory when they were operating at their peak. So, unless a person *internalizes* that a change has indeed taken place, acknowledging that they now must live with a new reality – they will not achieve an inner peace about their dissatisfaction. *Acceptance* is often one of the ways we can positively transform ourselves.

Your Investments & Resources

The 8th House rules your personal investments, possessions, assets, property, insurance, or resources that you share with others, be it a spouse, significant other, or business partner. Pluto's influence can bring a major change to your investments or your joint finances. I have known clients to amass a fortune or declare bankruptcy; or do both during the approximately 21 years that Pluto transits their 8th House. Clients have married and accumulated great wealth through their partnerships or have lost great sums of money. Some people will enter a partnership and make money the old fashioned way "by marrying it," while others will experience financial transformation when they go through divorce (or business dissolution) and are forced to split their assets with a spouse or partner.

Be aware that this is a time to be very cautious about incurring debt, making a personal loan, or even obtaining a mortgage, because you're under the control of others. It's a good time to be fiscally conservative and make your plans for the long-term, which may ultimately produce great success for your investments.

Keep in mind that since this House rules, estates, wills and trusts it's possible you'll receive an inheritance during this period of your life. Depending on other transits in your birth chart, it can be an ideal time for tax and estate planning, as well as matters concerning insurance.

Pluto's transit here gives you the potential to transform yourself on a very deep level by exploring your personal psychology, taking advantage of the opportunity to heal yourself, and thereby radically improving yourself. You may make a major breakthrough in self-discovery through personal growth workshops or individual therapy.

Your natural interest in all matters of sex, life and death may lead you to profound insights, whether through consulting with experts, taking classes, reading books or just talking with friends. You're drawn to spiritual teachings and discovering the mysteries of life that will enrich you. If you use these years wisely to transform and improve yourself, you'll better understand what is going on in your life.

Considerations, Actions, Decisions During Pluto in 8th House

1. Do you want to seriously transform yourself?
2. Begin therapy or some other transformative self-discovery process.
3. Do you want to heal a psychic wound within yourself?
4. Do you want to go on a transformative religious or spiritual journey?
5. Do you want to buy life insurance?
6. Do you want to settle a tax matter?
7. Do you want to apply for a long-term loan?
8. Do you want to make a major investment?
9. Do you want to plan your estate or prepare your will?
10. Do you want to have an intense, passionate sexual connection?

Transits to Use for Successful 8th House Decisions

You now understand the areas of life that are featured in your 8th House. We've discussed how each of the five transiting planets exerts its unique influence on the affairs of this House. This will help you better understand the changes you are experiencing, moods you're feeling, and the events taking place. Your awareness of this information may prompt you to:

> 1. *ACCEPT* the way things are and be content with what is going on in your life.
>
> 2. *CONSIDER* that you'd like to make some change, in which case you may evaluate your options and further contemplate your situation.
>
> 3. *DECIDE* that you're ready to make a change, take action, and make a decision pertaining to the affairs of this House.

If you make a decision, you'll want to learn how to pick the best transit to produce a successful outcome for it. Please know that the art of picking and interpreting transits requires very thorough analysis, normally done by a professional astrologer. Therefore, I've kept the discussion of selecting and using transits simple, for illustration purposes.

The key is to remember that each planet has the ability to bring a *different* positive quality of success to your decision. For example, *Jupiter's* effect may provide opportunities to expand and grow; *Saturn's* effect is more practical; *Uranus'* effect is sudden and exciting; *Neptune's* influence may bring you inspiration and idealism; *Pluto* may bring an intense and transformative effect for major change. This knowledge will help you understand how your decisions are affected by these planetary influences.

In the examples below, I chose a planetary transit to produce a favorable result for each individual's particular decision. This will help you see the many possibilities available to create the right outcome and make your 8th House decisions more successful.

Using a positive JUPITER Transit

DECISION: *I want to make a large investment in the stock market that will be profitable.*

Explanation: Earlier in this chapter, we discussed Marianne's desire to pick a lucky time to make a big investment in the stock market. We choice a long-term Jupiter transit that would bring luck and fortune during three separate periods of the year. By making her investment on specific days, she would have very fortunate results during these time periods. People she consulted about her investments would give her helpful counsel during that time as well.

* * *

Using a positive SATURN Transit

DECISION: *I am a "rageaholic" and need help to change my life.*

Explanation: We discussed earlier in the chapter how Eric emotionally and physically abused his wife through his uncontrolled anger. She made it clear that he would not get a second chance if he didn't change. He was willing to get help to transform himself in an effort to avoid losing her. We used a positive Saturn transit, which would bring serious commitment to his efforts to resolve his anger problems. This transit would be excellent for re-structuring his behavior and letting go of those abusive patterns. Using the exact timing of this transit, he went to an anger management clinic where he could understand why he behaved this way and learn strategies to create change in his behavior.

* * *

Using a positive URANUS Transit

DECISION: *I am gay and I am going to tell my family.*

Explanation: Marvin came from an ultra-conservative, judgmental family, who disapproved of alternative lifestyles. In fact, his father was homophobic, which led to Marvin keeping his secret of being gay for many years, too afraid of his family's reaction to tell them the truth. Finally, when Uranus transited Marvin's 8th House, he was ready to "come out" to them. This transit gave Marvin courage and a sense of detachment that lessened his feelings of fear and disapproval. It was the perfect time for him to assert his independence, be authentic, and let his family know the truth about himself and his lifestyle.

* * *

Using a positive NEPTUNE Transit

DECISION: *I'm writing a new will and want to leave my money to several charities.*

Explanation: Felicia was a widow with no children. She had family members who were successful in their own right and didn't need her money. She had always wanted to donate her money to the American Cancer Society. We used a Neptune transit because its influence fulfilled her dreams of helping others by healing them. We also planned this decision at a time when it would be unlikely there would be any lawsuits against her estate.

* * *

Using a positive PLUTO Transit

DECISION: *I want to divorce my spouse and find the best time to split our assets.*

Explanation: Madge had been married for 30 years and she and her husband were no longer happy together. For several years, they'd talked about separating and recently they talked about going through a divorce. Theirs had been a loveless marriage where they had just lived together as roommates. Madge was pretty confident that her husband would be fair in splitting their assets, but she preferred not to take any chances. We used a positive Pluto transit that was perfect for transforming merged assets, so each partner would receive a fair share, while minimizing the potential for upsets or litigation.

* * *

REMEMBER: You can use the FREE Transit Calculator that's discussed in Part IV of this book to go back in time to see which transits were occurring when a major event happened in your life. It might be a wonderful learning experience, especially since most transits repeat themselves over your lifetime. Also you can find out where your transits are today or in the future.

9th House

Travel, Education & Philosophy

Travel, education and philosophy all blend so well in this House to provide you with rich opportunities for learning as well as new views, beliefs and philosophies that will come as a result of your experience. It just depends on where you want to go, what you want to learn and how open you are to travel experiences that may educate you and change your beliefs.

- If you want to have a *Jupiter* vacation, filled with fun adventures, out of ordinary, bigger than life experiences – why not go to Disneyland.

- A great place for a *Saturn* trip would be to visit the great pyramids of Egypt where you could see pyramids built out of stone that have lasted thousands of years – solid and durable just like Saturn; and learn how they were built according to complex mathematical equations.

- For your *Uranus* vacation you might want to plan an exciting trip taking a shuttle ride to outer space. Right now they are on sale starting at a modest $200,000 per person, with longer vacation stays up to $20 million.

- You might enjoy a *Neptune* vacation where you can have a spiritual experience in nature swimming in the ocean with the wild dolphins in the waters off the coast of Bimini.

9th House: Travel, Education & Philosophy

○ Now, if you're ready for a highly transformational *Pluto* vacation, consider going to South America to participate in a "Shamanic Ecstasy of Consciousness" trip, guided by a shaman in the jungles of Ecuador where you'll discover mystic phenomena that will allow you access to the secrets of life.

Learning is stimulating to your heart, mind, spirit and psyche. Most of us find it extremely interesting to talk to well-educated people of intelligence, because we learn so much by hearing their ideas, opinions and philosophies. It's also intellectually invigorating to sit down and listen to the adventures of those who have spent years traveling all over the world visiting various foreign countries. Their stories can take us to all the places we've never been but dream of going. What makes many of these travelers so interesting is that they've spent months or years living like a native in a unique foreign culture, so they have the power to mesmerize us with fascinating stories of the people they've met and lived among.

The 9th House of your Horoscope is about learning whether through travel or school. It rules the higher education you've attained, the philosophies you espouse, long-distance journeys you take and your foreign travel excursions. This is an intellectually stimulating House because it also concerns the journeys you take mentally, such as in a classroom and physically on a plane, train or bus – to places unknown.

This House has great practical value to you because it can give you excellent insights about whether education will play an important role in your life. After all, you may be the type that says, "I loved doing undergrad work, but I was even more excited to do my graduate work to get my advanced degree." You may also be someone who enjoys getting multiple degrees because of your own education or career goals. On the other hand, you may be the kind of person who says, "I hated school and I couldn't wait to graduate, get out into the real world and get a job." Or, you may have felt that your basic high school or college education was quite adequate because you were more excited about "doing it" then, learning about it.

This is the area of your birth chart that will tell you a great deal about your intellect and penchant for exchanging knowledge. For instance, you may enjoy talking with people about your philosophies of life or you may be the type who looks forward to going to a lecture where you can hear someone brilliant expound on his philosophy. One of the important affairs of this House is the study of philosophies, belief systems and religions. This area concerns your search for higher knowledge and finding new horizons for you to explore, as well learning more about spiritual matters. This House will reveal your sense of purpose, the personal truths you hold dear, and direction you hope to take in life.

Look here to sort out whether you're well suited for a certain profession. Higher-education professions such as a doctor, lawyer, judge, accountant or philosophy professor or member of the clergy, typically requiring three to 11 years of advanced education. That's a major commitment of time to make if you aren't sure which of those professions are right for you.

This House governs all areas of higher learning, advanced education, college, advanced training, teaching, justice, law, politics, religion, publishing, literature, books, media, publicity, philanthropy, and prophecy. Many great teachers, lawyers, doctors, politicians, writers and athletes have prominent 9th Houses.

If you've fantasized traveling around the world, consult this House to find the ideal time to take a trip to another country. This House is the place to look if you're interested in learning through long distance travel and meeting foreign people from other cultures; especially if you're interested in living in a foreign country. This area of the birth chart will explain why some people have the aptitude and interest to learn three foreign languages while others can barely speak their native language correctly.

Other affairs ruled by this House include organized sports, the outdoors, your in-laws, intuition, churches, airlines, vacations, and international commerce.

Your Body in the 9th House

This house rules the liver, hips and thighs and sciatic nerve. Since there is nothing more important than your health, pay special attention to these areas of your body whenever a planet transits this House. It may indicate a period of time when you'll experience health benefits, issues or even problems you should be aware of. If you observe anything unusual, you'll have the opportunity to consult with a medical doctor or a health care practitioner.

9th House: Travel, Education & Philosophy

Your 9th House Decisions

You now understand that the 9th House of your birth chart primarily concerns your interest in travel, higher education and philosophy.

As you read about the description of this house, it's time to ask yourself a few questions. Has your education properly equipped you for a successful career and a fulfilling life? Do you want to go back to school? Is there any type of advanced education that would benefit your career or life interests? Do you enjoy reading or discussing politics? Do you find it stimulating to talk philosophy and exchange ideas? Do you find great satisfaction is discussing religion? Has sports been a big part of your life because you played competitively or because you enjoy watching it?

Is traveling of interest to you? Are you the type who loves learning about other cultures or would you prefer to stay local in your own country? Have you ever had an interest in learning a foreign language, knowing foreigners, or actually living in a foreign country?

These are all significant questions and your answers may lead you to make important decisions to change your life. Here are a few examples of decisions clients have made based on the activities and issues of the 9th House.

Situation: It's taken Patty a few years to save enough money for a trip around the world.

DECISION: *I want to pick the best time to travel around the world that will be educational and transformational.*

* * *

Situation: Ben never finished college. He knows that a degree will get him a better job and more pay.

DECISION: *I want to pick the best time to finish my college degree.*

* * *

Situation: Chip has been a straight-A student and gifted athlete, playing football on his school team. He's not sure whether to pursue a career as a professional football player or as an athletic coach.

What the Hell Is Going On in My Life?

DECISION: *I want to use my astrological transits to help me decide which career path might bring me the most satisfaction and success.*

* * *

Situation: Molly has never learned to speak a foreign language.

DECISION: *I want to pick the best time to successfully learn how to speak French.*

* * *

During the transits of *Jupiter, Saturn, Uranus, Neptune,* and *Pluto* – Patty, Ben, Chip, and Molly will have many opportunities to implement their decisions at a favorable time to produce the outcome they want.

The Transiting Planets Reveal Your Past, Present & Future

Your main focus is using astrology to understand *what the hell is going on in your life*. Once you do – this book will show you the best time to make a decision to change it, should you have a desire to do so. As you read about the five planets transiting the 9th House, notice the way each planet exerts its unique influence and effect, bringing specific opportunities, issues, problems, and events into this area of your life. But if you're curious as to how these planets are personally affecting YOU *today,* in your *past,* or in your *future,* you can find out where each transiting planet is in your birth chart by using the *FREE Transit Calculator* (see Part IV).

JUPITER in Your 9th House of Travel, Education & Philosophy

A Great Time for Education

Jupiter's transit through your 9th House brings you great learning experiences that will help you develop a more sophisticated view of the world. Under Jupiter's influence learning is fun, stimulating and filled with adventure. You may have a chance to learn through additional education or some advanced training. Or, you may also teach others formally or informally and increase their knowledge as well. Should you desire to go to college or enroll in a trade school this Jupiter transit provides you with a fabulous opportunity to expand your mind and grow through education. Imagine that Jupiter is a good luck charm you can use to have a successful educational experience as Percy discovered.

As a young boy, Percy had come with his family to the United States from Angola. Finishing grade school, he went to a high school in New York but dropped out after three years and took a job as a taxi driver to help support his family. After being so excited about coming to this country, going to school, learning a profession, and getting ahead in the world, he deeply regretted having to quit high school. But thanks to his commitment to his education, eventually he went back to receive his GED. Now as Jupiter transits his 9th House he's excited about enrolling in college either in a full time or night program, depending on whether he can qualify for scholarship assistance. He wants to study to be a teacher so he can teach other students what he's learned about the world. Making his application to a special scholarship fund for foreigners during his Jupiter transit will bring him good fortune in getting the financial assistance he needs.

It's a time when you're feeling idealistic and mentally optimistic about your quest for knowledge. You drink in knowledge the way a thirsty man drinks water, with a natural curiosity to discover *truth* in many areas of your life. Your brain has a unique capacity to see the whole picture, while enjoying a balance between your intuitive abilities and your logical reasoning mind.

Your interests may range from abstract to profound subjects where you're engaged in all types of reading and studying in such areas as philosophy, religion, politics, sports or any topic that interests you. This is a time when you find yourself concerned with morals and ethics as you develop principles on which to operate your life. Your interest in these areas may lead you to study these subjects in school or to pursue a career that's consistent with your philosophy and beliefs such as being a teacher, writer, lawyer or some other professional.

You may want to join a reading group to discuss the great classics of literature or enroll in a series of technical seminars to advance in your job. If you want adventure, you can join a branch of the military, enjoy traveling the world, while pursuing a hi-tech education that may be available. Since philosophy, spirituality, religion and improvement are all experiences of Jupiter in your 9th House, this is an excellent time for spiritual retreats, workshops, or religious classes that will help you grow as a person.

If you like to write, this is an excellent time for it, since the 9th House rules publishing and other communications media that reach the world at large. If you've dreamed of writing a blog, an article for a magazine, or even a book that you would publish, this is when your efforts are likely to be very successful.

As you are exposed to the broader world, your views on life will change since this transit provides you with a powerful opportunity to grow and mature in a way that will help you make more sense of the world around you. During this time you develop wisdom as long as you are enthusiastically open to the process of learning and being educated. In fact, the only problem you may encounter is if you're an arrogant or conceited person who thinks he already knows everything there is to know. In that case, you may find your opinionated or self-righteous behavior resulting in conflict with others. Undoubtedly, you'll find yourself interacting with people smarter than you who'll bring you down a peg or two. Jupiter's influence brings you confidence that should always be tempered with humility. Remember: A wise man knows what he *doesn't* know.

A Great Time for Foreign Travel & Learning

We've discussed how Jupiter's transit through your 9th House is a huge opportunity to gain an education through books, studies and school. But

9th House: Travel, Education & Philosophy

you can also expand your mind and knowledge through extensive traveling, making this a magnificent time to acquire knowledge about people in other parts of the world. By visiting various countries you'll learn about foreign people and cultures different from your own and even learn another language. This is a year that was made for the joy and adventure of traveling. I encourage people busy in their careers to take a sabbatical or lengthy vacation to enrich their mind and life. I counsel parents that one of the best school graduation gifts they can give their child is a month or more traveling in a foreign country.

One client left high school, not mentally ready for college and traveled with his backpack throughout Europe, feeling the need to be free to explore the world. Interestingly, he experienced two very Jupiterian experiences: traveling for adventure and then upon his return, great enthusiasm to enroll in college to begin his studies in earnest. What he'd learned in his travels matured him and made him grateful for the opportunity to pursue an advanced education.

I created this opportunity for myself in my senior year of college by joining an international marketing organization that assisted me in obtaining a three-month internship to work in Norway. On reflection, my work experience, the chance to live day-after-day in another culture, and the fantastic people I met made that time one of the major highlights of my life.

Jupiter's influence raises your consciousness and interest level in learning, motivating you to seek new information. This gives you the opportunity to replace outmoded beliefs or ignorant prejudices with a more accurate view of your world. In this way you can now replace what you "believe" to be true – with what "is" true. Advancing your learning and expanding your worldview is one of the gifts you'll enjoy as Jupiter transits your 9th House – as Andrew discovered.

Andrew had some very stereotypical views of minority groups based on growing up in a wealthy "WASP" suburb. (i.e., white Anglo-Saxon Protestant). He was sheltered from the poorer neighborhoods where people of poverty lived, so his ignorance led him to believe that people of certain ethnic groups were not as smart or ambitious as he was.

After college he took a job with an international export-import company and spent the first few years learning about their operations in the United States. One day his boss came into his office and said, "Andrew, I want you to fly to Mexico to meet with several of the executives who run our Mexico City Office."

Much to his surprise, the week he spent in Mexico City was eye opening as he observed a city buzzing with commerce and activity. He saw many businessmen and women, well dressed, looking rather smart and sophisticated; and the downtown area had the feel of a large metropolitan city like the ones he had visited in Europe. As he looked up at several of skyscrapers that made up the skyline, he said to himself, "Wow, this is an impressive city – not the Mexico I had envisioned. It's new and modern." He was actually starting to feel pretty stupid as he thought of some of the stereotypes he had of the Mexican culture.

The Mexican executives from his office all spoke fluent English as well as French and German. They talked to Andrew about their business backgrounds and some of their ideas on how to expand business operations in Mexico. By the end of the week, Andrew had gone through their budget proposals and marketing plans – thoroughly impressed with their presentations and vision of the future.

He and Ramon, one of the executives he met, hit it off so well that Ramon invited him to his home to have dinner and meet his family. Ramon lived in a gorgeous home that was even larger than the house Andrew had grown up in. He had a wonderful time meeting Ramon's family, finding them warm and gracious hosts. When he left back to the United States, he was excited to report on his business trip to the Mexico City office. He'd made a new friend and realized it was time to let go of some stereotypes that were based on his own ignorance.

Considerations, Actions, Decisions During Jupiter in 9th House

1. Attend school or finish your education.
2. Broaden your philosophy and worldview.
3. Learn something new that will stimulate your mind.
4. Apply to law school or send off your writing to a publisher.
5. Travel to some place where you've never been.
6. Live in a foreign country and learn the language.
7. Become a teacher.
8. Pursue a career in politics or join a political organization.
9. Begin a spiritual or religious activity
10. Join an organized sports team.
11. Take an adventurous outdoor trip.

SATURN In Your 9th House of Travel, Education & Philosophy

A Great Time to be Responsible for Your Education

Saturn in this House begins a period of time when you're accountable for the education you acquire and the philosophies you espouse. Part of being responsible is facing reality if you are having difficulty learning. I experienced this dilemma in high school when I started failing my German language exams. I had a choice of being irresponsible and continuing to fail the entire class or making some adjustment that would improve my situation. I chose to be responsible by asking for the help of a tutor. Another way Saturn can make you be responsible is that in order to afford your education you may need to work an additional part-time job in order to pay for it.

During this Saturn transit, education has an important purpose and learning is of *practical* importance in your life now. You're getting very serious about your beliefs and goals. What's happening in your life is that you're developing wisdom about the best ways to be successful and effective in achieving your long-term ambitions. You may realize that you'll never get ahead if you don't complete your high school education; or obtain a college degree; or attend a trade school; or take some sort of advanced training to make yourself more promotable. Your emphasis is on broadening your intellectual horizons and reaching out for new experiences that can help you grow. Saturn's influence causes you to want to learn because it's of practical value to you. Your search for knowledge and information helps you grow, mature and know yourself better.

Now is the time when you're in pursuit of understanding the meaning of life. This is when you sit down on the couch absorbed in the deepest book on philosophy or business ethics since you're more serious about defining your beliefs and morals. But since Saturn energies are not prone to airy-fairy philosophies or anything too idealistic, you'll be focused on how this information can be used in a practical and useful way in your life. You're searching for the unabashed truth, so you'll no longer accept the ideas and opinions of others, as you have in the past. You'll find yourself engaging in serious discussions about topics such as politics, philosophy and religion, challenging anyone whom you disagree. You're becoming your own person with your own views.

A Great Time for Learning the Truth

Because you're in the process of learning and establishing your own independent views, you may find yourself frustrated or disappointed with old mentors, teachers or experts you previously looked up to and respected, including family members you've known for years.

As Mandy grew up from childhood to young adulthood, she always loved to listen to her Aunt Elsa. She was very opinionated, but seemed so wise, often sighting personal experiences to support her beliefs. One evening when she was home from college, Mandy went to a family function where she heard Aunt Elsa espousing her views to some of her younger cousins. However, what she heard come out of Aunt Elsa's mouth were actually bigoted and opinionated comments that were factually incorrect. Mandy was disappointed in her and wondered how someone she had idolized as a child could make such ignorant and misinformed statements. As she listened to her aunt speak she was grateful that she'd developed her own intellectual curiosity, always motivated to learn the truth and ready to investigate when she wasn't sure. But most all, Mandy took pride in the fact that she was someone who now thought for herself.

The one mistake to avoid is thinking that you *know* more than you actually do, because it's important that you remain open to new knowledge in your quest to learn and make discoveries about your world. If you're overconfident in believing you know more than you do, you may underestimate what is necessary to achieve your goals. Make sure to use this time to re-evaluate what you "think you know," and to throw out ideas and beliefs that have no solid basis or foundation.

Avoid Settling Law Suits at This Time

The 9th House is the House of Law and since Saturn's influence can result in limitations, restrictions and difficulties over legal matters, this is usually not an ideal time to settle disputes in court. I've had clients who've been punished for their irresponsibility during this transit. One client was a landlord who didn't want to spend money paying someone to shovel the snow on the steps of his building. Subsequently, a tenant slipped and experienced a bad fall that required hospitalization. The landlord was sued for neglicience and was unwilling to settle, eventually losing his court case. Other clients have gone to court during this transit and received a far smaller settlement than they thought they deserved.

Since this House also rules long distance journeys, Saturn's energies may also cause the purpose of your travel plans to be less about fun and adventure and more about fulfilling responsibility and obligations. There's usually some burden or serious matter that comes into play with Saturn's transit here. One client of mine rarely traveled in his position, but with his company now embroiled in patent violation lawsuits in several European countries, he was traveling to cities like London, Paris and Rome to face litigation – not to have fun. He worked long days and had no time for sightseeing, because his evenings were filled with phone calls and writing legal briefs as he prepared for the next day.

A Time When Your Morals May Be Tested

The 9th House governs your ideals, morals and philosophy, and Saturn's influence brings tests and lessons to this area of your life as well. I had one client who was in a car when her friend caused an accident. Later, her friend asked her to testify in court, in essence to perjure herself, that she hadn't caused the accident, even though she clearly had. The high principles of Saturn require you to always operate with integrity and distinguish between issues of right and wrong or pay the consequences for your dishonesty.

You can expect that your morals and ethics may be tested during this time. For example, you're shopping at a store one day and you see a homeless person shoplifting and you must decide how you'll handle the conflicting values of feeling compassion for someone who might be hungry, while morally unable to passively standby and allow this thievery to go unreported. One client had this experience and chose to confront the homeless person in the store, reminding him that his shoplifting would be reported. However, since she felt a sense of moral responsibility to help someone in need, she offered to pay for the items he was prepared to steal. Additionally, after the homeless person left the store, her sense of integrity demanded she report the incident to the store manager so that the manager could be aware of this person in the future.

This is an excellent story to illustrate how Saturn's principle of accepting responsibility and operating with integrity can play out in one's life during this transit. After all, "virtue is not virtue until it has been tested." Many of the experiences you have in day-to-day life or even traveling during this time may test your values and beliefs as you engage in the process of determining your own ideas of what is right or wrong – just as my client discovered.

Learn About Other Cultures

Since this House rules long distance and foreign travel, Saturn's influence may create obstacles, difficulties and delays in your travels. The restrictions and personal limitations you experience may be uncomfortable or burdensome, but they teach you valuable lessons, perhaps to be more tolerant or more adaptable as you experience other cultures.

Candice was living in Rome on a summer work assignment for the magazine that employed her. She was getting upset and frustrated, having to wait so long to pay her utility bill. Anthony was living in Mexico as his company's marketing representative. He couldn't believe the people in his city waited in line for one hour to pay their phone bill. How did they have time do it? He was ready to pull his hair out over the long wait. Eventually they both learned that to overcome these obstacles they would need to make adjustments in the way they lived in their respective foreign countries. They found out that postal systems were not the preferred way of transacting business; credit cards were not used by many people; sophisticated computer systems to transact business through the Internet were not readily available or dependable. In fact, many people in the countries they worked felt more secure paying utility bills and other purchases in cash, thus obtaining a receipt as proof of payment.

When Candice and Anthony returned to the USA they had learned some real lessons about overcoming limitations, and being more tolerant and adaptable in their experiences of living in other foreign countries. Saturn's influence brought them maturity as well.

A Time to Finish What You Started

Have you ever started something only to quit doing it before it was completed? Then, months or years later you looked back, wishing you'd finished what you'd started. Well, if your efforts yielded disappointing results or even failed, this Saturn transit gives you a second chance to finish something you started a long time ago as long as your willing to work hard with a serious sense of commitment.

Saturn brings a high level of responsibility to your learning, so if you quit school years ago, this will be a time when you'll have a serious motivation

9th House: Travel, Education & Philosophy

to finish or advance your education. If by choice or circumstance you were prevented from finishing a book you were writing, this may be a time you'll be very serious about completing it. If you went to law school but never took the bar exam, you may now have another opportunity to do so. If you always wanted to teach but never got your licensing, you may now finish the process.

In my case, I always dreamed of being a professional baseball player. At age 17, it was doubtful that I had the talent to earn a baseball scholarship to a college, so I quit playing baseball after school and instead, worked part-time to pay for my education. When Saturn went through my 9th House, 30 years later – at age 47, I found an opportunity to play baseball in a senior's baseball league for men over 30. That transit gave me a second chance to complete my dream of playing organized baseball. It turned out to be one of the big joys of my life. So, remember an old astrology adage: "Saturn never denies even though it may delay."

This two and a half year period is a time when you're practical and realistic about what you want to do in all matters that this House governs: higher education, law, publishing, philosophy, spirituality, religion and travel.

You can use your serious dedication to make something "real" in your life that you were unable to bring into reality at another time. I've heard clients excuse themselves for not finishing something they had started years ago, saying, "At that time, I was just young, immature, not very responsible." Well, the good news is that Saturn's transit through your 9th House allows you to say, "Now I'm a mature and responsible, ready to accomplish what I set out to do."

Considerations, Actions, Decisions During Saturn in 9th House

1. Finish school or an advanced degree.
2. Learn something of practical importance to your profession or life.
3. Finish writing a book or some other important document.
4. Join an organized sports activity that you'd enjoy participating in.
5. Change a rigid philosophy or belief into one that is more expansive.
6. Travel for business or some practical purpose.
7. Be realistic and ethical in pursuing legal matters.
8. Commit to some action that demonstrates your integrity.

URANUS In Your 9th House of Travel, Education & Philosophy

A Great Time to Search for Your Truth

Something wonderful and invigorating is happening to your mind when Uranus transits your 9th House. Learning is exciting and stimulating. You're totally plugged into your intuition and capable of profound insights. For example, you make an observation about life to a friend and she says, "Wow…that's brilliant! How did you figure that out?" You say, "I was just walking down the street and I had this epiphany that made that idea so crystal clear to me."

You're able to broaden your intellectual and philosophical horizons as you search for the truth. You're free of a reliance on conventional wisdom. You now trust your own feelings and perceptions of what 's true, instead of relying on the traditional teachings from your past. You're mind is open as it has never been before. During this period of your life you shed old, rigid and obsolete beliefs that you've long held. You're feeling inspired, imaginative, with your mind open to innovative ideas and methods. On a deeply personal level you'll examine the morals and principles you live by so that fit your unique beliefs.

I remember talking to a client who made a shocking discovery, realizing that he'd treated people with callous disregard. One day, he was extremely rude to his neighbor. The neighbor confronted him about his lack of civility, pointing out his unkind behavior. The neighbor calmly asked him how he would you like to be "talked to" and treated that way. A light went on in his head and he realized that he would hate it. This confrontation brought him back to a memory of a grade school teacher, who urged him to live his life by the *Golden Rule*: *Do unto others as you would have them do unto you.* Suddenly he realized how disrespectful his behavior was and that it was time to change how he treated others. As he shared his discovery with me, I realized the beauty of Uranus' influence was that in the flash of a second it can make you aware of a new truth to live by, like the Golden Rule.

9th House: Travel, Education & Philosophy

A Time to Change Old Conventional Views

When Uranus transits your 9th House you have a keen awareness and the potential for unique insights into the world around you. However, the key to having this positive experience is to be totally open to new ideas, approaches and ways of experiencing your life. The energies of Uranus keep you young – often physically, and certainly mentally. You may know an elderly person who seems to thrive on new ideas and interests, often appearing much younger than her years. She's the living embodiment of someone who embraces change. People who fight change, the moment it comes into their life, live with a stress that stunts them mentally and ages them physically.

Be conscious that the purpose of this Uranus transit is to expose you to new, liberating and different ways of seeing the world in order to free you from old, conventional views you've always had. However, the influence of Uranus demands that you be flexible and adaptable to change. If you're this way by nature, you'll find Uranus' energies invigorating and exciting. But if you tend to be rigid, closed, or resistant to change; or if you're so attached to old, familiar ideas and approaches to the point that new ones threaten you, you'll encounter problems and conflict. This may be a disturbing time where you find your interactions with others upsetting and disruptive – as Humphrey found out.

Humphrey was an ultra conservative politician running for re-election. He'd held his position as a state senator for 20 years. His friends joked he was so conservative – he was "to the right of Attila the Hun." Humphrey agreed and said he would never change his beliefs. He proceeded to espouse his personal views such as "the church needed to be more involved in governing the country." Whenever he was on the stump talking to crowds, he let everyone know he was violently pro-life and saw no grounds for a woman to have an abortion under any circumstance.

One sunny, humid day at an election rally, a young, attractive woman, dressed very casually in a low cut blouse and short skirt, asked to be recognized and speak. She proceeded to tell the audience a very touching story about how she had just been through the trauma of rape. She felt she had the right to an abortion and confronted Humphrey, demanding to know why he was so extreme and inflexible in his views on abortion for rape victims. Humphrey stood in front of the crowd, glaring at her, speaking loudly into the microphone, "Well, it's no wonder you were raped, dressed so provocatively!" The crowd collectively gasped. The local news cameras captured his angry and insulting response on video.

By the next morning, his picture and the comment he made at the political rally were in the local paper and by the afternoon the video of his outburst was shown on news stations throughout the country. Despite 20 years of being the incumbent, when the votes were counted a week later, Humphrey lost the election.

If you have an open mind, the positive side of Uranus' influence is that your mind is very stimulated and you're receptive to innovative solutions to old problems. You'll be exposed to new and exciting ways of thinking and you'll make discoveries that will enhance your life and all your relationships. I tell my clients that this transit can turn them into a charismatic person that everyone wants to be around. People see you as fascinating and interesting, someone refreshing and invigorating to be around and exchange views. You'll be seen as original, employing unique, avant-garde ideas and methods that no one else has tried.

Go On an Exciting Vacation

Since the 9th House rules long distance and foreign travel, the influences of Uranus can make this an exhilarating and illuminating time to travel, where your experiences can revolutionize and radically change you. This is when you can take an unusual vacation trekking through the Himalayas or visiting the giant tortoises in the Galapagos Islands.

Of course, the influence of Uranus can bring tension and disruption as well, so if you're someone who prefers routine and being at home, this can be an unsettling time as well. I'm reminded of a married couple both talking about their vacation plans, one spouse wanting to stay home and garden in the backyard, while the other wanted to travel to a foreign country during their time off. In their case, Uranus created a great deal of tension in their home. You can counter these effects by being flexible and adaptable. If you're willing to experiment and step out of your normal comfort zone, you might enjoy the most exciting vacation of your life.

My friend Holly had always taken relaxing vacations to destinations like Hawaii or Mexico, staying at 5-star hotels where she could enjoy first class service. She told me the only place she'd every camped was at a *Holiday Inn*. Suddenly, she had an impulsive urge to take an unconventional and intriguing vacation different from any she'd ever taken before. Looking at a *National Geographic Magazine*, she saw an article on the great adventure of "going on a safari in Tanzania!" She became enthralled with the adventure of seeing African wildlife, hiking in the jungle, camping out in the fresh air and being near the danger of wild animals. She no longer needed the security of a luxury hotel because Uranus was transiting her 9th House.

Other Exciting Things to Do

Uranus' influence brings you a creative consciousness and feeling of limitless potential. Your writing is original and inventive and a perfect time for publishing a literary work; or to pursue your interest in law, politics, philosophy, religion, or broadcasting. You may have said, "One day, I'm going to write a book." Well, when Uranus transits your 9th House, you may finally to do it. You may decide you have a sudden passion to be an attorney, run for office, become a priest, or anchor a news program.

It's also an ideal time to participate in any activity that allows you to bring social change and help others. You may come up with a scientific advancement or technological innovation that benefits the community or the world. I had one client whose dream was to introduce solar stoves in Africa so the population there didn't have to spend so much time searching for wood.

It can be an exciting and stimulating time to take classes for higher learning, attend school or college where you're likely to meet interesting people and learn from brilliant teachers. Instead of telling friends that you'd love to take a course at the community college, now you're driving to the campus to look over their course offerings. You may walk into a classroom and meet a gifted professor who's discussing a breakthrough scientific paper on a new technology only a few people have ever heard about. When it comes to your education, you're ready to break the boundaries of normal convention and study metaphysical subjects, yoga, astrology or other New Age studies.

Be Aware of Emotional Explosions

The energies of a Uranus transit can be explosive when they're unexpressed or restricted. Generally, you'll feel their effects when there's a need for you to escape some form of restriction or limitation that's blocking you from being free. If that's the case, you'll rebel, as you've never done before.

That's exactly what happened to Jeremy, normally a very meek person. He had just graduated college and was still living at home. However, his parents still treated him like a child, trying to control his life. Recently, Jeremy had told his parents that he and a friend wanted to go on a special tour in Australia where he would have some exciting adventures in the outback, visiting tribes of Aborigines. His parents thought he was crazy, insisting that it wasn't safe for him and his friend to go on such a trip.

At first, he accepted their pressuring tactics, but after a few weeks the tension and anxiety of his parent's trying to control his life and restricting his freedom came to a head. At the dinner table one night when his parents made another suggestion about what he should do with his life, Jeremy exploded! He pounded on the dinner table and yelled at them, letting them know that he'd met with his friend, made travel arrangements and bought tickets. They were going to Australia whether his parents liked it or not. Then, he got up from the table and stormed out of the house.

When Uranus' energies manifest in your life they may create tensions within you that need to be expressed – not repressed. If you're deprived of the normal opportunity to express your ideas and feelings, you may find that the pent-up energies of Uranus will come out in an explosive outburst like Jeremy's, or even in an accident. That's why, during a Uranus transit, the best advice is to find ways to assertively express yourself, your ideas, and opinions. It's a time to vent your upset feelings before you blow up and injure your relationships or create a problem even bigger than the original one that brought about your upset.

But because "an ounce of prevention is worth a pound of cure," I advise clients to always know the area of life that Uranus is transiting in their birth chart. Then, during the time that Uranus transits that House, pay attention to any tension or upset you're noticing in that area of your life. Are you feeling restricted? What changes would you make to feel freer? Then, use your creativity and rational mind to come up with ways to bring change to that area of your life.

Not a Good Time for Resolving Legal Matters

The influence of Uranus brings unexpected surprises and not always the most pleasant ones. Since the 9th House rules law, this isn't the best time for resolving legal matters, since it's extremely difficult to know how they'll turn out. Court decisions are likely to have surprising or unusual outcomes or even be reversed. So, just be aware that if you're involved in litigation, you may be in for a surprise.

9th House: Travel, Education & Philosophy

This is an exciting and stimulating transit if you're willing to be receptive to new ideas, insights and ways of interacting with the world. If you have an open mind, willing to be adaptable and make changes, this can be an important time for your personal growth.

Considerations, Actions, Decisions During Uranus in 9th House

1. Be open to radically new ideas and views.
2. What new philosophies have you discovered?
3. Would you be excited to pursue any unconventional education courses?
4. Is there any activity or sport that would be exciting to try?
5. Plan an exotic trip somewhere.
6. Journey to a foreign country where you can have an adventure.
7. Avoid litigation.
8. Vent your upset before you blow up and try to discover a way to feel less restricted.

NEPTUNE in Your 9th House of Travel, Education & Philosophy

Are You Inspired or Confused?

As Neptune transits your 9th House you'll seek to understand your spirituality and how it applies to the world you live in. You may seek your own spiritual path by attending a regular religious service, joining a spiritual group, meditating, or through the volunteer work you do.

It's a time when you explore your higher consciousness in order to seek answers of a deep and personal nature. As you examine your outer world, Neptune's influence can be both mystical and inspirational as well as abstract and confusing. Of all the planets, Neptune is the least ego-oriented. In simple terms, Neptune energies cause you to remove your focus from gratifying yourself to serving others. Its effect on most people is to bring out their concern and compassion for all of society.

However, if your general outlook in the world has been focused primarily on satisfying your own needs with the attitude of "what's in it for me?" and "let everyone just take care of themselves," this may be a disorienting time for you. The reason why is that during this lengthy transit you'll experience an internal shift where you find yourself caring more about others than you ever have in the past. At first, you may find it odd, to go from the attitude, "I'm just too busy and can't be bothered," to "Sure, I can take some time out to help other people." What's happening in your life is that you're starting to see yourself as part of a larger group and less as a self-focused individual. When Neptune transits this House your learning is inspired with a spiritual orientation.

A Time to Care About Others

Patricia was much too busy to ever volunteer to help others, since she had a demanding career and family that required lots of attention. She took care of herself and her family and felt other people should do the same. As far as those who were less fortunate, "they weren't her problem." After all, social agencies were there to provide whatever help was needed. So, Patricia was able to emotionally detach herself from feeling any responsibility for helping others who were less fortunate.

That changed the day she got in her car and went to a store on the other side of town. As she walked back to her car after her errand, she saw a woman with her child sitting on the sidewalk. The woman had a canister with some coins it. A sign above the canister said, "Any Help Appreciated." She walked right by as if no one were there. Suddenly she heard a voice say, "Please stop, Patricia." In shock, she turned around in disbelief that the woman with the child was calling her name. She walked over to her and said, "Excuse me. Did you call my name?" The woman said, "Patricia, you don't recognize me, but my name is Maxine. We went to the same high school 20 years ago. We were in some of the same classes together. When I was a freshman, you once came to my rescue and scared away a couple of bullies who were beating me up at a park near the school."

Even though it was many years ago, Patricia never forgot the sight of this poor girl being kicked to the ground, yelling and screaming, as she ran over to rescue her. "Yes, I remember you, Maxine. What's happened to you that you're here begging on the street?" Maxine proceeded to tell Patricia a heart-breaking story of how her husband abandoned her and her child; being evicted after not being able to find a job to pay rent; then becoming sick and having no family to help her. Maxine explained there was a limit to the help she could get from social service agencies. She was now staying at a homeless shelter, but finding it impossible to get enough money to change her life. Patricia's heart was touched. Realizing that she couldn't walk away from what she'd just heard, she agreed to help Maxine.

As you can see, it took a personal experience to bring out Patricia's caring and compassionate nature. Subsequently, her assistance to Maxine brought Patricia in contact with her homeless shelter, which resulted in Patricia's continued volunteer efforts with the shelter. Now Patricia was contributing her time and money every week to help many women in circumstances similar to Maxine.

If You're Confused – Get Help

Neptune's influence can inspire you to new visions or bring you ideas that at first may seem accurate and then eventually seem blurry or confused.

Imagine looking at a chameleon, an animal that can suddenly change colors before your eyes. When you look at the chameleon, his color is yellow, and then his skin turns to green and then blue. That can be quite a confusing image to watch. Neptune's energies can have a similarly confusing effect where one moment you're sure you know something to be true, only to find out the next moment that it may not be so. For that reason, Neptune's passage through your 9th House is an excellent time to accept that you may not know the truth about something *for sure*. If you've ever felt wishy-washy in your ideas, confused, or unclear as if you were in a fog, you may have had Neptune transiting in your 9th House.

Ironically, Neptune's influence can also bring you clear inspiration that makes you confident that your ideas or perceptions about something are accurate. However, just like the magician who does the old magic trick where the object in his hand disappears before your eyes, "Abracadabra… Now you see it – now you don't." – Neptune can bring you illusion, delusion and deception. That's why it's of paramount importance that you carefully consider all your decisions when Neptune transits any House in your birth chart.

This is a period in your life when you would do well to find trustworthy individuals to counsel and assist you. They should be practical people whose wisdom is grounded in reality, preferably individuals you respect for having given you good advice in the past. Discuss your ideas and decisions so that you get the benefit of a reality check that will help you see whether your idea is a well thought-out and visionary or illogical and impractical. You'll benefit from someone with a strong voice who can bring you back to reality and help you see if there is anything missing in your thinking. Helpful advisors to consider may be a spouse, parent, relative, friend, a teacher, an employer, or some professional expert that you consult before you commit to any action.

This is the exact advice I gave Raul when he was ready to invest his life savings to open a sporting goods store in his neighborhood. He was all set to sign a lease, buy inventory, and set up his store's operations. Raul was excited about organizing this on his own. There were certain things he didn't know about running this type of business, but was sure he could learn whatever he didn't know, along the way. Within 30 days, he started having second thoughts, so I encouraged him to talk about his plans with a few people he had a close relationship. He decided to meet with a friend who sold commercial real estate. After Raul discussed his excitement about opening up a sporting goods business, his friend informed him it wasn't a good idea since a national sporting goods chain would be opening up a large outlet store less than two miles away. His friend pointed out that this sporting goods chain would have the advantage of offering customers a larger variety and deeper inventory, all at lower prices than Raul could afford.

Additionally, Raul talked to a banker friend about his business idea. Raul confided that he was having second thoughts because he'd just found out he would be competing with the sporting goods chain opening nearby. The banker said, "Raul, according to the latest statistics from the Small Business Administration, about 50 percent of all businesses fail in the first year, with the number of failures even higher within five years. You won't be well enough capitalized, and in light of such huge competition, the odds of your failing are very high. I suggest you re-think this idea and be more realistic. Personally, I think you're dreaming if you believe this new business is viable."

Raul was so happy that he'd taken the time to talk with these two people, realizing they had saved him from making a big financial mistake. He was also grateful I had pointed out how he might be suffering from a Neptunian delusion that caused him not to be realistic. Of course, I was confident that by his talking with his advisors he would see reality for himself. Raul's experience is another example of how your personal transits can help you understand *what the hell is going on in your life*. I continually remind clients to make their financial commitments and important decisions when they have favorable transits occurring. Timing... timing... timing.

Great Time for Spiritual Pursuits

When Neptune transits your 9th House, you're inspired to seek knowledge and search for the higher spiritual truths about your existence. This is an inspired time to take a metaphysical class or discover the mysteries of life by learning a mystical teaching such as the Kabbalah. You're open to finding answers through a philosophy or religion as long as it speaks to you on a heavenly or mystical plane. I've had clients who fulfilled this desire by taking a trip to Israel to visit the Holy Land or a tour of the Vatican.

It's a time when your strong feelings of faith may bring you a desire to lead a more self-reflective life like one client who went to India to study under a guru while another joined an ashram. Perhaps you may study religion or pursue a religious calling where you can do God's work, whether it's teaching a Bible studies class, entering the priesthood or becoming a rabbi. You may even find yourself attracted to a non-traditional spiritual movement.

This is an excellent period in your life to practice meditation or attend personal growth workshops or partake in other metaphysical experiences. You're in a contemplative state of mind where your ego is not tied to the material life but more to how you can be of benefit to the mass collective of all people. You feel drawn to being of service to others, perhaps deciding to do missionary work or volunteering for the Peace Corps.

Great Time for a Spiritual Journey

When you live in a material world, where your life is focused on work, paying the rent or mortgage, and all the other demands of day-to-day life, there doesn't seem to be time for thoughtful reflection about weighty questions like, "What is your purpose in life?" or "How could life be more fulfilling for you?"

Have you ever dreamed of just dropping out of the responsibilities of life and going on your own personal contemplative journey to discover answers for such questions? You have that opportunity when Neptune transits your 9th House, because it's an inspirational and mystical time to gain knowledge. One client used this transit to plan her transcendental trek to India, where she took an extended vacation joining a meditation group to go on a tour of all the holy sites, including the Taj Mahal. On her trip she spent time with various spiritual teachers who advanced her studies and self-understanding.

Beware of a Delusional Spiritual Journey

Neptune's influence can also bring misunderstanding and deception in your encounters with foreigners and those engaged in religious or spiritual teachings. So, be careful not to be overly optimistic or idealistic where you can be taken advantaged of or duped. In extreme cases, this can be a time when a person falls prey to phony gurus or cults that promise answers if you relinquish your personal responsibility to their authority. Be particularly careful if the leaders of the group advise you to sell your property and give them the proceeds to "further their work."

In a positive vein, the influence of Neptune in the 9th House can bring you to a holy place where you feel a deep connection to God, your religion and spirituality. In fact, this is a time to when a person may "see the light," perhaps through a religious experience, and as a result become spiritually enlightened.

At the other extreme, this same individual can become arrogant and self-righteous, fooling himself into thinking he has a vision where he's answering a divine calling, becoming holier than everyone else. The person believes he has found the answers, so he becomes overzealous and proselytizes in an effort to convert friends. Unfortunately, one of my clients fell into such a Neptunian illusion on her spiritual journey.

Eleanor joined an ashram run by a religious order. She was totally swept up with the chanting and divine direction she was given. It was clear to her that the gurus who were instructing her were showing her the true path to enlightenment. Now, for the first time, she understood why all her "superficial" friends would never find happiness. They didn't understand that the path to true bliss required abandoning the material. The head guru leading the ashram was going to personally instruct her on all her decisions so she'd be assured she was embarking on the road to true joy and contentment. He would soon find a partner for her and arrange a marriage with someone she could build a life. Eleanor was sure the guru knew what was best for her.

However, after two years of living in the ashram and an unsuccessful marriage, the fog lifted (as Neptune moved out of her 9th House) and she saw the reality: the guru was controlling her life, not leading her on a path to enlightenment. Fortunately for her, her awakening came just before she signed over all her assets to the guru. Finding your true path seldom requires signing over your life savings although under Neptune's spell you may be too confused to see that truth. Under this transit, beware of a spiritual wolf in lamb's clothing.

Take the Bus...Not the Jet to Spiritual Enlightenment

Neptune in your 9th House is a genuine opportunity to seek enlightenment and the divine truth if you avoid anyone's offer to fly you over the clouds – directly to nirvana. The true path is usually not a "non-stop" flight. It's normally a long journey that can lead to meaningful discovery and revelation as long as you aren't overly attached to what you learn, since your vision of the truth may change during this period of your life as it did for Eleanor. I suggest to clients they take – what I call, "the spiritual bus." If you decide to hop aboard, it will *stop* off at many wonderful places where you'll experience genuine spiritual enlightenment. For most, it's best not to get off the transcendental bus too soon. Instead take the entire trip because it will allow you to experience the joy and bliss of learning about yourself and others on your journey.

One revelation you'll have is that you're not alone in the world, because we're all interconnected as fellow human beings. This is a time to be compassionate to others, especially as you travel your world. The rich experiences you have on your travels may touch your heart as you learn that people of other cultures are just like you in ways you hadn't realized.

Considerations, Actions, Decisions During Uranus in 9th House

1. Volunteer in an organization that's helping people.
2. Choose a spiritual calling that inspires you.
3. Consult reputable people to assist you in evaluating your ideas and plans.
4. Travel somewhere on a spiritual journey that will enlighten you.
5. Participate in a religious activity that will have meaning for you.
6. Enjoy religious, mystical or metaphysical classes.
7. Take up yoga and meditation.
8. Go to a meditation retreat where you can reflect in quiet solitude.

PLUTO in Your 9th House of Travel, Education & Philosophy

A Great Time to Transform Your Purpose

This is a time when you're eagerly seeking knowledge, while having an intense desire to learn from your experiences by immersing yourself in them. Rather than just reading about a topic like global warming or gun control, you may decide you want to join a group that regularly debates the subject so that you can totally understand both sides of the issue. You're not interested in superficial learning, because you're looking for more in-depth and profound ways to grow in the world. Your learning is deep, intense often with a psychological orientation. You want to be an expert and are willing to take the time to fully inform yourself, exploring such subjects as philosophy, religion and the metaphysical. Whereas before, you may have had little interests in such meaty topics, now they're fascinating because they hold answers for you that aren't available in your day-to-day world.

Rather than just learning through books, you may find yourself interested in actual experiences that allow you to feel deep inside your being. Thus, instead of reading about people from another country, you may decide you want to spend an entire year living in a foreign city where you can learn the language and immerse yourself in their culture.

When Pluto transits your 9th House, you become intensely focused on the meaning of life, and the philosophies you espouse take on a more serious tone. Your friends will probably see you as "intense," because you're searching for universal truths. Your journey may cause you to investigate why people behave the way they do or learn more about your own spiritual connection to God; or whether you even have one. You're deeply interested in exploring new ideas and understanding weighty questions such as your life's purpose. You're in a process of transforming your view of the world as a result of major changes in your philosophy. You may have been egocentric thinking the world revolved around you, however now you're having second thoughts and deeper insights into your own behavior. The discoveries you'll be making will bring you wisdom and maturity that will be of positive benefit to the way you live your life.

You may experience some sort of crisis in your thinking if the values, ideas and beliefs you've operated with aren't valid, and demand to be drastically altered. I have seen people discover that making money in a high-paying job was not everything that thought it was; or being single, free from a long-term marriage was not as much fun as they expected. The purpose of this transit is to broaden and expand your worldview by forcing you to more deeply examine your beliefs to assure they are still appropriate for you. This was the dilemma that Allen faced.

Allen was in the middle of a crisis as he realized his own values and interests had been changing over the past two years. He had started college with the idea of getting a business degree, opening up a business and making millions. However, his beliefs about what was important changed during the months he volunteered to be part of a medical study at a local hospital. That's when he personally got to know some of the doctors and observe the way they used the miracles of modern medicine to heal and restore sick people back to health.

Now the idea of working to make lots of money seemed shallow and unimportant when he compared it to the more meaningful work of being a physician. He had changed his life philosophy, which centered on material success and found a far greater purpose to fulfill the desires of his heart. With Pluto transiting Allen's 9th House he felt a powerful shift in his psyche that brought him to a clear realization he was going to change his major to pre-med and become a doctor.

A Time of Profound & Deep Experience

Pluto's influence has the capacity to affect you in such an intense and powerful manner that in the course of your learning, it's possible you'll make a discovery that moves you very deeply. In some cases, Pluto's energies can turn your experience into a fanatical obsession that changes you in a deep and profound way. This was the case for Will who was raised in a reformed Jewish family. While his parents taught him to be proud of his religion and heritage, they rarely observed Jewish holidays or customs. He often joked with his non-Jewish friends, "I grew up eating baby-back pork ribs and *Oscar Mayer* bacon."

However, during Pluto's transit of his 9th House he traveled to Washington DC and visited the Holocaust museum. It was a deeply moving experience that put him in touch with his Jewish roots, making him aware of the suffering his people had endured, not just during the war, but also over the centuries. When he returned home, he went to a lecture at a synagogue on "What It Means to Be a Jew." He was profoundly moved by what he learned and filled with pride about his heritage. Soon he was doing research and reading scores of books on Judaism, feeling a deep conviction about his newfound awareness of what it meant to be a Jew.

He decided he would become a more devout Jew, committed to studying and keeping kosher laws, following such restrictions as not mixing meat with dairy products; and he would wear a skullcap as a way of displaying his deep commitment to the orthodox sect of his religion. Eventually, he became critical of his parents, admonishing them for eating pork and not observing the sacred kosher laws. He told them that because they didn't keep a kosher home, he wasn't comfortable eating any meals there any longer.

Be aware that Pluto's energies can cause you to be obsessive and judgmental as in the case of Will. So, be mindful of not crossing the line where you become so fanatical about your beliefs that you push them on others, or become rigid and intractable. During this transit, the intensity of what you learn and believe can cause you to develop very strong views and opinions and as a result you may find yourself engaged in intense discussions about topics you feel deeply about. Make sure you are cognizant of being assertive in expressing your strong beliefs, and not aggressive and humiliating when you find others do not share them.

Great Time to Serve Society

If you use Plutonian energies in a self-serving way to benefit yourself, such as abusing your power, you may encounter great opposition from others. We see this Plutonian principle play out when someone manages a company and is exposed for defrauding stockholders or when it's discovered that a politician was given "insider stock" tips or guaranteed a large lobbying contract at the end of his term in return for passing legislation that benefits a particular company or industry. Such abuses will inevitably result in intense conflicts and power struggles for the perpetrators.

In a dynamic way, Pluto's influence brings power and will to your actions. If your motivation is to use this energy for the good of everyone in society, you can accomplish a great deal and achieve positive transformation in all matters governed by the 9th House: law, politics, philosophy, higher education, religion, spirituality, publishing and travel. Being of genuine public service to others is one of the best ways to use the power potential of Pluto.

Kate always dreamed of becoming a U.S. Senator and after receiving her law degree she went to work for the district attorney's office where she successfully prosecuted several high profile cases. For 10 years she'd been a volunteer on several campaigns, attended lots of fundraisers, and networked with many of the powerful and influential people in her party. She made her ambitions known and when Pluto transited her 9th House, she was asked if she would run as the party's candidate for the state senate. This is what she'd been aiming for and she enthusiastically accepted the opportunity. Kate's political ambitions were well placed because she was clearly working to benefit society.

One of the ways you may discover the answers you seek is through long distance travel, especially to other countries where you can experience foreigners and their cultures. If you're the type of person that wants to immerse yourself in a culture, learn their language and customs, becoming a native in a foreign country, you'll have this opportunity during Pluto's transit through your 9th House. The experience will transform your view of yourself, people and the world. This is also a powerful time to be a teacher either in your own country or one that's foreign, because you'll bring forth an intensity to your teaching that will deeply move and transform others to learn. Whether it's by studying, teaching or working abroad, you'll find yourself expanding your horizons and worldview during this transit.

Considerations, Actions, Decisions During Pluto in 9th House

1. Find a course of study that you feel passionately interested in.
2. Are you open to a major change in your philosophy?
3. Research and find a profession that you might dedicate your life
4. Journey to a foreign country where you can immerse yourself in their culture.
5. Teach something that will change people's lives for the better.
6. Go into politics to improve the system and weed out corruption.
7. Write a mystery novel or do some in-depth psychological research.
8. Begin a spiritual or religious activity that will unlock some of the mysteries of your life.

9th House: Travel, Education & Philosophy

Transits to Use for Successful 9th House Decisions

You now understand the areas of life that are featured in your 9th House. We've discussed how each of the five transiting planets exerts its unique influence on the affairs of this House. This will help you better understand the changes you are experiencing, moods you're feeling, and the events taking place. Your awareness of this information may prompt you to:

1. *ACCEPT* the way things are and be content with what is going on in your life.

2. *CONSIDER* that you'd like to make some change, in which case you may evaluate your options and further contemplate your situation.

3. *DECIDE* that you're ready to make a change, take action, and make a decision pertaining to the affairs of this House.

If you make a decision, you'll want to learn how to pick the best transit to produce a successful outcome for it. Please know that the art of picking and interpreting transits requires very thorough analysis, normally done by a professional astrologer. Therefore, I've kept the discussion of selecting and using transits simple, for illustration purposes.

The key is to remember that each planet has the ability to bring a *different* positive quality of success to your decision. For example, *Jupiter's* effect may provide opportunities to expand and grow; *Saturn's* effect is more practical; *Uranus'* effect is sudden and exciting; *Neptune's* influence may bring you inspiration and idealism; *Pluto* may bring an intense and transformative effect for major change. This knowledge will help you understand how your decisions are affected by these planetary influences.

In the examples below, I chose a planetary transit to produce a favorable result for each individual's particular decision. This will help you see the many possibilities available to create the right outcome and make your 9th House decisions more successful.

Using a positive JUPITER Transit

DECISION: *I want to pick the best time to successfully learn to speak French.*

Explanation: Molly has never learned to speak a foreign language but is excited to learn French. We chose a Jupiter transit because it was perfect for self-improvement and would expand her ability to learn a foreign language, giving her the confidence to speak it while she was learning. The positive influences of Jupiter would also bring her a helpful teacher to assist her in learning a new language.

*   *   *   **

Using a positive SATURN Transit

DECISION: *I want to pick the best time to finish my college degree.*

Explanation: Ben knows that a degree will get him a better job, more pay and give him a sense of self-respect he desires. We chose a Saturn transit because it was favorable time for him to complete something he had started in the past but not finished. A Saturn transit would bring him energies to be committed to his goal, work hard and produce tangible results.

*   *   *   **

Using a positive URANUS Transit

DECISION: *I want to pick the best time to live in a foreign country for a fantastic and exciting experience.*

9th House: Travel, Education & Philosophy

Explanation: Rene has always loved people of other cultures. Her parents were from the Far East and she wanted to spend a year in a foreign study program living in their country of origin. We chose a Uranus transit because it would bring Rene new experiences and the excitement of living in a foreign country and unique culture. Under Uranus' influence she would meet many new people and make interesting and unusual friends.

* * *

Using a positive NEPTUNE Transit

DECISION: *I want to write and publish a religious book.*

Explanation: We chose a Neptune's transit to Charisse's 9th House, since it's excellent for writing and publishing a book. Neptune's energies would bring an inspired and creative quality to her religious writing. Neptune's influence would assist her in writing in a healing and compassion way, which would make her book appealing to readers.

* * *

Using a positive PLUTO Transit

DECISION: *I want to pick the best time to travel around the world to have an educational and transformational experience.*

Explanation: It's taken Patty a few years to save enough money for a trip around the world. She'd like her vacation experience to be one she will never forget. We chose a Pluto transit because the experiences that she would have visiting different countries would be intense and profound. Her experiences would stay in her memory for years with the trip having the potential to change her forever.

* * *

> REMEMBER: *You can use the FREE Transit Calculator that's discussed in Part IV of this book to go back in time to see which transits were occurring when a major event happened in your life. It might be a wonderful learning experience, especially since most transits repeat themselves over your lifetime. Also you can find out where your transits are today or in the future.*

10th House
Career & Status

There is no better way to understand how well things are going in your world than to ask yourself if you're happy in your career. Are you doing *what you wanted to do when you grew up?* Is your career progressing or is it growing stagnant. Are you on the fast track…or, no track?

The 10th House is the house of your profession, career and status. This House rules fame, honor, prestige, authority, hierarchy, life direction, achievement and mastery. If you once said, "I always knew I wanted to be a musician, writer, lawyer, hockey player, or a entrepreneur," or, if you've said, "I'm not sure what I really want to do for a career," – then this is the House that will assist you in understanding your career choices.

This House rules your ambition, aspirations, success, recognition, and standing in the community. It will tell whether or not you yearn to be in the public, have position in society, or attain status in the world. It also reveals a great deal of information about your character as well as insights into the personality of people who have authority over you.

Are you obsessed with status and impressing other people? Or, are you a high-achiever, who is disciplined, organized and patiently works hard to get ahead? Let's face it: some people have so much ambition that they won't stop until they reach the top and become president of the company. Other people are content to work for the president because they're only interested in having a simple dependable career, with less responsibility, and no need for any of the trappings of power, status or success.

Since this is the House of Career, look here to understand which professions you're best suited for and which ones would be unfavorable for you to pursue. This is the place to see the likelihood of your receiving promotions and recognition in your profession. You can also learn a great deal about whether your relationships with colleagues, bosses, and those in authority are likely to be harmonious, and thus bring you their help and support. Or, are those relationships destined to be acrimonious where you'll receive little support from them because you're constantly engaged in quarrels and disputes.

This House concerns your public image and political success, which makes it an especially important House for celebrities and politicians. In fact, it will give insights as to whether you'll be famous as a celebrity or achieve success as a politician. I once had a friend who spent 30 years of his life trying to pursue a career as an elected politician. He was wasting his time, only he didn't know it. The reason was that the 10th House of his natal chart indicated it was the wrong career choice for him and any attempts to pursue this profession would lead to frustration and failure. There were no transits that were going to change this likelihood. Unfortunately, he ignored this reality. Subsequently, he was frustrated over many years of failure, all the while stubbornly clinging to his ambition.

I've had many clients who spend years tackling a career that's inappropriate for them and despite their hard work and dedication, they experience great difficulty and frustration, as if they were trying to push a boulder up hill. Conversely, I've known others who pursued occupations they were meant for, with great ease and success. The 10th House can be your career compass pointing you in a life direction that is really your destiny.

Note: An astrologer, much like a vocational counselor, can analyze your birth chart and offer you great insight into the career choices you're best suited, and likely to achieve success and satisfaction.

This House concerns your sense of duty, responsibility and authority. It's the place where *public karma* play out. (Karmic law says: As you sow, so shall you reap; what goes around comes around.) In that sense, this area of the birth chart reveals how a person who ruthlessly ascends to the top of his profession may one day pay for any lack of integrity and dishonesty. This is the place to look to see a great deal about a person's character, especially if you want to know whether they're likely to live up to their commitments and be concerned about their professional as well as personal reputation. Looking at clients' charts, I find it intriguing to analyze a person's 10th House to see if they are ambitious and have a high likelihood of achieving power and status. Many of our presidents, distinguished leaders and generals have a birth chart indicating very a powerful 10th House that shows great integrity and unusual charisma.

This is the House that concerns long-range goals, large-scale organizations, chief executives, presidents, political position, government, affairs of state, military, ranks; as well as your father or whoever was the main breadwinner and person who taught you about the outer world.

Your Body in the 10th House

This house rules the teeth, skin, bones, knees, joints and back. Since there is nothing more important than your health, pay special attention to these areas of your body whenever a planet transits this House. It may indicate a period of time when you'll experience health benefits, issues or even problems you should be aware of. If you observe anything unusual, you'll have the opportunity to consult with a medical doctor or a health care practitioner.

Your 10th House Decisions

You now understand that the 10th House of your birth chart concerns your career, reputation and social status.

As you read about the description of this house, it's time to ask yourself a few questions about these areas of your life. Are you happy and fulfilled in your career? What are you meant to do in your career? Are you in the right profession? Are you achieving success in your career or are you constantly being frustrated in your attempts to succeed? Should you be changing jobs to increase your upward mobility and meet your goals? If you have been in one career, is it satisfying? If you seem to change your profession often, have you asked why you've had so many occupations?

If you don't like working for others and resent having a boss or someone with authority over you, maybe it's time to consider that you should be on your own as an independent consultant or entrepreneur. Should you be working for a profit-making company or doing public service work through a non-profit organization? Should you be in hi-tech, low-tech or no-tech?

These are all significant questions and your answers may lead you to make important decisions to change your life. Here are a few examples of decisions clients have made based on the activities and issues of the 10th House.

Situation: Hank never got along with his boss, because their personalities clashed. He realizes that his strained relationship has affected his bonus and promotional opportunities.

DECISION: *I have decided to find a new job at a time when I'll have a positive working relationship with my new boss.*

* * *

Situation: After 30 years of marriage, Betty and her husband have decided to divorce.

DECISION: *I want to divorce at a time when I can be assured that my status and life-style will continue as it has always been during my marriage.*

* * *

Situation: Jason has spent the last 10 years acting and winning small parts.

DECISION: *I want to aggressively promote my career at a time when I am likely to get bigger parts that will make me better known and famous in the public.*

* * *

Situation: After 10 years as an engineer, Natalie realizes she no longer wants to be an engineer.

DECISION: *I want to plan a career change at a time when I will experience success in a rewarding new profession where I can make a difference in the lives of others.*

* * *

During the transits of *Jupiter, Saturn, Uranus, Neptune,* and *Pluto,* Hank, Betty, Jason and Natalie will have many opportunities to implement their decisions at a favorable time to produce the outcome they want.

The Transiting Planets Reveal Your Past, Present & Future

Your main focus is using astrology to understand *what the hell is going on in your life.* Once you do – this book will show you the best time to make a decision to change it, should you have the desire to do so. As you read about the five planets transiting the 10th House, notice the way each planet exerts its unique influence and effect, bringing specific opportunities, issues, problems, and events into this area of your life. But if you're curious as to how these planets are personally affecting YOU *today,* in your *past,* or in your *future*, you can find out where each transiting planet is in your birth chart by using the *FREE Transit Calculator* (see Part IV).

JUPITER in Your 10th House of Career & Reputation

Be Out in the World to Receive Your Luck

When Jupiter enters your 10th House, you receive great opportunities to expand or improve your career, profession, social status or reputation. This is usually a fortunate time when you can make great progress in your occupation or business and achieve successful results. You may find yourself walking around the world with a confident swagger and a spring in your step. You'll feel courageous, enthusiastic and have a very positive attitude, which everyone around you notices. This is a time when you're happy because you're pursuing the work you were meant to do and your career climbs to new heights. It's when your business expansion efforts pay off big time. In fact, any career moves that you make are destined to produce results and strike pay dirt in the long run. This is a year of your life when you should be out in the public: networking, meeting people and making contacts with those who'll be valuable in helping you achieve success in your career or business.

Often in life you work hard; you talk to people; you reach out and ask for help, and you get nothing. No response. You might be tempted to say: "Hellloooo…is anyone there?" It just seems like the world is not acknowledging your existence, only throwing roadblocks your way. It's frustrating because despite your earnest efforts, requests and pleadings, you can't seem to make a breakthrough to accomplish your goals. However, get ready for the opposite effect.

Here are some of positive responses you may receive during the year that Jupiter transits your 10th House:

- "We've been looking for someone with your talent to join our company. You're hired!"
- "After interviewing all the candidates, the board has decided to offer you the presidency."
- "We're downsizing and re-organizing the company, but we'd like you to remain."

10th House: Career & Status

- "Congratulations on starting your own business. We'd like to be your first customer."
- "You've just won the lead in a movie directed by Steven Spielberg."
- "You've been chosen to light the torch at the Olympics and be honored as an outstanding athlete."
- "We want you to head the philosophy department at the university."
- "We want to promote you to 1st Chair violinist in the symphony orchestra."
- "Congratulations on being elected "Homecoming Queen!""
- "We want to recognize you for your outstanding service to the community with a special award banquet with the mayor and a feature in the newspaper."
- "Congratulations! You have won the lottery and will be receiving a check for $10 million dollars."

These are examples of statements that a person might hear when Jupiter transits their 10th House of career and reputation. Don't forget that luck is not only defined in terms of a big job offer, pay raise or a large product order or a civic award for meritorious achievement. After all, you can't always tell bad luck from good luck at first glance. What, at first appears as bad luck, may turn out to be good luck in the long run. Because of Jupiter's beneficent influences your good fortune may be that you are saved from *bad fortune*. Consider these examples:

- Not fired after making a costly mistake.
- Not laid off from your company when other people are.
- The company that didn't hire you goes bankrupt.
- In a bad car accident but not injured.
- Visited your doctor for a minor medical problem that accidentally reveals you have an early cancer.

A Jupiter transit can make you feel expansive and grandiose where you are only looking for "big things" to happen, so it's good to manage your expectations when you have this transit. After all, one person might consider himself lucky to find a $1 bill on the street; another would insist that he'd have to find a $100 bill to feel lucky. While Jupiter's energies generally brings good luck and great opportunity, avoid the tendency to have such grand ideas of what "luck" means that you lose all sense of proportion or gratitude for the fortune you've been blessed with. Often luck brings you opportunity. But what you do with that opportunity is up to you. However, you must be pro-active to take full advantage of the luck, fortune and opportunity that Jupiter brings to your career during this year. In fact, you must take steps to reach out in an extroverted way, even if it's not your normal style, because it will pay off during this year.

Here are some actions that clients, who wanted to advance their careers, have taken during this transit. I had one client agree to a commitment of having one lunch a week with a new contact; another said she'd make 10 phone calls a day to a new organizations asking if they would be interested in sponsoring her workshop to their membership; another person agreed to consult his weekly newspaper to attend three networking events at such places at his local chamber of commerce, country club and church; one job-seeker agreed to network each day on *LinkedIn*, attend job fairs, and call old bosses and colleagues on a daily basis until she found a new job. Someone who wanted to buy a franchise business agreed to research five franchise operations a week and attend the national franchise show to learn of the many possibilities. These are just a few action plans. But each of these clients achieved their career goals.

The secret to their career success was in knowing that Jupiter was transiting their 10th House – and then taking steps to capitalize on it. Don't let your year expire without making full use of your Jupiter transit. If you couple this transit with a real commitment to action, you'll experience good fortune in your career, status, and reputation. Your success equation is: *Action + Jupiterian Luck = Opportunity*.

Jupiter's passage through your 10th House may change your professional status where you become known for who you are and what you do. It may even be a time when you become famous as Bobby found out. *Bobby's Home Boy Band* had been a popular local musical group for many years. The group's leader, Bobby, was the lead singer and lead guitarist and he was extremely talented and known for writing his own music and lyrics. Everyone who'd heard his songs agreed, "This guy is going straight to the top." Despite his talent, for years he remained a great lead singer in a local band and started losing his ambition and motivation. There was no denying he'd wanted to make it to the top but he was now questioning whether he and his band had the talent to get a big entertainment contract at a major club in a large city like L.A. or New York.

When I met Bobby for his transit consultation, I saw that in a few months Jupiter was going to transit his 10th House (and he would have other excellent transits occurring as well). I said, "Bobby, this next year is your year for fame and fortune. You're going to get that big opportunity you've wanted for so long where you'll be recognized by the public." He was excited, but understandably skeptical. I told him that one of the key words that Jupiter symbolized is "luck." I explained that with Jupiter transiting his 10th House he had a lucky opportunity that only came along once every 12 years.

I counseled him that his optimism and his confidence would return, but he must be very proactive and make full use of his career luck. He explained he was ready to work with a new manager; and a new agent he liked, who could promote him to larger venues and take his career to the next level. He was also hiring a first class publicist to make sure his band was properly promoted. Bobby started to feel the enthusiasm of Jupiter and vowed to take aggressive action to take advantage of the extraordinary opportunity before him.

Within four months Bobby had put together his a first class team: a new manager, agent and an excellent publicist. Demos were sent out and he started flying to out-of-state auditions. One day his agent called him with the amazing news that he and his band had just been signed to a six-month contract to perform at a major Las Vegas casino hotel. He was told that if they drew well and the crowds liked their music, the band would be in line to be the opening act for one of the biggest vocalists in the country who played the hotel annually. Bobby was off and running. He had Jupiter in his 10th House.

Great Time to Advance in Your Profession or Change It

It's also a fortunate time for career advancement and finding a new profession because opportunities come your way to expand your career or to change it. In your current job this a favorable time to win a promotion or receive recognition for anything you've accomplished. By the way, if you've achieved any success or reached any noteworthy goal, this is the year to let people know that your success has filled you with confidence and the desire to achieve more.

The positive influence of Jupiter causes people to like and value you. During this transit you'll receive the recognition and respect of colleagues, co-workers and authorities who will be happy to hear of your successes. This is an ideal time to win acceptance for your ideas or the projects you've completed, so make sure to be assertive and let others know you're ready for new responsibilities. When others recognize your career achievements, your successful efforts may be acknowledged in the form of awards, bonuses or other gifts. Jupiter's influence brings an almost "spiritual" feeling to your career that you're doing something good for yourself and society and really making a difference. One of the positive benefits of Jupiter's influence is that it makes you confident and brings you opportunities for growth and expansion.

However, in a negative vein, it can also cause you to be so sure of yourself that your ego takes over and you become conceited, arrogant, or even overbearing to the point where others resent your cocky attitude. Remember a dose of humility when you sing your own praises. That means that when you do something well, avoid any tendency to run around your boss' desk like an NFL football player who's just made a touchdown.

During the year this transit takes place, it's important to honestly assess your skills and accomplishments so that your confidence is grounded in reality, not in self-puffery. The great boxer, Muhammad Ali said it well, "It's not bragging if you can back it up."

Winston, while less flamboyant than Muhammad Ali, had the same confidence and talent. He was a hi-tech geek who was a genius at understanding the most complicated elements of computer designs and implementations. He had worked at APPLE and GOOGLE, and at 27 he was already known in his industry. When Jupiter transited his 10th House, an international hi-tech consulting firm came to him and said, "Winston, our firm has a very hi-profile client who wants to know if we can do a very complicated 'migration.' We've never done that type of consulting work before."

The head of the consulting firm shared his concern of not wanting to ruin the firm's reputation with their client by promising to do something they couldn't accomplish. He told Winston that if he thought he could do the job, the firm would like to hire him. Winston looked at the CEO and said, "Sure. I can get the job done for you. I'd enjoy the challenge." Winston accepted their job offer and then assembled a team of the consulting firm's best technical consultants to tackle the assignment. His team met to discuss several approaches that might produce results and then flew to the client's office to begin the migration changeover from the old telecommunication system to the state-of-the-art system they were implementing. After many weeks of working out the bugs, problems and glitches in the new system, no more errors were reported. The telecommunications migration that had "never been done before" was now working perfectly. It was a huge success.

The following Monday, when Winston returned back from the client's office, the CEO came into his office to personally congratulate him, bring over a large bonus check, and discuss a big company promotion.

Great Time to Start a New Business

This is also an excellent time to start a new business or expand an already existing one. Jupiter's fortunate influence makes this a time when your work efforts flourish and you receive acknowledgment for your efforts. You may even see an opportunity to create a business of your own – as Cynthia experienced.

Cynthia had been working as a travel agent for the past 5 years. She enjoyed the work and was so sharp that her boss, recognizing her talent, trained her in each area of the travel business in order to prepare her to one day be an assistant manager. Subsequently, Cynthia learned all aspects of the business from sales and marketing to customer service and client development. She learned all about accounting, components of travel, tourism, accommodations, working with tour operators, hotels, and the various ticketing systems. In simple terms, Cynthia had learned the travel business.

That got her to think about starting her own travel agency operation. She had accumulated a wealth of experience and had many ideas on the new ways she'd like to grow her own business. It was also encouraging to have so many corporate clients say, "Cynthia you're so fabulous to work with. If you ever go out on your own, please let us know. We'd love to do business with you."

When Jupiter transited her 10th House she felt a great deal of confidence and was ready to make her goal a reality. Within a short time she gave notice and made arrangements to leave her job. Soon she found an ideal location for her travel business, a financial partner to assist her, and her first new clients. Because of her high sense of morals and ethics she planned to abide by the terms of the "non-competition agreement" she signed, and not contact old clients "for at least one year." She was confident she could be a successful entrepreneur operating her business with honest principles and practices.

Other Jupiter Benefits

This is a wonderful time for you, personally, because you're confident and keenly aware of your talents and abilities. For this reason, this is also a fortunate time to engage in other Jupiterian activities such as traveling for work. If you have any special opportunities to be considered for work assignments, take advantage of them because they're likely to work out to your benefit. If you travel abroad, you may meet foreigners who will provide great opportunities for your career advancement. If you have any career aspirations in publishing, the law, teaching, higher educational pursuits, medicine or healing, these are all favored this year.

Interestingly, you should know that the 10th House governs the parent who was the main breadwinner and the person who taught you about the outer world – often your father, but in many cases your mother. This is a time when you're likely to have a happy and joyful relationship with that parent. You're able to express your appreciation and gratitude for all that they have done to make you a success. Enjoy having an especially warm and cordial relationship with them during this year.

Considerations, Actions, Decisions During Jupiter in 10th House

1. Seek a promotion to a job where you could learn, grow and enjoy.
2. Change careers to one that offers greater opportunity.
3. Start a new business or confidently expand the one you're in.
4. Use your popularity to become famous.
5. Improve your social status by going out in public and making your presence known.
6. Take classes to learn something new; or go to school full-time for a degree.
7. Publish some literary work
8. Enjoy traveling for your career.
9. Show appreciation and gratitude to your parents

SATURN in Your 10th House of Career & Reputation

A Time To Take Responsibility for Your Career

During Saturn's transit you are accountable for whatever career, status, and reputation you've built. You're ready to harvest the rewards for all your hard work and efforts to attain your goal. Now is the time when your diligence and preparation pay off and you achieve excellent results; or *whatever results you deserve*. Do you remember those long hours and months of working overtime, not seeing much of your kids, and your spouse giving you the "evil eye" as you rolled in after 8 p.m. each night? Or, do you remember those weeks or months when you found a way to take leisurely lunches, leave work early and do only what was required? This is when "the chickens come home to roost."

Be aware that if you haven't worked in good faith or improperly prepared yourself, you may encounter great difficulties now. In fact, old astrologers had a saying: "Saturn in the 10th is a time of a rise or fall." In other words, during this period of your life you'll receive cosmic *payback*, for the good and bad deeds you've done. None of us is perfect, so most of us experience elements of both the positive and negative in our own personal career harvest. Don't forget that one of Saturn's lessons and benefits is re-evaluating your actions so you can let go of unproductive ways in favor of more beneficial behaviors that will improve you. That means, for example, if you've been a slacker at work, taking long lunches, leaving early and doing the minimum required, you have the opportunity to re-dedicate yourself to doing a more conscientious job.

Now is when you can discover what work you're really committed to doing in your life. Saturn's energies help you in this regard, because you will receive *feedback* from the outer world, be it the public or your employer, about your job performance. The response you get will help you realistically evaluate your career accomplishments to see if you're doing the work you're meant to do. If you've had any illusions about your talents and abilities, during this time you'll receive some sort of objective evaluation you can use to decide whether to continue in your career or job; or consider a new one. Consider these assessments:

- "Based on your poor work habits and lackadaisical attitude, you'll be on probation for the next three months."
- "You're lack of patience makes it clear why you haven't been an effective teacher."
- "I'm not confident you know how to lead others, therefore, I can't recommend you for promotion."
- "Because of your creative culinary skills we'd like you to be our new chef."
- "Based on your dedicated efforts to help our department make the sales forecast, I'm approving you for a 20 percent raise."
- "With your superior grammar and writing skills you'll make an excellent editor."
- "Because of your leadership skills and ability to motivate others, I'm recommending you for promotion."

Saturn's influence demands that you critically evaluate your achievements in your career and outer world in order to decide whether to continue or change your direction. Here are some clients who received Saturn's message.

Growing up, Kenny loved playing baseball. Because of his tremendous talent, he was drafted, right out of college, by a major league team. After seven years playing minor league ball for a Triple AAA team in Arizona, he's never hit better than .260. He's just been told that he'll be cut because he's not considered someone who can hit major league pitching.

Rhonda was a fantastic salesperson for many years. Then, three years ago she was promoted to regional sales manager replacing the old manager who continually missed his sales goals. She ended up inheriting an under-achieving sales force, requiring her to fire, hire and train replacements. So, Rhonda has had to work 60-70 hour weeks on the road, re-building the reps in the field. Finally over the last 12 months her efforts have paid off with her sales team beating the company forecast by 20 percent. Rhonda has just been offered a promotion to be the company's new national sales manager.

Gene always enjoyed public speaking and it made him feel good to help people by delivering motivating lectures. He thought he had a great future as a paid public speaker. But before he "took the show on the road," he wanted to gain some experience and see how the hometown crowd liked his talks. Gene convinced several local business organizations to allow him to speak before their members. After a number of lectures, he was uncertain how to gauge their enthusiasm. Gene finally decided to sit down and get some feedback from several of the executives who had heard him speak. He was surprised to hear their feedback, "Gene, I hate to have to tell you this – but you're not a motivating or inspiring speaker." Another said, "Gene, you're boring; your voice could put babies to sleep." Gene has Saturn in his 10th House so this is a critical time for him to evaluate and determine if public speaking is a career he should pursue.

Walter was a senior executive for a major consumer food conglomerate. He was promoted to president of one of the company's consumer products division five years ago. At first, he was very hard-working and dedicated to increasing revenues, and in his first year of operations, sales and profits were modestly up. However, over the last three years profits have been negligible. His efforts and enthusiasm have slacked off. Instead of being seen as a leader who works day and night to increase company profits, he's well known by employees for leaving headquarters for personal reasons ranging from attending to problems with his errant son to taking Friday afternoons for long golf-weekends. Many of the department heads have suspected that his judgment at meetings may be impaired from too many three-martini lunches.

His boss, the group president, met with him today and fired him. Gene was told that he wasn't "cutting it," and they needed to make a change.

A Time for Recognition

From a positive perspective, Saturn brings rewards if you've worked hard, honestly, and to high standards. If so, this will be a time of major achievement in your career where your life's ambition and goals are realized. You may receive leadership opportunities, huge financial rewards, and public recognition for the work you've done. This is when your promotion is announced in the business section of the local newspaper or your face appears on the cover of an industry magazine announcing your success. You now have the opportunity to impress the outer world with who you are and your talents. You'll feel like the King or Queen of your profession.

Saturn's influence brings you responsibilities when it transits your 10th House, so if your goal is to be a leader, this can be a period of great achievement where you reach a high point and make your mark on the world. If you're not inclined toward taking on the responsibilities of leadership, this may be just a more demanding but productive time in your career. Either way, this is when you're able to work in a purposeful, disciplined, organized and diligent manner.

This was the case for Richard who for so many years made profits for his company while serving his community so generously. Richard could not believe he was standing at the podium accepting a lifetime achievement award from the Chamber of Commerce. He was now 62, and had successfully run his own business, employing 500 people; however, he still found time to have his company sponsor programs for the Little League, the Girl Scouts, and several other community organizations, as well as raise funds to build three parks in the inner city. Richard had organized and funded scholarship programs at several city high schools to help underprivileged children go to school. He was a generous and philanthropic individual, and this was his day to be recognized and acknowledged. Saturn was transiting his 10th House.

A Time for Karmic Payback

Saturn is a tough taskmaster if you haven't prepared properly, taking shortcuts, sloughing off to avoid hard work, not operating with integrity, or being dishonest in order to get where you are. If that's the case, you'll harvest the negative energies of Saturn, and you'll arouse extreme opposition from those in the outer world, perhaps people in your career, who are in a position to block your advancement and thwart your ambitions.

Since Saturn's influence holds you accountable for your past actions and behavior, you may receive criticism, disapproval, and dismissal for doing an ineffective job. Any time during the period that Saturn transits here, you may have to bear the consequences of what you've done in your past. A famous historical example of this *karmic bill* coming due was President Richard Nixon and the infamous Watergate scandal. The discovery of his involvement in the Watergate burglary and subsequent cover-up led to his fall from grace and eventual resignation from the presidency on August 9, 1974.

However, long before Watergate, Nixon's questionable actions and dirty tactics as a politician created a large opposition from those who were anxious to see him fall from high position. Ultimately, his dishonest and unethical behavior in the Watergate scandal brought about a near certainty of impeachment, public disgrace and his own downfall. This all happened to Richard Nixon when Saturn transited his 10th House of Career.

Always remember that just like Santa Claus, Saturn knows "whether you've been naughty or nice." Make sure to prepare diligently for your success, rather than taking shortcuts as you climb to the top. By working hard, striving to operate your life with honesty, principles, and ethics you can help assure that you experience the positive rewards of Saturn's transiting your 10th House. Remember: The values (*integrity*), morals (*be honest*), and principles (*Golden Rule*) you learned when Saturn was in your 9th House prepare you to live your life to the high standards required when Saturn transits your 10th.

A Time to Pay Attention to Your Overall Life – Not Just Your Career

Quite often, when Saturn transits your 10th House, you become so focused on your outer world – career, job, status and reputation that you overlook what's occurring in your personal life with the people you're close to. Despite the demands of your career and of your outer world, Saturn demands you be responsible for your actions and behavior in your personal world. If you ignore them, you'll feel the repercussions and negative effects there, as well.

I have had many clients who felt their dedication and hard work building a career excused them from leaving time for their personal life, family and loved ones. In essence, their life was in total imbalance. Therefore, in the years *before* Saturn transits your 10th House, it's important that you create a balance between your personal life and career. Otherwise, you'll eventually experience problems and their consequences when Saturn transits here. These problems can diminish the success you'll enjoy in your career and the outer world. This was the case for a client named Michael.

Michael was a hardworking accountant who spent 30 years of his life building his accounting practice by working six days a week and bringing clients' work home on weekends. Other than taking some time out for meals and an occasional family outing or brief vacation, he was totally focused on building his practice. He didn't have much time for his wife or kids. His wife Barbara did her best to give their three children enough attention since Michael was always working. But his inattention caused them to act out and be resentful, with two of the children requiring therapy in their adolescent years. Barbara became lonely and looked for outside interests, and eventually had an affair. She finally admitted she no longer loved her husband and wanted a divorce. Consequently, when Michael became a partner at his accounting firm, he was depressed instead of happy, since this honor came at the expense of losing his family.

Michael's story clearly illustrates the negative consequences of Saturn when a person's life is so out of balance. To avoid problems, Saturn requires you to be responsible for your personal life as well career. However, if you've operated according to proper ethics, morals and principles, and you've worked hard and diligently over the years, this two and a half year period of Saturn transiting your 10th House may be the most rewarding time of your life as you realize the harvest of all your hard-won efforts.

Considerations, Actions, Decisions During Saturn in 10th House

1. Have you worked diligently in your career or not?
2. Are you in the right occupation or career?
3. Are you in the right job?
4. Have you received feedback about success or failure in your career?
5. Should you seriously consider changing your career or job?
6. You should expect to work very hard if you start a new job or business during this transit.
7. Objectively re-evaluate the business you're in.
8. Do you need to make any changes in the way you do your work?
9. Do you have a balance between your personal life and career?

Uranus in Your 10th House of Career & Reputation

You Are Ready to Be Independent

When Uranus transits your 10th House, you'll likely make radical changes in your career, reputation or social status, so get ready for excitement, surprises, and the unexpected in these areas of your life. This is a period when you're motivated to find new ways to express yourself in the outer world. You're not concerned with pursuing conventional or traditional career paths. In fact, you're likely to be excited about experiencing some new life calling. You have your own ideas and principles you think should be adhered to, so the thought of independence and being your own boss thrills you. You're ready to begin a new phase in the work you do in the external world. It's a time when you feel a limitless potential.

You'll also have a desire to break away from any routine or unchallenging work. It's when all those years of doing the same job or monotonous type of work finally catches up with you, and you start feeling like you can't stomach it any longer. Another effect you may encounter is no longer being able to accept orders from bosses or those in authority. This will be especially true if you've had to put up working with people you don't like or respect. Now it will become intolerable.

Beverly had worked for her sexist boss Lou for the past year in a routine office job. The most irritating part of the job was those times when she had to interact with him. Every time Lou wanted her to do something, his requests began with, "Honey, do this," and "Sweetheart, please get me that." She once politely said, "Lou, this is the 21st century. Men at work don't call women by those names or endearments." However, no amount of reminding him made any difference to the inappropriate ways he addressed her. He always excused himself by saying, "I don't mean anything by it," or "Don't be so sensitive," or "Are you one of them 'women's libbers? What's the big deal?'"

It was useless for Beverly to explain to Lou why his behavior was offensive, since Lou was old enough to be her grandfather and clearly from another era. He was stuck in a time warp where it was commonplace for men to feel entitled to display chauvinistic or inappropriate behavior to women whenever it suited them. Eventually she stopped correcting him or requesting he call her "Beverly." But it still grated on her when she heard him say those words. When Uranus transited her 10th House, his behavior became too upsetting to endure any longer. Within one week, Beverly answered an ad and took another job. She left a letter of resignation on his desk and never came back.

A Great Time to Take Career Risks

Have you ever had the opportunity to change your career or job; or start a new business, but you were too afraid to take the risk, perhaps because of practical concerns or normal fears? Well, during this period of your life, you'll have the courage and will no longer hold back. Uranian influences will compel you to make a change in a dynamic way without being inhibited by any restrictions you may encounter in the outer world.

This is an ideal time to start a new business that you'll build through your own innovation and creativity. You're ready to take a risk, having the courage to go off on your own, often with little or no safety net, guided by a keen awareness and intuition of what you want to do. You're fearless. Best of all, you're not bound by the conventional rules of what's possible. When people ask your secret to success, you'll reply, "I didn't know *it couldn't be done*...so, I did it."

Sharon was a client who had worked for almost a year at a cupcake baking shop. She had never worked in the food or retail industry before, so it was interesting and fun to learn something new. The owner, Helga taught her a great deal about cupcake baking. Sharon was so enthused that she also did some basic research on the Internet, looking at different recipes and learning more about industry practices.

Surprisingly, the more Sharon learned, the more it became clear that Helga was using the cheapest ingredients in her recipes. The flour and frostings were not of the highest quality and key ingredients like butter were substituted with margarine. She also understood why the cup cakes weren't always fresh, since Helga sold them again the next day instead of donating them to charities, as other bakers did. When Sharon started sharing her observations and discoveries with Helga, Helga became angry and told her, "I know what I need to do to make a profit. Why don't you let me worry about how to run this bakery?"

After visiting Helga's competitors over the next few weeks, it was easy to understand why the competition made much tastier and fresher cupcakes than Helga's. Then a light came on and two exciting thoughts came to her mind, *I'd love to open up my own bakeshop and make high quality, gourmet cupcakes. And my mother makes the most delicious, yummy cupcakes I've ever tasted!*

A week later Sharon told her mother her idea and received an enthusiastic offer to help; and she also enlisted her uncle's financial and business support to start her own cupcake business. Within six months, Sharon had opened up her own gourmet cupcake store. She was going to appeal to those customers who wanted the special treat of a delicious cupcake, made fresh daily with natural ingredients. Sharon was excited to finally be in business for herself.

At Time for Clashes, Restrictions & Freedom

The influences of Uranus have the potential for excitement as well as disruption. So, the seven-year cycle may be a period of ups and downs in your career, reputation, and social status. Imagine your career is a roller coaster ride and one moment you're enjoying the thrill and excitement, the next you're yelling because you want to get off. Expect that it's likely to be a time of growth, change and instability in your career.

During Uranus' transit through your 10th House, it's possible that radical changes in your career may come about because of severe conflicts with bosses or other authority figures resulting in either possibility: "Take this job and shove it!" or, "Clean out your desk, your fired." You may find that the way you express your identity in the world through your profession, reputation or social status will be radically altered, challenged or disrupted in some way. Unpredictably, you may be on the cover of *Fortune* as an icon; or perhaps on the cover of *The Enquirer* for something a bit less iconic.

If your job or profession has become boring, routine or old, no longer providing you with fresh experiences for growth, you can expect that this is where change will occur in your life. I have found that the degree my clients were affected depended upon how much freedom and creativity they had woven into the work they had been doing over the years.

There are many catalysts that could bring about exciting or upsetting changes into your life. As you work in your job or career, your independent nature may be threatening to those in authority. You may encounter personality clashes with superiors because of your individualistic attitudes. However, on the other hand, this is an excellent time to make discoveries and use unique methods to produce success in your profession.

Over these seven years you may experience several manifestations of transiting Uranus in your 10th House. You may find that authority figures in your life such as bosses, employers, teachers or parents place severe restrictions on you that will cause you to rebel or break free from their domination over you. If that's the case, you'll have to determine if these restrictions are too limiting, or if you're just feeling a need to have more freedom from your routine responsibilities because they're no longer challenging to you. I tell clients to ask themselves an age-old question: "What price freedom?" You may have to decide if the trade-offs you receive (e.g., salary, benefits, status) provide enough incentive for you to compromise and tolerate the restrictions (or boredom) you're experiencing.

In the event that you're indeed being repressed or severely limited, you'll likely make a change in order to gain your freedom. But be careful of acting too impulsively, because you'll face repercussions and upsets in your life if you make a sudden, hasty decision. The ideal is to make a thoughtful, prudent decision instead of a knee-jerk response out of anger and frustration. However, trying to manage the energy of a Uranus transit is a bit like riding on the back of a bull at a rodeo. No matter what advice someone gives you before you get on the bull, it's a little bit different once you're on it.

Sammy was in business with two older partners named Elias and Dennis. Sammy had come into the business after completing his MBA program five years ago, and he had been excited to join because he had many ideas on how to market and promote products. The three of them worked hard during the first three years of building the company, with each partner doing whatever it took to bring in sales and make the business successful. However, as the business grew, the three of them started having a major difference of opinion on how to run it. A particular point of contention was that Elias wanted to buy merchandise from a source that Sammy suspected was selling stolen goods. When Sammy voiced his objections, an argument ensued.

Disagreements over the best way to operate the business profitably, inevitably led to more and more discord among them. Elias continually reminded Sammy how young, naïve and inexperienced he was. Sammy stood up for himself and said, "My age has nothing to do with the fact that I don't want to be involved in a business where we make money by doing anything dishonest." The other partner, Dennis, was a very non-assertive individual, who always took Elias' side in order to avoid conflict. In actuality, Dennis didn't care how profits were made as long as the business made money.

One day, the three partners met for breakfast and had a fight over the same issues of running a business with integrity. Elias saw Sammy as an impediment; while Sammy saw his partners as two dishonest men he no longer wanted as business partners. It was collectively agreed that it was best for Sammy to exit the partnership and sell his one-third ownership to Elias and Dennis. Uranus' influence made Sammy aware of how intolerable his partners' dishonesty was to him, and he felt a compelling need to break free from them.

A very positive outcome of these seven years may be to suddenly and surprisingly find an opportunity to change your career to an entirely new field or perhaps, to do your job in a revolutionary, creative way. The opportunity may come into your life, out of the blue offering you a chance to do your work in a very exciting, liberating and different way then before. This is how Uranus' influence motivated Sharon to leave Helga's cupcake business and start her own shop.

To truly understand what is going on in your life, realize that the energies of Uranus are telling you that you need a change. This is a period in your life when the work you do must provide you with opportunities for growth and stimulation. Pay attention to the warning signs, where you begin to find your career or job boring, restrictive and unsatisfying. Be aware that if you choose to ignore the tensions and discontent you're feeling, a problem will occur within you or at work, as was the case for Sammy.

Uranus transiting your 10th House provides you with a second chance to try a different job or a new profession that will excite you more than the previous work you did. The more conscious you are about your needs, the easier you'll find changing to another career that will be more satisfying. This may involve experimenting, taking risks and knowing that you may not hit pay dirt and find the perfect career immediately. Instead, focus on the joy and excitement of your mental juices being stimulated because you're no longer stuck in your old routine. You're now able to break free.

A Time for Radical Change in Your Career

The best advice I can offer you as you experience Uranus transiting here is not to make the mistake of *ignoring* Uranus' energies that call for radical change, thinking that your feelings will go away if you just re-focus on your job and work harder (because they won't); or *denying* your feelings, rationalizing that every job has boredom and restrictions you just have to live with (because you don't); or *resisting* these energies by telling yourself that you're not going to let your upset or dissatisfaction get the better of you (because they will).

There is a hazard to you if you *consciously* ignore, resist or deny Uranian energies that call for you to make a radical change in your life. The danger is that you'll *unconsciously* attract events to suddenly occur, forcing you to make the needed changes you tried to stop from happening on a *conscious* level. Here's a simple example to illustrate how this phenomenon plays out:

- A competent person (consciously) knows he wants to quit his job but resists doing so.
- Eventually, he starts (unconsciously) making mistakes that create a major problem (that results in a sudden "costly" event) for which his employer now fires him.
- Now this person is forced to make the change he tried (consciously) to stop from happening.

Carl Jung, the famous Swiss psychiatrist and founder of analytical psychology, was an astrologer who cast horoscopes of all his patients. He said, "Until you make the unconscious – conscious, it will direct your life and you will call it fate."

One of my clients, Lee, tried very hard for years to live with an oppressive situation at work, but when Uranus began its transit through her 10th House, she could no longer acquiesce. Lee had been upset with her boss's controlling nature, because she could never make the simplest decision without him watching over her shoulder. She'd had several meetings with him requesting he give her more freedom and less unnecessary supervision. He always listened, agreeing her work was professionally done and then dismissed her by saying he'd think about their conversation. However, he still continued to micro-manage her. She'd thought of quitting her job a hundred times, but because she liked the challenge of her work and the people in her company, she always convinced herself she could live with the situation.

On the day that she felt Uranus' energies overwhelm her, she was having a meeting with her boss and he reminded her that he needed to review a weekly report before she sent it to headquarters. Lee had prepared the same report countless times, including when her boss was on vacation, with never a problem. As she heard his request, she felt herself becoming angry, finally exploding at him. "Despite the conscientious job I've done over the past 12 months, you still don't trust me to do my work correctly. I'm tired of your over-controlling, micromanaging behavior. You're a control freak! Why don't you spend more time doing your own job instead of worrying about me doing mine." They proceeded to have a horrible shouting match, resulting in his firing her for insubordination. She left the building in shock, yet strangely happy, because she had wanted to leave this job for a long time. Even though she'd played out this event in her mind many times, it took the explosive energies of Uranus for it to manifest in her life on a conscious level.

I have noticed that Uranus' energies can be explosive when they're not allowed an outlet. They can bring unexpected events into your life, that seem out of your control, as Lee found. As you'll see in this next story, people who exhibit Uranian behavior will often say, "I had to do it...I just couldn't take it anymore!" – like Reggie.

Reggie the policeman sighed in frustration as he looked at the homeless people he saw on his beat, and the fact that day after day he had to roust them from loitering and panhandling. He was getting tired of so many of them hanging around the streets disturbing businesses by urinating near shop entrances and annoying people walking down the streets. Every day Reggie grew angrier at the monotony and restrictions he felt these homeless people imposed on him when he preferred going after "real criminals."

One afternoon, as he had done many times before, Reggie confronted a particularly aggressive homeless person who was disturbing patrons as they walked into a retail shop. He walked up to the man and told him to move along and to "stop getting into people's face" because they weren't giving him money. The panhandler wouldn't move and started arguing and yelling back at Reggie to "mind his own business." That's when Reggie snapped and took out his baton and roughly pushed the panhandler against the building wall. The man's head hit the wall, knocking him unconscious as he started bleeding profusely. A passerby who witnessed the policeman's attack videoed the incident on his cell phone and sent it to the media. It was all over the 6:00 news, igniting the wrath of the public and Reggie's superiors. He ended up being put on probation for using unnecessary force, the department faced a lawsuit, and the incident ultimately damaged Reggie's career prospects.

Repressing Uranus' energies can lead to losing your job or damaging your career, resulting in a drastic fall from a position of leadership or power. Both Lee and Reggie ignored the Uranus' energies present in their life, and bottled up their anger until it reached the breaking point with a sudden explosion and subsequent disastrous fallout. When Uranus goes through your 10th House, pay attention, don't go unconscious on the job.

A Time for Radical Change in Your Social Status

We've talked about Uranus' effects as it pertains to your career or job. However Uranus' influences can affect your social status and the way people in the world experience you. When Uranus transits your 10th House, you may find that people may see you as being original and innovative. I once had a client who made a major discovery in his profession and all of sudden people saw him as a genius causing his social status to change immediately. He was sought after to attend public gatherings and parties because he was such a novelty and celebrity.

The other manifestation of Uranus is characterized by behavior that is seen as unconventional and socially unacceptable, thus causing your public status to radically change. This can be a time when your actions may be perceived as weird, strange, and aberrational to your peers or society, resulting in a sudden fall from grace as Wiley experienced.

Wiley had been supervisor for many years with his company and he was liked by co-workers and admired in his community for the volunteer work he did with young kids. But he had a problem that he'd managed to keep hidden for years, and one day that problem became public.

At the mall, he stopped at a store to buy some dress slacks and brought several of them into the dressing room to try on. When he came out of the dressing room, he casually told the salesperson that none of them were to his liking and he preceded to walk out of the store. The department store's security team followed him out the door and confronted him. They insisted he come back into the store and promptly escorted him back to the dressing room where he was told to undress in front of them. As he pulled down his pants, the security team saw that he was wearing an additional pair of slacks underneath his pants, still with a price tag on it. Wiley sheepishly said that he had a memory lapse and couldn't explain why he hadn't paid for the slacks.

10th House: Career & Status

Obviously, Wiley was caught shoplifting and was arrested on the spot. Once all the embarrassing details came out, people at church looked away from him when he tried to make eye contact. Then, he was asked to resign by his two volunteer groups. Wiley wasn't sure how all of this would play out at work but he knew he was deeply distressed and would need professional help to deal with the shame and embarrassment he was feeling because of what he'd done. Uranus in his 10th House had brought a radical change to his social status.

In a positive vein, Uranus can bring very liberating and exciting change to your career, reputation and social status. I once had a client who, for many years was a successful cement contractor. When Uranus came to his 10th House, despite making a tremendous amount of money, he made a sudden decision to quit his profession. His occupation, which involved working in the field and getting his hands dirty, no longer fit his upscale image of himself. Another client, tired of his years as a white-collar executive working in an office, quit his job abruptly, preferring to be a custom cabinet-maker because he loved the freedom he felt being a craftsman.

Considerations, Actions, Decisions During Uranus in 10th House

1. Is your career exciting and stimulating? If not – how can you make it so?
2. Do you want to change your career or job because it has gotten too routine?
3. Do you want to start an innovative business?
4. Are you ready to radically change the way you do business?
5. Do you have any tensions with bosses or those in authority?
6. Are you repressing, denying or ignoring a need to make changes in your career or outer world?
7. Are any upsets occurring in your personal world because of your focus on your career?
8. Is there anything exciting you could do that would change your reputation or social status?

NEPTUNE in Your 10th House of Career & Reputation

A Time to Be of Service

Neptune transiting your 10th House is a time to *dream* of doing something new with your life. This is when you may become interested in how your job or career can serve those in the outer world. No matter how much of your life you've spent climbing the corporate ladder or building your company into a huge enterprise, you're starting to feel like it's time to give back to others. You want to serve those in your immediate community or even society as a whole.

Since you're feeling a sense of idealism and compassion for others, you may ask yourself: how can I contribute to others beyond my personal world. This is when you use your position of authority in your company to influence them to do something for the community. Even if your focus has been solely on your career, you feel a professional obligation to expand your life's purpose by doing some sort of humanitarian good. It's no longer *just about you,* now your focus is on others.

Frank was client of mine who typified many of the CEOs and presidents I've known who have had Neptune transit their 10th House. Waking up every day and coming to work just to build more company profits made Frank feel empty and dissatisfied. I explained that his focus was changing from working to make money to "working in service" of others. I asked, "Frank, have you ever dreamed of doing something for other people, their kids, or your community?" He said, "Absolutely," and proceeded to tell me some of his great ideas to help people who didn't have his advantages.

During his Neptune transit, Frank ended up delegating many of his corporate responsibilities to his senior executive team and took time off from the business. He then met with community leaders and local government officials to see how he could help to improve the lives of local residents. Thanks to his efforts, his company-sponsored youth soccer teams, raised funds to build a sports park and a recreational facility used by kids from the poorer side of town.

10th House: Career & Status

A Time to Be Confused or Inspired

A Neptune transit of your 10th House can bring confusion and a sense of disorientation to the outer world of your career, reputation and social status. I've known people who've felt safe and secure in their career, as if it were built on a solid foundation, but during this transit they started feeling insecure and ungrounded. Imagine being ensconced in your career and enjoying it for years, then one day you wake up and you're disillusioned because you're no longer sure you're doing what you should be doing or that it makes any difference. You may feel fear and anxiety about your life's purpose, who you've become, where you're going, and why you even chose to go there. Perhaps you're feeling discontented in your current job and have clouded vision about where you're headed in life. You're a ship without a rudder as you feel the confusion of Neptune's energies. The good news is that you'll get over your disorientation and find your bearings again if you learn to adapt to the influences of Neptune and its effects on you.

As an astrologer, I find that the influences of the planet Neptune are the most difficult to explain to people, because understanding how they'll affect you has a great deal to do with your level of consciousness and whether you're oriented to the spiritual or only the material world.

Neptune is a planet that brings spirituality, mysticism, faith, ideals and compassion into your life. If that sounds like a lot of *"woo...woo talk"* because you're not comfortable with the ethereal, then Neptune's energies may sound strange and difficult to grasp. If your orientation is focused only on material results, with work success being the sole purpose for your existence, Neptune's transit will be a very disorienting and distressing time for you, because the answers you seek will not be found in the physical realm.

When you have a major Neptune transit you don't exclaim to your business partner, "How are we going to make our next million, Fred?" Instead, you say, "Fred, we could help a lot of people with a million dollars!" Your total orientation changes from a desire for money and material goods for yourself – to a sincere interest in serving others.

After I briefly discussed how Neptune's influence was bringing confusion to one client's career aspirations, he responded as if he still didn't understand. He said, "I'm just a bottom-line guy...none of that airy-fairy stuff for me." My reply to him was, "Well, you'll have great difficulty making sense of *what the hell is going on in your life,* because there's nothing tangible about Neptune."

What the Hell Is Going On in My Life?

You can begin to understand how Neptune is affecting your psyche by imagining that everything you want to accomplish for yourself (and your company) does not have the same importance as it did before. Neptune's energies demand that you detach yourself from your normal ego drives, which are usually geared toward pursuing success for selfish purposes. Please understand this is *not* to say you are a self-centered person because you pursue your own success. But it *is* to say that Neptune's energies are not directed toward your individual success, such as Jupiter's would be. Neptune's energies function best when they're used to benefit all of humankind – not just yourself. Now, if you want to quit your job and work in some humanitarian organization to make the world a better place, for a paltry salary, Neptune will help you be successful. Let's discuss some of Neptune's influences to help you understand what you might be experiencing during this time of your life.

A Time to Be Disillusioned

Imagine taking a sunny afternoon walk by the ocean, pondering some very serious questions like, "What am I doing with my life?" and "What kind of work could I do that would bring me greater satisfaction?" You're enjoying the beauty of nature as you feel yourself having a crisis of confidence. You're wondering what's happened because it was just yesterday, maybe last month, or "was it last year" when you remembered feeling content? Your eyes scan the movement of the water as you watch the waves roll into shore and suddenly you feel a sense of disappointment because of the failures you've experienced in the outer world. Your memory plays them back in your head like a slide show. Where did these memories come from and when did these feelings start? All you know is that what you're doing is no longer satisfying and you yearn for something more fulfilling to do as your life's work.

Rodney wanted to find a sales position with a company that offered a service that genuinely helped people. He answered an ad, interviewed with the firm's executives, and was impressed with their commitment to making a difference in their customers' lives by the unique services they offered. He was sure this was the perfect company for him and delighted to accept their employment offer. He started out very successfully selling the firm's services based on all the great benefits clients received. Once he brought in a new client, he was paid a commission, and told that the operations department would take care of his client. So, Rodney lost contact with the clients he had originally sold. However, a few of them had his home phone and called to say they were upset and angry because they were not receiving the service Rodney had promised them. He assured them he would get some answers as to what had happened.

The following week, Rodney sat in a sales meeting with the company's president where he voiced his concern about the many client complaints he had received, asking if they were being addressed. Several other salesmen immediately spoke up, sharing the same experience of being contacted by dissatisfied clients. One salesperson raised a question, "If these clients are unhappy, it will cause the company problems and damage our reputation." The president started yelling at the salespeople, telling them not to worry about the occasional complaint and to just do their job of "closing deals" and bringing in new clients. He said that if any client gets too upset, "we're always open to settling with them, to avoid legal problems." The President showed no interest in the talking about the concerns that were voiced. He was only interested in one thing: Sell more clients!

By the time the meeting was over, Rodney walked out disappointed and depressed, questioning why he was working for a company whose leadership had only one motivation: making profits with little concern for properly satisfying clients. Rodney's disillusionment occurred during his transit of Neptune in his 10th House, causing him to question what he was doing with his life, as he realized he wasn't being of service at all. He was actually deceiving people.

Sabotage & Deception

Neptune's influence can bring discouragement and disappointment in your career or job. Some people experience this when they work for a large organization and find themselves involved with company politics instead of enjoying the *esprit de corps* and the opportunity to fully focus on doing their work productively. Neptune's influences can also bring dishonesty and deception into your job. Thus, you may find that during this transit a co-worker unexplainably challenges you or someone you thought you were friendly with is deceiving you. You may also discover that people in positions of power and authority have withdrawn their support for your advancement, for no apparent reason.

In extreme cases, you may find that people at your job sabotage your efforts to work effectively. Neptune's influences can bring mystery, intrigue, and strange happenings into your career during these years, so if you have Neptune transiting your 10th House, do not become paranoid, but *do* become ultra sensitive and aware that these things may occur. Trust your intuition and if you notice any unusual events or strange interactions, make sure to investigate and bring closure to any problem that exist. Be sure to confront people diplomatically and directly about any unusual behavior you encounter.

Because the energies of Neptune can bring confusion into your life, it's an important time to avoid miscommunication. This is when it's easy to have a casual conversation and think you and the other person really understand each other only to find out later that the two of you are worlds apart. I remind clients that it's a good practice during this transit to have witnesses to important discussions; put agreements in writing; and reconfirm your verbal agreements by writing a confirming letter or e-mail, and save a copy for yourself. By being ultra cautious, you'll avoid unnecessary misunderstanding and upset.

However innocent your actions or associations, during this transit you may meet people of dubious character, so be careful to avoid business dealings with anyone engaged in deceptive or fraudulent activities that could lead to scandals that could damage your career, reputation and social status. Trust your intuition and investigate those you associate with in any of your important dealings.

A Time to Make a Difference

Neptune's transit to your 10th House is when you'll reflect on your life's purpose and try to find out what kind of work would give it meaning and value. You may be searching for the "right" profession or realizing that your present profession is not right for you, and that it's time for you to find a new career path. Ask yourself how can you make a difference. What can you do for a living that allows you to find joy in your job? The answer may lie in finding work that allows you to be of service to others. You may have noticed that many people in service businesses love what they do. They bring a special passion and enjoyment to the idea of serving others and working with the public.

Under this transit any business or occupation where you can be of service may be the best place to look. This is the ideal time to pursue a career in social work, medical service, enroll in nursing school, become a paramedic, flight attendant or even a waiter. This transit especially favors professions that help disadvantaged people or those with any type of addiction problems.

One of my clients decided to join the Peace Corps after working 12 years in the corporate world. She complained of spending half of her time embroiled in company politics, in-fighting, and even backstabbing. She was ready to leave the material world and help people in less advantaged countries.

This transit is a call for you to give of yourself through the work you do, in ways that benefits others, not just you. You can also enjoy helping others by engaging in humanitarian projects where you volunteer your time outside of work.

Considerations, Actions, Decisions During Neptune in 10th House

1. Do you have a fantasy career that you'd like to pursue?
2. Does your career satisfy you spiritually?
3. Does your job allow you to contribute to society in some way?
4. Do you want to volunteer to help those in need?
5. Are there any strange occurrences at work that suggest deception or even sabotage?
6. Is there anything in your career that is disillusioning you?
7. Have you been clear in your communications with people?

PLUTO in Your 10th House of Career & Reputation

You Are "The Man That Can!"

When Pluto transits your 10th House you are intensely concerned with your life's purpose. This is an important time when you're focused on your career and achieving your goals. You may find yourself wanting to do something extraordinary that would make a contribution to society. Pluto's influence gives you the opportunity to focus your will and use your personal power to achieve your ambition.

Superman was "faster than a speeding bullet, more powerful than a locomotive, able to leap tall buildings in a single bound." Well, during this transit you'll actually feel powerful as well. While you probably won't be able to *bend objects using your will*, liked the caped crusader, you'll feel exceptionally capable and resourceful. People will feel your intense presence.

When I was working at Nabisco many years ago, I had a reputation for taking an idea and quickly turning it into reality. My old boss called me, "The man that can!" That's how you'll feel during much of this Pluto transit. I remind clients who have Pluto transiting their 10th House: You have awesome powers you can use to make improvements in your job, organization, or career. You have a vital energy that makes you resourceful, brings you determination and creativity. Your leadership abilities are enhanced, making this an ideal time to take on any position of power and authority where you can take direct and decisive action to produce results in the external world.

Jocelyn was a member of the executive committee of her company, always respected for her well thought-out ideas and suggestions. She'd had a successful record of managing many of the company's most profitable ventures. Others on the committee were much more conservative than Jocelyn and shied away from any projects that might fail.

When the president met with the committee, he discussed a new product line that could conceivably add $100 to $300 million in revenues. Everyone was excited to hear this news. He continued, "Of course, there's no way of being sure whether the new product line will be a boom or a bust, so we have to be realistic, since we all know that 90 percent of all new products fail." With that last statement, a hush fell over the room and the excitement of being picked to assume responsibility for this new product line wafted out of the air. Only Jocelyn spoke up, "This sounds like an challenging project with lots of potential. I'd like to take charge and be responsible for it." The President smiled and said, "Excellent, Jocelyn. I know you'll do a great job. Keep me posted on your progress."

Over the next two years, she worked tirelessly with senior executives in research, marketing, sales, and distribution. By the end of the second year, the product line was well established on chain grocers' shelves, selling in all 50 states with current revenues totaling well over $350 million dollars and highly profitable. At the annual year-end meeting, the President congratulated Jocelyn for the brilliant job she had done, praising her organizational ability, motivational skills, and courage in coordinating the entire undertaking. He announced, "Jocelyn, you embody the qualities of leadership that this entire division needs in order to continue growing over the next decade. That's why it gives me extreme pleasure to give you the news that since I'm retiring this year, I have recommended to the board that you be my replacement as the next president."

Jocelyn's story is a perfect illustration of the leadership, motivation skills, resourcefulness and power you possess to achieve your career ambitions when Pluto transits your 10th House.

A Time to Transform Your Career

In the past, if you've not felt a spiritual connection or been drawn to helping others, this may be a time when you'll want to pursue work that allows you to make a difference and improve the lives of others in society. While Neptune gives you the compassionate ideals, the energies of Pluto will give you the ambition and resources to accomplish them.

Pluto energies give you the desire to do work that has profound meaning for you. If you've had a job that didn't seem to matter, that you weren't committed to and wasn't satisfying, you'll likely choose this time to change jobs or careers. I had a client who, during this transit, went from being partner in a law firm for 20 years to pursuing a career as a psychotherapist. As a former mergers and acquisitions executive of 25 years, I left my career to become an astrologer because I felt a powerful drive to help people transform their lives by showing them how to use astrology in a *practical way* in their everyday life.

If you're not clear about your ambitions or what you want to achieve in your career or life, this may be a period when you change jobs often on your path to discovering the work you'll ultimately do. If this is the case for you, don't let yourself become discouraged or feel lost, as you learn through the trial and error of trying different work experiences, what you should be doing.

Let's take a look at Matt's story, a client who found that each job drew him closer to the right one. But the process began for him by investigating and trying out different career opportunities before he settled on one that he finally felt passionate about. Matt always enjoyed helping people by providing medical assistance, starting as a teenager when he took an emergency first aid course and volunteered at a hospital. His job journey began as a lab technician, then an x-ray technician, and for a few years an EMT (emergency medical technician), a job he found exciting and demanding, but not totally fulfilling.

Still, during Pluto's transit through his 10th House, he made a commitment to completing his Bachelor of Science in Nursing, enjoying his time as a nurse in the pediatrics ward of a local hospital. His desire to learn more about healing others led him back to school to become a physician's assistant. Matt has been a PA for past eight years and loves the career he chose, even though it took many years to finally achieve it. Who knows, maybe one day he'll decide to become a doctor.

Play By the Rules or Else!

The positive energies of Pluto gives you drive, ambition, and strong will to successfully achieve your goals. This transit can bring you honors, recognition, and even make you famous. Many powerful politicians, generals, corporate presidents and show business personalities reach the pinnacle of their success when Pluto transits their 10th House. However, to receive the highest benefits of Pluto's energies, your motives must be pure and your dealings with others honest. You'll receive the most positive results if you operate at high standards of ethics and values that benefit society – not just your own personal aggrandizement. Pluto energies demand you play by the rules of society in a fair and honest way as you pursue your goals in life.

Of course, since Pluto rules the underworld and crime, there are criminals and mobsters who've risen to power using the dark forces of Pluto to obtain their nefarious objectives, profiting from the illicit services they provided the masses. Eventually, these criminals received Pluto's retribution for the evil they perpetrated on society, often suffering a violent death for their misdeeds.

There are some people who behave in a sociopathic, often criminal manner, lacking any sense of moral responsibility or social conscience. Pluto metes out a harsh punishment to such individuals. Therefore, in an effort get what *you* want, be careful not to resort to Pluto's negative influences, which include using aggressive and ruthless tactics that are devoid of morals and ethics. We've all known people who would "walk over dead bodies" and use any means possible, if it would further their personal or career goals. Such people are sadly mistaken in thinking they can achieve their ambitions and *not* encounter opposition from anyone. Eventually, they're proven wrong and are often brought down by Plutonian forces that always prove to be more powerful then they are – as Stanley found out.

Stanley owned a large clothing distributorship that marketed blue jeans in the United States. He'd been turned down as a *Levis* distributor because another company was already the licensed distributor for his sales territory. Since the jeans manufacture refused to sell him the *Levis* brand, Stanley found a way around that. He set up an overseas manufacturing company in a third world country, solely for the purposes of making "knockoff" jeans with the *Levis* label.

Stanley then hired a disreputable general manager who was willing to use child labor to manufacture the jeans, reducing the cost of production by 50 percent. This was Stanley's ruthless manipulation to obtain a huge inventory of cheap "knockoff" *Levis* to sell to his customers. By exploiting underage children and the *Levis* brand name, he created millions in profits. Stanley considered himself a pretty shrewd businessman until he was served with a lawsuit from both the manufacturer and the licensed distributor, detailing a step-by-step chronicle of his fraudulent scheme. Based on the size of the lawsuit and the damages, his business would soon be bankrupt. The powerful energies of Pluto in the 10th House can bring a death to any illegal or dishonest activity, another reason to use them wisely and responsibly.

What If You Haven't Found the Right Career?

Pluto's influence brings you a major change in your life's purpose. Instead of becoming the president who tries to save a "dying company," you may decide to become a doctor and save lives. This is also when you may change your career direction and the kind of work you want to do. You may decide you'd rather be a dentist than a dental hygienist, a racecar driver rather than an accountant or a dress designer instead of an engineer or vice versa. You realize that you'd rather work for a non-profit organization than a for-profit corporation; or you'd rather work for yourself instead of someone else. No matter what your discovery, the results will be – you'll become a very different and transformed person than you were before this transit began.

Pluto's transit in your 10th House brings intensity to your efforts to achieve success in the outer world. So, this is an excellent time to figure out your life's purpose, who you are, and what you want to accomplish. If this is a period of your life where you're not sure where you're going in the outer world or what career, job, or business to pursue, it's important that you persevere and not become discouraged. If you're one of these people, I have great news for you: You'll likely find your deeper calling during Pluto's transit through your career House.

But if you need help finding your answers, make an appointment to see a career counselor, a life coach or an astrologer to discuss the various careers or businesses you're suited for; and the best times to put out maximum effort to find the right career opportunity.

Have confidence that the energies of Pluto will give you the power and drive to achieve your career ambitions. Additionally, under this Pluto transit you'll have the capacity to be extremely resourceful. Therefore, this transit is perfect for investigating your career options and looking with high intention for jobs (or businesses to start) through networking, professional contacts, friends, Internet postings, human resource professionals, employment specialists and business brokers who can give you insights that will help you discover your next career.

By taking the time to know yourself and what you want to achieve, you'll develop the confidence that comes with having prepared yourself to succeed. However, before you get there, the process may involve many work experiences before you discover *what it is you want to be when you grow up.*

Considerations, Actions, Decisions During Pluto in 10th House

1. Are you feeling powerful in your current profession?
2. Are you interested in assuming greater authority in your job or career?

3. Would you like to make a big change from your present career to a new one?
4. What professions would give you the opportunity to transform others?
5. Are you involved with any people of questionable morals or ethics?
6. Do you want to volunteer or contribute to society in any way?
7. What efforts could you undertake to have a more powerful reputation and social status?

Transits to Use for Successful 10th House Decisions

You now understand the areas of life that are featured in your 10th House. We've discussed how each of the five transiting planets exerts its unique influence on the affairs of this House. This will help you better understand the changes you are experiencing, moods you're feeling, and the events taking place. Your awareness of this information may prompt you to:

1. *ACCEPT* the way things are and be content with what is going on in your life.

2. *CONSIDER* that you'd like to make some change, in which case you may evaluate your options and further contemplate your situation.

3. *DECIDE* that you're ready to make a change, take action, and make a decision pertaining to the affairs of this House.

If you make a decision, you'll want to learn how to pick the best transit to produce a successful outcome for it. Please know that the art of picking and interpreting transits requires very thorough analysis, normally done by a professional astrologer. Therefore, I've kept the discussion of selecting and using transits simple, for illustration purposes.

The key is to remember that each planet has the ability to bring a *different* positive quality of success to your decision. For example, *Jupiter's* effect may provide opportunities to expand and grow; *Saturn's* effect is more practical; *Uranus'* effect is sudden and exciting; *Neptune's* influence may bring you inspiration and idealism; *Pluto* may bring an intense and transformative effect for major change. This knowledge will help you understand how your decisions are affected by these planetary influences.

In the examples below, I chose a planetary transit to produce a favorable result for each individual's particular decision. This will help you see the many possibilities available to create the right outcome and make your 10th House decisions more successful.

10th House: Career & Status

Using a positive JUPITER Transit

DECISION: *I want a singing career that will make me famous and successful.*

Explanation: We discussed Bobby's Home Boy Band and how much Bobby wanted to finally break into the big time. We used the Jupiter transit because it would bring him a year of luck and opportunity and he'd likely be paid a good deal of money. He could look forward to working with lots of people, agents and managers who would be beneficial for him. It was the perfect time to expand and seek fame on the national stage of a Las Vegas Hotel.

* * *

Using a positive SATURN Transit

DECISION: *I want to divorce at a time when I can be assured that my status and lifestyle will continue as it was during my marriage.*

Explanation: We discussed Betty's situation earlier in the chapter. After 30 years of marriage, Betty and her husband have decided to divorce. We took advantage of Saturn transiting her 10th House in favorable aspect to another planet in her birth chart. This transit would assure that she received a fair settlement that would assure she would be prosperous in her new status as a single person. Her affluent lifestyle would continue in the manner she was accustomed.

* * *

Using a positive URANUS Transit

DECISION: *I want to plan a career change at a time when I'll experience success in an exciting new profession.*

Explanation: After 10 years as an engineer, Natalie realizes that she's bored with being an engineer. She's ready to change her career and find a more vibrant job that will utilize her skills. We chose a Uranus transit because it would yield a totally different job from what she had been doing. She would have an opportunity to work more independently in a way that was new and stimulating

* * *

Using a positive NEPTUNE Transit

DECISION: *I want to quit my job and join the Peace Corps.*

Explanation: We discussed how Meg was tired of the corporate world and ready to make a difference by volunteering with the Peace Corps. Meg wanted the committee to recognize that she was an inspired, compassionate person filled with strong ideals, and this Neptune transit would help her display those traits. Also, the self-sacrificing nature of Neptune would help convey to the committee that she understood the hardships she would encounter. The fortunate energies of this transit would bring her the opportunity to be of service to those in need.

* * *

11th House: Career & Status

> ## Using a positive PLUTO Transit

DECISION: *I want to start a hazardous waste company.*

Explanation: Neil has worked in the nuclear waste and bio-remediation industry for many years and he is ready to start his own hazardous waste business. Pluto rules wastes, so businesses in this area are favorable to Plutonian energies. We choose a very positive Pluto transit that affected his 10th House so that he would have the good fortune, longevity, and public recognition to make his business successful and well known.

* * *

> REMEMBER: *You can use the FREE Transit Calculator that's discussed in Part IV of this book to go back in time to see which transits were occurring when a major event happened in your life. It might be a wonderful learning experience, especially since most transits repeat themselves over your lifetime. Also you can find out where your transits are today or in the future.*

11th House
Friends, Hopes & Dreams

When you think of the 11th House, think of a best friend you take long walks; the one who'll bring you chicken soup when you're sick; or the one you call to tell about the exciting date you had last night. This House also embodies the organization you belong to where you have fun in the company of like-minded people; or the one where you do philanthropic work, raising funds for those in need.

The 11th House rules your friendships and the socializing you do in larger groups. It also concerns your hopes and wishes. Since this house concerns your friends, acquaintances, and associates, it will tell you a great deal about how you value friendships. Are they important in your life? Are you likely to make friends for a reason, a season or a lifetime? This House describes the type of friends that you'll gravitate to, ranging from powerful friends in high places who'll help you reach your goals to down-to-earth, modest types who just offer you friendly conversation.

Perhaps, you're attracted to friendships with people who are affluent and in the upper income classes; or to the contrary, eschew anyone who's materialistic, preferring friendships with those on the lower social rungs, who don't need lots of money. You may be drawn to friends who are caring, nurturing types, who'll give you a hug when you're depressed and listen to the drama taking place in your life; or you might value friends who are always recommending fascinating books, suggesting suspenseful movies, and entertaining cultural events you'd enjoy; or you may prefer those who are of practical assistance because they'll tell you about a great stock tip, the right person to contact for a job, or even where to shop to get the best bargain.

This House also rules groups, organizations and their activities. It concerns your role in your community and your social life in it. Some people thrive on joining an organization for the fellowship and opportunity to express themselves within a group. This House describes how you relate as an individual to groups of people, the quality of your social interactions with them, as well as your effect on them. Do you come alive when you're a member of a group, making innovative suggestions, clearly showing your leadership abilities, or do you tend to become shy and let others have the limelight? Perhaps you're someone who only occasionally enjoys being with a crowd of people, preferring mostly to be alone.

You may be the type of person who lives for the opportunity to socialize with different groups to broaden your sphere of social contacts. I remind clients that to receive the benefits of many positive transits they'll need to *network*, which may mean reaching out to others and meeting people, whether it's dropping in on a chamber of commerce networking event, joining a group dedicated to dancing the salsa, or just joining a few people for a cup of coffee.

Life can become much more fulfilling when you volunteer your time and energy in service of others, so this House is important because it governs volunteering, societies, philanthropic groups, humanitarian causes, charity groups, associations, leagues, clubs, membership groups, and fraternities. I enjoy talking with clients about this House because I can give them insights about their penchant for volunteering to help others as well as the type of humanitarian causes that might inspire them. One client may find excitement in joining a group that teaches English as a second language; another enjoys participating in a group that delivers gifts to underprivileged children at Christmas; while another finds spiritual satisfaction in an organization that promotes peace.

This House governs your hopes and wishes. It's the place to look to see what your dreams are and if they'll come true, whether it's finding your soul mate, experiencing the joy of having a family, owning a dream home in a tropical paradise, finding the cure for cancer, or working in a career that will satisfy your longing to make a difference in people's lives.

Your Body in the 11*th* House

This house rules the arteries, legs, shins, calves, and the ankles. Since there is nothing more important than your health, pay special attention to these areas of your body whenever a planet transits this House. It may indicate a period of time when you'll experience health benefits, issues or even problems you should be aware of. If you observe anything unusual, you'll have the opportunity to consult with a medical doctor or a health care practitioner.

What the Hell Is Going On in My Life?

Your 11th House Decisions

You now understand that 11th House of your birth chart concerns your friends, hopes and wishes. As you read about the description of this House, it's time to ask yourself a few questions about these areas of your life.

What kind of friends do you have in your life? Are they helpful and supportive to your achieving your hopes and wishes or are they negative and unsupportive of your dreams and goals? Are they there when you need them in a pinch or are they "fair-weather" friends who tend to contact you when they need something? Or, perhaps you have friends who would prefer only to be with you when you're feeling up and life is going well? What qualities do you look for in the friendships you seek? What qualities turn you off from being someone's friend?

Are you involved in any organizations and groups that allow you to socialize as well as contribute to a larger cause? Are you interested in joining any groups to volunteer? Are there any opportunities for your personal growth working with others in a social group? Could you be making social contacts they might help you reach your goals?

Do you have any special hopes and wishes that you would like to achieve now or in the future? Do you dream of a life where great things happen to you, whether it's achieving inner peace or having great health, a loving partner, happy children, supportive friends, a beautiful home, or fulfilling work? Do you have dreams of writing a book, screenplay, or becoming a professional football player or ballerina?

These are all significant questions and your answers may lead you to make important decisions to change your life. Here are a few examples of decisions clients have made based on the activities and issues of the 11th House.

Situation: Rachel is moving to a new city where she doesn't know anyone.

DECISION: *I want to find the best time to meet friends of my social background and seek membership to an exclusive country club.*

* * *

Situation: Albert has always wanted to volunteer at an organization that helps the homeless community. His volunteer efforts have never worked out because he gets distracted with other activities that are going on in his life.

DECISION: *I want to pick the ideal time to have a successful volunteer experience.*

* * *

Situation: Sandy has inherited a great deal of money.

DECISION: *I want to find the ideal time to establish a successful philanthropic organization.*

* * *

Situation: Judy's old friends drink, party too much, and aren't into a healthy lifestyle.

DECISION: *I want to find the ideal time to participate in activities where I'm likely to meet new friends that I'll enjoy.*

* * *

During the transits of *Jupiter, Saturn, Uranus, Neptune,* and *Pluto* – Rachel, Albert, Sandy, and Judy will have many opportunities to implement their decisions at a favorable time to produce the outcome they want.

The Transiting Planets Reveal Your Past, Present & Future

Your main focus is using astrology to understand *what the hell is going on in your life.* Once you do – this book will show you the best time to make a decision to change it, should you have a desire to do so. As you read about the five planets transiting the 11th House, notice the way each planet exerts its unique influence and effect, bringing specific opportunities, issues, problems, and events into this area of your life. But if you're curious as to how these planets are personally affecting YOU *today,* in your *past,* or in your *future,* you can find out where each transiting planet is in your birth chart by using the *FREE Transit Calculator* (see Part IV).

JUPITER in Your 11th House of Friends, Hopes & Dreams

Friends and Groups Are Lucky For You

When Jupiter transits your 11th House, you focus on your hopes, wishes and friendships because they bring you a great deal of happiness. Pay close attention to your friends, because they will be of special help and support to you. Your social life will be busy because you're making new acquaintances and meeting interesting people. New friends who come into your life are valuable to your growth and success; and conversely, you'll benefit them as well. The positive interactions you'll have with others makes this is a perfect time to work with groups of people instead of going it alone.

You may be very effective at getting what you want by yourself, but this Jupiter transit gives you the opportunity to learn how to work with others to achieve *group* goals. This is a valuable chance to learn more about how groups operate, as well as how you function by being a part of a larger whole. When Jupiter transits 11th House, I encourage you to find some group or organization to join as a way of enriching your life and receiving benefits that will only be realized through your participation with others. This is also the ideal transit to use to make new friends who will enrich your life as Diane found out.

Diane had a classic experience with friends who brought her great fortune during this Jupiter's transit. She went with her friend Fran to the mall to shop and meet some of Fran's friends for lunch. They were fun, down-to-earth people. During lunch the conversation moved to each of their careers. One friend worked for a retail clothing company and told Diane that since she was a friend of Fran's, she would extend a special 20 percent discount off any clothes she bought. Another friend invited Diane to come to a party that evening. A third friend said, "I've got a really cool guy to introduce you, too. He's a real gentleman, very intelligent, has a great job and wants to settle down. I think you two would really hit it off." Now all of Fran's friends easily became Diane's friends, too.

11th House: Friends, Hopes & Dreams

A Great Time for Group Activities & Networking

You might not be a person who normally participates in many group activities, but now you'll find yourself drawn to them. If you already enjoy all kinds of social events, during this Jupiter transit your social life will be on *steroids,* and in a very positive way, since you'll be meeting even more interesting people who can become new friends, acquaintances or just valuable contacts.

You'll feel a wellspring of humanitarian feelings, which will make it enjoyable to engage in group activities of all types: community service projects, associations, fraternities, and country clubs. During other times in your life, you may have been too busy to join a formal organization or just not in the mood for group involvements but you won't feel that way now, because such efforts seem comfortable and valuable. It's a fantastic time to network and make mutually beneficial social contacts – as Gabby discovered.

Gabby had dreams of one day joining a television news team and being an anchor during the prime time news hour. She had a journalism degree and for the last several years she'd worked as a newspaper reporter. Now Gabby had much bigger ambitions and desired to break into TV. Unfortunately, there were many other people who wanted to do the same thing and she knew that landing a TV job was usually based on personal contacts and connections – none of which she possessed.

Gabby's friend Hal had invited her to the grand opening of a new, trendy restaurant owned by a famous chef. It was a dressy event, with lots of classy, interesting people walking around with Champagne-filled glasses and waiters offering trays of tasty hors d'oeuvres. All of sudden, Hal looked at Gabby and said, "Gabby, I'd like you to meet Herbert Wilson. He's the station manager for WKWZ-TV here in town." Gabby almost spilled her Champagne as she excitedly shook Herbert's hand."

Herbert Wilson surprised Gabby by being genuinely interested in knowing her, asking questions about where she grew up, where she went to school, and how she liked her job. Eventually he asked, "So, Gabby where do you see yourself in 10 years?" She gave him a big smile and said, "I see myself anchoring the 10 p.m. news at your station." He looked at her for the longest time, grinned and said, "You're serious, aren't you?" She told him that she was, sharing with him that anchoring a news program had been her dream ever since she was in college. She explained that she just needed a more personal connection to be considered for an opportunity. He looked at her and said, "Well, you have it: me. Here's my card. Call me Monday morning. I can't promise you a job, but I can promise to get you in to meet a few people you should know." He gave her an encouraging smile as he said, "It will be a good start toward the day you do our 10 p.m. newscast."

Great Time to Volunteer

Because you're feeling idealistic, genuinely wanting to improve the world you live in, you may decide to volunteer for humanitarian projects. No matter how selfish you may have been in the past by focusing only on your needs, now you want to give of yourself. You're very interested in contributing in ways that will benefit your friends and organizations, as well as improve society. Your involvement with other people makes you aware of the significant impact you have on the lives of others, as well as their impact on you.

Franklin decided not to go home to celebrate Thanksgiving with his family. His friends had left town already and he suddenly realized, "I'm all alone for this holiday." Later he received a phone call from an old friend inviting him to join group of people volunteering to serve a Thanksgiving dinner at a homeless shelter. At first, Franklin thought the experience would be totally disheartening but quickly admitted to himself, "How selfish am I a being? These people are probably depressed a lot of days." He told his friend, "Sure. Count me in." By the end of his six-hour shift at the shelter, Franklin realized that he'd done the right thing by volunteering. It made him feel good to put a little cheer in the life of so many downtrodden people. Ironically, seeing the satisfaction on their faces had given him a warm feeling inside he had never experienced before.

Considerations, Actions, Decisions During Jupiter in 11th House

1. What are your hopes and wishes?
2. What is your dream?
3. Do you want to make new friends?
4. What are ways that you and your friends can help each other?

11th House: Friends, Hopes & Dreams

5. Plan an activity for a group of friends.
6. Join a social organization where you can have fun and make new friends and social contacts.
7. Join an organization and volunteer your time and talents.

SATURN in Your 11th House of Friends, Hopes & Dreams

A Time to Re-Evaluate Your Goals and Involvements

As a kid, I remember telling people that I was going to become a professional baseball player. That was my dream. Eventually the baseball coach cut me from the team and brought me back to the reality: I didn't have the talent to be a major leaguer. Then, in my early high schools years, I was sure I wanted to become a medical doctor. However, my distaste for dissecting frogs in my biology class and my "F" grade in analytical chemistry helped me realize I would never be taking the physician's Hippocratic Oath.

We all have hopes and dreams of what we want do and become in life, so when Saturn transits your 11th House you take stock of the goals and objectives you've established for yourself. You accept responsibility for them by deciding if they're realistic, obtainable, and can bring you the happiness as well as the fulfillment you seek. This Saturn transit is a call for you to responsibly assess whether you can reach your goals. I could have ignored my reality-checks and pursued my dream of being a baseball player or a doctor. And I would have failed at both. This may be a serious time when you'll consider your options and re-evaluate whether your goals can be achieved or not. If your conclusion is that they aren't realistic, you'll have to modify, change, or let them go.

Rachelle's story is an excellent illustration of Saturn's process at work. When she wasn't at her job as a waitress, Rachelle worked diligently towards her dream of becoming a symphony violinist, practicing for several hours a day and going out on numerous auditions whenever she heard of an opportunity. It's been seven years of hard work trying to join a symphony orchestra. So far, she's had no tangible success with her musical career, so it may be time for her to re-consider her dreams and goals. Maybe she needs more preparation in terms of violin classes or perhaps she'll have to accept that she doesn't have the talent to achieve her goal of playing with a symphony. Rachelle will have to realistically evaluate her situation and consider making changes that will help her succeed; or let go if she can't. Perhaps, she can make an adjustment in her musical career aspirations where she can find satisfaction joining a string quartet and performing at weddings instead playing first violin at symphony hall.

Wherever Saturn transits, you have the opportunity to make something "real" in that area of your life. So, if you've worked hard to accomplish a goal and achieve something you really wanted, this is the time when results may occur. If not, as in Rachelle's case, it's time to develop a more realistic perspective. The good news for Rachelle is that Saturn's energies will bring her the practical experience and wisdom to re-engineer her plans so she can be more successful; or it may bring her the maturity to accept that she can't. If you're meeting with frustration and failure in reaching your goals, this is the time to critically evaluate them. Saturn's process is there to help you be realistic about what's possible.

Examine Your Involvement in Groups

When Saturn was in your 10th House, your focus was on being recognized for your achievements. However, Saturn's influence in your 11th House is a time of incorporating yourself into group efforts with other people to achieve group goals, for the benefit of others. So, during this time: It's no longer just *about you.* It's about the group, the organization, and society. Your commitment to a group is important, so you may want to work with others who are as dedicated as you.

Additionally, Saturn's energies require you to examine your involvements in social groups or organizations in order to make sure that they're still appropriate to your life. You may be over-committed as a volunteer and not have sufficient time to contribute any longer, or you may find that changes in a group's objectives may no longer fit with yours. One client spent years working for a service organization that at one time was engaged in important humanitarian pursuits benefitting society, but in recent years had gotten very political. This Saturn transit caused him to reevaluate his membership and decide that he no longer wanted to be part of this organization. Saturn's energies bring tests, lessons and restrictions to any socializing you do with others at this time. For example, if you've always worked alone or if you haven't enjoyed working in groups, this may be a time when the idea of working with others feels especially uncomfortable and restrictive to you.

My client Rooney was a very introverted author, spending hours writing, preferring his own company to being around lots of people. He'd written two books, neither of them sold many copies, because he wasn't much of a promoter. The idea of attended a crowded gathering to publicize his books made him ill at ease. While he enjoyed one-on-one meetings or even small groups, large social events and parties were intimidating and uncomfortable.

He'd recently met a fellow author named Harvey who loved to network and attend numerous organizational events where he found excellent opportunities to promote his books. Harvey tried to encourage Rooney to attend similar events, explaining to him that these social gatherings were a way of hearing about promotional opportunities where Rooney could sell his books. He reminded Rooney that he'd never have any success if he just stayed in his one-bedroom apartment every night. Rooney listened to Harvey's advice and agreed it might be time to re-evaluate his attitude about networking, since on a practical level it would help him sell more books.

Rooney's experience illustrates the need for a person to get out of their "comfort zone," find ways of overcoming their limitations, and make a necessary adjustment that will be to their benefit. Saturn doesn't make it easy, but it does make it worthwhile.

It May Be Time to Weed the Garden of Friendship

Saturn's influence may bring you difficulties, restrictions and limitations in your friendships, forcing you to resolve any problems they may be causing you. Therefore, if you're involved in any friendships that are unsupportive, detrimental or more trouble than they're worth, you'll end them and instead focus on relationships that help you achieve your goals and objectives. Strong friendships that bring value to your life will pass the test of this time and grow stronger. In fact, this is an especially good time to make friends with older, wiser people who can be a source of counsel to you.

Ryan had a drinking problem for many years and finally went through a detox program, joined AA, and for the last year he'd been sober. He still smoked but wanted to quit. His AA sponsor, Roy, was a close friend and implored Ryan to understand that part of his recovery was ending old friendships with friends who were "drinkers and druggies," and finding new ones. At first Ryan thought he was strong enough to keep his old friends despite Roy's warnings that it wouldn't work. He finally realized there was no point in being around friends who were committed to the

11th House: Friends, Hopes & Dreams

very habits and addictions he was dedicated to removing from his life. With that "sobering" evaluation, Ryan was finally ready to make new friends who really fit his new lifestyle and personal goals. By exposing himself to old friends, he underwent a Saturnian test that made him realize he had to *let go* of his old friends for his own well-being. This is an excellent illustration that shows while Saturn's lessons may be hard; they bring rewards for those who learn them well.

Recognize that your friendships may test you, making you realize they're limiting you in some way. They may even be destructive to you as was the case for Ryan. During Saturn's transit you may find yourself not really enjoying socializing with lots of people, unless it's for some practical purpose. Let's face it: you're serious and practical about your social relationships, which means they must count for *something*.

This is a period when you'll examine your friendships and their importance to you. After all, we often have friends for a reason, a season or a lifetime, so Saturn's passage through the 11th House may be a time when you should consider "weeding the garden of friendship." Ask yourself: Do you have friendships that you've outgrown or that are no longer positive, supportive or even healthy to have any longer? This may be the time to let them go, so you can create new friendships that are of real value to you and better meet the practical needs you have at this time. This was the awareness that Helen came to during this transit.

Helen has noticed that her friend Ruth Ann only calls when she wants Helen to accompany her to social functions or clubs to meet men. Ruth Ann once told Helen, "Look girlfriend, you're beautiful and a real 'man magnet.' When I go out with you, I always meet lots of men. That's why it's so much fun to party with you." Helen has tried to enjoy their friendship but it has dawned on her that she gets very little out of it because they never talk about anything personal or intellectual – only about men. Helen has tried to get to know Ruth Ellen on a deeper level, but Ruth Ellen always changes the subject back to herself or men. She's clearly self-involved with no interest in getting to know Helen beyond superficially.

When they do go out to a club together, it's not much fun because while men show Helen a great deal of interest, they seem to ignore Ruth Ellen after they've had a brief conversation with her. Helen is tired of being the bait to attract men to Ruth Ellen. The truth is she has little in common with Ruth Ellen and has finally come to the realization she's no longer interested in their friendship. It's her responsibility (Saturn) to say "no thanks" the next time Ruth Ellen invites her out to a club.

This is the exact process of critical evaluation you'll encounter as Saturn transits this House. By consciously trying to improve good friendships, they'll become better; and by recognizing the ones that don't serve you, you can let them go, giving you more time to find new friendships. This is Saturn's evaluative process at work in this area of your life.

Considerations, Actions, Decisions During Saturn in 11th House

1. Re-evaluate your hopes and wishes to make sure they're realistic.
2. Do you have a dream that needs to be re-evaluated?
3. Do you want to make new friends and let go of old ones?
4. Are you interested in worked hard to help an organization meet its goals?
5. What are the practical benefits you might gain by volunteering?
6. Do you want to expand your social life and contacts in ways that will be of practical value to you?
7. What changes or adjustments can you make in order to feel more comfortable socializing in groups?

URANUS in Your 11th House of Friends, Hopes & Dreams

A Great Time to Save the World or Just Help the Community

When Uranus transits your 11th House, you experience radical changes in your hopes and desires. Like a thunderbolt out of the sky, you may suddenly see a new vision for how you can achieve goals that you've never even considered before, because now your imagination is stimulated and vibrant. Your mind begins to dream of possibilities of how you could make the world a better place. This is a time when you may be drawn to experimenting and investigating even unconventional possibilities in order to find out your life's purpose.

This may be when you have a clear vision of your social role in improving your community or society by pursuing volunteer work or engaging in a humanitarian project. I had a client donate an empty lot and help organize a community garden for people to collectively raise produce and plants because he thought it would be an innovative way for people in the neighborhood to share food production and feel connected to their environment. Just like my client, you may find yourself interested in being part of an activity that will build a better future for everyone.

A Time to Change Friendships & Social Affiliations

Be aware that the influence of Uranus can make you defiant and rebellious against any group pressures that you may encounter. What's happening for you is that you're feeling fiercely independent, so you'll resist the attempts of any group of people who try to make you conform to their wishes. You'll be especially resistant to friends or groups that are traditional or too conservative, because you're yearning for new relationships that free you from outmoded ways of thinking. This may cause you to suddenly decide that some of your long-term friendships are too stifling and seek new ones that better mirror the person you've become at this time in your life.

For many years you may have identified with certain groups, associations, organizations or clubs that you've always been involved. Uranus' energies will demand that your involvements with such groups offer you freedom from the routine and commonplace. If they don't, you may find yourself rebelling against them and what they stand for. This was the case for Richard. Richard had been a member of a "good old boy" country club for the past 30 years. Over that time, he'd made many friends who clearly had very conservative views. While some of them shared prejudices that bothered him, he chose not to respond to them when they were voiced. But that's changed lately, because he's found himself feeling angry and rebellious when he hears such ignorant comments.

A big controversy erupted at the club when a person of color wanted to seek membership. As a board member, Richard had been pressured to cast his vote against admitting this person. This prejudicial behavior was the last straw for him as he suddenly realized he was in a country club with a bunch of bigots. "I'm not a bigot. And I don't want to be in a club with these type of people." Richard is resolved to quitting the club and finding a more liberal membership he can relate to. This is an example of the fiercely independent action you might take when Uranus transits your 11th House.

A Time for Finding New Friends & Getting Rid of Old Ones

Since this is the House of Friendships and group activities, Uranus' influences will bring new and unusual friends into your life. Their uniqueness will be exciting, stimulating and a contrast to the more traditional friends you have. This is a time when a person you would call eccentric or a "weirdo" is now your new best friend. Even though the closest you've ever come to a *body piercing* was the time you accidentally stabbed yourself with a sewing needle, now you're enjoying a new buddy who sports a nose ring. What's even stranger, you're starting to like it and thinking about getting one, yourself. You may also find that old friends may suddenly bring you new experiences and adventures that are quite liberating as well. In fact, it's because these friends bring excitement and stimulation to your life that they'll remain your friends through this transit.

Because of Uranus' unpredictable influences, friends can be a source of upsetting and disrupting experiences, which may result in you suddenly breaking off a friendship with someone you've known a long time.

11th House: Friends, Hopes & Dreams

I remember having a friend of many years, Darla, who was upset that my committed relationship with a girlfriend prevented me from spending as much time with her as I used to. It was very upsetting to her. She abruptly ended a 25-year friendship with one phone call as Uranus transited her 11th House.

Another reason that break-ups may occur is that your current set of friends no longer feel appropriate to your hopes, wishes and goals; or their conservative nature may no longer fit with who you are. That happened for a newly divorced client who threw over all his married friends in favor of a new batch of single friends he could pal around with. He needed a total liberating change from the friends he had as a married person, now that he was single.

During this transit, you're no longer interested in conforming to the *status quo* in order to preserve these friendships. Instead, you may be amazed that now you prefer the friendships of younger people because there's nothing more exciting than youthful vitality and their openness to all that is new and modern. You may also attract the company of friends who are younger, fun-loving, exciting and unconventional people, which is what happened to a client of mine named Wally.

Wally was retired now so he was able to pack a lunch and go to the beach every day. He noticed that a particular group of young kids would come by and sit near him. There was a whole beach available, but for some reason they'd throw their blankets near him, set up their volleyball net, start drinking beers from a cooler, and then toss Frisbees with their dogs. A little later, the group would set up a charcoal grill and cook burgers and just party all afternoon, having a great time together.

One day, while at his usual beach spot, a young girl from the group walked over and asked if he'd like to join them and have a burger. He was rather surprised, since he was a 66-year-old man and these kids appeared to be in their late teens. The cute gal who made the invitation could tell he was going to refuse, so before he could say "no thanks," she grabbed his hand and brought him over to the group.

For most of the summer he joined them as they laughed and poked fun about their adventures and each other. One of them explained they were on their summer vacation and were all close friends who were entering college in the fall. Everyone showed a great deal of interest in Wally, asking him questions about who he was, what he had done in life, how he was enjoying retirement at age 66, the books he had read, and the movies he had seen. They loved hearing him recount some of the historical experiences he had lived through before they were born.

Wally began his summer sitting on the beach with a bunch of young kids he didn't know, but by the end of it he couldn't believe how close he felt to this group of young people. Being friends with them had made this one of the best summers of his life. He would never have imagined that he could have such amazing friendships, especially an old man like him. Like Wally, you can experience the unexpected surprises that Uranus can provide, bringing the most exciting and liberating experiences you've ever known. All that's required is being open to partaking in the adventure.

I encourage you to take advantage of this rare time in your life when you'll be exposed to an exciting social life, meeting interesting people, and making new friends. If you derive any pleasure from giving to others, you will find this an invigorating time be involved in humanitarian groups and forward-thinking organizations. What you learn and experience will be surprising and unexpected. Consider joining organizations that are engaged in unique or unusual activities that may bring new discovery and insights into your life so that it's even richer than it was before.

Considerations, Actions, Decisions During Uranus in 11th House

1. Do you have any hopes and wishes that inspire you?
2. Do you have an unusual dream or fantasy goal?
3. Is there any dream that you are ready to let go?
4. Do you want to make unique and exciting new friends?
5. Volunteer for an organization that innovatively helps society.
6. Plan an exciting outing with a group of friends.
7. Host a party for your old and new friends.

NEPTUNE in Your 11th House of Friends, Hopes & Dreams

A Time to Be Inspired to Help Others

When Neptune transits your 11th House your hopes, wishes and ideals are very important to you and you'll be inspired to bring them into reality. For some people their *wish* is to be of service to others. If that's you, your dream will come true because during this period of your life you'll feel a wellspring of compassion and desire to help anyone in need. Neptune's energies cause your personal ego needs to be unusually detached from your actions, enabling you to put your attention on helping others instead of only focusing on "what's in it for you." In life there are often "givers" and "takers." Neptune's influence brings a selfless influence that helps even "takers" generously give under this transit. Your heart may be so moved to benefit others at this time that you'll finally take action to work in service of an organization, community or society, as was the case for Edith.

Edith was a wealthy widow and spent most of her time playing mahjong, bridge, watching late-night TV, or tending to her grandchildren. But she longed to have greater purpose for her life during her senior years. She'd moved the year before to a smaller apartment, since her needs were modest. Her building was a typical high-rise in downtown New York City, surrounded by many neighbors.

One day as she was on the elevator a young woman in her 40s got on at one of the floors. Edith wouldn't have paid any attention to her were it not for the young woman's crying, obvious bruises and black eye. When Edith asked what happened, the dazed woman explained her husband had beaten her again. Edith was outraged to see such abuse, and quickly decided to take the woman to an emergency clinic for treatment. As she sat in the waiting room, she began thinking about other women who were victims of abusers. Her thoughts were interrupted when the doctor came out to tell Edith that this was one of the most serious cases of domestic violence he'd seen and he would be reporting it immediately to the police. That experience gave Edith just the purpose she'd been looking for, because it inspired her to volunteer at a shelter for abused and battered women.

Avoid Self-Delusion

Neptune's energies give you the capacity to feel a real connection to spiritual activities or religious organizations at this time. You're feeling inspired and able to tap into the ethereal side of life. Yet, under Neptune's influence it's easy to fantasize and engage in self-delusion. I met with a client whose birth chart indicated this tendency toward self-deception, which was further amplified when Neptune transited his 11th House.

My client described an experience that typified how Neptunian delusion operated in his life. He was an active member of his church choir where he met another female member he started going out with. They enjoyed having wonderful philosophic discussions about religion and found time to go to a movie or grab a burger together. Despite this woman telling him how much she enjoyed him "as a friend," he saw the relationship as the beginning of a significant love relationship. All doubt was removed in his mind when they spontaneously had sex one night. Afterwards, he admitted being disappointed when she said "sex had been fun," and then abruptly invited him to leave because she had plans the next day and needed her sleep.

While he was taken aback at her casualness, he was sure their intimacy meant this was the start of a more serious relationship. So, he felt betrayed and deceived when he saw her at choir practice a few weeks later, oblivious to him and holding hands with another man. In reality, he had deluded himself by being unrealistic and over-idealizing his friendship with this woman, convincing himself they were now in the midst of establishing a serious relationship. He wasn't able to comprehend that to her – their evening of spontaneous sex was just a sexual fling and their relationship was only a casual friendship. I pointed out that he had created a fantasy of the relationship he'd *hoped* they'd have, instead of correctly perceiving the relationship they were *actually* having. He ignored or missed all the signs that should have made it clear to him, "she's just not that into you."

Be Realistic & Don't Get Attached to Your Fantasies

This is a special time in your life when your altruistic feelings and compassion may lead you to explore how you can contribute to the benefit of an organization or society. The key is to pursue your dreams and vision while grounding yourself in practical judgment about what's possible.

One of the benefits of this Neptune transit is that your intuition and imagination give you the ability to be creative and even fantasize dreams you'd like to make a reality. You feel a great deal of optimism to the point where you may need to be more realistic about achieving your dream. Otherwise you may end up disillusioned and discouraged. The influences of Neptune make this a time to pursue an ambition or dream as long as you're not overly *attached* to it becoming a tangible goal. This is the lesson that Morrie learned when Neptune transited his 11th House.

Morrie met most of his friends at his temple and was a big promoter of a plan to build a Hebrew school. He spent his own money hiring an architect and consultant to put together an architectural proposal showing his vision of the new school. When he told friends and members of the congregation about it, they were very encouraging and complementary. Three months later he learned that the temple board had voted not to act on his Hebrew School plan but agreed to consider it the following year.

He felt very disappointed and deceived that members of the board had "led him on," now deciding that other projects were of higher priority. Morrie's reaction was an example of someone who was overly optimistic and absorbed in a fantasy of what he thought should happen based on what he wanted, without consideration for the reality that others might not see things the way he did. He deluded himself. When you give of yourself during Neptune's transit, it's important to be *unattached* to having results occur on *your* terms. The energies of Neptune are geared toward selfless giving, devoid of one's own ego desires.

Selfless Friendship

Since the 11th House also rules friendships, you'll feel a special bond with friends who inspire you because of their compassionate, loving nature, as well as their benevolent desire to help and support you. I remember one client, Beth, who embodied Neptune's self-sacrificing energies. She dropped everything in her life to run over to help her good friend Angelica who broke her leg while hiking. Beth spent many days at Angelica's house, cooking her food, doing her laundry and running numerous errands for her. Beth emailed her networking group and found a caretaker in the area who could assist Angelica when Beth needed to go back to her job. Of course Angelica was eternally grateful because no one was available to help her were it not for her friend Beth.

This is also a wonderful time to make friends with people, who are spiritually oriented, with whom you share a deep heart connection. They're likely to be as generous and kind as you are. Be creative and join volunteer organizations; and church or spiritual groups where you can make new friends.

Be Sensitive to Your Friendships

Neptune's influences seem to mysteriously change the character of your friendships, without you noticing their effect. Old associations may go from closeness to just fading away, while others may disappear altogether. You may find yourself saying, "We used to be close, but we seem to have lost touch," or "I use to see him a lot but now that he's into a different lifestyle, I don't have much in common." If you find yourself making those comments about old friendships, it might be because Neptune is transiting this House.

Be aware of some of the influences that Neptune will bring to your friendship during this period of your life. Don't let your compassionate nature cause you to give so much to a friendship that you end up feeling taken advantage. It's a good time to recognize whether the basis of your friendship is your giving and the other person only receiving, or whether it's a healthy, mutually giving relationship.

While Neptune's energies include faith and inspiration, be mindful that they also include illusion and confusion as well. So during this period of your life be careful that you don't deceive your friends through your behavior, even unconsciously; and be careful that you aren't deceived by friends as Lee Ann was.   She'd just met a very attractive man named Reid, whom she brought to a party at the home of her new friend Sally. They were all having a great time when Lee Ann noticed that Sally and Reid were spending a lot of time talking and laughing. She started feeling ignored and felt insecure, but she said nothing about it. Then, a few weeks later after not hearing from Reid again, she was extremely hurt when a mutual friend told her that Reid and Sally were now in a serious dating relationship with each other.

With new friendships like the one Lee Ann had with Sally, you never know whether it will be meaningful or not; or even disappointing. When Neptune transits this House, don't become paranoid, but trust your intuition so that if you notice any strange behavior or sense a misunderstanding has occurred with a friend, you have the option of discussing it openly to gain clarity.

Considerations, Actions, Decisions During Neptune in 11th House

1. What hopes and wishes inspire you?
2. Do you have a dream or fantasy you'd like to make a reality?
3. Are you interested in sharing friendships with those who are more spiritually oriented?
4. Is there give and take in your friendships?
5. Are any friends taking advantage of you or deceiving you?
6. Do you want to volunteer to help those less fortunate?
7. Do you want to join any organizations that serve the community?

PLUTO in Your 11ᵗʰ House of Friends, Hopes & Dreams

A Time to Make a Difference with Others

When Pluto transits your 11ᵗʰ House, you may radically change or transform your future hopes, wishes and goals. You may have dreamed of playing a musical instrument and now you want to be a singer; or perhaps you wanted to stay single forever and now you can hardly wait to get married and have your own family; or your goal was to be fabulously rich and now you want to devote yourself to helping those in poverty.

A powerful drive to fulfill your ambition has taken over your very being and you'll feel an extreme commitment to attaining your ideals. You're obsessed about doing something important that will fulfill your life's purpose and bring you happiness and meaning.

You're feeling an intense passion to socialize that will result in your being attracted to new activities and groups that you relate to and identify with. As your ideals and goals change, you may be attracted to new friends of depth with similar ambitions. This is a period in your life where you may meet powerful and influential friends. The relationship you have with them will have a profound effect on you and what you accomplish. Since shallow and superficial relationships will no longer be satisfying, you'll want to be with people who share your passion and intensity.

Mary Beth was a fascinating and brilliant new friend that Tiffany met at the health club. They had great conversations where Mary Beth would talk about all kinds of political and social topics that Tiffany had never taken time to explore. One day Mary Beth asked her to read an article on global warming. After reading it, Tiffany was fascinated, especially after recalling her father, contemptuously saying that it was "nonsense, a total hoax." When Tiffany told Mary Beth she was interested in knowing more about the issue, Mary Beth invited her to a lecture by a renowned scientist. After hearing the talk, Tiffany was so moved that she decided to join Mary Beth in volunteering at an organization that educated people about the threat this problem posed.

You may have grown up never reading books until a new friend exposes you to literary classics; or you may have never understood art until an artist you befriend shares his passion with you; or you may have never invested your savings until a new friend, a self-made millionaire, helps you put together your own stock portfolio. When Pluto transits this House, you'll meet friends who make a powerful impact on you, your thinking and actions, just as Tiffany did. You'll be transformed through their friendship with you.

You May Have Intense Friendships

You may find yourself feeling a deep psychological connection with friends you have or make at this time. You're able to have engrossing personal conversations where you share your inner motivations and your most personal secrets with them. This may result in your having intense relationships where, instead of relating superficially, you reveal your deepest thoughts, becoming vulnerable and open with each other. Your experience with friends will lead to deep connections that are more satisfying than any you've had in the past. However, Pluto's energies in this House often bring a tendency to control, dominate or manipulate in the area of friendship. You may have experienced the negative side of Plutonian behavior with friends who always need to be the center of attention, have a need to control the conversation, or who use *manipulation* get their way. Here are the four classic pressure tactics:

- *Flattery:* "You're the only one who can help me."
- *Sympathy:* "I'm really under pressure, I could lose my job."
- *Guilt:* "Remember the time I did that favor for you?"
- *Intimidation:* "If you don't help me, you'll regret it."

So, beware that if you or your friends exhibit these tendencies you can expect some upsetting interactions in your relationship with them. Pluto's influence gives you penetrating insights into the behavior and motivations of others, which may result in your deciding to end a friendship that's toxic for you. You'll have an almost psychic ability to discern which friendships are truly positive and which are negative. You can then *weed your garden* and transform your friendships by eliminating the ones that are no longer appropriate and allowing the ones of great benefit to blossom and grow.

When Pluto transits your 11th House, you're looking for empowering and supportive friendships that allow you to connect with people on a very deep level. It's a fantastic time to meet teachers and mentors who'll share their knowledge and resources, guiding you toward your life goals. You may find a friendship with someone who aids your personal development, helps you learn more about yourself, and affects your life on a profound, transformational level, just as Leonard experienced.

Leonard drove his motorcycle into the town square where he could have his cup of coffee and sit down to play a casual board game with whoever was there. That's where he met Walt and began their friendship playing chess, having lunch and talking about every topic under the sun.

When Walt heard Leonard admit he knew nothing about the arts, Leonard's eyes lit up and their friendship moved to a whole new level. Walt began bringing books of all kinds to their morning chess match, proceeding to introduce Leonard to the wonders of classical art, showing him pictures of the works of many great artists. Walt led him into a world he'd never known before, discussing paintings in a way that brought the historical period and subjects to life. Walt described paintings, so vividly that Leonard could see the colors and imagine the story the painter was trying to tell.

Leonard's experience is an example of the powerfully transformative influence that friendship can offer you during this period of your life. One of the ways you can promote such an important relationship is to make time for it and be willing to initiate contact. Three of my most important friendships resulted because I picked up the phone and invited these new friends for a walk or a cup of coffee; and with two of them I had to be persistent before they made time for me. If I hadn't been proactive, I may not have received the gift of their friendship. But I realized these were important people in my life who were worth my added effort; and these friendships have lasted a lifetime.

The Dark Side of Friendship

There is also a dark side to Pluto, since it rules criminal and underworld activities, and people who are socially disaffected, who often represent a threat to society (such as gangsters and terrorists). This planet also rules the elements of life that are secret and behind the scenes. You need to be aware of this facet of Pluto's energies, since it transits this area of your life for approximately 21 years, leaving plenty of time for you to experience its influences. Plutonian energies can manifest in behavior that's

11th House: Friends, Hopes & Dreams

controlling, intimidating, coercing, and power seeking. Therefore you need to be vigilant about the groups you socialize with and the friends you make during this time, since you could be affected by these influences.

You may have known someone who engaged in criminal activity, even though you may not have known what part Pluto played in influencing their behavior. I have analyzed the birth charts of people whose criminal tendencies were activated by this transit. So, while you may not be affected, you should at least be aware of how Pluto's dark forces may come into your life under this transit.

While it may be unlikely that during this transit you'll become close friends with people like *Bonnie and Clyde,* join the *Jesse James' Gang* and rob a bank, or start an organization called *Murder, Inc.*, you may be unexplainably attracted to certain people who may not have your best interests at heart. In fact, these people may be very bad for you (or your children), but nevertheless you may be drawn to them out of an unconscious compulsion you aren't even aware.

Years ago Rodney, a very conservative, single client, met a new friend at a sporting event. That friend invited him to an exclusive party at a swanky hi-risc apartment. Rodney walked into the social gathering and said hello to a very pretty hostess who brought him a drink and introduced him to a number of people, mostly women. One of the guests casually mentioned to Rodney that this was a private party hosted by a group of high-class prostitutes. He was told that no illicit activities were going on *now,* because it was just a party among their friends. Once he was told this, he relaxed, amazed at how everyone was laughing and having fun, just like any enjoyable party. Rather than grabbing his sports coat and leaving, he was amazed at how fascinated he was with the whole experience. He told me that he was thinking, *Oh my God, I'm at the apartment of a bunch of hookers! And, I'm having fun talking to these women like they were great friends.* He was enthralled. He felt a devilish pleasure as if he was doing something illicit.

Rodney could not get rid of his fascination and attraction, eventually inviting one of the women out for an innocent date with no agenda other than getting to know her like any new girlfriend. At the end of their evening, he went up to her apartment for a nightcap. It wasn't long before a loud knock on the door announced members of the vice squad, who came into the apartment and arrested Rodney as the woman's "john." Later on at the police station, he was told that even though he wasn't paying for sex, his date was a well-known prostitute, who had been implicated by another "john."

What the Hell Is Going On in My Life?

I tell that story because many of us are fascinated with criminals, underworld types, illicit (sexual) activities, as well as "bad boy/bad girl" types who live a life in direct contrast to the "white bread" world most of us live in. The county's obsession with gangster movies such as *The Godfather* and TV shows such as *The Sopranos*, illustrate our collective fascination with the underworld, sex and other taboos.

When Pluto travels through your 11th House, be careful of putting yourself in any precarious situation or attracting the type of friends who might put you in danger. Always trust your intuition during this period of your life. If you sense there is something not "right" about someone you've met or the environment you are in, you're probably right. While you may have the self-control and good judgment that Rodney didn't possess, it's still easy to find yourself in unusual circumstances, where fate takes you for a walk down a street you've never been. And you want to walk just a little further. . .even though it seems awfully dark and foreboding.

Sonny just moved into a new city, so he was eager to make new friends, stopping off at a local pub to have some dinner. Eventually, the bartender recommended he have a nightcap at a very "happening" club. Sitting down at a table, he was approached by a stylishly dressed fellow who offered him some great "coke," which he refused. In their friendly conversation, the fellow found out Sonny was new in town and invited him to a cool party where he could meet a lot of new people. What Sonny didn't know was that this guy was a gang member and his friends were felons with criminal records. Intuitively, Sonny felt something sinister about this person, as if he were trying to seduce him, so he politely refused.

Experiencing Pluto's dark side is an extreme but during Pluto's lengthy transit through the 11th House, it may manifest in your life on some innocent level even if you don't end up befriending, Don Corleone, the Godfather, or Tony Soprano. A more positive likelihood during this Pluto transit is that you'll make intense new friendships with people who will have a powerful impact on you, helping you grow and improve your life in extremely beneficial ways.

Participate in a Transformational Organization

Because Pluto's energies transform, re-make and improve, this is an excellent time to participate in activities and organizations that are geared toward reforming the world you live in. If you live in a community where a civic building needs to be rebuilt or modernized, or a park needs to be rejuvenated, this is where you may be excited to volunteer your time.

Perhaps, you'll have an interest in participating in humanitarian projects that benefit others which may result in your meeting likeminded people who'll play an important part in your life. The point to realize is that whether it's a project, an organization, or a person, the experiences you encounter and the people you meet will have a profoundly positive effect on you. Pluto's transit through your 11th House brings you the opportunity to build a stronger foundation for your life's purpose by transforming your goals and friendships.

Considerations, Actions, Decisions During Pluto in 11th House

1. Have you experienced any dramatic changes in your hopes and wishes?
2. Do you have a dream that would change your life?
3. Do you want to make new friends who you can enjoy a more intense relationship?
4. Do you have any friendships that are toxic for you that you should eliminate from your life?
5. Do you want to make social contacts with powerful people?
6. Do you want to join an organization that's dedicated to transforming society?
7. Do you want to volunteer at an organization that improves the lives of people in your community?

Transits to Use for Successful 11th House Decisions

You now understand the areas of life that are featured in your 11th House. We've discussed how each of the five transiting planets exerts its unique influence on the affairs of this House. This will help you better understand the changes you are experiencing, moods you're feeling, and the events taking place. Your awareness of this information may prompt you to:

> 1. *ACCEPT* the way things are and be content with what is going on in your life.
>
> 2. *CONSIDER* that you'd like to make some change, in which case you may evaluate your options and further contemplate your situation.
>
> 3. *DECIDE* that you're ready to make a change, take action, and make a decision pertaining to the affairs of this House.

If you make a decision, you'll want to learn how to pick the best transit to produce a successful outcome for it. Please know that the art of picking and interpreting transits requires very thorough analysis, normally done by a professional astrologer. Therefore, I've kept the discussion of selecting and using transits simple, for illustration purposes.

The key is to remember that each planet has the ability to bring a *different* positive quality of success to your decision. For example, *Jupiter's* effect may provide opportunities to expand and grow; *Saturn's* effect is more practical; *Uranus'* effect is sudden and exciting; *Neptune's* influence may bring you inspiration and idealism; *Pluto* may bring an intense and transformative effect for major change. This knowledge will help you understand how your decisions are affected by these planetary influences.

In the examples below, I chose a planetary transit to produce a favorable result for each individual's particular decision. This will help you see the many possibilities available to create the right outcome and make your 11th House decisions more successful.

11th House: Friends, Hopes & Dreams

Using a positive JUPITER Transit

DECISION: *I want to find the best time to meet friends of my social background and seek membership in an exclusive country club.*

Explanation: If you recall, Rachel decided she wanted to meet new people, make friends and broaden her social network by joining an exclusive country club. We chose a Jupiter transit because it would bring energies of her being well received at her initial interviews, and likely bring her the luck to have her membership approved. It would also result in members liking and enjoying her once she joined. Jupiter's positive energies would assure that fortunate experiences would occur from the friendships she made.

* * *

Using a positive SATURN Transit

DECISION: *I want to join the Navy and become a Seal.*

Explanation: Jarrett had always dreamed of joining the Navy and passing the challenging physical tests of becoming a Seal. He was an athlete, always staying in top-notch shape. We chose a Saturn transit because it would give him the discipline and determination to achieve that lofty goal. It would also put him in a mental and physical mindset to work hard and endure the rigorous training. Lastly, the transit was geared toward his positive cooperation with others in a group atmosphere where success depends on teamwork.

* * *

Using a positive URANUS Transit

DECISION: *I want to meet new and unusual friends.*

Explanation: We chose a Uranus transit because Uranus rules friendship. Uranian energies would bring Maggie exciting, unique friends who would liberate her from her previous loneliness. She would meet fascinating and non-traditional people who would bring adventure and change into her life.

* * *

Using a positive NEPTUNE Transit

DECISION: *I want to pick the ideal time to have a successful volunteer experience.*

Explanation: We discussed earlier in the chapter how Albert has always wanted to volunteer with an organization to help homeless people. In the past, Albert's volunteer efforts hadn't worked out well, because his own needs took greater priority than volunteering. By using a Neptune transit, Albert's compassionate nature would emerge and he could forget his personal needs by focusing on serving the needs of others.

* * *

Using a positive PLUTO Transit

DECISION: *I want to allow some friendships to die and others to be born.*

Explanation: We discussed earlier in the chapter how Ryan's alcohol rehab process led him to AA. Yet, he still continued to hang out with several of his old friends who drank, smoked and used drugs. He was ready to make a total change and let those relationships end, in order to focus on new friends who would be part of his sober life. We used a Pluto transit because its energies were transformational and would bring an end to the old connections he had, while helping him find new friendships that would be healthy and fit into his new lifestyle.

* * *

REMEMBER: You can use the FREE Transit Calculator that's discussed in Part IV of this book to go back in time to see which transits were occurring when a major event happened in your life. It might be a wonderful learning experience, especially since most transits repeat themselves over your lifetime. Also you can find out where your transits are today or in the future.

12th House
Psychology & Secrets

The 12th House is the most mysterious House in your birth chart. It rules faith, spirituality, and your secrets, as well as selfless service to humanity like volunteering to help others. It's embodied in your best friend Jane who has such a great heart, always volunteering for something, whether it's to read to elderly people at the convalescent home or collecting clothes from the neighbors to bring to the *Salvation Army*. You see it in action at your son's little league baseball game as you watch your neighbor, Bill, taking time out of his busy work schedule to volunteer to coach. You see this benevolent service to others, as you notice Aunt Sally always busy baking cookies for someone's fundraiser.

Additionally, this House contains the secrets of the man who trolls the Internet every night, visiting pornography web sites after his wife has gone to sleep; and the woman who lives with fear and shame because she's regularly abused by her spouse. It also hides the illicit affair that the minister's wife is carrying on with a member of the congregation.

This is the area in your birth chart where you connect to your mystical inspiration; or your spiritual or religious faith. It's also known as the House of Illusion, Secrets, Self-undoing and Self-deception. This House reveals all the things about "you" that YOU don't know, and can't see – that everyone else can. Located here are your hidden strengths, weaknesses, and what you don't want others to know about you. This is the House of *denial*. It's the rear view mirror that you look at to see *who you are,* but the image you view never quite matches reality. I once had a dear friend named Mary who deluded herself so much, we called her "Queen of De-Nile."

Like Mary, you may deceive yourself or just make excuses because there are things about you that might be too painful to recognize. Does that sound familiar? Many of us have a personal wound or deep hurt that might be painful to recall. If you have one, it lives in your 12th House and may explain a great deal about what is going on in your life.

The hurt may have occurred in the past, that day at school when a child wet his pants and everyone made fun of him, calling him names that stuck for years. For another person, their wound may be from a childhood memory of being sexually molested. These experiences can cause a person to repress the existence of their pain. In fact, the pain may be too great or too frightening to explore. Yet, these traumatic experiences can cause self-esteem issues, depression and even drive such individuals to various addictions because they can't live with the torment they suffer on a daily basis.

Some people unconsciously re-create their hurts by attracting relationships that bring them the same pain they experienced when they were young, such as the abused child who grows up and marries an "abusive spouse." In their effort to escape the pain they're feeling, they may follow a path to a destructive addiction. The most common are alcohol and drugs, however, there are people who are addicted to sex, compulsive eating, excessive TV, shopping or gambling as a means of escape.

The good news is that the inner workings of this House give such victims the possibility of bringing their pain and hurt to their consciousness where they can make the healthier choice of resolving what has bothered them. If you're willing to uncover truths about yourself that are buried deep within, you can find great wisdom and understanding that will allow you to begin the healing process for any hurt you've suffered.

Sometimes these revelations can come through some sort of self-discovery, therapy or psychoanalysis. It's also possible that the healing process occurs through volunteering, because you've suffered and experienced the pain others have. So, you want to help, out of the gratitude you feel for being helped. Or, you may be like Chiron, the centaur in Greek mythology who was the "wounded healer." He helped others because of his ability to empathize with their suffering, since it was like his own. It didn't make his wounds go away, but it gave his life more meaning and significance. You may find that in helping others heal, your own wound may heal, but even if your wound isn't healed physically, you may get healed spiritually, as a byproduct of your great work. The influence of the 12th House makes you want to help others because you see them as a part of your larger self. This House connects you to your compassionate nature where your service may, at the very least, bring you a quantum of solace.

What the Hell Is Going On in My Life?

This the area of your birth chart where you hide yourself from others. It contains the hidden side of yourself that's buried in your personal subconscious mind and in your dreams. Here is the place where you keep all your memories of past lives, even if you're not consciously aware of them. The 12th House should, be considered your "secret cellar," holding your treasures as well as your junk, and all those things about you that you'd rather others not know.

Here's the place where your dreams are stored that may help you uncover your emotional blocks. This area of your birth chart is where all your hidden fears, paranoia, mental health, and psychological problems live. This House is the secret location where you keep your "worries and secret sorrows, the ones that you bear alone, never telling anyone about." It's your own private retreat where your psyche goes to escape. This is the place to look within your inner self to see all the behind-the-scenes maneuverings you keep from everyone else, especially those things you *do* when no one else is watching you. This House rules your need for seclusion, your interest in the occult or psychic phenomena, clandestine affairs, hidden enemies, hidden talents and resources, karma, mysticism, meditation, sacrificial service, repression, neuroses and self-destruction.

If you've ever had fears of being locked up and hidden from the world, you should know this House rules confinement of all types that have the effect of removing you from society such as hospitals, prisons, restraints, institutions, asylums, anywhere you might be detained for whatever reason.

This is the last House of your birth chart and the end of a complete cycle. The 12th House is the most mystical, since it's about endings and the key to everything you've learned from all of the life experiences of the previous 11 Houses of your birth chart. Because this House is directly plugged into your subconscious, it offers you the psychic opportunity to abstract some meaning from your past. Consider this final House of your birth chart as the end of road and the accumulation of all your experiences, holding the secrets of your life and the subconscious motivations that have guided it. If you have the courage to explore this House, you'll be provided with a final opportunity for psychic liberation from the hurts, wounds and any secrets that have haunted you. This House's greatest gift to you is the special opportunity to selflessly serve others for their benefit.

12th House : Psychology & Secrets

Your Body in the 12th House

This House rules feet, toes and physical pain. Since there is nothing more important than your health, pay special attention to these areas of your body whenever a planet transits this House. It may indicate a period of time when you'll experience health benefits, issues or even problems you should be aware of. If you observe anything unusual, you'll have the opportunity to consult with a medical doctor or a health care practitioner.

Your 12th House Decisions

You now understand that 12th House of your birth chart concerns your faith, spirituality, volunteering, psychology, self-deception, and your secrets.

As you read about the description of this house, it's time to ask yourself a few questions about these areas of your life. Are you a spiritual person? What kind of spiritual life do you have? Do you want to develop greater spirituality? Do you volunteer and serve others? If you don't like volunteering – why not? If you don't have the time – how come? Do you have a mystical or deeply religious side? Do you practice meditation or go on spiritual retreats to renew yourself? Have you ever been removed from society as a result of some long-term hospitalization, alcohol or drug rehabilitation, or imprisonment?

What are your secrets? Do you have any psychic wounds you are aware of? Have you ever confronted a deep hurt? If so, are you healed? Is there any self-destructive behavior or neuroses that you have struggled with? Do friends tell you about qualities in yourself that you find hard to believe because you're not aware of them? What are the secret things you do when you are alone that you never do when others are around? Have you ever been in therapy to discover any hidden psychological issues that have plagued your life? Do you have any addictions that you keep hidden, whether it's eating chocolate late at night, gambling, or using more serious drugs? (Note: my editor insists that chocolate is not an addiction, it's an avocation! Furthermore, cacao is a vegetable, and you should eat your veggies every day.)

Do you need a great deal of seclusion from the rest of the world? Are you interested in the occult or psychic phenomena? Have you ever been involved in a clandestine love affair? Do you know someone who might be a secret enemy?

These are all significant questions and your answers may lead you to make important decisions to change your life. Here are a few examples of decisions clients have made based on the activities and issues of the 12th House.

Situation: Rita is a nurse and has always felt she had a special calling to minister to the terminally ill.

DECISION: *I have decided to find a new job where I can do hospice work with those who are dying.*

* * *

Situation: Tina was raped as a teenager and has lived with guilt and shame for many years. She has never told anyone of the experience.

DECISION: *I want to seek counseling to discuss my secret and heal the deep pain I feel inside.*

* * *

Situation: Edgar's mother has Alzheimer's disease and taking care of her has created a great strain on the family.

DECISION: *I want to find the best geriatric facility to care for my mother.*

* * *

Situation: John has struggled with ADHD (attention deficit hyperactivity disorder), causing him to have erratic moods, anger issues, and a lack of sustained concentration, making it difficult for him to have meaningful relationships.

DECISION: *I want to find an effective way to control my health disorder.*

* * *

During the transits of *Jupiter, Saturn, Uranus, Neptune,* and *Pluto* – Rita, Tina, Edgar and John will have many opportunities to implement their decisions at a favorable time to produce the outcome they want.

The Transiting Planets Reveal Your Past, Present & Future

Your main focus is using astrology to understand *what the hell is going on in your life.* Once you do – this book will show you the best time to make a decision to change it, should you have a desire to do so. As you read about the five planets transiting the 12th House, notice the way each planet exerts its unique influence and effect, bringing specific opportunities, issues, problems, and events into this area of your life. But if you're curious as to how these planets are personally affecting YOU *today,* in your *past,* or in your *future,* you can find out where each transiting planet is in your birth chart by using the *FREE Transit Calculator* (see Part IV).

JUPITER in Your 12th House of Psychology & Secrets

A Time of Healing

When Jupiter transits your 12th House, you have the capacity to grow in the spiritual or religious realm of your life by expanding your consciousness. This is when a window to your heart and soul opens up for you to peer within and take a deep look at your inner self. If you like what you see, you may feel a sense of bliss and contentment. If you don't, you now have the opportunity to do something about it. This is a wonderful time of feeling psychologically and spiritually good inside. Whatever grip past fears and phobias have had on you begin to loosen and you feel a sense of faith and confidence that you can overcome them (or you feel even better because you overcame them long ago).

What's happening is that emotionally and mentally you're ready to confront some of your deep-seated fears and heal the psychic wounds you may have been living with. It's so easy for most people to avoid the pain or depression they feel by busying themselves in work, activities or addictions that distract them from facing whatever may be at the root of their torment. Through this Jupiter transit you can learn and understand more about the hidden or secret dimensions of your life that previously you've had fears about facing. This is when you can go back to your childhood and tap into any painful experiences or phobias that need to be confronted because you now have the courage to heal yourself.

I had one client who was mystified about why he avoided intimacy, touching, hugging and kissing in his relationships; another client didn't understand why she had a fear of germs that made her wash her hands thirty times a day; while a third couldn't understand why she got so angry over the smallest matters. Thus, this is a very fortunate time to uncover any psychological mysteries that have troubled you.

Imagine that despite your fears and insecurities someone gave you a hug and made you feel safe and secure about whatever was bothering you. Jupiter's effect is to provide you with that loving "hug." You're now able to confidently approach life because you're in a spiritually trusting place with great faith that your problems can be resolved as Jake finally realized.

Jake felt abandoned at the age of five when his mother died, and he carried those fears of abandonment into his romantic relationships. He subconsciously acted out the psychic wound that was buried within him, by sabotaging his intimate relationships. Whenever he went from dating a woman casually to a more serious commitment, he got scared. Becoming vulnerable and intimate with a woman reminded him too much of the painful experience of being close to his mother, only to have her leave him unexpectedly. He felt that if he totally gave his love to a woman, he couldn't trust that she'd always be there for him. So, whenever he was involved in a promising romantic relationship, and his girlfriend pushed to get closer for more of a commitment, he'd find some reason to break up, saying he just couldn't handle such an intense relationship now.

I've had many clients, just like Jake, who repeat their unsatisfying relationship patterns. Whether it's fear of abandonment, as in Jake's case, often there's some fear hidden in their unconscious that blocks their ability to love, trust and be vulnerable. Other clients deceive themselves by thinking that because they're *aware* of a childhood wound such as abandonment, they no longer sabotage their relationships. I remind clients that having an *intellectual* awareness of their psychic wound usually doesn't heal the damage it's done or the effect it has on their relationships. For such clients to heal, they need to go below the surface of mental understanding, deep inside to the source where the pain resides. If you're a person grappling with these issues, this Jupiter transit provides you with an opportunity to seek professional assistance to really heal yourself.

A Time to Teach or Be Taught

Jupiter's influence in the 12th House minimizes your normal ego drive so that you can be more detached and openly look at yourself uncritically. You won't react defensively to comments made by others, because you feel more peaceful inside. You have a very generous nature and a capacity to be empathetic, showing yourself and others in the world a higher level of compassion. There's a feeling within you that says, "I feel a connection to the rest of humanity." You're no longer content to satisfy your needs alone because you have a sincere desire to help others. This is a beautiful time in your life when you feel a genuine spiritual connection to your fellow man and you're sincerely interested in seeking wisdom and discovering your own spiritual truth. I encourage you to take classes, read books, and participate in discussions that give you an outlet to share what you've learned and further your learning and growth.

If you do have something important that you need to learn, this may be a time when you'll find someone who can act as a teacher to you. That person may not literally be a teacher, but perhaps a friend or associate who ends up teaching you a great deal. Since the 12th House is where we keep our secrets and psychic wounds, if there is something within you that needs healing, this person may assist you in that process. Because of your benevolent nature, you may help others by teaching them in some way.

A client who was an only child always wished he had an older brother to help and guide him. He grew up as a member of the *Boy Scouts* in his town and enjoyed doing fun activities with kids. As he got older he thought more about the kind of volunteering he'd like to do. One day he saw the perfect opportunity in an ad that said, "Be a Big Brother." He called up, got details, and was totally excited about interviewing for the opportunity to mentor some younger boy. Instead of longing for a big brother, he realized he could be the big brother he had always wanted. That's how easy it is to give of yourself when Jupiter transits your 12th House.

A Time for a Spiritual Journey & Volunteering

Because you're in a compassionate and charitable mindset, this is an ideal time to volunteer for hospital work or some other humanitarian project. You'll feel a special calling to help those who are in need and less fortunate. You understand that the purpose of your life includes being of service to others, not just yourself. Since you're interested in your spiritual growth, you may want to further develop your spiritual consciousness or your relationship with God. In order to tap into these areas, you may decide to go on a spiritual retreat, engage in meditation, yoga or religious classes.

You feel extremely creative. Your intuition is strong and your perceptions are keen. This is a wonderful time to enjoy and be inspired by any interest you have in art and music. You may find yourself in a blissful state where you're ready to reach out to others or be willing to allow others to reach out to you.

Considerations, Actions, Decisions During Jupiter in 12th House

1. Are there any hurts or wounds you want to resolve?
2. Begin therapy or some self-discovery process
3. Is there anyone who has hurt you that you're ready to forgive?
4. Is there a spiritual or religious activity that would expand your consciousness?
5. Is there any volunteer work that would bring you joy?
6. Begin a humanitarian or charity project that would benefit others.
7. Go on a meditation retreat.
8. Make travel plans to go somewhere for spiritual adventure.

SATURN in Your 12th House of Psychology & Secrets

Time to Evaluate Your Accomplishments & Your Life

When Saturn transits your 12th House it's time to seriously examine matters of this House such as your spirituality, your desires to serve, volunteer efforts, psychological issues, and secrets that are part of your life. Have you developed yourself spiritually? Do you want to make any changes in your volunteer efforts? Have you addressed any important psychological issues that have affected you, including secrets that have been a burden? This is an important time to take stock of your successes and failures as you reflect on your life experiences. If you find yourself discontent because you have not achieved as much as you've wanted, you might feel some personal regret; or even a crisis, or fear that you've failed.

However, this is when you should count your blessings for what you've accomplished and not let your ego become too attached to your failures. One of the few things you probably *won't* say on your deathbed is, "If only I had spent more time at work, my life would have turned out so much better." I tell my "bottom-line" oriented clients, "This is when your faith and ability to be grateful is tested, because during this Saturn transit it's easy to be discouraged if you feel you've fallen short of your goals, especially if you're a *perfectionist* who finds that – whatever your success, it's never enough!"

This is meant to be a time for you to compassionately view the experiences you've had in the most important areas of your life, recognizing that you've done the best you can (if not you'll get another chance). I tell clients who are going through this transit, it's time to move into the space of *acceptance*. If that seems difficult for you to do, then to find peace, heed the words of the inspirational Buddhist teacher, Jack Kornfield, and "give up hoping for a better past."

You must understand this is a time of completion for your undertakings, a time of resolution for work you may have been involved in, and a time of endings for ventures that have run their course. If your life were a "game," it would be the 9th inning or the 4th Quarter. The game is almost over (that is until the next one begins). That's really what is going on in your life, as my client Joanna found out.

Joanna had built a very successful retail cosmetics company with six outlets. She had grand plans of taking her retail concept and going national, but that had never panned out. Instead, she spent the last 24 years building six profitable shops throughout the state. Many years ago she'd tried opening up new locations in two surrounding states; however, it was a costly mistake since those stores were unprofitable and eventually closed. Joanna's ego was bruised and she found it hard to accept that her expansion plans failed. Later on, she came to realize that her best success was in operating the retail locations right in her own backyard. The good news was that her statewide business had given her a great lifestyle and made her wealthy. Joanna had a lot to be grateful for. Aside from her tremendous business success, she was very proud of her two daughters and the success they'd created for themselves, as well as the three grandchildren she now had. Joanna was now ready to retire, after accepting a generous offer from a competitor who was buying all her stores.

Saturn rewarded her hard work with a comfortable retirement, allowing her some important time of reflection. She'll now have the opportunity to seriously evaluate the experiences she had, as she begins a process of introspection that will lead her to self-discoveries she'll use to make a new start in the coming years.

I have had many clients like Joanna with a similar story of a life filled with some "bumps," but mostly with success and good fortune. Saturn's transit in their 12th House is meant for these people to stop what they're doing, evaluate their failures and accomplishments, and to show some gratitude for whatever blessings and good fortune they've received.

A Time for Finishing, Not Starting

Saturn's two and a half year transit is a time when you'll be finishing up anything you have been engaged in over recent years. For example, if you've been involved in an activity, project, job, or even career that has reached a conclusion and should be over, you'll do so during this transit. You'll be receiving ample warning signs that the "2-minute" buzzer has sounded and the game is near over. You'll feel a bit like a singer who can no longer hit the high notes or a baseball pitcher whose 90-mile per hour fastball has slowed down to the high 70s.

What the Hell Is Going On in My Life?

During my Saturn transit to the 12th House, I started noticing that I wasn't as effective at the job I was doing at the time. It was more difficult to interest clients in my firm's services, traveling started becoming drudgery; I hated being away from my home and family; and no amount of money from the job was enough to compensate for my waning interest in my work. So, from personal experience, I can tell you that Saturn's transit here is a time of finishing, not a time of starting new ventures or enterprises. Even if you're antsy to start something new or make a change, this isn't a good time to begin your efforts. The energies of Saturn can be draining and limiting to the point when you'll wonder: "What happened to my energy and ambition?"

This is when aspects of your life no longer seem to work very well. For example, you may find that the job that you used to do so easily and successfully, seems more difficult (as was my case). You find that tried and true methods that always worked before, no longer produce good results. In fact, you may realize that you don't enjoy your job as much. This same dynamic may be operating in other areas of your life as well.

You may also notice that during this time your normal ways of handling people and situations aren't producing the usual positive results. For example, you may find yourself thinking, *My creative ideas used to flow so naturally, but now they don't come as easily,* or *I used to think I was a great salesman but I don't know what's happened lately.* It seems as if you need to find a whole new way of doing something to produce success, yet you don't know where to begin to get better results. You're feeling totally frustrated without knowing what you should do to correct the situation.

Before you make any final judgments, the best thing you can do is re-evaluate what's really happening in this area of your life. Take stock of what you've achieved and what you haven't. Maybe what you've been doing has run its course. Perhaps, you've had a long run doing something and it has matured like a ripe fruit. Now, it is ready to be over, as was the case for Joanna with her cosmetics business. Saturn's transit through your 12th House is time of endings, not beginnings. The message on the scoreboard of your life is: "Complete what you began and finish what you've started." This was Keith's lesson during this Saturn transit.

Keith had worked for a governmental health organization for the past 20 years, traveling extensively to many poverty-stricken places in the world. It had been a rewarding job, but the routine and grind of travel was taking its toll. His boss was demanding, rarely showing appreciation for his hard work and successful results. While he had enjoyed dedicating himself to helping others, he was emotionally drained. He felt a need to step back and re-evaluate the work he was doing and what might be the next step. After some reflection, he came to the conclusion that the best thing was to take early retirement, put his possessions into storage, and do something he had always dreamed of doing. He decided to enter a meditation retreat he had discovered during his travels, where he could rest, go on an inner journey to contemplate his life, and open up to spiritual guidance. Keith had Saturn in his 12th House, a perfect time to re-evaluate his life and his future.

The important point of this transit is not to become discouraged about the failures or disappointments you may experience during this Saturn transit. If you haven't achieved 100 percent success, it's easy to be depressed over your inadequacies and failures. Saturn's energies require you to *let go* of whatever no longer works. If you haven't been as successful as you would have liked, ask yourself: what obstacles have prevented you from accomplishing the results you've wanted? Become aware of any impediments that have interfered with your success or happiness in order to make sure that in your next venture they don't limit you again.

Starting over may give you an excellent opportunity for success, so for now this is when you may need to clear the decks of what you're doing and make plans to do something new. This may mean researching the Internet for information that might stimulate your creative juices, or calling up old colleagues to brainstorm ideas and opportunities. Rather than succumb to any self-imposed pressure to begin something too quickly, use this period of your life to step back and evaluate what you'd like to do next. You're in between destinies, which will become clearer when Saturn's transit leaves your 12th House and heads into your 1st House.

In summary, if you're feeling as if the old "tried and true" is no longer working or that something is ending in your life at this time, you're not crazy – it IS! This insight is important as you try to find some understanding about what is going on in your life.

An Opportunity to Confront Your Secrets

Since the 12th House rules the secrets that are hidden in the subconscious mind, Saturn's influence is perfect for evaluating and addressing any psychological problems, complexes, or phobias that have emotionally burdened you. Saturn's energies often bring a crisis into your life or a test that forces you to face personal problems or psychological issues that have limited you.

If you have any fears or personal wounds from your childhood, this is when you'll have an opportunity to resolve them and let them go from your life. One client who was asked if he was ready for a big promotion immediately became afraid of failing when asked if he was willing to accept more responsibility. As a child, he'd been told he was stupid and would never amount to anything. He heard those parental rantings in his psyche every day, causing him to question his own competency any time there was talk of his promotion. Another client grew up hating his mother, finally learning that his anger and contempt were causing him to mistreat his wife who reminded him of his mother. Yet another client who was constantly told how beautiful she was, saw only an ugly person in her mirror because she grew up thinking she wasn't pretty. This may be an opportune time to confront your secrets by seeking psychotherapy, participating in personal growth workshops, or by going on a meditation retreat. If you commit to the hard work of healing yourself, Saturn will reward you later on.

The purpose of Saturn transiting your 12th House is to evaluate what you've accomplished and to re-consider whether any of the activities in your life have come to their completion. It's also a time to re-examine your secrets, phobias, neuroses, or any psychological issues that have limited you by confronting them directly and seeking resolution.

Considerations, Actions, Decisions During Saturn in 12th House

1. How would you evaluate your successes and failures?
2. Are you a perfectionist who's never satisfied with your successes?
3. What have you learned from your failures?
4. Are you finishing or ending something in your life such as your career?

12th House : Psychology & Secrets

5. Are you planning on starting anything new?
6. How can you improve your weaknesses and limitations?
7. Are there any secrets, wounds or hurts that you want to address?
8. Seek help for any psychological problems.

URANUS in Your 12th House of Psychology & Secrets

A Time for Psychic Liberation

Transiting Uranus in your 12th House is a time when you free yourself from many of the behaviors that have originated in your unconscious mind, where psychic activity takes place that you are *not* aware of. Your mind contains feelings, thoughts, urges and memories that may be outside your *conscious* awareness. The liberating energies of Uranus give you the potential to become aware of your fears, psychological issues, and neuroses, so that you can set yourself free of them. Your intuition assists in you in discovering the truth about secrets you may have repressed, but are now ready to confront.

You experience flashes of insight into the vary emotions that may have burdened you in the past such as fear: "I'm afraid when I meet someone new they won't like me," or guilt: "I'm noticing how I manipulate to get my way," or anger: "I see how my impatience causes me to react angrily." This can be an exciting time when you have the potential to be psychologically and spiritually free. This exhilarating feeling of liberation occurred for a very special client of mine whose fear was that if she told the truth, she would be punished.

Rose was a young Jewish woman from Poland who as a teenager was taken from her home, along with her family, to a concentration camp. She lived through the horrible experience of the Holocaust, coming to the United States when she was 21. Rose was granted citizenship and has lived here for 6seven years, all the while being tortured by an irrational phobia that she might still be deported at any time.

Her fear comes alive as she thinks back to the year 1945, when she and her only surviving family member, a younger sister were booked on a ship headed for the freedom of the United States. There was a great deal of confusion that day with thousands of refugees trying to get on the ship headed to New York City. Her sister was booked on the next ship.

As they said, goodbye, Rose panicked as she realized that she'd lost her passport, which meant she wouldn't be allowed to board the ship. Her sister quickly gave her – her passport, since they were close enough in age and appearance to fool the authorities. She assured Rose she would find Rose's passport and use it in place of her own. Rose got on the ship impersonating her sister, and after a long voyage landed at Staten Island, where she looked up at the Statue of Liberty and cried at the freedom it represented to her. At Passport Control, the immigration officer looked carefully at her passport and asked her to raise her right hand and swear that she was *Rose Bronsky*. That was 6seven years ago.

Since then, no amount of reassurance by her own children that she was safe and would never be deported was sufficient to motivate her to tell her secret to the U.S. immigration authorities. Even her immigration attorney told her, "Rose, there was so much confusion in those days after the war that your legal entree into the USA would never be contested after this long. Besides, the most important point is that your citizenship and passport are now legal after all these years."

Those reassurances didn't matter to Rose, since her phobia was stronger than her secret. It took Uranus going through her 12th House to give her the courage to confront her fear and finally go to the U.S. Immigration office with her attorney and tell the authorities her story. Once the chief officer understood the circumstances, he gave her complete assurance that she was a full U.S. citizen in good standing. Rose finally felt free at last.

All Alone with Your Fears

Not everyone is open to being liberated from the fears, psychological issues, or neuroses that emanate from their subconscious. This is especially true for people who feel no connection to the spiritual, religious, or even the metaphysical aspects of life. Often such individuals are rigid and opposed to change, and find new discoveries so disturbing, they resist any opportunities for enlightenment.

If this is the case for you, this transit may be a difficult period in your life when you feel all alone as you encounter your hidden fears, repressed psychological problems, and the psychic wounds that have troubled you in your life. Be mindful that you may feel tense without understanding why you're upset. It's possible that you'll experience the instability of Uranus, which may bring you unexpected incidents that are disruptive.

What the Hell Is Going On in My Life?

You may even have your secrets exposed, causing you to exclaim, "I can't believe someone found out," or "Why is this happening to me?"

Beware of Dishonest Dealings

Since the 12th House rules illusion, deception and self-undoing, when Uranus transits this House you may experience some unexpected deception that you never saw occurring before. You may find out that someone you thought was your ally is more of an enemy, working against your interests. A surprising event may occur that was a result of something you did in your past. You may discover you have been behaving compulsively, even though unconsciously.

Always remember: Uranus' influence brings surprises, disruptions, and often shocking and unexpected events into you life. The disruption and instability may occur out of nowhere, leaving you unaware as to how it happened. However, if this happens to you, the first place to look is your own actions, both on a conscious and unconscious level.

Pauline and Brett were both senior managers at the same company and they were friendly colleagues, often having lunch together where they talked about the company, senior management, and ideas on how to grow their business. Brett was a clever opportunist and consummate corporate politician, always listening intently to Pauline's great ideas with an ulterior motive. After such a lunch discussion with Pauline, he'd make sure to stop off at the president's office and have a chat with him. Brett would be sure to discuss his new ideas, claiming Pauline's ideas as his own. The president had been uninspired by Brett's ideas in the past, but now he was growing more and more impressed with Brett based on some of the newer ideas he'd heard lately. Of course, the new ideas were actually Pauline's.

It was a big surprise to Pauline at the next departmental meeting when the president announced the promotion of Brett as the company's new senior vice president. Her face turned red and she grew upset as she listened to the president discussing several innovative ideas and projects that Brett had proposed to management. The president was sure they would increase company sales by one-third! Every idea was one she'd discussed in detail with Brett over lunch.

Pauline experienced one of the outcomes of Uranus transit in the 12th House: hidden enemies. She discovered that someone she thought of as a friendly colleague was really working secretly against her interest. She had every right to feel betrayed, but she also shared some responsibility for what happened. This is where the unconscious part of her behavior helped produce this outcome. There was something within her psyche that held her back from expressing her ideas to anyone but Brett.

Maybe Pauline didn't have the confidence to sit down with the president and present her own ideas for fear that they'd be quickly disapproved. Or, was it possible that she was content to informally discuss her ideas because she didn't want to attract attention; or want the responsibility and challenge of a promotion? Pauline was creative and brilliant, but not assertive or self-promoting. She sent out signals that she was happy to share her original ideas and unlikely to talk to the president to get them adopted. Brett picked these signals up and used them to his advantage.

Pauline had to suspect on some level that a corporate politician like Brett might take her ideas and present them directly to the president. Brett's lack of integrity and his shameless ambition made it easy for him to take credit for her ideas and use them for his own advancement. While Pauline was clearly the victim, she had to accept some responsibility for what happened, even if it was in not taking some action on her own. This story clearly illustrates how unconscious behavior can drive one's actions or inactions.

Beware of Surprises That Come from Secrets

Your unconscious mind may protect you from experiences your conscious mind would rather not acknowledge. Perhaps you've had a traumatic experience as a child or an embarrassing moment as an adolescent or an indiscretion during the early years of your marriage that you'd rather not remember. This part of your brain can guard your deepest secrets because you find them too painful and would rather keep them buried. Or, it can cause you to imagine that if you deny or ignore them, they'll go away. But people who have such secrets often pay a high price, unconsciously plagued with feelings of shame, inferiority and low self-esteem that they may not be consciously aware.

Uranus energies attempt to liberate you from your secrets, even by exposing them. If you resist Uranus' energies that demand you face the truth and make a radical change, they may sabotage you by triggering events or consequences that will be disruptive to your life. You may experience psychological upheaval, shock, unexpected outcomes, and surprising events that force you to face personal issues that you must address.

Often during this transit, if you've kept a hidden secret – the energies of Uranus can cause it to be revealed in an unexpected way.

This happened to a client of mine who had pledged fidelity to his wife, and for many years he had been faithful. However, on a recent business trip he'd cheated for the first time in their 12-year marriage. He was at the hotel bar having a nightcap where he met a very attractive graduate student. After sharing a few drinks with her, one thing led to another and they went up to his hotel room and had sex.

Afterwards, he felt horribly guilty about his infidelity, but he rationalized that being honest about his affair would only hurt his wife's feelings. Unfortunately, for my client, he had Uranus transiting his 12th House, so he wasn't prepared for the shock of his doctor telling him that he'd contracted an STD (sexually transmitted disease). The doctor advised him, for obvious health reasons, to send his wife into the clinic for an examination (and contact the graduate student). He was forced to make a full, upsetting confession to his wife and pay the consequences. In his case, Uranus' influences freed him from having to carry around the guilt of lying and being unfaithful to his wife. This incident also gave him and his wife the opportunity to confront the underlying reasons that led to his infidelity.

Being Confined by Your Secrets

The 12th House also rules all types of institutions such as hospitals, rehab clinics, asylums, prisons, and other places of confinement. These facilities hide many aspects of our life that we may wish to keep secret from others. This is in no way to suggest that you'll be in prison or confined. (Of course, who knows? After all, it may depend on *your* secrets.)

However, this may be a time when your life suddenly brings you into contact with these institutions in some way, either personally or in connection with people you know. I had one client who suddenly decided to volunteer at an elderly care facility; another found a job at a correctional facility; another was a danger to herself and had to be institutionalized; while another violated his parole and was sent back to prison. With Uranus, you never know what may suddenly happen.

The purpose of Uranus transiting your 12th House is to free yourself of secrets, phobias, neuroses, or any psychological issues that have limited you, by confronting them directly and seeking resolution. If your intuition leads you to discover some psychic wound from the past, you now have the opportunity to take advantage of this Uranus transit to liberate yourself once and for all.

Considerations, Actions, Decisions During Uranus in 12th House

1. Liberate yourself from any dark secrets with the help of a therapist.
2. Make discoveries about yourself by enrolling in a personal growth workshop.
3. Free yourself by forgiving someone who has hurt you.
4. Use your intuition to make yourself aware of any hidden enemies?
5. Participate in an unusual spiritual or religious activity.
6. Do volunteer work that will be exciting.
7. Discover a humanitarian or charity project that you'd like to be involved in.

NEPTUNE in Your 12th House of Psychology & Secrets

A Time to Be Spiritual & A Time to Smell the Flowers

When Neptune transits your 12th House your focus is on higher consciousness and the spiritual realm of your life. No matter whether you were a "captain of industry," a second grade teacher, or the bookkeeper for a non-profit organization, you'll want to connect to your inner spirit and soul. It's that time when you finally decide to "smell the flowers," appreciate the joy in nature, find meaning through quiet meditation, and even reach out to God. You're engaged in important work, searching for the meaning of life on both the conscious and unconscious level.

For years your focus may have been the external and material world, but now you seek the inner peace that comes with being satisfied with who you are – not what you have. This is a time when you want a break from the day-to-day world preferring an opportunity to privately examine your life and experiences. You'll realize that logic and rational thought don't provide sufficient answers, which is why you may find yourself drawn to spiritual or religious realms to gain more understanding. Neptunian energies will help you by giving you a heightened sensitivity, intuition, and psychic ability to aid you in your efforts toward self-discovery into the deeper dimensions of your soul. During this transit many people go on a meditative retreat, a spiritual journey, or a very long vacation to examine their life and deeds.

A Time for Serving Others

Neptune's energies provide you with insight and intuition to become more aware of the secrets in your psyche. If you've buried or suppressed experiences from your past that have created psychological problems, this is an excellent time to heal them. Now is when you'll feel compassion for others and a faith that will inspire you. If you've spent many years of your life angry with a parent or estranged from a sibling this transit brings you the opportunity to forgive them.

You may have noticed that there is a *lot of healing* going on in the 12th House because that's the place in your birth chart where the pain and wounds of your life are buried. All five outer planets provide their own unique character to healing you in matters of the 12th House.

There are many experiences that can assist you on your spiritual journey such as volunteering and being of service to others because such pursuits will be gratifying and lend meaning to your life, which is exactly what happened to Arlene.

Arlene had fought cancer twice in her life, going through radiation and chemo regimens. As part of her battle with cancer she attended a support group with other cancer patients, meeting all kinds of wonderful people. While she was now in remission, many of the friends she made in the group were dying with level three or level four cancers. Some had informed their families they weren't willing to go through grueling chemo or radiation treatments a second time and were prepared to accept death.

Arlene felt great compassion as she got to know many of these people, which is where she got the idea to volunteer for hospice work. There was a dignity and process to dying that she'd read about, believed in, and had seen first-hand. Next week she would begin her volunteer service at a hospice center that served many cancer patients she was looking forward to helping. The idea of making their transition out of this life meaningful gave her great satisfaction. Her own 12-year fight with cancer made her realize how much she loved serving people who suffered from a similar illness. Arlene's experience personifies the miraculous giving that human beings do for each other when Neptune transits their 12th House.

A Time for Self-Forgiveness

Neptune's transit through your 12th House can be a disorienting time, so if your main focus has been on achieving material success, this may be a period of confusion, disillusion, and anxiety. This is one of those sections in my book that I hope will help explain to someone: *What the hell is going on in your life?*

You may feel distracted during these years, not being able to understand the lack of motivation you're feeling in your career or job. This may be when you experience psychological fears that come from past experiences. Some of those fears may be based on old secrets that still remain in your cellar. Ask yourself if there are any that you've *intuitively* became aware of recently. You may be uncomfortable or upset about confronting the unknown. Or, you may experience depression that can come from your awareness of your own inadequacies and past failures. Be very aware that you're in a sensitive state with the possibility that your fears are making you feel vulnerable. If so, friends or counselors can assist you in discussing your feelings and experiences. This was the exact situation that a client of mine, Thomas, found himself in when Neptune transited this House.

Thomas attended Catholic school as a very young boy and while there, was molested by a priest. Thomas never told anyone because he was too afraid and ashamed. He also knew that if other kids found out what had happened to him, they might make fun of him, which would have been unbearable. Since his parents were very strict Catholics, he was worried that if he told them, they might not believe him, so he decided his only option was to live with the pain he felt inside. The pain never got better because the memory never went away. It got worse as he grew up carrying this upsetting secret, feeling shame for being molested, wondering if somehow it was his fault, and feeling guilty for having said nothing about it.

When Thomas saw me, he was in his 40s with Neptune transiting his 12th House. I encouraged him by saying this was the ideal time confront his secret and forgive himself. It took immense courage, but he called up a rape crisis center and talked with a counselor who was very understanding. The counselor listened to him with great empathy and gave him some gentle advice as to what he could do. Thomas felt better for having told someone and was now ready to join a support group that the counselor recommended and take meaningful steps to heal himself.

A Time to Reflect & Meditate

With this Neptune transit your focus will be on evaluating the meaning of your life from a spiritual perspective. This is a time of serious reflection when you realize that satisfaction in life does not come from material success. If you're like most people, you've heard such words before. What's amazing is that during this transit, you'll finally be able to understand the true significance of them. You'll begin to ask yourself, *who are you* on a spiritual level. Are you fulfilled inside? Or have you lived your life superficially, focusing only on the material plane with no concern for your spiritual development. Do you have a higher purpose you want to discover? During this period of your life you'll consider these questions and search for answers.

Because of the magnitude of these questions, you may decide to take time from your everyday life to evaluate what you've achieved and the meaning that it's held for you. This may cause you to be less focused on your career or job success because you're consciously or unconsciously searching for answers. You may find value in quiet reflection and meditation. There are many experiences that can assist you on your spiritual journey, such as going on a meditation retreat, participating in personal growth workshop or entering individual therapy. You may even consider taking a sabbatical from work or just going on a vacation to some spiritual destination that will give you the time, space, and peace to find answers to the questions you may ponder. This is an ideal time to be introspective and contemplate your life by walking along the ocean, hiking through the woods, or meeting a good friend for a cup of coffee to talk about what you've learned.

Peter has often looked back on his life and reflected on a tragedy that occurred when he was 23. He normally was not a heavy drinker but one night he did something uncharacteristic and got very drunk. Then he did the most irresponsible thing he has ever done: He got into his car, ran a stop sign, and killed a young child. The accident continuously plays out in his mind like his own private horror movie. A child unexpectedly runs out in front of Peter's car and he never knows whether he could have reacted in time and prevented the accident had he been sober. The reality was that he was drunk and a child was dead.

Peter spent several years in deep depression trying to work through his self-hatred and loathing. Part of his rehabilitation was quitting drinking, joining AA, and volunteering time to an organization that brought public awareness to drunk driving. He has worked a great deal to forgive himself and find peace through therapy and meditation, but he still can't forget that horrible day in his life. When you suffer a gut-wrenching tragedy as Peter did, your whole life is dedicated to working on self-forgiveness every day. But the benefit of Neptune's transit through your 12th House is you genuinely have the capacity to *finally* forgive yourself.

A Time to Examine Your Life & How You've Lived It

On some level you may feel that your life has been empty and meaningless. If so, you may even experience depression at this realization, as you say, "All I've cared about is making a lot of money," or "All I've done is live for my own pleasure, never concerned with anyone else," or "All I've ever accomplished is raising a family." This is not to say that these are not legitimate choices or accomplishments, because they are. It's just that at this time in your life, they may not be very consoling. But don't lose faith if you come to this awareness; instead recognize that Neptune's passage through your 12th House is an ideal time for compassion and finding new inspiration. If you realize you've not lived your life in a manner that brings higher meaning and fulfillment to your life, use your deeper awareness to change your life so that it does.

Old astrologers often associated the 12th House with an adage: *Serve or suffer*. It expressed the need you may feel during Neptune's transit of this House, where you decide to answer the call to volunteer and be of service to others, thus, deriving great satisfaction. Or, you choose to ignore this opportunity and suffer for doing so. What's important to note is that this is an ideal time to give to others through volunteer efforts or performing services to benefit the community or society, giving your life much more joy and meaning. Perhaps, more than any other time, you now have the unique ability to be compassionate, empathetic, and generous to your fellow man. Take advantage of these gifts and share them with the world.

Considerations, Actions, Decisions During Neptune in 12th House

1. Seek help for any psychology problems, secrets or wounds.
2. Forgive yourself or someone else for the hurt they caused you.
3. Use your intuition to become aware of any people in your life who might be hidden enemies.
4. Participate in a mystical, spiritual or religious activity.
5. Do volunteer work where by serving others you may end up healing yourself.
6. Begin a humanitarian or charity project that helps those who are less fortunate.
7. Attend a meditation retreat or personal growth program that may inspire you and connect you to your spiritual self.

PLUTO in Your 12th House of Psychology & Secrets

Take Out the Psychic Garbage

When Pluto transits your 12th House, your energies become intensely focused on your inner growth, spiritual development, and transforming yourself on a deep, profound psychological level. You'll become an excavator, digging into your past and bringing to the surface, fears, psychological problems and neuroses that have plagued your life. Think of Pluto as a *roto-rooter* that allows you to drill into the center of your psyche and find the psychic garbage that's contained within you. You can then bring it up to the surface of your consciousness to confront, change, and improve yourself for the better.

Get ready to connect into the psychology of who you are as you become aware of how your subconscious mind has repressed unpleasant experiences from your childhood. Pluto's energies give you the remarkable capacity to tap into your intuition and psychic abilities to discover knowledge you never knew before. Your keen ability to access your unconscious mind helps you become aware of compulsions and obsessions that have controlled you. This is a time when you seek enlightenment through activities that bring self-knowledge such as psychotherapy, meditation, or frequenting a spiritual retreat.

You feel like you have the capacity to regenerate yourself, and a desire to help and heal others. Pluto's energies are well utilized in any profession where you can transform, improve, rehabilitate or restore something. This may cause you to pursue occupations that serve institutions such as hospitals, clinics, rehab centers, asylums, and prisons.

Don't Let Your Secrets Poison You

You may have learned from childhood to hide elements of your personality and behavior that aren't likely to be approved of by others, as well as society in general. Since the 12th House rules your secrets, during this period of your life you may discover hidden aspects of yourself that you've avoided showing others or that are buried in your psyche. Pluto is like a high-powered flashlight that lets you see in places where the light has never shined, allowing you to understand things about yourself you never knew. Unless you confront those hidden secrets, their toxic effects can sabotage your self-esteem and life in a powerful way, as they did in Jonah's case.

Jonah came from a poor family with only one parent to take care of him, and his five brothers and sisters. In order to survive he learned how to shoplift food, clothing, and anything his family needed. Then, he graduated to committing worse crimes such as muggings, burglaries, and even armed robberies. He is now an adult, but he continues to feel a great deal of shame over his past criminal behavior. He searches his mind for how he can repay the debts he owes and ponders what he can do to right these wrongs. The stores he stole from are no longer there for him to make amends and his neighborhood victims have moved away. His punishment for his crime has been a life of feeling guilty, inferior and inadequate. It's now time to finally get help to confront the secret he's had for so many years, since he can no longer live with the pain and shame.

Confront Your Unconscious Compulsions

Pluto's energies bring your psychological motivations to the surface to help you understand the ways they empower you as well as how they may sabotage you. You may find your conscious efforts are undermined by unconsciously motivated actions that end up subverting you. This may result in your not understanding why, despite your sincere efforts, you aren't able to control certain behaviors, as you notice things not working out the way you intended. You may find yourself saying, "I can't seem to control my temper," or "I know I should stop eating so much," or "I'm addicted to pornography, but I can't stop." As a result, you may feel powerless to change a part of your personality that you know is unhealthy or unproductive.

This Pluto transit gives you the opportunity to confront unconscious behavior that has produced negative results in your life. This behavior may have originated during your childhood, only to cause you problems and upsets in your relationships as an adult. However, now you'll be able to purge it from your personality so it can be replaced with a new way of behaving. But to accomplish this transformation, you must get to the root of why you've behaved this way in the first place. This isn't always easy, as Danny found out.

Danny is a very handsome young man and easily attracts women with his intense personality, masculine physique, and seductive magnetism. He's grown used to getting his way sexually with women he dates, to the point that he seldom takes "no" for an answer when he wants a woman. Despite the many women he goes out with, he seldom has more than one or two dates with any of them. His dates complain that Danny seems to be interested in "only one thing!"

Danny tries to move slower and not be so sexually aggressive, but he ends up forgetting his intention and screwing things up by repeatedly behaving badly. A case in point was his last dating experience with a woman he met at a party. Danny was really attracted to this woman's personality, character and beauty. He could see she was a special woman he might be able to enjoy a relationship – not just a one-night stand. So, he wanted to make sure to restrain his sexual desires this time, promising himself he'd focus on letting them both get to know each other first.

The first dinner date went well and he felt in control of himself. On the next two dates with her, he made sure not to be alone with her at either of their apartments, for fear he would come on too aggressively. This strategy worked because they were having a nice time getting to know each other. Then, on their next date the young woman invited Danny into to her apartment. She made it clear that she wanted to enjoy a glass of wine and then go to bed early, explaining to him that dating was new to her, and that she liked going "slowly" before becoming intimate with a man.

He acknowledged he understood, realizing it was important he respect her wishes. But as he sat on the couch close to her, something changed as felt a real sexual attraction for her, no longer caring about his pledge to himself or her words to him. He leaned over to kiss her and when she pulled away Danny got angry, calling her a tease, and from there the conversation got ugly with his date asking him to leave. Danny left, and as he got into his car he tried to understand how he had suddenly lost control of himself. He asked himself, "What happened? I knew how I wanted to behave; yet I couldn't."

Danny experienced the power of Pluto's unconscious energy to interfere with his conscious intentions, especially because he was unaware of the psychological issue driving his behavior: he doesn't respect women, only seeing them only as sexual objects for his personal gratification. If he wants to really change his deep-seated behavior, he'll most likely require professional assistance.

Pluto's influence makes it possible for you to understand the hidden side of your personality. It's important to recognize that its energies can also activate the dark side of your nature. I consult with many clients who are sure – because they *intellectually* are aware of their bad behavior, they can now regulate their problem and remedy it. Most of the time, they are as powerless to control it as Danny was. The reason they fail is because their behavior emanates from their unconscious. Therefore, correcting it requires going to the root of the problem, not trying to resolve it just on a mental level. I had one client who had a similar problem to Danny's and she said, "Yes…I know I have that problem, so I just *watch myself* to make sure that I don't act that way." She was only fooling herself, since the same behavioral problem in her relationships came up each year that I consulted with her.

In summary, Pluto's transit to your 12th House may give you an awareness of how your behavior has caused your relationships or actions to succeed or fail. This provides you with the opportunity to confront your feelings and emotions so you have a better understanding of how they have positively or negatively affected your life. Then you can consider if you need to make any radical changes to improve yourself.

Secret Enemies & Transforming Bad Behavior

Some people think they can continue their misdeeds, or treat people badly because they've had a life where they've gotten away with such behavior. You may have known bullies, abusive types, or people who behave in morally dishonest or corrupt ways. These people are at very high risk of being exposed and facing retribution when Pluto transits their 12th House. Their unacceptable behavior is likely to get them into trouble, not only in relationships but also with other people, even the law. I remember a female client whose husband cheated on her in countless affairs. Unfortunately, in his last peccadillo, her husband picked the wrong woman to have an affair with because when the woman's husband found out about their affair, he hired a hit man who shot and killed him.

This is a good time to assess your life and your behavior and how you've treated others. If you're in denial about the inappropriate ways you've behaved, this may be a time when you'll face the consequences of not having confronted and resolved your misbehavior. Remember, the 12th

House rules secret enemies, so if you have offended someone purposely or innocently, this can be a time when you'll receive *pay back*. You may encounter people who will try to undermine or hurt you in some way.

Plutonian energies are drastic and can bring total upheaval and catastrophe into your life, including death and destruction. You may find yourself saying, "I never would have believed he would do such a thing." People who are angry or upset at you at this time are capable of horrendous outrage, revengeful behavior, and violent actions such as you've never encountered before. So, I remind clients to be hyper vigilant about their behavior, the activities they engage in, and the people they associate with during this transit. If you become aware of someone you've upset, the best strategy is to honestly talk with them, take responsibility for your actions, and attempt to repair the relationship or the damage you've done. This is the time to show great humility and ask for understanding and forgiveness. Err on the side of great contrition as a way of diffusing and resolving the upset you've created.

No doubt, if you've ever faced such a confrontation, you'll never forget it, because it will force you to finally confront your behavior and actions. You may be shocked as you recall, "He was so angry at me, I thought he was going to hit me!" or "He looked like he wanted to kill me!" Your experience will give you the opportunity to transform any bad aspects of your personality and character. The good news is that by honestly facing any inappropriate behavior or even modest shortcomings, they'll no longer control you, allowing you to remove them from your life once and for all. This is the secret to positively transforming your behavior as Gina found out.

Gina had been caught forging checks, but since she was a first time offender, the judge didn't ask her to serve time, instead he agreed to let her perform six months of community service. Yet, 18 months later she was again arrested and convicted of check forgery. Even though the forged check amounts were under $500, the judge lectured her on her total lack of morals, imploring her to examine her dishonest behavior and find out where it came from so that she could correct it, and function in society. He then proceeded to sentence her to two years at the state correctional facility.

Serving a prison sentence was the best thing that could have happened to Gina, although she certainly didn't think so at the time. While in prison she began on-line studies to be an aesthetician. She also counseled with the prison psychologist to understand *why* she engaged in such self-destructive behavior. Once she became aware of why she was acting out in such a dishonest way, she took steps to change her behavior. Gina looked forward to putting her life together when she got out and vowed never to return to prison again.

Considerations, Actions, Decisions During Pluto in 12th House

1. Seek help that will allow your secrets to die forever.
2. Do you have any behavior that needs to radically change for you to be more fulfilled?
3. Begin some intense therapy or self-discovery process.
4. Transform your psyche by forgiving yourself or someone else.
5. Do you know anyone who you suspect is a hidden enemy that you should resolve differences with?
6. Begin a spiritual or religious activity that will transform you in some way.
7. Do volunteer work for an organization that helps people transform themselves.

Transits to Use for Successful 12th House Decisions

You now understand the areas of life that are featured in your 12th House. We've discussed how each of the five transiting planets exerts its unique influence on the affairs of this House. This will help you better understand the changes you are experiencing, moods you're feeling, and the events taking place. Your awareness of this information may prompt you to:

> 1. *ACCEPT* the way things are and be content with what is going on in your life.
>
> 2. *CONSIDER* that you'd like to make some change, in which case you may evaluate your options and further contemplate your situation.
>
> 3. *DECIDE* that you're ready to make a change, take action, and make a decision pertaining to the affairs of this House.

If you make a decision, you'll want to learn how to pick the best transit to produce a successful outcome for it. Please know that the art of picking and interpreting transits requires very thorough analysis, normally done by a professional astrologer. Therefore, I've kept the discussion of selecting and using transits simple, for illustration purposes.

The key is to remember that each planet has the ability to bring a *different* positive quality of success to your decision. For example, *Jupiter's* effect may provide opportunities to expand and grow; *Saturn's* effect is more practical; *Uranus'* effect is sudden and exciting; *Neptune's* influence may bring you inspiration and idealism; *Pluto* may bring an intense and transformative effect for major change. This knowledge will help you understand how your decisions are affected by these planetary influences.

In the examples below, I chose a planetary transit to produce a favorable result for each individual's particular decision. This will help you see the many possibilities available to create the right outcome and make your 12th House decisions more successful.

Using a positive JUPITER Transit

DECISION: *I want to seek counseling to discuss my secret and heal the deep pain I feel inside.*

Explanation: We discussed Tina being raped as a teenager and wanting to enter therapy to heal herself. We used a Jupiter transit to provide her the good fortune and confidence to finally resolve the hurt she experienced. This transit would assure she would work with a professional who could offer her the help she required to heal herself.

* * *

Using a positive Saturn Transit

DECISION: *I want to leave my job.*

Explanation: We discussed earlier in the chapter about Keith being emotionally burned out from the work he was doing for a governmental health organization. We used a Saturn transit because it was ideal for him to contemplate his career, prepare himself for a transition to retirement and evaluate the positives and negatives of his work experience.

* * *

Using a positive URANUS Transit

DECISION: *I am going to tell U.S. Immigration my secret.*

Explanation: We discussed earlier in the chapter Rose's fear about telling her secret of using her sister's passport to gain

12th House : Psychology & Secrets

admittance into the United States, 6seven years ago. We used a Uranus transit because it was the perfect energy to give her the courage to take the risk of revealing her secret, and liberate herself from her fears.

* * *

Using a positive NEPTUNE Transit

Explanation: *I want to forgive myself for the molestation experience I had as a child.*

Situation: We discussed earlier in the chapter Thomas' being molested as a child. We used a Neptune transit because its energies were ideal for Thomas to feel compassion and self-forgiveness for himself. It would help him heal the deep psychic wound he had experienced.

* * *

Using a positive PLUTO Transit

DECISION: *I want to pick the best time to find a job in the state prison system.*

Explanation: Wilson had just received his degree in criminology and wanted to pursue a career working in the state prison system in the hopes of rehabilitating criminals. Pluto's energies are powerfully effective for dealing with the criminal element and transforming them. Pluto's influence would help Wilson be successful in his job and make it a rewarding career.

* * *

REMEMBER: You can use the FREE Transit Calculator that's discussed in Part IV of this book to go back in time to see which transits were occurring when a major event happened in your life. It might be a wonderful learning experience, especially since most transits repeat themselves over your lifetime. Also you can find out where your transits are today or in the future.

Part VII   Applying the New Astrology to Your Life

You've Learned About Your Own Transits

I hope you've taken the opportunity to find out in which areas of your life the planets are transiting by obtaining your FREE transits (discussed in Part IV) and then reading about how those transits may be affecting you.

This exercise was designed to give you *general* information about the many events that occur during the time of a particular transit. Congratulations – if you looked up your personal transits. You now understand the many activities, challenges and opportunities that you may encounter as each planet transits the 12 House areas of your life.

Keep in mind – the entire length of time each transiting planet will spend in a House.

- Jupiter transits a House for one year.
- Saturn transits a House for 2 ½ years.
- Uranus transits a House for seven years.
- Neptune transits a House for 14 years.
- Pluto transits a House for 21 years.

Now…It's time to Go From the General to the Specific

It's valuable to have general knowledge that "during the year" that Jupiter transits your 7th House of Relationships – *you will have a great opportunity to meet someone for a wonderful relationship*; or that when Uranus transits your 10th House of Career, *you might have a sudden change in jobs*.

But you may want to know exactly, "WHEN" these events are going to happen in your life???

The good news is that an astrologer can tell you the *"when"* – by calculating *all* your specific transits and the dates when they'll occur. This will give you the precise timing to understand what's going on in your life, what events are happening, and the best time to make decisions.

Are You Ready to Use Astrology in Your Life?

Someone once said: "Knowledge is not power. It is the USE of knowledge that makes you powerful." He was right. If you're ready to make full use of the powerful tool of astrology, it's time to consider consulting with a professional astrologer. He will cast your birth chart and do a complete analysis of your transits.

An astrologer devotes years of study and works with thousands of birth charts, analyzing the effects of various transits and their meanings. There is no substitute for the value and expertise a professional astrologer can provide you. In essence, the practice of astrology is as complicated as brain surgery. When you need that type of operation, you want the best surgeon. When you need a thorough analysis of your transits, you want the best astrologer. It's that simple.

Going to an Astrologer for Your Annual Transit Consultation

An annual *transit consultation* with a professional astrologer can be just as important as going to your doctor once a year for a complete physical checkup. Your transit consultation is a map that shows what's going on in your life, including the fortunate events you should take advantage of and the pitfalls you should avoid. Your consultation offers you valuable insights so that you can make sense of those events that might be frustrating or hard to understand. By knowing all your important transits in advance, you can strategize how to take full advantage of opportunities that are coming your way.

It's not a good idea to walk through your life blind, any more than you would walk through a heavily wooded forest with your eyes closed, unable to see what lies ahead of you. Your transit consultation can light your path through life so you see clearly *where you've been, where you are,* and *where you going.*

Using an Astrologer as Your Life Coach

Through the analysis of your birth chart and your current transits, your astrologer begins to know you quite intimately. He is then in a position to guide and advise you with recommendations based on your personality, goals and objectives. Together, you can discuss issues such as the best time to find a romantic partner, marrying, divorcing, changing jobs, moving, investing, or making an expensive purchase, such as a new home; or any other important matter in your life.

Your astrologer can also help you understand why you may be feeling anxious, depressed, unsettled, angry, or any other emotion you may be experiencing. You may have said, "How long, O' Lord, how long will I be going through this? When will it end?" That's where your astrologer can discuss why a transit has been so upsetting, what are the lessons you should learn from it, how might it benefit you in the long-term; and when it's likely to be over.

Your astrologer can discuss the major transits to use to help you create change and make your decisions successful. It's like having a personal strategy meeting with a life coach to examine your options, choices and possibilities. Your astrologer will give you the exact dates when an important transit will occur in your life, so you can implement your decision with that timing in mind. He can also assist you in creating *Astro Action Plan* (which we've discussed in great detail in Part III.) to implement on the days that your transit is in effect, in order to assure maximum success.

What Happens at Your Transit Consultation?

Let me answer by illustrating how I conduct a client *transit consultation*. I discuss with a client the specific activities, events, problems, challenges, goals, and desires they have at that time in their life. In our consultation, I will ask: "Please tell me what is going on in your life. Do you have any problems you want to resolve? Is there anything about your life that you're unhappy about? In what areas are you most satisfied? Do you have any goals or objectives you want to accomplish this year? If you could make your life *more perfect*, what do you wish would happen? What changes, if any, are you seeking?"

Usually out of this discussion a client will reveal the areas of their life that are working well, as well as the parts of their life they want to better understand, change or improve. Sometimes, a client wants help in making more sense of some experience that has occurred in their life, such as depression, divorce, or death. Out of our discussion a client will often decide that they want to make some important decisions to create a change in their personal life, relationships, career, investments, or home. At that point I can recommend specific transits they can use (and the dates they will occur) to help bring about the change they desire.

Choose Your Astrologer Carefully

Selecting an Astrologer: There are excellent astrologers all over the world. To choose the right one for you – use referrals from friends who have had a personal experience with a particular astrologer. The Internet is a great place to find many well-regarded astrologers. Look for testimonials of satisfied clients through referral services such as *YELP*. Go to the astrologer's web site and learn more about them. Most astrologers post testimonials of satisfied clients. Make sure that you are comfortable with the astrologer's style and approach. My style is to use astrology in a very practical, useful way. Other astrologers might focus more on the spiritual and metaphysical ways that astrology can be applied to your life. There is no right or wrong. Just make sure that their approach fits with your expectations.

Astrological consultations no longer have to be given face-to-face. You don't have to select a local astrologer because they live in your town or because you can sit in their office. Modern communication devices give you the entire world to choose from. Your consultation can be given on the phone, or with live video-feed through Skype, or through the Internet. A recording of the entire conversation can be made and sent to you via email or snail mail, so choose your astrologer based on their competence, not their location.

Cost: Fees charged by an astrologer for a natal or transit consultation vary. A one to 1 ½ hour customized client consultation ranges from $150 to $400. (Note: before an astrologer meets with you, they'll typically spend 30 minutes to 3 hours preparing your chart and analyzing it.)

Have Perspective: You may spend $150 or more going for a spa treatment; or $350 an hour to consult with an accountant, attorney or some other specialty consultant. Your astrologer offers you a unique consulting service you can use to understand what's happening in your life on an emotional or psychological basis. Plus, your astrologer can help you create an action plan for an entire year that may include making important decisions on such life matters as: romance, marriage, divorce, finding a job, career change, investing, buying a home or real estate; or even the best time to take a vacation or buy a car. In evaluating this service, ask yourself: What would this information be worth to you?

Bottom-Line: The best *birthday* or *holiday gift* you can give yourself (or a friend) is an annual transit consultation to understand *what the hell is going on in your life*, and to discuss any important decisions you want to make.

Important Tip: There are astrologers who offer a cheaper, more "assembly line," mass-market approach to doing a transit consultation. They will take your birth data, plug it into a software program, and e-mail you a transit printout for $50 or $75. Don't waste your money. That type of transit analysis is overly generalized, rarely customized, and certainly not personalized. It's not the kind of analysis that you want to use to understand what's going on in your life. Nor is it a thorough analysis to make a major decision. There is nothing personal about a computer printout. When you have surgery, you expect to talk directly with your surgeon about the procedure. You should not settle for less when you have a transit consultation. You deserve a one-on-one conversation with your astrologer about your transits and natal chart, and a reading tailored to your individual needs and goals.

My Invitation: If you or your any of your friends would like to schedule a *transit consultation* with me, you are welcome to e-mail me at Larry@AstroDecision.com. Or, you can visit my web site AstroDecision.com or this book's website WhatTheHellisGoingOnInMyLife.com. (My phone number is listed on my web site, if you'd like to call me.) I'd be delighted to have you as my client.

Good Luck!

Made in the USA
San Bernardino, CA
21 May 2013